T0207467

Lecture Notes of the Institute for Computer Sciences, Social Informatics and Telecommunications Engineering 405

More information about this series at https://link.springer.com/bookseries/8197

Telex Magloire N. Ngatched ·
Isaac Woungang (Eds.)

Pan-African Artificial Intelligence and Smart Systems

First International Conference, PAAISS 2021
Windhoek, Namibia, September 6–8, 2021
Proceedings

Springer

Editors
Telex Magloire N. Ngatched ⓘ
Memorial University of Newfoundland
Corner Brook, NL, Canada

Isaac Woungang ⓘ
Department of Computer Science
Ryerson University
Toronto, ON, Canada

ISSN 1867-8211   ISSN 1867-822X (electronic)
Lecture Notes of the Institute for Computer Sciences, Social Informatics
and Telecommunications Engineering
ISBN 978-3-030-93313-5   ISBN 978-3-030-93314-2 (eBook)
https://doi.org/10.1007/978-3-030-93314-2

This Springer imprint is published by the registered company Springer Nature Switzerland AG
The registered company address is: Gewerbestrasse 11, 6330 Cham, Switzerland

Preface

We are delighted to introduce the proceedings of the first edition of the Pan-African Artificial Intelligence and Smart Systems Conference (PAAISS 2021). This conference brought together leading academic research scientists, industry practitioners, independent scholars, and innovators from across the African continent and the world to explore, exchange, and discuss the challenges and opportunities of harnessing the capabilities of Artificial Intelligence (AI) and Smart Systems (SS), which have emerged as the engine of the next wave of future innovations.

The theme of PAAISS 2021 was "Advancing AI research in Africa". The technical program of PAAISS 2021 consisted of 19 full papers in oral presentation sessions at the conference tracks. The conference tracks were as follows:

Track 1: Artificial Intelligence (Theory and Framework), Track 2: Smart Systems Enabling Technologies, Track 3: AI Applications in 5G/6G Networks, and Track 4: Applied AI and Smart Systems. Apart from the high-quality technical paper presentations, the technical program also featured four keynote speeches and one tutorial presentation. The four keynotes presenters were Attahiru S. Alfa, Professor Emeritus, Department of Electrical and Computer Engineering, University of Manitoba, Canada; Ndapa Nakashole, University of California at San Diego, USA; Ernest Fokoue, School of Mathematical Sciences, Rochester Institute of Technology, USA; and Telex Magloire N. Ngatched, Department of Electrical and Computer Engineering, Memorial University of Newfoundland, Canada. The tutorial presenter was Ernest Fokoue, School of Mathematical Sciences, Rochester Institute of Technology, USA.

An international conference of this size requires the support and help of many people. A lot of people have worked hard to produce a successful PAAISS 2021 technical program and conference proceedings. Our steering chair, Thomas Ndousse-Fetter, was essential for the success of the conference. We sincerely appreciate his vision, constant support, and guidance. It was also a great pleasure to work with an excellent organizing committee team, in particular, the General Co-chair Victoria Hasheela-Mufeti, University of Namibia, and the Technical Program Committee. We are grateful to our webmaster Justice Owusu Agyemang, Kwame Nkrumah University of Science and Technology, Ghana, for his diligence and hard work. We are also grateful to the University of Namibia for agreeing to host the conference had it been run in-person. We also would like to thank all the authors who submitted their papers to the PAAISS 2021 conference.

We strongly believe that the PAAISS 2021 conference will continue in the coming years to be an excellent forum for all researchers, developers, and practitioners to discuss the up-to-date scientific, technological, and practical aspects of AI and SS and their applications. We also expect that future PAAISS conferences will be as successful and stimulating as this first edition, as shown by the contributions presented in this volume. We do hope that you enjoy reading the conference proceedings.

October 2021

Isaac Woungang
Telex Magloire N. Ngatched

Organization

Steering Committee

Thomas Ndousse	Imhotep Research Institute, USA
Isaac Woungang	Ryerson University, Canada
Telex Magloire N. Ngatched	Memorial University of Newfoundland, Canada
Jules-Raymond Tapamo	University of KwaZulu-Natal, South Africa
Serestina Viriri	University of KwaZulu-Natal, South Africa

Organizing Committee

General Chair

Thomas Ndousse — Imhotep Research Institute, USA

General Co-chair

Victoria Hasheela-Mufeti — University of Namibia, Namibia

Technical Program Committee Co-chairs

Isaac Woungang	Ryerson University, Canada
Telex Magloire N. Ngatched	Memorial University of Newfoundland, Canada

Sponsorship and Exhibit Chair

Victoria Hasheela-Mufeti — University of Namibia, Namibia

Local Organizing Chair

Justice Owusu Agyemang — Kwame Nkrumah University of Science and Technology, Ghana

Tutorials/Workshops/Program Chair

Jules-Raymond Tapamo — University of KwaZulu-Natal, South Africa

Publications Co-chairs

Isaac Woungang	Ryerson University, Canada
Telex Magloire N. Ngatched	Memorial University of Newfoundland, Canada

Web Chair

Justice Owusu Agyemang   Kwame Nkrumah University of Science and
                                Technology, Ghana

Panels Chair

Thomas Ndousse   Imhotep Research Institute, USA

Tutorials Chair

Serestina Viriri   University of KwaZulu-Natal, South Africa

Technical Program Committee

Jules-Raymond Tapamo	University of KwaZulu-Natal, South Africa
Shadrack Maina Mambo	Kenyatta University, Kenya
Antoine Bagula	University of the Western Cape, South Africa
Mohammed-Sani Abdulai	Advanced Information Technology Institute, Ghana
Serestina Viriri	University of KwaZulu-Natal, South Africa
Shibwabo Benard	Strathmore University, Kenya
Ismail Ateya	Strathmore University, Kenya
Lawrence Githuari	University of Nairobi, Kenya
Herve Frackin	University of Le Havre Normandie, France
Petros Nicopolitidis	Aristotle University of Thessaloniki, Greece
Lu Wei	Keene State College, USA
Luca Caviglione	CNIT, Italy
Khuram Khalid	Ryerson University, Canada
Megha Gupta	University of Delhi, India
Hamid Mcheick	Université du Québec à Chicoutimi, Canada
Rohit Ranchal	IBM Watson Health Cloud, USA
Cui Baojiang	Beijing University of Post and Telecommunications, China
Vinesh Kumar	University of Delhi, India
Sanjay Kumar Dhurandher	University of Delhi, India
Andrea Visconti	University of Milan, Italy
Joel Rodrigues	University of Beira Interior, Portugal
Glaucio H. S. Carvalho	Sheridan College, Canada
Zelalem Shibeshi	University of Fort Hare, South Africa
Danda B. Rawat	Howard University, USA
Ilsun You	Soonchunhyang University, South Korea
Neeraj Kumar	Thapar Institute of Engineering and Technology, India

Nitin Gupta	University of Delhi, India
Amir Mohammadi Bagha	Ryerson University
Marcelo Luis Brocardo	University of Santa Catarina, Brazil
Alain Richard Ndjiongue	Memorial University of Newfoundland, Canada
Ahmed Mohamed Ali Ibrahim	Carleton University, Canada
Olutayo Oyeyemi Oyerinde	University of the Witwatersrand, South Africa
Narushan Pillay	University of KwaZulu-Natal, South Africa
Lilatul Ferdouse	Ryerson University, Canada
Mkhuseli Ngxande	Stellenbosch University, South Africa
Ignace Tchangou Toudjeu	Tshwane University of Technology, South Africa
Glenford Mapp	Middlesex University, UK
Raphael Angulu	Masinde Mulino University of Science and Technology, Kenya
Clement Nyirenda	University of the Western Cape, South Africa

Contents

Deep Learning

A Critical Analysis of Deep Learning Architectures for Classifying Breast
Cancer Using Histopathology Images 3
    Yusuf Seedat and Dustin van der Haar

A Patch-Based Convolutional Neural Network for Localized MRI Brain
Segmentation 18
    Trevor Constantine Vambe, Serestina Viriri, and Mandlenkosi Gwetu

Facial Recognition Through Localized Siamese Convolutional Neural
Networks 33
    Leenane Tinashe Makurumure and Mandlenkosi Gwetu

Classification and Pattern Recognition

Face Recognition in Databases of Images with Hidden Markov's Models 55
    Mb. Amos Mbietieu, Hippolyte Michel Tapamo Kenfack,
    V. Eone Oscar Etoua, Essuthi Essoh Serge Leonel,
    and Mboule Ebele Brice Auguste

Brain MRI Segmentation Using Autoencoders 74
    Kishan Jackpersad and Mandlenkosi Gwetu

Effective Feature Selection for Improved Prediction of Heart Disease 94
    Ibomoiye Domor Mienye and Yanxia Sun

Convolutional Neural Network Feature Extraction for EEG Signal
Classification 108
    Liresh Kaulasar and Mandlenkosi Gwetu

Race Recognition Using Enhanced Local Binary Pattern 120
    Eone Etoua Oscar Vianney, Tapamo Kenfack Hippolyte Michel,
    Mboule Ebele Brice Auguste, Mbietieu Amos Mbietieu,
    and Essuthi Essoh Serge Leonel

Detection and Classification of Coffee Plant Diseases by Image Processing
and Machine Learning 137
    Serge Leonel Essuthi Essoh, Hippolyte Michel Tapamo Kenfack,
    Brice Auguste Mboule Ebele, Amos Mbietieu Mbietieu,
    and Oscar Vianney Eone Etoua

Plant Diseases Detection and Classification Using Transfer Learning 150
   Emma Genders and Serestina Viriri

Neural Networks and Support Vector Machines

Hybridised Loss Functions for Improved Neural Network Generalisation 169
   Matthew C. Dickson, Anna S. Bosman, and Katherine M. Malan

Diverging Hybrid and Deep Learning Models into Predicting Students'
Performance in Smart Learning Environments – A Review 182
   Elliot Mbunge, Stephen Fashoto, Racheal Mafumbate,
   and Sanelisiwe Nxumalo

Combining Multi-Layer Perceptron and Local Binary Patterns for Thermite
Weld Defects Classification 203
   Mohale Emmanuel Molefe and Jules-Raymond Tapamo

Smart Systems

An Elliptic Curve Biometric Based User Authentication Protocol for Smart
Homes Using Smartphone 219
   Amir Mohammadi Bagha, Isaac Woungang,
   Sanjay Kumar Dhurandher, and Issa Traore

Efficient Subchannel and Power Allocation in Multi-cell Indoor VLC
Systems 237
   Sylvester Aboagye, Telex Magloire N. Ngatched, and Octavia A. Dobre

Autonomic IoT: Towards Smart System Components with Cognitive IoT 248
   Justice Owusu Agyemang, Dantong Yu, and Jerry John Kponyo

Study of Customer Sentiment Towards Smart Lockers 266
   Colette Malyack, Cheichna Sylla, and Pius Egbelu

Author Index 279

Deep Learning

A Critical Analysis of Deep Learning Architectures for Classifying Breast Cancer Using Histopathology Images

Yusuf Seedat$^{(\boxtimes)}$ and Dustin van der Haar

University of Johannesburg, Kingsway Avenue and University Roads, Auckland Park, Johannesburg, South Africa
201071785@student.uj.ac.za, dvanderhaar@uj.ac.za

Abstract. Cancer is the classification given to a group of diseases that occurs when abnormal cells divide uncontrollably, often destroying normal, healthy tissue. Cancer which is a genetic disease is often caused by the change in the genetic makeup of living cells. Medical research has identified and classified over 100 subcategories of cancer, with the names given to each being derived from the organ where the cell mutation occurs. Medical professionals often utilize pathology reports to aid in the diagnosis and treatment of cancer; these reports contain a vast amount of information and include histopathology scans. The article uses varying techniques to learn the patterns found in histopathology scans so that the use of deep learning architectures in the classification of cancerous tissue can be compared and analysed. The results of the research have shown that the AlexNet model achieves an accuracy of 79%, the DenseNet model achieves an accuracy of 84% while the NASNet Mobile model achieves an accuracy of 88%.

Keywords: Breast cancer · Histopathology · Computer vision · Deep learning · Neural network

1 Introduction

Cancerous cells develop when mutations in the genetic makeup of the anatomy occur. These mutations allow for cells to multiply uncontrollably. The World Cancer Organization reports that breast cancer is the most common type of cancer found in women across the world. The average risk of a woman in the United States of America developing breast cancer at some point in her lifespan being as high as 13%. Further, The American Cancer Society estimates that for the year 2020, 277 000 new cases of breast cancer will be diagnosed in America, with an estimate of at least 50 000 breast cancer related deaths [1].

The identification and classification of cancer are highly dependent on the use of biomedical imagery. A widely used image is known as the histopathology scan, which shows the structure and formation of tissue as seen under a microscope. The analysis of such scans is complex and requires the expertise of highly specialized medical

T. M. N. Ngatched and I. Woungang (Eds.): PAAISS 2021, LNICST 405, pp. 3–17, 2022.
https://doi.org/10.1007/978-3-030-93314-2_1

professionals and as such the proposed research aims to use computer vision to study computer aided diagnostic techniques to aid medical professionals in the classification process of determining whether certain tissue is cancerous or malignant [2]. The goal of the proposed research is not to replace highly trained medical professionals but rather to aid in their decision making, allowing for more accurate and informed life changing decisions to be made with higher precision and at a faster rate.

The reason this research area was selected is due to the widespread occurrence, mortality, and impact breast cancer has on millions of lives. Furthermore, with the aid of advancing technologies, the study and enhancement of computer aided diagnostic tools could have life changing positive impacts on just as many lives. It has been shown that the early detection of breast cancer can significantly improve the treatment that follows as well as the results of these treatments. This article focuses on comparing deep learning methods that can be used to solve this task, utilizing multiple pipelines, consisting of varying architectures, and processing techniques to gain insights into the type of algorithms that are suitable for the task of breast cancer image classification. A key feature of deep learning models is their ability to automatically extract features and learn abstract information about the data which the model is being fed, as such, this work compares different deep learning models to produce an understanding of how each model performs in the task of classifying breast cancer using histopathology image scans.

This paper begins with a literature review in Sect. 2. Section 2.1 defines the problem background; Sect. 2.2 examines related works which have been studied in the field of breast cancer and deep learning. The experimental setup is discussed in Sect. 3, with its implementations and the proposed model explored in Sect. 4. Section 5 dives into the results which have been achieved by the research. Section 6 provides recommendations to consider. Lastly, Sect. 7 concludes the paper with a view on the scope for potential future work.

2 Literature Review

2.1 Problem Background

Medical professionals use varying techniques when making a diagnosis. The diagnosis of cancer can be achieved using varying methods, common approaches are not limited to physical examination, imaging tests, laboratory tests, and biopsies [3] but also include the use of artificially intelligent systems to aid in the diagnosis and treatment of breast cancer. As the world has advanced, healthcare has seen a shift and with that, we see medical professionals utilizing computer aided diagnostic tools more frequently. The identification and classification of cancerous tissue are highly dependent on the analysis and study of biomedical images. Due to the power of advanced computational processes, we have seen a rise in the use of computer aided diagnostic tools in medical oncology to aid in the avoidance of oversight of abnormalities found in medical scans.

The domain that the proposed research aims to address is medical, with a focus on the diagnosis of breast cancer using histopathology images and computer vision. The research aims to utilize varying techniques and processes which are common to big data and machine learning, to classify unseen histopathology image scans as either cancerous or malignant. The novelty of the work stems from the comparison of deep learning architectures without forming hybrid pipelines which use deep learning models at its feature extraction phase, supported by other techniques such as support vector machines, boosting, bagging, and decision trees at its classification phase. The proposed system consists of an environment that encompasses users and different constraints. The end users of the proposed system would be medical professionals, more specifically, pathologists and oncologists.

2.2 Related Works

The core focus of the proposed research is to analyze the performance of deep learning architectures used in the classification of breast cancer. To ensure that a sufficient benchmark is established, the following section will examine related works in the field whereby the structure and architecture of each work will be evaluated.

Nahid et al. conducted a study on the use of deep neural network techniques guided by local clustering for breast cancer image classification using histopathology images. The authors of this work believe that the use of state-of-the-art deep neural networks can effectively solve the problem of breast cancer image classification. This research was guided using a convolutional neural network, A Long Short-Term Memory network, and a combination of the two. The work aimed to tackle the problem of breast cancer image classification by using an unsupervised learning method. Nahid et al. made use of Mean-Shift and K-Means clustering algorithms to achieve feature partitioning. The model proposed in this work defines three pipelines. Each pipeline was structured differently so that results could be compared. Pipeline one compromised of a convolutional neural network, pipeline two made use of the LSTM model, and pipeline three adopted a combination of pipelines one and two. The experiment made use of classical image classification evaluation metrics including F-Scores, precision, recall, false positive and negative rates, and Matthews Correlation Coefficient. The work obtained its best accuracy of 91.00% and its best precision of 96.00% across all pipelines however it was shown that the worst precision of 80.00% was achieved by pipeline two when using K-Means and Support Vector clustering. In terms of the best precision obtained, pipeline one was shown to outperform the other two pipelines. The best accuracy score was also achieved by pipeline one when using the Mean-Shift clustering and SoftMax activation approach. When comparing these metrics to similar works, the authors found the performance to be comparable [2].

In the work authored by Jian et al., the authors aimed to solve the problem of using a computer aided diagnostic system to provide a second opinion on medical image diagnosis, allowing for improved reliability of a medical professional's diagnosis. The research done in this work is aimed at reducing the training parameters of a deep learning model, introducing a new learning rate function, and creating a novel architecture in solving the problem. This work uses a convolutional neural network at its core, this custom neural network, named: Breast Cancer Histopathology Image Classification Network, was built using a small Squeeze and Excitation Network. To enhance its novelty, the work makes use of a Gaussian Error Scheduler. To efficiently analyze the performance of this novel architecture in combination with the Gauss Error Scheduler, the model was trained and tested on the Breast Cancer Histopathology Image dataset (BreakHis) [4]. The data set was collected and compiled at the P&D Laboratory in Brazil. The work performs both binary and multi class image classification experiments. The model's performance was evaluated using several common performance metrics, results show that the model achieved its best accuracy of between 98.7% and 99.34% for the binary image classification and between 90.66% and 93.81% for the multi class image classification. The reason for these ranges is due to the model being trained and tested using differing scan magnifications. A clear advantage of this work is its novelty, the authors compared their results to several other well-known approaches, and they report significant performance gains. The work was comprehensively done; however, it should be noted that the model does not consider any social aspects of the data, meaning when making new predictions for different racial groups, the model could perform less optimally [5].

In the work titled Optimizing the Performance of Breast Cancer Classification by Employing the Same Domain Transfer Learning from Hybrid Deep Convolutional Neural Network Model, the authors aim to tackle a common problem found when using deep learning techniques to classify breast cancer images, that is, the problem of the lack in training data available. To address this problem, Alzubaidi et al. proposed a solution to optimize the performance of classification models using transfer learning and image augmentation. This research indicates that the proposed solution aims to solve the problem by allowing a deep learning model to train on a task and then fine tune the model for another task. The research accomplished this fine tuning in two ways which were: training the proposed model on the domain dataset and then training the model on the target dataset as the first approach and the opposite of this, training the model on the target data set and then on the domain dataset as the second approach. The work makes use of two datasets, the domain dataset, and the transfer learning dataset. The authors used the microscopy BACH 2018 grand challenge [6] as the target dataset. The second dataset that was used in the research was combined from multiple sources of microscopy images.

The sources used were the erythrocytesIDB dataset which contains images of blood smears taken from Sickle Cell Disease and collected by the Department of the General Hospital from Santiago de Cuba. The second source used was a dataset containing 367 white blood cell images. The two remaining sources were a dataset containing 150 blood scans and the ALL-IDB2 dataset [7]. The authors make a point of noting that this second data set is within the same domain of the first dataset and goes on to define a third dataset of unrelated images which will also be used in the transfer learning stage. The architecture was chosen after studying state of the art models such as GoogleNet and ResNet. The hybrid architecture that the authors refer to consist of 74 layers, of which 19 are convolutional layers with different filter sizes, to extract features such as shape, color, and edges. The convolutional layers are then followed by Batch Normalization and a Rectified Linear Unit. The ReLU activation function was found to be a good choice as it performs a mapping that suits the objectives of the work. Lastly, a SoftMax function was applied to finalize the model's output. From the experimental results, it was concluded that the results of transfer learning from the same domain dataset to be the most optimal. The results were also compared with similar works and when compared to the ICIAR-2018 dataset, image classification was shown to surpass its results, in terms of patch wise and image wise classification. It was further shown that the use of transfer learning can slightly improve performance when the source dataset is completely different from the target set but it can significantly improve results when the source dataset is similar to the target dataset, in terms of the domain [8].

A new tool developed by Google designed to analyze mammograms has seen its claim to fame raise recently. This is largely because Google has shown the work to be at its least, as effective as human medical professionals. The system has been developed by a team of experts from Google's Deepmind in collaboration with the Cancer Research United Kingdom Imperial Centre, the Royal Surrey County Hospital, and the Northwestern University. The model was trained using a total of 91 000 mammograms and their relevant biopsy results. The team then fed the model an additional 27 000 mammograms on which predictions were made. According to the authors of the work, the system consisted of an ensemble of three deep learning models with each of these models operating on different levels of analysis. The levels of analysis used were the full case, the individual breast, and the individual lesions. Each model will then produce a cancer risk score, ranging between zero and one. The final prediction score is then calculated using the mean of the three independent models. The model also makes use of a convolutional neural network architecture as the problem of breast cancer detection is understood to be of an image classification nature [9] (Table 1).

Table 1. Summary of key limitations found in related works.

Authors	Dataset	Key limitation
Nahid et al. [2]	BreakHis	No use of data augmentation or transfer learning
Jian et al. [4]	BreakHis	Scan size could omit key nuclei features
Alzubaidi et al. [8]	BACH 2018 erythrocytesIDB ALL-IDB2	No use of same domain dataset, i.e., histopathology dataset of other tissue

The table above presents a summary of key limitations found in related works, with these in mind, the sections that follow dive deeper into the selection of models for this work as well as the results achieved by each model.

3   Experimental Setup

The proposed solution handles breast cancer image classification, cancerous tissue can either be classified as benign or malignant and as such, the problem is binary. The dataset for the proposed model has been collected and labeled from a dataset containing 162 whole mount slides of breast tissue scans at a magnification of 40×. The data set which is authored by Aksac et al. at the University of Calgary contains 198 783 benign scans and 78 786 malignant scans. Using these scans, patches of the size 50 × 50 were extracted. Each patch is named in the format uxXyClass where u is the patient ID, X is the x coordinate where the patch is located, Y representing the y coordinate of the patch, and class being either zero or one. Class zero represents a benign patch and class one represents a malignant patch [10]. This dataset was chosen as it contains histopathology scans which are all the same dimension, the data is well structured and labeled and each image scan contains a localized part of a patient's histopathology scan.

The dataset was split with an 80:20 train-test split. 80% of the data set was used to build the model and 20% of the data set was used to evaluate the model's performance on unknown data. The dataset was also initialized using a random state to ensure that the train-test split remains deterministic in all iterations of the model's execution. These parameters were kept consistent across each pipeline.

The experiment will be divided into three pipelines, the first pipeline is composed of a convolutional neural network modeled after the AlexNet architecture, the second pipeline uses a DenseNet model while the third pipeline makes use of the NASNet Mobile architecture. Each of these pipelines is broken down into 4 phases. These phases are image capture, image preprocessing, feature extraction, and image classification. Each pipeline will differ by using different pre-processing and classification techniques however, each pipeline will serve the same function to the end user. The image capture phase involves the capturing and transformation of image data to transform the image data into a machine-readable format. The image preprocessing step allows for the images to be enhanced by means of varying algorithms, this allows for the image to be converted into varying formats, which enhances the ability for it to be used in classification. The feature extraction phase converts the image to a vector of features that uniquely identifies objects within an image. Lastly, the classification phase performs the classification of the image, assigning each image in the data set an image class [11].

The end user will be presented with a graphical user interface allowing them to choose which classification pipeline they want to use and upload their image for classification, this graphical user interface will also serve the purpose of showing the user important metrics. The proposed system will need to be put under constraints to ensure optimal results. These constraints include the use of histopathology scans by the end user which conforms to the standards of the scans used by the training model, this includes the image magnification factor as well as the dye color being used. Section four of the article will discuss the reasons behind the selection of these architectures.

4   Method Comparison

Each pipeline that was used followed the high-level pattern recognition steps which are used in classical computer vision systems, namely: image pre-processing, feature extraction, and class classification. The section that follows will discuss each pipeline in detail, delving into the different approaches used across each step. Each pipeline uses a common input phase whereby images are captured using common image capture libraries.

All three models utilized grey scaling with noise reduction preprocessing techniques. Grey scaling of an image transforms the image into what looks like a black and white representation of the image to the naked eye. The process is an image matrix transformation that converts the original image matrix of three channels into an image matrix of weighted intensity. All grey scaling algorithms use the same three step process. First, the red, green, and blue values of the image pixels are found, next these values are then converted into a single value representing the grey scale pixel intensity and lastly, the original red, green and blue pixels are replaced by the grey scale pixel value, resulting in a grey scaled image. The grey scaling of an image allows us to utilize a simple color space, saving on computation time as well as eliminates the effect colors could have on the feature extraction phase. This study uses a grey scale algorithm that considers the human perception of color and used the following weights in calculating the intensity values of each pixel [12]. The reason why a weighted approach to grey scaling was used was to allow for a gradual change in intensity across the black to white color spectrum which results in a more acerate representation of the original RGB image.

$$I = 0.3R + 0.58B + 0.11G \tag{1}$$

To denoise the image data, a Gaussian blur was applied to remove noise. Image noise can be thought of as random variations in the color or brightness of an image. When the image noise is significant, it can have a negative effect on a computer vision pipeline and as such, the removal of image noise is often thought to be a fundamental step in image preprocessing for computer vision systems. The Gaussian blur algorithm works by scanning over each pixel of an image and recalculating each pixel based on the average of the pixels which surround it [13]. The area which is scanned is known as the kernel, this work utilized a 3×3 kernel size. In one dimension, the Gaussian function can be defined as:

$$(x) = 1 \Big/ \sqrt{2\pi \, \Phi^2} e^{\frac{x^2}{2\theta^2}} \tag{2}$$

Where $\varnothing$ represents the standard deviation of the pixel distribution. When applied to images, the Gaussian blur function will need to be used in a two-dimensional space as it maintains the Gaussian shape and rotational invariance of an image, to derive this function, we compute the product of two one dimensional Gaussian functions [14].

The learning rate of a deep learning model is a hyperparameter that controls how a model should change in its response to the estimated error rate each time the model updates its weights. Deciding on an optimal learning rate can be challenging, if the learning rate has been set to be too small the time taken to train the model can increase at a rapid rate. On the other hand, when the learning rate has been set to be too high, we could be left with a less than optimal set of weights or an unstable training phase. As the model is trained using an adaptive gradient descent algorithm, optimizing the performance using a learning rate scheduler could yield positive results. This article makes use of a learning rate on plateau approach that will adjust the learning rate when a plateau in the model's performance has been reached. The plateau is defined as an instance when no change for a set number of epochs has been detected. The learning rate scheduler for this work was based on the validation accuracy, so if the validation accuracy does not improve after several epochs, the learning rate is adjusted.

All three models also make use of model checkpoints. This approach is a fault tolerant method for ensuring the optimization and safety of long running processes. The learning rate of the model was used as a callback to train the network and stop the training when no significant performance gains were observed over a set number of epochs. This strategy allows for the checkpointing of model performance over time, allowing for the most optimal parameters to be used in the final model output.

4.1   AlexNet Model

The AlexNet model was chosen due to its popularity in the field of image classification. The model has been shown to produce outstanding results and somewhat altered the general approach to image classification using a convolutional neural network (CNN). As this model utilizes a CNN, deep learning feature extraction methods native to convolutional neural networks will apply. The CNN will treat the pre trained network as an arbitrary feature extractor meaning the input image will propagate forward, stopping at a specific layer and using the outputs of that layer as the features. In essence, the weights of the convolutional layers are used as feature maps [15].

This model makes use of the AlexNet architecture, which was developed by Alex Krizhevsky, Ilya Sutskever, and Geoffry Hinton in 2012. A convolutional neural network (CNN) is a type of multi later neural network that is designed to recognize patterns. The AlexNet architecture has been based on a widely cited and studied work.

The architecture consists of eight layers which are made up of five convolutional layers followed by three fully connected layers. AlexNet also makes use of Rectified Linear Units (ReLU) as an activation function applied to its fully connected layers, the aim of this being to speed up training time [15]. This model makes use of a sigmoid activation function in its last dense layer so that inputs can be transformed into a value ranging from 0.0 to 1.0. The model is compiled using an Adam optimization function, this function is adaptive in nature and allows the model to find individual learning rates for each parameter. As the task is binary in nature, the model was compiled using a binary cross entropy loss function (Fig. 1).

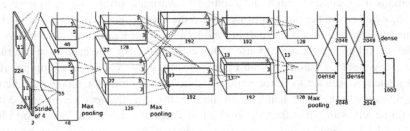

Fig. 1. Architecture of the AlexNet convolutional neural network [15].

The architecture of the AlexNet model which has been briefly described can be seen in the image above. The network consists of filters with varying sizes for its five convolutional layers and often employs transfer learning which utilizes weights of the pretrained network on the ImageNet dataset. This study does not make use of these pretrained weights, instead defining a CNN architecture that mimics that of AlexNet. The reason why this approach was chosen was to allow the study and analysis of the AlexNet architecture without employing transfer learning from pretrained weights.

4.2 DenseNet Model

The DenseNet model was chosen as the architecture was developed with the aim of simplifying the connectivity pattern between layers of exiting CNN architectures. The DenseNet model was also one of the first models which eliminated the need to learn redundant feature maps, using this model allows for the work to see the full effects of said improvements to traditional CNN models. This pipeline aims to use transfer learning to classify histopathology breast scans. To achieve this, the pipeline makes use of a Densely Connected Convolutional Neural Network in the form of the DenseNet-201 model, with pretrained weights. This model aims to decrease the gradient vanishing problem as well as improve feature propagation and support feature reuse. The DenseNet model connects each layer to every other layer in a feed forward manner and uses pretrained ImageNet weights to employ transfer learning. DenseNet uses concatenation, meaning each layer receives collective data from its previous layers. This means that the network should produce more diversified features with stronger features [16]. The figure below shows the architecture of the DenseNet-201 model (Fig. 2).

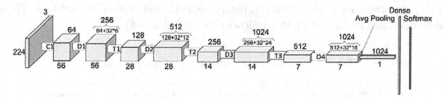

Fig. 2. Architecture of the DenseNet convolutional neural network [16].

4.3 NASNet Mobile Model

The NASNet Mobile model is a convolutional neural network that has been trained on over a million different images from the ImageNet dataset. As a result, the model has learned deep feature representations for a wide array of images. The NASNet Mobile architecture was chosen as it allows for the use of transfer learning from existing works. The NASNet Mobile architecture is pretrained with images of input size 224 × 224. The model consists of two core concepts, namely cells and blocks. A block is the smallest unit of the architecture while a cell is a combination of blocks. Blocks are operational units of the architecture and serve the purpose of convolutions, average pooling, max pooling, and mappings [17]. Cells can take the form of either a normal cell that returns feature maps or reduction cells that return feature maps where the feature map's height and width are reduced by division. The model makes use of an Adam optimizer with a binary cross entropy loss function and is compiled using GlorotUniform initialization. The high-level architecture of the model is shown in the figure below, it should be noted that cells and blocks are not predefined and are free parameters that are useful for scaling (Fig. 3).

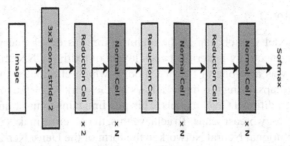

Fig. 3. Architecture of the NASNet mobile convolutional neural network [18].

5 Results

The work makes use of a quantitative research approach, where experimental pipelines for each method are implemented allowing for several metrics commonly used in computer vision pipelines to be analyzed and compared. The section that follows will discuss the results achieved across all three pipelines. These metrics include but are not limited to precision score, F1-score, accuracy, recall, support, and confusion matrices. These will be discussed in the section that follows (Tables 2, 3 and 4).

Table 2. Summary of results for the AlexNet model.

	Precision (%)	Recall (%)	F1 score (%)	Support (%)
Benign	75	88	81	8080
Malignant	85	71	68	8080

Table 3. Summary of results for the DenseNet201 model.

	Precision (%)	Recall (%)	F1 score (%)	Support (%)
Benign	88	91	89	8080
Malignant	90	87	89	8080

Table 4. Summary of results for the NASNet mobile model.

	Precision (%)	Recall (%)	F1 score (%)	Support (%)
Benign	92	84	88	8080
Malignant	86	92	89	8080

The tables above provide a summary of the results achieved across each pipeline, the AlexNet model achieved an accuracy of 79%, the DenseNet model an accuracy of 84%, and the NASNet model an accuracy of 88%.

The precision metric represents the number of actual positive cases that are contained in the total prediction set. The AlexNet model shows a significantly lower precision score across both benign and malignant cases with the precision score of benign cases being the highest for the NASNet model while the DenseNet model shows the most promising precision score for malignant cases.

The recall metric is an indication of the true positive rate. The results presented in the tables above show how the AlexNet model produced a higher recall rate for the benign class when compared to the NASNet model, however, the model also produces the lowest recall rate for the malignant class, this tells us that the AlexNet model predicts benign cases better than the NASNet model but at the same time, performs the worst when predicting malignant cases. The best recall rate for benign cases is produced by the DenseNet model, with the NASNet model far outperforming both other models in predicting malignant cases.

The F1-score is a metric that aids in the measure of the recall and precision metrics It is a measure of the weighted average of these two metrics.

The support measure is the number of total occurrences of each class in the dataset, as such, each model will have the same support as the same data augmentation and preparation was used across each model. The confusions matrices for each model were also generated and are shown below. The matrices represent a summary of the classification results of each model and indicate the true positive, false positive, true negative, and false negative for each model. The confusion matrix of the AlexNet model is presented below (Figs. 4 and 5).

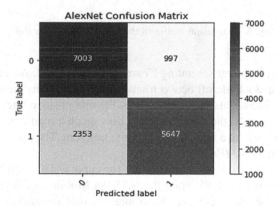

Fig. 4. Confusion matrix of the AlexNet model.

The DenseNet model presented above shows the highest true positive value for the benign classification. This indicates that the DenseNet model correctly predicted the highest number of benign cases. The NASNet model's results, which is shown below, shows the most promising true negative value, meaning the model performed best at correctly predicting malignant cases. The NASNet model also produces the highest false positive value, which means the model had the highest number of incorrect predictions for the benign classification but also performs the best for malignant classification as it produces the lowest false negative malignant predictions (Fig. 6).

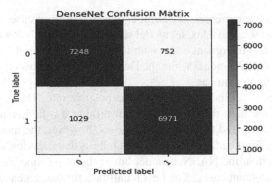

Fig. 5. Confusion matrix of the DenseNet model.

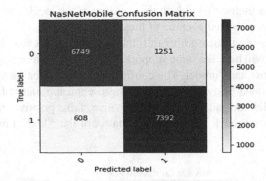

Fig. 6. Confusion matrix of the NasNetMobile model.

The ROC curve, Receiver Operating Characteristics, of a classifier shows the classifier's performance as a trade-off between sensitivity and selectivity, in most cases, the curve consists of a rate of false positives versus the true positive rate, with a threshold parameter [19]. In essence, the curve indicates how much a model is capable of differentiation between classes in a binary classification problem. The figure below shows the ROC curve for each model (Fig. 7).

The AlexNet model produces an area under the curve (AUC) of 0.88, the DenseNet model produces an AUC of 0.95 while the NASNet Mobile model produces an AUC of 0.96. This AUC measure represents the probability that a randomly selected positive sample would be ranked higher than a randomly selected negative sample. The ROC curve and AUC measure indicate how well a model can predict benign and malignant samples.

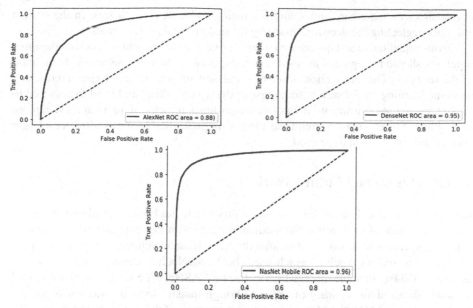

Fig. 7. ROC curves for the AlexNet, DenseNet and NASNet models.

6 Recommendations

Several constraints exist on the system, these include the quality of the data set as well as the environmental parameters of the histopathology image scan which the end user feeds into the model. The constraint on the end users scan is of importance as the scan would need to conform to standards and specifications of the histopathology data set which has been used in the training of the model. For example, the dye color which is being used should be the same as the dye which was used across the original dataset. These constraints are to ensure optimal conditions in the training and prediction of the proposed model.

The proposed research intends to solve the problem of analyzing and comparing deep learning architectures in the classification of breast cancer using histopathology images, due to the nature of the research being done, several ethical and social implications are prevalent. The implications around data usage can cause a tradeoff between data usage and the level of care available. If a medical professional has adjusted to using the proposed system and patients do not wish to share their data, the level of care could easily decrease. The implication of this is that any patient expects a doctor to make judgments based on their education and training and not rely on computer aided techniques [20].

It is also important to consider the values and bias that the algorithms being used will introduce. This means consideration needs to be given to the way in which the proposed system may maximize any false negatives over false positives, it becomes imperative to understand how the proposed system introduces a level of bias, whether intentional or not. The effect of the outcome of the proposed solution could also see the possibility of medical professionals becoming overly dependent on the system resulting in incorrect diagnosis or on the other hand, could see patients placing all their trust in the system and thus neglecting the decisions made by trained medical professionals.

From a qualitative and quantitative perspective, the results achieved across the three pipelines should be regarded as insufficient, especially due to the nature of the domain of the research. The intersection of the medical domain and computer vision requires a machine learning model with optimal results due to the ethical and legal factors tied to it. The image data that was used was of a magnification factor of 40, to achieve a more desirable result set, the work could use a lower magnification factor to allow for a larger surface area of the scan to be used.

7   Conclusion and Future Work

Each proposed model discussed throughout this article has been a valuable experiment into an approach of intersecting the medical domain with the computer vision domain. The first pipeline which was modeled after the AlexNet architecture achieved an accuracy of 79%. The second pipeline which uses the DenseNet201 architecture achieved an accuracy of 84%. Pipeline three, which utilizes a NASNet Mobile convolutional neural network achieved an accuracy of 88%. Although transfer learning was employed for the DenseNet and NASNet Mobile models, future work of this study should include the use of transfer learning from models within the same domain, this can be achieved by training a network on a different magnification level and using these weights to further train a final network. Further, a pretrained neural network can be employed to perform object detection, eliminating the risk of the end user providing an arbitrary image instead of an accepted histopathology scan. Due to the potential of fatality involved in the study domain, the results achieved in this work need to be improved to be useful, to improve these results, reinforcement learning should be considered for future work. As an added future enhancement, the study can analyze the scans where the patient was known to have passed away because of the cancer and train a model with the knowledge that these scans resulted in mortality. Overall, the study has shown the potential of using newer deep learning methods to perform a diagnosis of breast cancer, using histopathology image scans.

References

1. Motlagh, M., et al.: Breast cancer histopathological image classification: a deep learning approach. bioRxiv (2018)
2. Nahid, A., Mehrabi, M., Kong, Y.: Histopathological breast cancer image classification by deep neural Network techniques guided by local clustering. Biomed. Res. Int. **2018**, 1–20 (2018)
3. Cancer - Diagnosis and treatment - Mayo Clinic. https://www.mayoclinic.org/diseases-conditions/cancer/diagnosis-treatment/drc-20370594
4. Jiang, Y., Chen, L., Zhang, H., Xiao, X.: Breast cancer histopathological image classification using convolutional neural networks with small SE-ResNet module. PLoS ONE **14**, e0214587 (2019)
5. Spanhol, F., Oliveira, L., Petitjean, C., Heutte, L.: A dataset for breast cancer histopathological image classification. IEEE Trans. Biomed. Eng. **63**, 1455–1462 (2016)

6. Aresta, G., et al.: BACH: grand challenge on breast cancer histology images. Med. Image Anal. **56**, 122–139 (2019)
7. Labati, R., Piuri, V., Scotti, F.: All-IDB: The acute lymphoblastic leukemia image database for image processing. In: 2011 18th IEEE International Conference on Image Processing (2011)
8. Alzubaidi, L., Al-Shamma, O., Fadhel, M., Farhan, L., Zhang, J., Duan, Y.: Optimizing the performance of breast cancer classification by employing the same domain transfer learning from hybrid deep convolutional neural network model. Electronics **9**, 445 (2020)
9. de Carvalho, T., Noels, E., Wakkee, M., Udrea, A., Nijsten, T.: Development of smartphone apps for skin cancer risk assessment: progress and promise. JMIR Dermatol. **2** (2019)
10. Janowczyk, A., Madabhushi, A.: Deep learning for digital pathology image analysis: a comprehensive tutorial with selected use cases. J. Pathol. Inform. **7**, 29 (2016)
11. Elgendy, M.: Deep Learning for Vision Systems. O'Reilly Media, Sebastopol (2020)
12. Loch, F.: Image Processing Algorithms Part 3: Greyscale Conversion
13. Flores, T.: Gaussian Blurring with Python and Open CV (2019)
14. Gaussian Filtering. University of Auckland (2010)
15. Krizhevsky, A., Sutskever, I., Hinton, G.: ImageNet classification with deep convolutional neural networks. Commun. ACM **60**, 84–90 (2017)
16. Ruiz, P.: Understanding and Visualizing DenseNets (2020)
17. Radhika, K., Devika, K., Aswathi, T., Sreevidya P., Sowmya, V., Soman, K.P.: Performance analysis of NASNet on unconstrained ear recognition. In: Rout, M., Rout, J., Das, H. (eds.) Nature Inspired Computing for Data Science. Studies in Computational Intelligence, vol. 871, pp. 57–82. Springer, Cham (2020). https://doi.org/10.1007/978-3-030-33820-6_3
18. Tsang, S.: Review: NASNet neural architecture search network (Image Classification) (2020)
19. Bir, P.: Image classification with K nearest Neighbours (2020)
20. Carter, S., Rogers, W., Win, K., Frazer, H., Richards, B., Houssami, N.: The ethical, legal and social implications of using artificial intelligence systems in breast cancer care. Breast **49**, 25–32 (2020)

A Patch-Based Convolutional Neural Network for Localized MRI Brain Segmentation

Trevor Constantine Vambe[1]([✉]), Serestina Viriri[2], and Mandlenkosi Gwetu[1]

[1] University of KwaZulu-Natal, King Edward Avenue, Scottsville,
Pietermaritzburg, South Africa
219095439@stu.ukzn.ac.za, gwetum@ukzn.ac.za
[2] University of KwaZulu-Natal, University Road, Westville, Durban, South Africa
viriris@ukzn.ac.za

Abstract. Accurate segmentation of the brain is crucial for many clinical processes. Traditionally, manual segmentation was used, but this had several limitations. Several algorithms have since been proposed, but the advent of deep learning, particularly Convolutional Neural networks (CNN), ushered in a new era in image processing. Additionally, Patch-Based Segmentation (PBS) provided an alternative form of data argumentation. Unfortunately, all algorithms proposed to date still provided accuracy rates below 100% due to over-segmentation or under-segmentation. However, much effort has been put into improving these rates, but there is still room for improvement. Additionally, most medical applications of brain segmentation require the precise segmentation of a few components. In the current study, an algorithm was proposed based on previously proposed algorithms. The study aimed to test if localized segmentation would improve the hippocampus, thalamus-proper, and cerebellum-cortex segmentation. The evaluation metrics used showed that localized segmentation improved the predictive power of the proposed algorithm.

Keywords: Convolutional neural network · Localized brain segmentation · Magnetic resonance imaging · Patch-based segmentation

1 Introduction

The brain is a crucial organ in the body. It has several functions, which include the control and coordination of other organs of the body. Neurological disorders that affect it could result in the sub-normal functioning of the body. X-rays, Computed Tomography (CT) scans, and Magnetic Resonance Imaging (MRI) are some of the medical imaging technologies that could be used in dictating these disorders [19]. MRI is preferred for soft tissue because it has no known side effects [27]. Segmentation of these images forms an important clinical step. The segmented regions could be used for volumetric analysis during disease diagnosis or treatment planning and monitoring [8,24]. They could be used in diagnosing

© ICST Institute for Computer Sciences, Social Informatics and Telecommunications Engineering 2022
Published by Springer Nature Switzerland AG 2022. All Rights Reserved
T. M. N. Ngatched and I. Woungang (Eds.): PAAISS 2021, LNICST 405, pp. 18–32, 2022.
https://doi.org/10.1007/978-3-030-93314-2_2

diseases such as epilepsy, Alzheimer's Disease, schizophrenia, bipolar disorder, multiple sclerosis, attention-deficit and tumor identification [22,26].

Machine learning algorithms have done exceptionally well in image processing. Unfortunately, they require large volumes of training data [7,25,30]. This data is expensive, difficult to get, and is strictly protected by patient-doctor confidentiality regulations. Additionally, several MRI segmentation algorithms have been proposed in the past few decades [10]. The majority of these algorithms under-perform when presented with complex and volumetric medical image data. Irrespective of this fact, the application of Convolutional Neural Networks (CNNs) have produced exceptionally high accuracy rates. The work by Toan et al. [8] summaries some of the state-of-the-art deep convolutional neural networks.

Segmentation was traditionally done manually by seasoned radiologists [10,13]. Additionally, radiological laboratories have to deliver results promptly due to the urgency associated with the medical field. This made manual segmentation inefficient as it is time-consuming and results are not reproducible and highly subjective [10,11,13,17,21]. There was, therefore, need for fully automated algorithms that do not over-fit given data. To date, several fully and semi-automated algorithms have been proposed. Additionally, in diagnosing diseases, medical practitioners zero in on particular components and these are located in specific regions of the brain [4,5,9,14,23].

This work is an extension of the work by Cui et al. [10]. The first significant experiment mainly focused on developing an algorithm for accurate human brain segmentation into White Mater (WM), Gray Mater (GM), and Cerebrospinal Fluid (CSF). The second section of the current study focused on the development of a localized component-based Patch-Based Segmentation (PBS) algorithm. In this section of the current study, two significant experiments were carried out. The first experiment focused on the segmentation of two components, that is, thalamus-proper and hippocampus. In the second experiment, three components were segmented, that is, cerebellum-cortex, thalamus-proper, and hippocampus.

The remainder of the paper is arranged as follows: Sect. 2 discussed the general concepts involved in brain image segementation, that is, the brain structure and its function, MRI concepts, segmentation concepts and the general concepts in CNNs. Section 3 then discussed the methodology, that is, data preprocessing, patch-based CNN, the CNN architecture and the proposed algorithm. Section 4 presented the experimental results and discussions and Sect. 5 provided conclusions and recommendations.

2 MRI Segmmentation

Common ways of segmenting the brain include population-specific atlas-based segmentation and pattern recognition methods [24]. There was a need for spatial information if pixels/voxels are to be segmented correctly. The need to include specific spatial features and intensity information is mitigated by using CNNs [24]. The following section covers the brain's general structure, MRI technology, brain segmentation, and CNNs.

2.1   The Brain

The brain interprets signals from the outside world and processes them into information. The brain governs memory, emotion, creativity, and intelligence [3]. The brain has several components that work as a system to achieve its functions. Figure 1 [2] shows some of the human brain's components and what they control in the body. The seven components shown here are the frontal lobe, temporal lobe, pituitary gland, brain stem, cerebellum, occipital lobe, and parietal lobe.

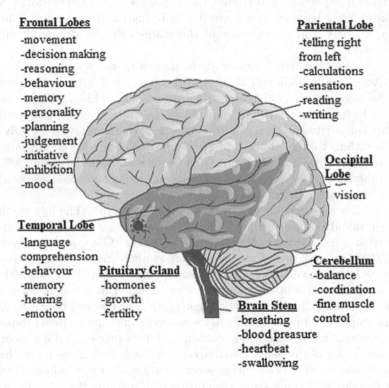

Fig. 1. The brain structure and some of its functions [2]

From the diagram, it can be observed that neurological disorders affecting the cerebellum could result in challenges with balance, coordination and fine muscle control. The diagram gives more details on the components and what they control. Ultimately, damages to any part of the brain could result in the body performing sub-optimally.

2.2   Magnetic Resonance Imaging (MRI)

Magnetic Resonance Imaging (MRI) is derived from the work done by Bloch and Purcell on Nuclear Magnetic Resonance (NMR) [15]. Magnetic Resonance

(MR) imaging makes extensive use of atoms' properties when they interact with external magnetic fields [12]. Due to the constituents of the hydrogen's nucleus, there is a magnetic moment generated resulting in the generation of a magnetic field [18]. A strong external magnetic field (β_0) is then applied that aligns the nucleus in one of the two states, either high energy state or low energy state. They can be further excited within the field β_0 by applying a Radio-Frequency (RF) field β_1. The RF waves are produced to target hydrogen atoms and their frequency is given by the Larmor frequency (Eq. (1))

$$f = \gamma \beta_0 \tag{1}$$

In Eq. (1), f is the angular frequency of the protons, γ the gyromagnetic ratio and β_0 the field strength. The RF signal results in energy changes from high to low and vice versa during the nucleus' relaxation. The energy emitted by an atom can be captured, stored and used for MR image processing [12,15,18].

2.3 Segmentation

Voxels/pixels of a brain component or region of the brain would have the same texture, depth, and other attributes. The outputs of the segmentation process are annotated images or images with contours that logically describe the different regions of interest. Additionally, segmentation requires the classification of pixels. Also, the research work that was done by Despotovic et al. [11] demonstrated that the classification of pixels/voxels depended on their neighbors [11]. The current study used a patch-based CNN algorithm in segmenting the brain.

2.4 Convolutional Neural Networks (CNN)

Image and video data frequently come in array-like data structures. Convolutional Neural Networks (CNNs) can process this data by learning sets of convolutional kernels that enable it to learn important details about the classification problem. Convolutional Neural Networks are built from a combination of convolutional and pooling layers. These consist of multiple hierarchical architectures of feature maps. The model used for these can be depicted by Eq. (2).

$$y = \{a, b\} \tag{2}$$

In Eq. (2), a is the convolutional operator whilst b is the bias [20]. Additionally, CNNs learn to optimize kernels using the training data [6,24]. In this way, CNNs automatically learn important features about the problem at hand. Spatial and intensity information will be learned if it is important for the problem and implemented accordingly. The work that was done by Moeskops et al. [24] summarises some of the applications of CNN in brain image segmentation, even though their research work mainly looked at the infant brain segmentation.

3   Methodology

Google's colab was the Integrated Development Environment (IDE) used during the neural network training. Additionally, this paper was an extension of the work done by Cui et al. [10]. In the current study, the dataset used by Cui et al. was used since it was publicly available [1].

3.1   Data Preprocessing

All experiments in the current study used brain MRI slices for the first patient suffering from Bipolar Disorder with Psychosis. The slices were originally in the NIfTI file formats. This format was converted into NumPy arrays (.nii). Additionally, all the slices used in the experiments were cropped. The slices used for the first experiment were cropped to a size of 170 * 170. The slices for the rest of the experiments were cropped to a size of 80 * 80. Additionally, patches that comprised of only background pixels were eliminated, and class weights were also used during training to reduce the majority classes' dominance during parameter tuning. Additionally, patches were generated using Tensorflow's extract_patch() function. Also, datasets were split into training and validation splits using Tensorflow's train_test_split(), in which 25% of the patches were used for validation. Finally, Tensorflow's crop_to_bounding_box() function was used to extract the central pixel value for each patch.

3.2   Patch-Based CNN

Patch-based segmentation uses neighborhood information to estimate the value of the central voxel or pixel. Researchers have made several considerations. These considerations can be grouped into 2D, 2.5D and 3D considerations. 2D considerations use horizontal or vertical 2D slices. The information contained in the patch was used to estimate the central value of the pixel. 2D considerations leave out information from the neighborhood pixels that are not in the same dimension as the slices. 2.5D use information from sagittal, axial and coronal axis during pixel voting. On the other hand, 3D models use information in a volume to vote for the central voxel's value. 3D models are known to provide more information for the segmentation process and hence are expected to produce better results as the tissues' morphology is considered in all dimensions other than just 2D. 3D models process much information hence usually are resource-intensive as opposed to 2D models [7,23]. The current study focused on 2D localized PBS.

3.3   CNN Architecture

The neural network used convolutional, pooling, drop_out, and dense layers. Additionally, the architecture proposed by Cui et al. was adopted for the current study. In the current implementation, the Softmax layer was removed, and the activation function for the last layer was set to Softmax. Additionally, all convolutional layers used Rectified Linear Units (ReLU) as their activation function.

Also, Stochastic Gradient Descent (SGD) was the optimizer while categorical-crossentropy was the chosen loss function for the neural network. Additionally, the learning rate, momentum, decay rate, and drop-out probability were set to 0.001, 0.9, 0.005, and 0.5, respectively. Also, connecting weights were initialized from a random normal distribution with mean zero and standard deviation of 0.01. Also, the bias for each term was initialized to 0.0 [10]. Lastly, the final classification depended on the number of classes that were being segmented in each of the experiment.

The architecture of the neural network was as discussed in the paragraph above. Also, patch generating functions were set to extract patches of size 32 * 32 with stride size set to one and padding set to 'SAME'. Additionally, several parameters were set for the neural network. Some of the parameters were as stated in Sect. 3.2, while the rest were as shown in Table 1. The table showed the chronology of connecting layers, input and output sizes for each layer and the number of feature maps produced at each layer.

Table 1. A summary of the layers of the neural network model

Layer number	Layer type	Layer	Number of feature maps	Input-size	Output-size
1	Conv2D	Conv	48	32	28
2	MaxPooling2D	Pool	48	28	14
3	Conv2D	Conv	96	14	10
4	Drop-out	Drop	96	10	10
5	MaxPooling2D	Pool	96	10	5
6	Conv2D	Conv	700	5	2
7	Drop-out	Drop	700	2	2
8	Conv2D	Conv	4/3	2	1
9	Dense	Dense	4/3	1	1

The first layer was a convolutional layer with a kernel size of 5 * 5, input size 32 * 32, and producing 48 feature maps. The second layer was a pooling layer that scaled-down input images with a scale factor of 2. The third layer was a convolutional layer with a kernel size of 5 * 5, an input size of 14 * 14, and producing 96 feature maps. The fourth layer was a Drop-out layer, and its drop-out rate was 0.5. The fifth layer was a pooling layer with the same rate as the initial one. The sixth layer was a convolutional layer with kernel size 4 * 4, an input size of 5 * 5, and producing 700 feature maps. The sixth layer was another convolutional layer with kernel size 2 * 2, input size 2 * 2, and producing 4/3 feature maps (depending on the experiment). The seventh layer was a dense layer with the number of classes parameter set to 4/3, and the output size was 1 * 1. In the current study, all the images used were grayscale. The neural network was designed to segment patches from brain slices using supervised learning. The following images showed the first patch's raw and ground_truth images. The patches were for the segmentation of the brain into hippocampus, thalamus-proper, cerebellum-cortex, and background.

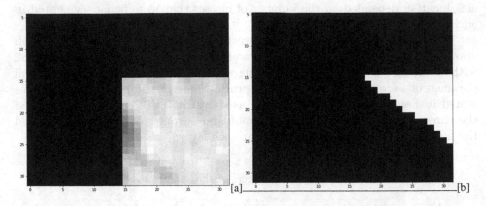

Fig. 2. Images showing a raw patch [a] and its ground_truth patch [b]

Figure 2 [a] and [b] showed the raw and ground_truth patch images, respectively. An inspection of the patches would show that the various tissue regions and their boundaries are not clear. This then makes manual, semi-automated and fully-automated segmentation a difficult task. The neural network's task was to learn to segment [a] into [b].

3.4   The Proposed Algorithm

Algorithm 1 provides a general framework of the proposed algorithm with a number of components missing. Firstly, all conversions from one data structure to the other were not provided. Additionally, the algorithm excludes the function responsible for mitigating class imbalance' effects and the label encoding function. Also, the details of the neural network model were not provided in the algorithm but were provided in Table 1. In the algorithm a number of built in Python functions such as extract_patches() and crop_to_bounding_box() amongest others were used.

Algorithm 1: Proposed Algorithm

Result: Segmented Brain Slices

```
1  ns = number_of_slides
2  images= [ ], images1=[ ]
3  for i = 0; i < ns; i++ do
4  |    y_train1 = y[:,:,i]
5  |    x_train1 = x[:,:,i]
6  |    y_train = crop_center(y_train1, 80, 80)
7  |    x_train = crop_center(x_train1, 80, 80)
8  |    images.append(y_train)
9  |    images.append(y_train)
10 end
11  batch_size, epochs, inchannel, x, y, num_classes = 4, 185, 1, 32, 32, 4
12 for i = 0; i < ns; i++ do
13 |    y_patches.append(extract_patches1(y_train[i]))
14 end
15  y_patches = tf.image.crop_to_bounding_box(y_patches, 16,16,1,1)
16  y_patches = to_categorical(y_patches)
17  x_patches1 = [ ]
18 for i = 0; i < ns; i++ do
19 |    x_patches1.append(extract_patches(x_train[i]))
20 end
21  x_patches = x_patches1 x_train, x_valid, y_train, y_valid =
      train_test_split(x_patches, y_patches, test_size=0.25, random_state=0,
      shuffle = True)
22  sgd= SGD(lr = 0.001, decay = 0.005, momentum = 0.9)
23  model = Model(input_img, encoder(input_img))
24  model.compile(loss="categorical_crossentropy", optimizer=sgd,
      metrics=['accuracy'])
25  CNN_train = model.fit(x_train, y_train, epochs=epochs, verbose=1,
      validation_data=(x_valid, y_valid), shuffle=True, callbacks =
      [cp_callback])
```

In the algorithm 80 * 80 slices were used as input to the algorithm. The algorithm also initialises several variables used in the neural network. Some of these variables included batch_size and num_classes. Patches are then extracted using built in Python functions. The function, train_test_split() is then used in splitting the patches into training and validation datasets. The other model parameters are set as provided in Sect. 3.2 and the algorithm.

4   Experimental Results and Discussions

The current study was made up of three experiments. The initial experiment was for training an algorithm that would rival start of the art neural networks in MRI human brain image segmentation. This algorithm was based on a neural network architecture proposed by Cui et al. [10]. This first experiment implemented the algorithm in segmenting whole brain slices into the background, WM, GM, and CSF. Additionally, the algorithm was implemented in localized patch-based segmentation. This implementation was done in two separate experiments. The first experiment (referred to as the second experiment) segmented a localized region of the brain into hippocampus, thalamus-proper, and background. The last experiment (referred to as the third experiment) segmented it into background, hippocampus, thalamus-proper, and cerebellum-cortex. The graphs in Fig. 3 showed the performance of the neural network in the third experiment.

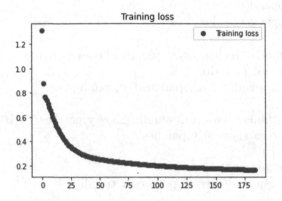

Fig. 3. Training losses for the third experiment

Figure 3 showed the loss function graphs of the algorithm's implementation in the the the third experiment, respectively. The graph showed an exponential decrease in the training losses. Furthermore, the graph was asymptotic to zero, which implied that the neural networks were learning and its parameter tuning was approaching optimum levels. Additionally, after training, the neural networks were then used in classifying central pixels of given patches.

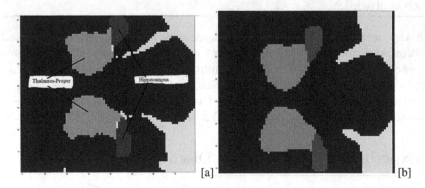

Fig. 4. Images showing the ground-truth [a] and the corresponding image segmented by the proposed model [b]

The number of patches used in the first, second and third experiment were 2481, 3299 and 6326 respectively. Additionally, Fig. 4 gave a comparison of the ground-truth and the segmentation results of the proposed model in the second experiment. Also, the results of the classifications were then used in the calculation of several test statistics. These were then used in evaluating the performance of the neural network in each implementation. Table 2 showed the test statistics values for the first experiment.

Table 2. Test statistic values for the first experiment

Test statistic	Background	GM	CSF	WM	Averages
Accuracy	99.48	96.37	99.72	95.45	97.06
Recall	98.53	96.14	66.67	91.90	84.90
Precision	98.74	92.05	44.44	96.49	77.66
Null_Error Rate	80.81	60.58	99.76	60.18	75.33
False_Positive Rate	1.26	8.31	83.33	3.34	31.66
F1_Score	98.63	94.05	53.33	94.13	80.50

Table 2 showed the values for predictive Accuracy, Recall, Precision, Null_Error rate, False_Positive rate, and F1-Score for the first experiment. The table showed a high performance of the algorithm in most statistics except for the classification of CSF. In which only one test statistic showed high performance, the rest showed poor performance. This implied that the algorithm poorly segmented CSF. The low performance was attributed to its low prevalence rate. Additionally, the Null-Error rate was low for WM and GM. On the other hand, Table 3 showed the performance of the algorithm in the second experiment.

Table 3. Test statistic values for the second experiment

Test statistic	Background	Thalamus-proper	Hippocampus	Averages
Accuracy	95.18	94.998	98.30	96.16
Recall	99.53	72.54	87.90	86.66
Precision	94.66	99.3	77.86	90.61
Null Error Rate	21.58	82.11	95.94	66.54
False Positive Rate	20.37	0.11	0.99	7.16
F1_Score	97.03	83.94	82.53	87.83

Table 3 shows a high-performance rate for the algorithm. The values were slightly low in recall for the classification of thalamus-proper and precision for the Hippocampus classification. Additionally, Table 4 showed the performance of the algorithm in the third experiment. In the table, C-Cortex stood for cerebellum-cortex, and T-Proper stood for thalamus-proper.

Table 4. Test statistic values for the third experiment

Test statistic	Background	C-cortex	T-proper	Hippocampus	Averages
Accuracy	95.32	96.54	99.07	98.81	98.14
Recall	96.16	93.59	76.86	91.82	87.42
Precision	97.63	87.94	98.41	62.93	83.09
Null error rate	24.26	82.01	96.17	97.87	92.12
False positive rate	2.34	12.83	1.24	54.09	22.72
F1_Score	96.89	90.68	86.31	74.68	83.89

Table 4 showed the high performance of the algorithm. The low performance was recorded for recall in the cerebellum-cortex classification and four test statistics for the hippocampus. This indicated the algorithm's low performance in segmenting the hippocampus, which was attributed to its low prevalence rate. Additionally, almost all the Null error rate values for all the tissue classifications were very high indicating that the model had to do more than just predicting the dominant class during classification.

A comparison was also made of the test statistics in Tables 2, 3 an 4. It was evident that in 4 out of the 6 (excluding Prevalence) test statistics, localized segmentation produced better results. Additionally, in two test statistics, two-component segmentation produced poor results compared to whole-brain segmentation, while three-component segmentation produced better results than the first experiment. The results from the current study were also compared with results for other state-of-the-art algorithms. The algorithms' segmentation results were acquired from the study done by Cui et al. [10]. Table 5 gives the results of the second and third experiment and the predictive accuracies of other algorithms.

Table 5. Accuracy rates for the proposed CNN and other state-of-the-art CNNs

Neural network	Total no. of labels	Average no. of correct labels	Accuracy rates
Proposed CNN (2 Components)	3299	3110	94.27%
Proposed CNN (3 Components)	6326	6000	94.84%
Cui CNN	24725	22 458	90.83%
CNN1	24 725	22 246	89.97%
CNN2	24 725	22 299	90.18%
CNN3	24 725	21 326	86.25%

In both implementations, the algorithm showed improved accuracy rates as compared to state-of-the-art neural networks. Additionaly, Table 6 showed the dice similarity coefficient results for the proposed neural network compared against other state-of-the-art neural networks. In Table 6, EC stood for Error Correction.

Table 6. Dice ratios for the proposed CNN and other state-of-the-art CNNs

Neural network	Dice ratio	Neural network	Dice ratio
Proposed CNN (2 Components)	87.83%	FreeSurfer with EC [28]	86.9%
Proposed CNN (3 Components)	83.89%	ANIMAL with label fusion [28]	86.2%
Cui CNN [10]	95.19%	ANIMAL with label fusion	
CNN1 [10]	94.12%	with EC [28]	86.9%
CNN2 [10]	94.83%	Patch-based [28]	87.9%
CNN3 [10]	92.62%	Patch-based with EC [28]	88.9%
Nonlinear patch-based with EC [28]	89.4%	Nonlinear patch-based [28]	88.6%

In Table 6, Dice ratios from the work done by Zhang et al. [28] showed the results for the segmentation of the hippocampus from several methods. The proposed model did better than three other methods. It performed as good as the patch-based algorithm and slightly less than the patch-based algorithm with Error Correction (EC) and Non-linear patch-based method. Additionally, the dice ratio showed poor performance when compared to the rates in [10]. This was attributed to the fact that all the classifications in that work were binary classification problems. The proposed algorithm segmented three regions in one implementation and four in other implementations. From the classification results from the current study, it was evident that the more components segmented, the lower the dice ratio. Additionally, the proposed algorithm showed better segmentation results as compared to all the methods in the work done by Haegelen et al. [16] and Zhang et al. [29]. Additionally, to pave the way for a fair comparison, the classification results for the first experiment were compared with those of the third experiment. Localized segmentation showed increased rates in Accuracy, Recall, Precision, Null_Error rate, False_Positive rate and F1-score of 1.08%, 2.58%, 5.52%, 16.79%, −8.94% and 3.39% respectively. These increase/decrease rates indicated that localized segmentation increased the predictive power of an algorithm.

5   Conclusion and Recommendations

In the first experiment, the proposed algorithm improved the training accuracy from 90.83% to 93.37% compared with the results of the algorithm it was based on. Additionally, the several test statistics used showed that the proposed algorithm had exceptionally high predictive power. The performance of the algorithm was also compared with its implementation in localized patch-based segmentation.

In most cases, medical diagnosis, treatment planning, and treatment monitoring require the segmentation of a section of the brain or just a few components that are important for the neurological disorder being investigated [4,5,9,23]. In that light, the average training accuracy for the localized segmentation experiments was 95.15%, which was higher than 93.37% for the first experiment. Additionally, comparing the results for the first experiment and the last experiment (same number of classes) showed that training accuracy slightly increased from 93.37% to 93.70%. On the other hand, other test statistics showed that localized segmentation increased the neural network's predictive ability. In general, all the statistics used showed significantly high-performance rates for the algorithm with a few sub-optimum performance rates on classes with limited training data.

5.1 Limitations

Deep learning neural networks require large volumes of training data. This compounded by the fact that medical image data is significantly large strains the computational resources. In each of the current study experiments, only a few slices from a single patient were used. This resulted in a neural network that did not generalize well due to the lack of variability in the samples used during the training and validation of the neural network. Additionally, Google-Colab had a 12-h limit and use limitations, which made extensive experimentation during training very difficult. In addition to these limitations, training the neural network to small segment organs presented challenges as there was limited training data for the neural network.

5.2 Future Work

Future research could experiment with data augmentation for small organs. It could consider using multi-dimensional pixel voting as an augmentation strategy. Also, researchers could experiment with integrating transferred learning of small organs into medical image segmentation algorithms. Additionally, future research could experiment with reinforcement learning. Also, training accuracy did not reach its peak hence training for more extended periods could be considered. Additionally, considerations could be made of hybrids of the proposed algorithms with state-of-the-art algorithms like U-net, V-net, and many other algorithms. Lastly, future work could also consider proposing algorithms for automated cropping and patch generation that maximizes the output of the neural network.

References

1. NeuroImaging & Resources Collaboratory. https://www.nitrc.org/projects/candi/_-share. Accessed Sep 2020
2. UNDERSTANDING BRAIN TUMORS. https://braintumor.org/brain-tumor-information/understanding-brain-tumors/. Accessed Sep 2020
3. Anatomy of the Brain (2018). https://mayfieldclinic.com/pe-anatbrain.htm. Accessed Sep 2020
4. Basher, A., et al.: Hippocampus localization using a two-stage ensemble Hough convolutional neural network. IEEE Access **7**, 73436–73447 (2019)
5. Bateriwala, M., Bourgeat, P.: Enforcing temporal consistency in deep learning segmentation of brain MR images (2019). arXiv preprint arXiv:1906.07160

6. Bernal, M., et al.: Deep convolutional neural networks for brain image analysis on magnetic resonance imaging: a review. Artif. Intell. Med. **95**, 64–81 (2019)
7. Bernal, J., Kushibar, K., Cabezas, M., Valverde, S., Oliver, A., Lladó, X.: Quantitative analysis of patch-based fully convolutional neural networks for tissue segmentation on brain magnetic resonance imaging. IEEE Access **7**, 89986–90002 (2019)
8. Bui, T.D., Shin, J., Moon, T.: 3d densely convolutional networks for volumetric segmentation (2017). arXiv preprint arXiv:1709.03199
9. Carmo, D., Silva, B., Yasuda, C., Rittner, L., Lotufo, R.: Hippocampus segmentation on epilepsy and Alzheimer's disease studies with multiple convolutional neural networks (2020). arXiv preprint arXiv:2001.05058
10. Cui, Z., Yang, J., Qiao, Y.: Brain MRI segmentation with patch-based CNN approach. In: 2016 35th Chinese Control Conference (CCC), pp. 7026–7031. IEEE (2016)
11. Despotović, I., Goossens, B., Philips, W.: MRI segmentation of the human brain: challenges, methods, and applications. Comput. Math. Methods Med. **2015**, 1–24 (2015)
12. Forshult, S.E.: Magnetic Resonance Imaging-MRI-An Overview. Fakulteten för teknik-och naturvetenskap (2007)
13. Frid-Adar, M., Klang, E., Amitai, M., Goldberger, J., Greenspan, H.: Synthetic data augmentation using GAN for improved liver lesion classification. In: 2018 IEEE 15th International Symposium on Biomedical Imaging (ISBI 2018), pp. 289–293. IEEE (2018)
14. Garzón, B., Sitnikov, R., Bäckman, L., Kalpouzos, G.: Automated segmentation of midbrain structures with high iron content. Neuroimage **170**, 199–209 (2018)
15. Grover, V.P., et al.: Magnetic resonance imaging: principles and techniques: lessons for clinicians. J. Clin. Exp. Hepatol. 5(3), 246–255 (2015)
16. Haegelen, C.: Automated segmentation of basal ganglia and deep brain structures in MRI of Parkinson's disease. Int. J. Comput. Assist. Radiol. Surg. 8(1), 99–110 (2013)
17. Hai, J., Chen, J., Qiao, K., Zeng, L., Xu, J., Yan, B.: Fast medical image segmentation based on patch sharing. In: 2017 2nd International Conference on Image, Vision and Computing (ICIVC), pp. 336–340. IEEE (2017)
18. Hendrick, R.E.: Breast MRI-Fundamentals and Technical Aspects. Springer Science+Business Media, LLC (2008)
19. Joseph, R.P., Singh, C.S., Manikandan, M.: Brain tumor MRI image segmentation and detection in image processing. Int. J. Res. Eng. Technol. 3(1), 1–5 (2014)
20. Lee, N., Laine, A.F., Klein, A.: Towards a deep learning approach to brain parcellation. In: 2011 IEEE International Symposium on Biomedical Imaging: From Nano to Macro, pp. 321–324. IEEE (2011)
21. Ma, Z., Tavares, J.M.R., Jorge, R.N.: A review on the current segmentation algorithms for medical images. In: Proceedings of the 1st International Conference on Imaging Theory and Applications (IMAGAPP) (2009)
22. Mayer, A., Greenspan, H.: An adaptive mean-shift framework for MRI brain segmentation. IEEE Trans. Med. Imaging **28**(8), 1238–1250 (2009)
23. Milletari, F., et al.: Hough-CNN: deep learning for segmentation of deep brain regions in MRI and ultrasound. Comput. Vision Image Underst. **164**, 92–102 (2017)
24. Moeskops, P., et al.: Automatic segmentation of MR brain images with a convolutional neural network. IEEE Trans. Med. Imaging **35**(5), 1252–1261 (2016)

25. Shin, H.-C., et al.: Medical image synthesis for data augmentation and anonymization using generative adversarial networks. In: Gooya, A., Goksel, O., Oguz, I., Burgos, N. (eds.) SASHIMI 2018. LNCS, vol. 11037, pp. 1–11. Springer, Cham (2018). https://doi.org/10.1007/978-3-030-00536-8_1
26. Wang, L., et al.: Benchmark on automatic six-month-old infant brain segmentation algorithms: the ISEG-2017 challenge. IEEE Trans. Med. Imaging **38**(9), 2219–2230 (2019)
27. Yi, L., Zhijun, G.: A review of segmentation method for MR image. In: 2010 International Conference on Image Analysis and Signal Processing, pp. 351–357. IEEE (2010)
28. Zandifar, A., et al.: A comparison of accurate automatic hippocampal segmentation methods. NeuroImage **155**, 383–393 (2017)
29. Zhang, D., Guo, Q., Wu, G., Shen, D.: Sparse patch-based label fusion for multi-atlas segmentation. In: Yap, P.-T., Liu, T., Shen, D., Westin, C.-F., Shen, L. (eds.) MBIA 2012. LNCS, vol. 7509, pp. 94–102. Springer, Heidelberg (2012). https://doi.org/10.1007/978-3-642-33530-3_8
30. Zhang, X., Fu, Y., Zang, A., Sigal, L., Agam, G.: Learning classifiers from synthetic data using a multichannel autoencoder (2015). arXiv preprint arXiv:1503.03163

Facial Recognition Through Localized Siamese Convolutional Neural Networks

Leenane Tinashe Makurumure[✉] and Mandlenkosi Gwetu

University of KwaZulu-Natal, King Edward Avenue, Scottsville,
Pietermaritzburg, South Africa
217076701@stu.ukzn.ac.za, gwetum@ukzn.ac.za

Abstract. Facial images offer a reliable means of physical biometric identification. However, image modularities, geometric distortions, partial deformations, and obstructions could easily lead to false positives or false negatives. This paper explores the viability of a patch-based siamese Convolutional Neural Network (CNN) for region-specific extraction in situations described above. The idea is to create a facial recognition model that will still perform even when only partial facial information is available. We extract nine patches and create nine patch-specific models. We explore the accuracy of three patch-based models that use different combinations of patch-specific sub-models against one that uses a global facial image. Training and testing are performed on the AT&T face dataset. Experimental work shows that carefully combined patch-specific CNNs can perform better than a global CNN. The global CNN classified image pairs with an Equal Error Rate (EER) of 0.090. A patch-based siamese CNN of all nine patches achieved an EER of 0.045. Two patch-based siamese CNNs, one with carefully chosen patch-specific sub-models and the other with random patch-specific sub-models, achieved an EER of 0.037 and 0.098, respectively.

Keywords: Facial recognition · Siamese convolutional neural networks · Equal error rate · Image patches

1 Introduction

To date, facial recognition has been successfully incorporated into simple social media applications as a means of object identification. However, it is not reliable enough for biometric identification or authentication to access a system or some resource. Facial recognition could offer a relatively cheap solution to biometric authentication [15], however, it is not very reliable, and this has kept it at the forefront of research in the past decade. There have been vast improvements due to the advancement of deep learning and faster processing of enormous data. Nevertheless, there is still more to be done. Ken Bodnar, an Artificial Intelligence (AI) researcher, is quoted in an article [16] saying that AI facial recognition technology is excellent but not very robust. This means that the technology could misidentify someone as a genuine client (False acceptance)

T. M. N. Ngatched and I. Woungang (Eds.): PAAISS 2021, LNICST 405, pp. 33–51, 2022.
https://doi.org/10.1007/978-3-030-93314-2_3

or an imposter (False rejection), thereby causing a breach into the system or inconveniencing legitimate clients, respectively.

A study from Massachusetts Institute of Technology (MIT) shows that facial recognition tools had significant problems identifying people of color [16]. Bias and potential invasion of privacy have kept facial recognition as an essential research topic. Facial images are typically required in two different electronic tasks: verification and identification, as shown in Fig. 1. Verification (authentication) performs one-to-one matching, while identification is a one-to-many matching problem. In both cases, the underlying objective matches a test image (known or unknown) to another image to determine if both images belong to the same person or are from different people.

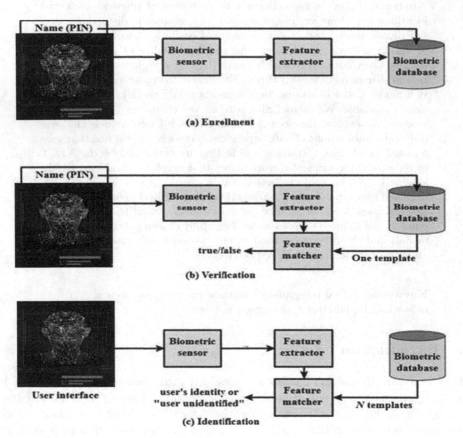

Fig. 1. A generic giometric system. Enrolment creates an association between a user and the user's biometric characteristics. Depending on the application, user authentication either involves verifying that a claimed user is the actual user, or identifying an unknown user [15].

Conventional strategies use classifiers like Neural Networks (NNs) or Support Vector Machines (SVMs) to measure similarities between two images and classify them as the same person or imposter using some threshold. However, these methods have limitations in facial recognition due to the sheer volume of data that requires processing before a decision can be made. Better results of neural networks applied to the facial recognition problems have come from siamese convolutional neural networks. Convolutional Neural Networks (CNNs) are non-linear, multi-layer neural networks that operate pixel by pixel to learn low-level features and high-level representations in a unified way. Past research techniques tend not to perform any significant pre-processing to the image pairs, and features are typically extracted from the entire facial image (global CNNs). They do not address the shortcomings that come up when the facial image is disfigured or deformed. We propose an improvement to the conventional siamese CNN architecture by creating a neural network whose input is not the whole face but patches/regions of the face (patch-based siamese CNN). This technique would allow the network to specialize on a smaller area and is less likely to give a false acceptance or false rejection when the entire face is unavailable. This research aims to design and implement techniques and experiments to evaluate the viability of patch-based siamese CNNs for facial image matching.

This study seeks to answer the following research questions: Can patch-based feature extraction be more effective that global feature extraction when applied to facial images taken in real environments? Can less information (partial face) be used instead of the entire face and still get the same or better results.

The remainder of this paper is structured in the following manner: Sect. 2 consists of the literature review which explores some existing research on the use of deep learning models for facial recognition. Section 3 explains the main methods and techniques used to implement this study. In Sect. 4 the experimental protocol followed by this study is justified. The outcomes of this study are presented and discusses in Sect. 5. Section 6 concludes the paper by summarising its findings and highlighting possible future work.

2   Literature Review

Facial verification studies, prior to 2014, generally compared features extracted from two faces separately before the idea of a siamese architecture. The concept of siamese architecture was first introduced by [2], who applied it to signature verification. A siamese neural network is an architecture of twin neural networks with identical weights that take different inputs and work simultaneously to compute similar output vectors. Chopra [4] replaced the siamese neural network subnets with CNNs and applied the resulting model to face verification. The CNNs map input patterns into a low-dimensional target. This idea started with the PCA-based eigenface method [18], which is invariant to geometric distortions and small differences in input pairs. This drives the computing of a similarity metric between the patterns. The learned similarity metric later allows the matching of new persons from faces not seen during training. The authors in [4] trained and tested this technique on input face images from a combination of the AR[1] dataset

---

[1] http://www2.ece.ohio-state.edu/~aleix/ARdatabase.html.

and the FERET[2] dataset. They achieved a verification Equal Error Rate (EER) of 2.5%, though the network partially saw subjects used for testing during training. This technique's strength is that invariant effects do not come from previous knowledge about the task, but are learned during training. This overcomes the shortcomings of previous techniques that are sensitive to geometric transformations and distortions in the input image pairs. However, due to the complex architecture of CNNs, this system is inefficient in terms of speed. The authors in [10] improved Chopra's design in terms of computational speed and complexity by fusing the convolutional and subsampling layers of the CNNs in the model, making it a four-layer CNN architecture (an idea introduced by [13] in handwriting digit recognition). Figure 2 shows the change in the architecture of the convolutional neural subnets. These authors applied this model to the AT&T[3] dataset and achieved an EER of 3.33%. This technique could classify a pair of images in 0.6 milliseconds, which is significantly faster than [4]. It could also verify test subjects not seen during training. There have been different variants of deep convolution networks that differ in model architecture through the past years. Some popular ones are explained in the papers [6,7,9,11,14,17,20]. Some say the paper [12] was the pioneering publication, but [11] is regarded as the most influential paper. The architecture of the network, called AlexNet, paved the way for CNNs. It has a relatively simple layout architecture, and it achieved a top 5 test error rate of 15.4% (top 5 error is the rate at which, given an image, the model does not output the correct label with its top 5 predictions). In 2012 the model ZF Net [20] fine-tuned AlexNet to improve GPUs' performance and achieved an 11.2% error rate. In this paper, the authors clearly show how to visualize the filters and weights correctly. Most past proposed models and techniques extract features from global facial images. None of them explore the viability of patch-based feature extraction. In this paper, we will explore the viability of region-specific feature extraction with siamese CNNs.

3   Methods and Techniques

3.1   Convolutional Neural Networks

CNNs or ConvNets have had a significant advancement in image analysis due to their specialization characteristics by detecting patterns and making sense of them. The main three layers of a CNN that enable this specialization are: the Convolution layer, pooling/subsampling layer, and fully-connected layer. The network's convolution layer receives an input image and outputs a stack of filtered images (feature maps) to the next layer using the convolution operator. The number of output feature maps is determined by what we have set as the number of filters. This layer detects different features using different filters (edges, shapes, texture, objects, etc.). A filter is simply a small matrix, and we determine the dimensions. The values of the filter are initially randomized and are learned during

---

[2] https://www.nist.gov/itl/products-and-services/color-feret-database.
[3] https://www.kaggle.com/kasikrit/att-database-of-faces.

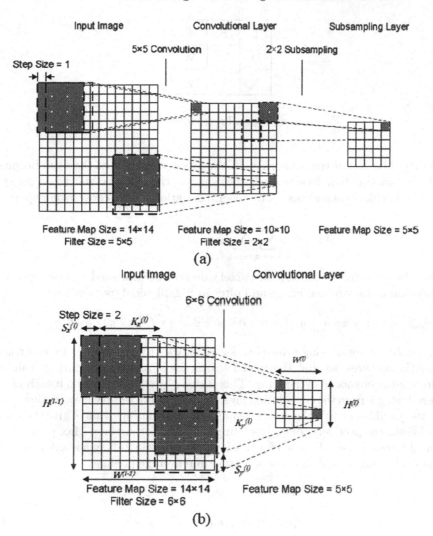

Fig. 2. Convolution layer (a) Convolution (with stride of 1) followed by subsampling; (b) convolution operation (with stride of 2) [10].

a	b	c
d	e	f
g	h	i

Fig. 3. Original image pixels

r	s	t
u	v	w
x	y	z

Fig. 4. Image filter

training. The deeper the network goes, the more sophisticated the filter becomes such that rather than detecting edges or shapes, they may be able to detect specific objects like eyes and nose. The general equation for the convolution operator is:

$$g(x,y) = \sum_{s=-a}^{a} \sum_{t=-b}^{b} w(s,t)f(x-s,y-t) \tag{1}$$

Using this operator, a filtered image pixel value can be expressed as shown in Eq. 2, in relation to the original image and filter in Figs. 3 and 4, respectively.

$$e_{out} = v*e + z*a + y*b + x*c + w*d + u*f + t*g + s*h + r*i \tag{2}$$

The pooling/subsampling layer shrinks the stack of feature maps by downsampling the features, so that the model learns fewer parameters during training, reducing the chance of over-fitting. This is done by stepping through each of the filtered images from the convolution layer with a filter of a particular window (usually two) and by a particular stride (usually two). Equations 3 and 4 give the width and height (respectively) of the resulting images after pooling. Max pooling is a typical filtering operation used for this layer. It works by taking a maximum value from each window, and this works better than average pooling.

$$output_w = Image_w - Filter_w + 1 \tag{3}$$

$$output_h = Image_h - Filter_h + 1 \tag{4}$$

The pooling/subsampling layer usually includes an activation function or put as a separate layer. We will use the Rectified linear activation function (ReLu) [3]. The function steps through every pixel in a given image, returning it directly if it is positive. Otherwise, it will return zero [3]. Instead of the sigmoid or hyperbolic tangent activation function, we will use this function to avoid the vanishing gradient problem.

The last layer of the network is the fullyconnected layer. This layer takes a list of flattened feature values from the last pooling layer into a one-directional feature vector. This architecture's rationale is that the convolution layer provides a low dimension, invariant feature space, and a fully connected layer learning a non-linear function in that space. The learning happens through back-propagation and gradient descent. The model learns features (filter values) in the convolution layer and weights in the fully-connected layer.

3.2   Siamese Architecture

The siamese architecture is a network of two identical neural networks that share weights. It receives two inputs and returns a similarity measure that tells us how similar the two inputs are. The two neural networks are replaced with CNNs and applied to facial recognition. The CNNs get us two feature vectors that give us a similarity measure by taking the element-wise absolute difference. Through this, we can deduce if they are genuine pairs or imposter pairs. A distance function is learned between the two vector representations produced by the same neural networks, such that two equal faces would have: similar feature vectors, a small absolute difference, and a high similarity score. In contrast, two different faces would have: different feature vectors, a high absolute difference, and a low similarity score. Equation 5 is used to compute the pair-wise distance between the two output vectors using the p-norm. During training, we propagate and update the model parameters so that the conditions above are satisfied.

$$||x||_p = (\sum_{i-1}^{n} |x_i|^p)^{\frac{1}{p}} \tag{5}$$

where p is the norm degree.

4   Loss Function

A loss function is used to calculate the model error. Its job is to represent all aspects of the model into a single number, and improvements on that number signify a better model. We use the pair-wise ranking loss which can be expressed as Eq. 6 or 7. The functions compare a query input image (q) against a reference input image (r). The query may be a genuine match (qp) or an imposter (qn). A margin (m) is used to create a minimum distance between positive and negative queries.

$$L(r_a, q, m) = \begin{cases} d(r_a, q) & \text{if } q = q_p \\ max(0, m - d(r_a, q)) & \text{if } q = q_n \end{cases} \tag{6}$$

$$L(r_a, q, m) = y||r_a - q|| + (1 - y)max(0, m - ||r_a - q||) \tag{7}$$

4.1   Cascade Classifier Model

Patch detection and cascading are vital steps in this experiment. We train our own Haar cascade classifier to detect the eye region, illustrated in Fig. 5, an approach adapted from [19]. Viola and Jones describes a machine learning approach to visual object detection that uses three techniques: Integral image, AdaBoost, and Cascading. The integral image is a representation of an image that allows any Haar-like feature used by the detector to be computed more efficiently. AdaBoost [5] allows the detector to focus on a smaller set of Haar-like features given a more extensive set. The third technique is combining increasingly complex classifiers

Fig. 5. Face and eye region patch detection.

in a cascade structure such that the detector focuses on promising regions of the image. In creating our own Haar cascade, we use the Cascade Trainer Graphical User Interface (GUI) [1] that allows comfortable use of OpenCV tools for training cascade classifier models. We used the GUI in the following steps:

1. Collect a dataset of positive images (those containing the object to be detected) and negative images (those that do not contain the object to be detected) images.
2. Create a folder p of positive images.
3. Create a folder n of negative images.
4. Use the Haar Trainer GUI to train by specifying the path to the two folders, set the number of stages, and set the width and height of positive images.

For this research a classifier described above was trained on 200 positive samples of 62×22 window size, which gives about 905498 Haar features per window. One thousand negative samples were used. The training was done in 20 stages, which took approximately 8 h.

4.2 Model Architecture

The CNN structure below was used for all models in this research. All input images to each convolutional layer are padded using reflection padding of size 1. We make normalization a part of the model architecture by performing batch normalization on each output feature map to the next convolutional layer. CX denotes a fused convolutional/subsampling layer. FX denotes a fully connected layer that applies a linear transformation to input data.

- C1-feature maps:5; kernel size 3×3; stride:2; input: $1 \times 100 \times 100$ image; output feature maps: $5 \times 50 \times 50$.
- C2-feature maps:14; kernel size 3×3; stride:2; input: $5 \times 50 \times 50$ image; output feature maps: $14 \times 25 \times 25$.
- C3-feature maps:60; kernel size 3×3; stride:2; input: $14 \times 25 \times 25$ image; output feature maps: $60 \times 13 \times 13$.
- F4-input: 10140 features; output: 3200 features.
- F5-input: 3200 features; output: 1600 features.
- F6-input: 1600 features; output: 40 features.

A siamese CNN, Fig. 6, is then two of the CNN subnets described above where each outputs 40 features describing an input image. Equation 6 is used to compute the pair-wise distance between the two output vectors using the p-norm. Equation 7 or 9 gives us the pair-wise ranking loss. Weight updates are back-propagated using the Adaptive Momentum Optimization Algorithm (Adam), with a learning rate of 0.0005, which is an optimization of both the Stochastic Gradient + momentum (Stochastic Gradient Descent (SGD) + momentum) and the Root Mean Squared Propagation (RMSProp).

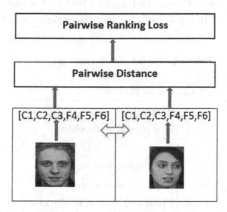

Fig. 6. Siamese CNN architecture with an imposter input pair.

5   Experimental Methodology

5.1   Dataset

The model described above was trained and tested on the AT&T dataset [8]. The dataset consists of 40 different subjects, each with ten different gray-scale facial images. These images are taken against a dark homogeneous background with subjects in an upright and frontal position (with tolerance for some side movement). The images vary in facial expressions (open eyes/closed eyes/smiling/not smiling) and facial details (glasses/no glasses), and lighting. The dataset was partitioned into two disjoint sets: the training set with thirty five individuals and the testing set with five individuals. Though this research assumes accurate detection, detection is, however, still a required step. Therefore, the dataset is preprocessed to remove challenging cases in which the face or eye region could not be detected, such that only 274 were used for training and 42 for testing. From these images, genuine pairs (images of the same person) and imposter pairs (images of different people) were created—37401 for training and 861 for testing.

5.2   Data Preprocessing

Eye region detection and patch extraction performed for the Patch-based CNN prior to feeding each patch to the respective model. The eye region is detected using the method described above. The positions of the rest of the patches are deduced and extracted from there. Nine patches were extracted, as shown in Fig. 7.

5.3   Global Siamese CNN

The global siamese CNN is shown in Fig. 8. The CNN's output is a dissimilarity measure of the two input images: high for imposter pairs and close to 0 for genuine

Table 1. Facial patch descriptions.

Patch	Facial region
1	Eye region
2	Eye region + forehead
3	Nose
4	Eye region and nose
5	Jaw region and mouth
6	From eye region to the chin
7	Nose and cheeks to chin
8	Left half of the face
9	Right half of the face

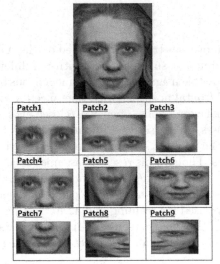

Fig. 7. Example of 9 patches extracted from a single input image.

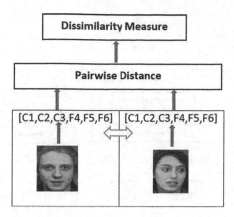

Fig. 8. Global siamese CNN architecture.

pairs. By comparing the dissimilarity measure to a given threshold, the model predicts the pair as genuine or imposter.

5.4   Patch-Based Siamese CNN

The patch-based CNN is a set of siamese CNNs where each siamese CNN specializes in comparing a specific patch described in the sections above. We trained 9 siamese CNNs. Any combination of patch-specific CNN would make up a patch-based model, as illustrated in Fig. 9. Each model in the combination outputs a dissimilarity measure. We aggregate them into an ensemble by a voting mechanism. The combination predicts a given pair to be genuine if most of the patch-specific models are predicted as genuine, given some threshold. Otherwise, the pair is predicted as an imposter pair.

6   Results

We test the effectiveness of the proposed technique through accuracy. Accuracy is deduced from the EER derived from a combination of False Acceptance Rate (FAR) and False Rejection Rate (FRR) on our test dataset. FAR is the likelihood of the model incorrectly accepting an imposter sample, as shown in Eq. 8. FRR is the likelihood of the model incorrectly rejecting a genuine sample, as shown in Eq. 9. EER is the value when FAR is equal to FRR. The lower the EER, the higher the accuracy of the model.

$$FAR = \frac{FA}{FA + TN} \tag{8}$$

$$FRR = 1 - TPR \tag{9}$$

where

$$TPR = \frac{TP}{TP + FR} \tag{10}$$

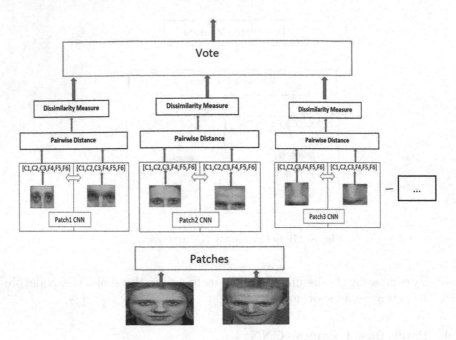

Fig. 9. Patch-based siamese CNN architecture.

FA is the False Acceptance count, TP is the True Positive count, TN is the True Negative count and FR is the False Rejection count.

6.1   Global Siamese CNN

Results for the global CNN on the dataset described above are shown in Figs. 10, 11 and 12. The model achieved an EER of 0.090 at a threshold of 0.27.

6.2   Patch-Specific CNNs

To create accurate combinations of patch-based CNNs, we first evaluated the performance of each CNN in isolation. Results are shown in Table 2. From the nine patches extracted, one could create many combinations; we evaluated three combinations:

– Combination 1: made of patches 1, 2, 3, 4, and 5.
– Combination 2: made of patches 4, 5, 6, 8, and 9.
– Combination 3: made of all the patches.

6.3   Combination 1

Combination 1 achieved an EER of 0.098 at a threshold of 0.33. Results are shown in Figs. 13, 14 and 15.

6.4   Combination 2

Combination 2 achieved an EER of 0.037 at a threshold of 0.35. Results are shown in Figs. 16, 17 and 18.

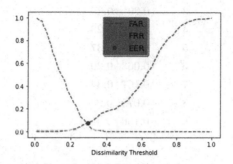

Fig. 10. Global CNN: FAR, FRR and EER.

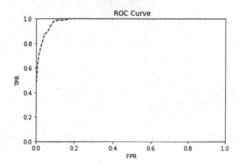

Fig. 11. Global CNN: ROC curve.

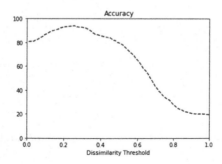

Fig. 12. Global CNN: accuracy per threshold.

Table 2. EER and threshold of each patch-specific model

Patch	EER	Threshold
1	0.247	0.29
2	0.30	0.32
3	0.29	0.36
4	0.074	0.23
5	0.173	0.37
6	0.063	0.29
7	0.167	0.34
8	0.079	0.23
9	0.166	0.35

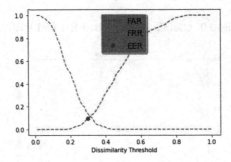

Fig. 13. Patch-based CNN of the first combination of patches: FAR, FRR and EER.

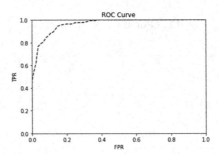

Fig. 14. Patch-based CNN of the first combination of patches: ROC curve.

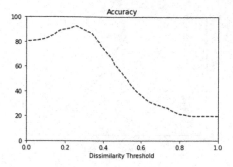

Fig. 15. Patch-based CNN of the first combination of patches: accuracy per threshold.

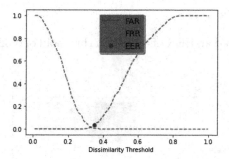

Fig. 16. Patch-based CNN of the second combination of patches: FAR, FRR and EER.

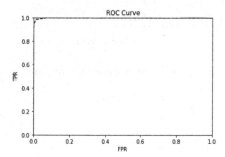

Fig. 17. Patch-based CNN of the second combination of patches: ROC curve.

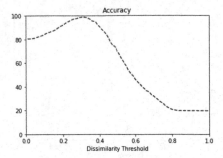

Fig. 18. Patch-based CNN of the second combination of patches: accuracy per threshold

6.5   Combination 3

Combination 3 achieved an EER of 0.045 at a threshold of 0.32. Results are shown in Figs. 19, 20, and 21.

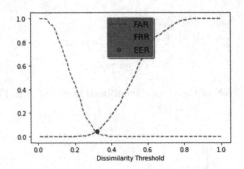

Fig. 19. Patch-based CNN of the third combination of patches: FAR, FRR and EER.

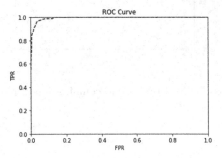

Fig. 20. Patch-based CNN of the third combination of patches: ROC curve.

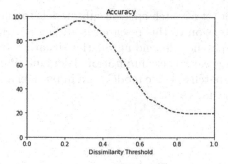

Fig. 21. Patch-based CNN of the third combination of patches: accuracy per threshold.

7   Discussion and Conclusion

This paper describes a new insight that some specific patches are more effective in accurate facial recognition than others (Table 1). Detailed experiments presented in this paper confirm two facts.

Firstly, we could use more facial information as patches instead of one global face and achieve better accuracy. This is preferred when there is a possibility of presenting a partially deformed face. Since the combination (a patch-based siamese CNN) will predict according to the majority of its patch-specific siamese submodels, it will remain discriminative enough in such situations. Further experiments show that there is a task in choosing the correct combination of patch-specific sub-models. If a correct combination, like combination 2, that combines sub-models of a low EER is chosen, the results are favorable. Compared to the results of a random combination, like combination 1. The dissimilarity threshold at the EER position of a patch-based CNN is more than that of a global CNN suggests that the patch-based CNN is more lenient. A higher dissimilarity threshold means that the model maintains high accuracy even though it allows a greater difference between the two input images and still predicts them as a genuine pair.

Secondly, Table 2 shows that if a correct patch is chosen (like patch 4), one patch that is less than the entire face can be more accurate than presenting a global face. We could create a facial recognition system that uses less facial information, therefore, decreasing computational demand.

We can conclude that this study answers two questions: A Patch-based feature extraction can be more effective than global feature extraction. Less information (a partial image) can be used instead of the entire face and maintain accuracy.

8   Future Work

The performance of the proposed technique depends on accurate detection that leads to patch extraction. Exploring various detection methods and pre-processing methods may increase the accuracy of a patch-based CNN. Accuracy also depends on combining the right set of patch-specific sub-models to make up a patch-based model. A possible extension to this research is adding a method to dynamically choose and combine patches depending on the situation presented. The more patches extracted, the greater the computational demand. Parallel computing can be explored such that patch-specific models run in parallel and present a decision to a central component for voting.

References

1. Ahmadi, A.: Cascade trainer GUI (2016)
2. Bromley, J., et al.: Signature verification using a "siamese" time delay neural network. Int. J. Pattern Recogn. Artif. Intell. **7**(04), 669–688 (1993)
3. Brownlee, J.: A gentle introduction to the rectified linear unit (RELU). Mach. Learn. Mastery. **6**, 1–10 (2019)
4. Chopra, S., Hadsell, R., LeCun, Y.: Learning a similarity metric discriminatively, with application to face verification. In: 2005 IEEE Computer Society Conference on Computer Vision and Pattern Recognition (CVPR 2005), vol. 1, pp. 539–546. IEEE (2005)
5. Freund, Y., Schapire, R.E.: A decision-theoretic generalization of on-line learning and an application to boosting. J. Comput. Syst. Sci. **55**(1), 119–139 (1997)
6. Girshick, R.: Fast R-CNN. In: Proceedings of the IEEE International Conference on Computer Vision, pp. 1440–1448 (2015)
7. He, K., Zhang, X., Ren, S., Sun, J.: Deep residual learning for image recognition. In: Proceedings of the IEEE Conference on Computer Vision and Pattern Recognition, pp. 770–778 (2016)
8. Hopper, A.: The ORL face database. AT&T (Olivetti) Research Laboratory, Cambridge (1992)
9. Jaderberg, M., Simonyan, K., Zisserman, A., et al.: Spatial transformer networks. Adv. Neural Inf. Process. Syst. **28**, 2017–2025 (2015)
10. Khalil-Hani, M., Sung, L.S.: A convolutional neural network approach for face verification. In: 2014 International Conference on High Performance Computing and Simulation (HPCS), pp. 707–714. IEEE (2014)
11. Krizhevsky, A., Sutskever, I., Hinton, G.E.: ImageNet classification with deep convolutional neural networks. Adv. Neural Inf. Process. Syst. **25**, 1097–1105 (2012)
12. LeCun, Y., Bottou, L., Bengio, Y., Haffner, P.: Gradient-based learning applied to document recognition. Proc. IEEE **86**(11), 2278–2324 (1998)
13. Simard, P.Y., et al.: Best practices for convolutional neural networks applied to visual document analysis. In: ICDAR, vol. 3 (2003)
14. Simonyan, K., Zisserman, A.: Very deep convolutional networks for large-scale image recognition (2014). arXiv preprint arXiv:1409.1556
15. Stallings, W., Brown, L., Bauer, M.D., Bhattacharjee, A.K.: Computer Security: Principles and Practice. Pearson Education, Upper Saddle River (2012)
16. Strahilevitz, M.: Facial recognition bans: what do they mean for AI (Artificial Intelligence)? Forbes (2020)
17. Szegedy, C., et al.: Going deeper with convolutions. In: Proceedings of the IEEE Conference on Computer Vision and Pattern Recognition. pp. 1–9 (2015)
18. Turk, M., Pentland, A.: Eigenfaces for recognition. J. Cogn. Neurosci. **3**(1), 71–86 (1991)

19. Viola, P., Jones, M.: Rapid object detection using a boosted cascade of simple features. In: Proceedings of the 2001 IEEE Computer Society Conference on Computer Vision and Pattern Recognition. CVPR 2001, vol. 1, p. I. IEEE (2001)

20. Zeiler, M.D., Fergus, R.: Visualizing and understanding convolutional networks. In: Fleet, D., Pajdla, T., Schiele, B., Tuytelaars, T. (eds.) ECCV 2014. LNCS, vol. 8689, pp. 818–833. Springer, Cham (2014). https://doi.org/10.1007/978-3-319-10590-1_53

Classification and Pattern Recognition

Face Recognition in Databases of Images with Hidden Markov's Models

Mb. Amos Mbietieu[1]([✉]), Hippolyte Michel Tapamo Kenfack[1,2],
V. Eone Oscar Etoua[1], Essuthi Essoh Serge Leonel[1],
and Mboule Ebele Brice Auguste[1]

[1] University of Yaoundé I, B.P. 337, Yaounde, Cameroon
{amos.mbietieu,hippolyte.tapamo,oscar.eone,serge.essuthi,
brice.mboule}@facsciences-uy1.cm
[2] UMMISCO, Bondy, France

Abstract. In this paper, we present a new approach to Facial Recognition (FR) that uses Hidden Markov Models. The method we propose enhances the HMMs by integrating a clustering step for the partitioning of each face image before building the associated model. We then apply this algorithm to a publicly available image databases FERET, which allowed us to obtain **98.02%** True Positive Rates (TPR) and **99.01%** True Negative Rates (TNR) for our enhanced HMMs method, compared to 96.04% of TPR and 98.81% of TNR with Grid + HMMs, then 77.14% of TPR and 79.05% of TNR with Discrete Markov Models. These performances are obtained on the basis of their confusion matrix, then the sensitivity and specificity of each of these methods.

Keywords: Database · Elbow method · Face recognition · Hidden Markov Models (HMMs) · Image histogram · K-means algorithm

1 Introduction

In the ecosystem of technologies aimed at improving our daily lives, the safety of people and properties has remained a major issue. By exploiting these technologies, we can provide mechanisms to identify a person uniquely and provide means to secure our environment. For a database of people face images, we want to know if a new image from the outside matches one of the images encoded in the database. During these last decades characterized by technological advances, several intelligent systems have emerged such as smart homes, automatic cars, smartphones, and many others that are thus equipped with advanced security systems such as fingerprint recognition and FR. It is therefore a question of setting up an authentication mechanism for an individual's access to these systems. Researchers in various fields have focused their work on keys and passwords that are difficult, even impossible to falsify, secure and, above all, effective. For example, in our environment within the confines of University of Yaoundé 1, courses

Supported by Ummisco, University of Yaoundé 1.

T. M. N. Ngatched and I. Woungang (Eds.): PAAISS 2021, LNICST 405, pp. 55–73, 2022.
https://doi.org/10.1007/978-3-030-93314-2_4

of the majority of first-year students take place in lecture halls with an average capacity of 500 seats. Due to the large size of the class, it is obvious that intruders can easily disrupt the smooth progress of a course. A face recognition mechanism would capture potential perpetrators and generate an alert.

Our objective in this paper is to contribute to the improvement of face recognition process in order to increase the recognition rate in image databases and thus make the systems using this technique more reliable. FR is an ubiquitous problem since the beginning of the digital age characterized by the presence of digital images, videos that are published through social networks for example. We can cite as an illustration in the field of biometric, companies or airports and other travel businesses where the implementation of a security policy is very important and necessary to block the voices to terrorists. The methods used today to deal with the problem of FR have always encountered a high number of difficulties including orientation, image size, hairstyle, and even aging ... etc. In this work, histograms are used as in several fields like musical processing (even if it means differentiating musical rhythms [1]), image processing and many other areas of statistics. Colors histograms of different partitions of the image in a conventional manner are first used, then in a second time the partitions is performing by applying the k-means algorithm, and the comparison of the images of faces will correspond to the comparison of histograms by evaluating the similarity between them through a suitable similarity measure. k-means is one of the best Data Mining (DM) algorithms for partitioning a set of data into groups or clusters, k being fixed beforehand at the input of the algorithm. By implementing the concepts of this powerful DM algorithm and by exploiting the information consulted in the histograms in depth, we manage to overcome the difficulties encountered by other applied face recognition methods.

The fact that the face has variable geometry and that the histograms also model the classification problems are the main reasons that allowed us to use k-means algorithms to find the different clusters in an image then associates a histogram for each class obtained. For the relevance of the results, we use the color images in the (R, G, B) color space; and the performance of this approach has led to very good conclusions, which offers a boost and shows the relevance of the work that we will have to do in this topic.

As the remaining of this paper, we devoted the first section to the related work. This review allows us to note that there is a large ecosystem of solution approaches around the problem of FR. We devoted the second section of our paper to the presentation of the HMMs while highlighting the corresponding use cases, notably the evaluation and the training problem. In the third section, we presented our approach compared to the existing ones to put in phase the interest of inserting a clustering step in the FR process.

2   Related Work

In the field of face recognition, several lines of research have attempted the problem raised. The oldest methods used the approaches based on the principles of statistics and linear algebra, then other approaches were based on connectionist methods, and finally stochastic approaches [9,12,14].

2.1 Approaches Based on Statistics and Linear Algebra

A FR system is made up of two fundamental phases: The learning phase and the recognition phase. During the learning phase, the systems which use the approaches of statistics and linear algebra make use of a good number of algorithms such as PCA, LDA, ICA [7,14] for the projection of the images learned in a database of the system. During the recognition phase, the appropriate similarity measures are used in order to carry out a comparison of the image models in databases. Existing approaches combine global and local methods [14,16,26].

2.2 Face Recognition Using Neural Networks

The problem of FR took another turn in 2014 with the DeepFace and DeepID [18] with the advent of deep neural networks. This achieved the SOTA accuracy on the famous LFW benchmark [19], approaching human performance on the unconstrained condition for the first time (DeepFace: 97.35% vs. Human: 97.53%), by training a 9-layer model on 4 million facial images. The concern with this CNN model is that training requires a very large amount of data.

Deep learning, such as Convolutional Neural Network, use cascade of multiple layers of processing units for feature extraction and transformation, and they learn multiple levels of representations that correspond to different levels of abstraction, as present in this recent survey [17]. The levels form a hierarchy of concepts, showing strong invariance to the face pose, lighting, and expression changes. In [9,17], the model is trained on a database of 350 million images, with 17,000 classes. Consequently, these models require height power from GPUs.

2.3 Stochastic Approaches in Face Recognition

The techniques used in the previous methods do not significantly exploit the relationships between the local characteristics of the images. Another more effective technique that exploits the drawbacks of the other previous methods is the HMM-based method [12]. This method characterizes the face as a random process that varies depending on several parameters. Samaria et al. [2,12] illustrated the usefulness of HMM-based FR techniques by emphasizing on their method where the face model is subdivided into five overlapping regions, including the nose, mouth, forehead, chin, and eyes. They present their HMM-based technique by considering that each region is a hidden state of HMMs. Figure 1 shows the DMM associated with the face. In this description, the set of states and the transition between them is noted. Thus, a_{ij} means to transit from state i to state j in the model.

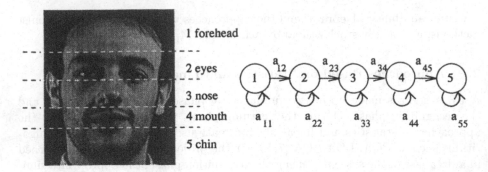

Fig. 1. Facial regions for 5-state left-to-right DMM. Extract from [12]

As shown in Fig. 2, the model will scan the different statistical properties of the face during the training phase. Thus, during the face recognition phase, the author only proposes to evaluate the plausibility of the trained model against all the sequences of observations extracted from this image. This likelihood is based on the evaluation problem which is solved by the Forward-Backward algorithm.

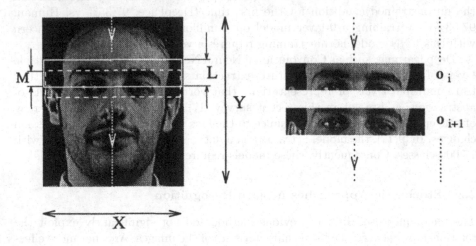

Fig. 2. Sampling technique. Extract from [12]

The sampling technique described in Fig. 2 allows to convert each still image into a sequence of vectors $O = O_1 O_2 \cdots O_T$, which are ordered from top to bottom. Each line block represents one observation vector (of size $X \times L$, where L is the number of lines in each block) and this sampling will result into a 1D sequence of observation vectors O. T is calculated as:

$$T = \frac{Y - L}{L - V} + 1 \qquad (1)$$

and V is the amount of overlap (expressed in number of lines) between successive blocks.

This approach introduced by F. Samaria Fig. 2 requires the face to be straight, i.e. under ideal conditions. However, FR systems can be exposed to non favorable environmental conditions. As an example, the person who presents himself in front of the system may be in one state or another (we mean he may be smiling, a little distracted and therefore the face is not presented straight anymore). From the regionalization proposed for the image of the face, we retain enough constraints that impinge on the quality of the results obtained in the end. In future approaches we are using color images because while it is simpler to manipulate greyscale images, there is a loss of color information when moving from a color image to a greyscale image. HMM has three main components (A, B, π), where A is the state transition distribution matrix; B the observation distribution matrix and π the distribution vector of the initial states of the model. However the DMM used here has only two mains components (A, π). Therefore, a DMM isn't a HMM since the states are not hidden in a DMM, and no symbol is observed [16,17]. The problem here is that in their modeling of HMMs, the notion of sequentiality is not taken into account. This is the reason why the term used has been much more the Discrete Markov Models (DMM).

3   Comparison of Images Based on Hidden Markov Model

The modeling of histograms generally deals with situations where a good number of classes are to be distinguished. In this case, classes most often have the same amplitude. All the desired information is then hidden in these histograms. Therefore, we must look a way to model these histograms in order to extract this information. With an image, we will associate a set of histograms, a normalization step will be necessary in order to extract the Markov chains as well as the possible observation sequences for a given model of the image like in [4].

3.1   Face Model Training Phase

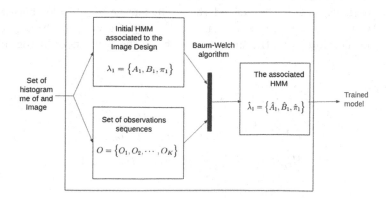

Fig. 3. Process of training of the model.

Figure 3 shows us the training process of a face model. In this process, the **Baum-Welch** algorithm takes as parameters the initial model, the set of observation sequences associated to this image as well as the maximum number of iterations. Once the initial model of the image has been built, it is trained on the different extracted sequences, as presented in the previous section to have a new model which "masters" better features of the image. During the training of a face HMM, it learns the statistical properties of the organization of the different pixels of the face image. And these statistical properties will tell us even more about understanding the texture of the image of each face as we can see in Fig. 8. This is the reason why, after having obtained the right parameters of the model by the **Baum Welch algorithm**, the stationary distribution of the model is first searched, because this distribution will allow us to better understand the behavior of the face model on the long term.

3.2   Calculation of the Normalized Similarity Rate Between Two Images

As we explained earlier, comparing two images will be like comparing the models associated with them. Thus, this involves calculating the similarity rate between these models. The appropriate measure of similarity for the comparison of two HMM has been proposed [28]; see Eq. 2:

$$\hat{\sigma}(H_i, H_j) = Sim(\lambda_{\hat{H}_i}, \lambda_{\hat{H}_j})(in\%). \tag{2}$$

3.3   Calculation of the Amplitude Coefficient

In the normalization phase, it was a question of bringing the histogram data into an interval where they are much more visual and easily representable. Indeed, if the similarity between $\hat{H}_i$ and $\hat{H}_j$ is 100%, we can easily interpret it by saying that $\hat{H}_i \approx \hat{H}_j$, and in the boundary conditions, we have equality. So this means that, for each $\hat{h}_i \in \hat{H}_i$, there exists $\hat{h}_j \in \hat{H}_j$ satisfying $\hat{h}_i = \hat{h}_j$, which is equivalent to saying with Eq. 3. θ is then called the coefficient of amplitudes between $\hat{H}_i$ and $\hat{H}_j$. We then have Eq. 4, so that the similarity is giving by the Eq. 5. This last relation therefore gives the similarity between the two sets of histograms H_i and H_j.

$$\frac{100 \times h_i}{H_{iMax}} = \frac{100 \times h_j}{H_{jMax}}. \tag{3}$$

$$\theta(\hat{H}_i, \hat{H}_j) = \frac{min(H_{iMax}, H_{jMax})}{max(H_{iMax}, H_{jMax})} \tag{4}$$

$$\sigma(H_i, H_j) = \theta(\hat{H}_i, \hat{H}_j) \times \hat{\sigma}(H_i, H_j)(in\%) \tag{5}$$

4   Face Comparison

4.1   Approach Based on Grid Partitioning

In this work, we started by adapting this process to the effect of comparing our images of faces. So we had to look for the right parameters that would allow us to obtain good comparison results. This was possible thanks to the determination of the minimum size for the image grid [4,10].

This partitioning approach consists in taking an image, there fragmenting into small pieces as we can see via Fig. 4:

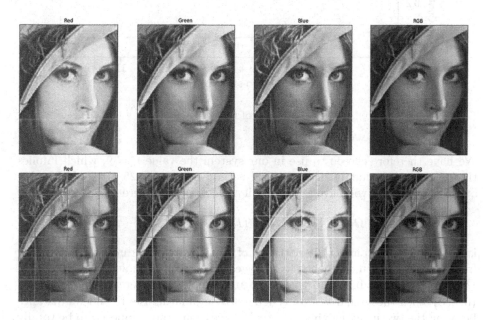

Fig. 4. Grid image: first step.

The available benchmark for FR are describe in [17]. We tested our model with the FERET dataset, as it is one of the most used datasets in this field of FR [17]. To validate our results in the section devoted to the comparison of the different approaches, we looked for the optimal size of the grid as elucidated in Fig. 5. For this experiment, we have simplified the task of finding the size of the generalized $n \times m$ grid to $n \times n$ grids. Thus, we can observe through the Fig. 5 that when our images are partitioned with a grid size of $n = 5$, almost no image wrapped in the base is recognized during the recognition phase, we have a TNR close to 1 and thus a FPR close to 0. The goal is that our system will be able to recognize people who have enrolled and also that people who have not enrolled will not be recognized, the TNR and the TPR must get closer to 1, while the FPR and the FNR get closer to 0. This is, in fact, a sought-after point of convergence, we note that for $n = 8$ these same parameters have stabilized.

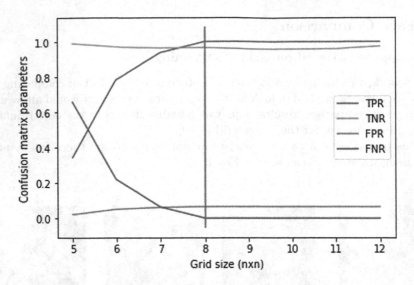

Fig. 5. Choice of the grid size.

We have therefore chosen to use in our system the value $n = 9$, which implies that the size of a thumbnail of the grid is on average 25×25 pixels. If I and J are two images, we will have the similarity vector of $\mathbb{R}^3$ where I_p, $p \in \{R; G; B\}$

$$\Omega_{IJ} = \{\sigma(I_R, J_R); \sigma(I_G, J_G); \sigma(I_B, J_B)\} \tag{6}$$

is the set of histograms of the partition of the image in the direction p. Starting from the observation that when two images I and J are completely similar, then $\Omega_{Max} = (100, 100, 100)$ and that they are completely different when $\Omega_{Min} = (0, 0, 0)$, then the similarity rate is defined by evaluating the Euclidean distance between the two images giving, and two images which are supposed to be totally similar: $d(I, J)$ is the Euclidean distance between Ω_{IJ} and Ω_{Max}, so,

$$d(I, J) = \sqrt{\sum_{p \in R, G, B} (100 - \sigma(I_p, J_p))^2} \tag{7}$$

This distance is increased by the Euclidean distance between Ω_{Max} and Ω_{Min}, i.e. $100\sqrt{3}$. The dissimilarity rate between the colors of image I and image J is then obtained by making $100 \times \frac{d(I,J)}{100\sqrt{3}}$, and the similarity rate is given by Eq. (8).

$$\chi(I, J) = 100 - \frac{d(I, J)}{\sqrt{3}} \tag{8}$$

Table 1 show us the result of the application of classical partitioning, grid size: 9×9. The image J_i represents the image wrapped in the system, and the image I_i represents the new test image that matches it. Equation (6) is then

Table 1. Results of the application of classical partitioning, grid size: 9×9.

Images		$\Omega_{I,J}$			$d_\sigma(I,J)$ $in\%$	$\chi(I,J)$ $(in\%)$
I	J	$\sigma(I_R,J_R)$	$\sigma(I_G,J_G)$	$\sigma(I_B,J_{Bc})$		
I_1	J_1	93.84	94.20	93.74	10.52	**93.93**
I_1	J_2	2.47	2.4	3.96	168.11	2.94
I_1	J_3	52.4	52.65	52.68	82.13	52.58
I_1	J_4	52.17	52.28	52.1	82.82	52.19
I_1	J_5	2.42	3.14	2.18	168.74	2.58
I_1	J_6	10.55	10.91	12.43	153.64	11.29
I_2	J_2	70.0	72.96	78.0	45.99	**73.45**
I_2	J_3	1.35	1.33	2.22	170.38	1.63
I_2	J_4	1.42	1.38	2.21	170.32	1.67
I_2	J_5	76.55	70.87	45.4	66.17	61.79
I_2	J_0	16.35	15.84	23.85	140.99	18.6
I_3	J_3	93.98	94.91	95.07	9.29	**94.63**
I_3	J_4	92.63	93.46	93.84	11.62	93.29
I_3	J_5	1.34	1.75	1.22	170.72	1.44
I_3	J_6	5.66	6.03	7.02	162.41	6.23
I_4	J_4	90.73	90.84	91.72	15.45	**91.08**
I_4	J_5	1.35	1.75	1.21	170.72	1.44
I_4	J_6	6.02	6.32	7.01	162.04	6.45
I_5	J_5	87.03	89.48	85.31	22.25	**87.16**
I_5	J_6	17.97	22.87	13.84	141.78	18.14
I_6	J_6	67.52	69.87	78.31	49.33	**71.52**

applied to obtain the similarity vector between two images, then from Eq. (7) the rate of dissimilarity between the colors of the two images is derived, and finally, Eq. (8) is applied to evaluate the rate of correspondence between the two images.

4.2   Enhanced HMM: Our Approach Based on Clustering

In this work, we made the observation that, in grid partitioning, the different pixels of the image are counted together to set up the histogram by "area", however, if there was a way to put together the pixels of the image which have a certain common neighborhood together, this would be beneficial to us since

Table 2. Results of the application of unsupervised learning with k-means, **for** k = 51.

Images	$\Omega_{I,J}$			$d_\sigma(I,J)\ in\%$	$\chi(I,J)\ (in\%)$
I J	$\sigma(I_R, J_R)$	$\sigma(I_G, J_G)$	$\sigma(I_B, J_B)$		
I_1 J_1	95.67	95.68	95.12	7.83	**95.48**
I_1 J_2	1.14	1.48	1.24	170.98	1.29
I_1 J_3	56.29	55.60	53.26	77.89	55.03
I_1 J_4	44.49	44.65	46.67	94.81	45.26
I_1 J_5	0.78	0.62	0.53	172.09	0.64
I_1 J_6	5.41	7.17	7.07	161.87	6.54
I_2 J_2	54.00	65.26	60.75	69.74	**59.74**
I_2 J_3	0.67	0.83	0.69	171.94	0.73
I_2 J_4	2.15	2.96	2.30	168.93	2.47
I_2 J_5	48.49	29.15	27.97	113.41	34.52
I_2 J_6	12.67	15.13	12.65	149.87	13.47
I_3 J_3	95.49	95.62	95.72	7.61	**95.61**
I_3 J_4	26.21	25.75	26.29	128.03	26.08
I_3 J_5	0.46	0.36	0.30	172.56	0.37
I_3 J_6	3.16	4.12	3.98	166.70	3.75
I_4 J_4	88.95	87.39	88.93	20.08	**88.40**
I_4 J_5	1.52	1.20	1.00	171.06	1.24
I_4 J_6	10.54	13.67	13.35	151.54	12.51
I_5 J_5	76.96	70.03	66.66	50.40	**70.90**
I_5 J_6	10.25	6.42	5.41	160.50	7.34
I_6 J_6	58.06	72.72	73.01	56.84	**67.18**

this notion of the neighborhood of the pixels is no longer a matter of locality in the image. This idea, therefore, made us to think of an unsupervised learning method, where we precisely allow the machine to "group" together pixels that look alike, or have the same neighborhood. The idea of clustering came to us following the observation that the data we manipulate, which are images, are not labeled; there is no way to distinguish the pixels of an image that looks similar when we have the image by looking at its texture. So there must be a way to classify these pixels in order to distinguish the texture of the image. In the literature, several clustering algorithms exist [5,11,23], and one distinguishes hierarchical and non-hierarchical clustering. **K-means** is an algorithm for partitioning a set of data into clusters or groups [5,6]. At least two factors influence the implementation of this algorithm to produce good results at the exit: The number of clusters to be formed at the exit and the problem of initialization of the centroids of each cluster.

(1) Choice of the number of clusters: In the literature, the choice of the number of clusters in the K−means algorithm is generally made either randomly, or the method of Forgy [3]. However, a method used recently is called "elbow" [25]. It consists of launching the K−means algorithm with several K values and choosing the value of k which minimizes the inter-class distance and maximizes the intra-class distance. This optimization is based on the fundamental Huygens' theorem:

Theorem 1. *The total inertia is equal to the sum of the inter-class inertia and the intra-class inertia.*

This theorem allows us to present the elbow method which is as follows: **Elbow method [25]**

$$WSS = \sum_{i=1}^{N_C} \sum_{x \in C_i} \left\| x \quad \bar{x}_{C_i} \right\|_2^2 \tag{9}$$

$$BSS = \sum_{i=1}^{N_C} |C_i| \times \left\| \bar{x}_{C_i} - \bar{x} \right\|_2^2 \tag{10}$$

(1.) Measuring the intra-class variance giving by Eq. (9), where C_i is the ith-cluster; N_C is the number of the clusters and $\bar{x}_{C_i} = \frac{1}{|C_i|} \sum_{x \in C_i}(x)$ is the means value of the cluster C_i for different values of the cluster;

(2.) Measuring the inter-class variance by calculating the energies giving by the Eq. (10), where $\bar{x}$ is the means value of all the data which is hier our image, $\bar{x} = \frac{1}{|\text{size of the Image}|} \sum x \in Image$ for different values of the cluster;

(3.) Summing all these energies: $TSS = WSS + BSS$ for each value of the cluster;

(4.) And finally, the optimal value of k will be the one for which $\frac{WSS}{TSS}$ is close to 0.2.

This method, applied to our images, made it possible to have the following graph giving the intra-class dispersion rate as a function of the number of classes. From this graph, four optimal values of k are available: 12, 25, and 45 and 51. In this work, we have used the value of $k = 51$ clusters.

We note through the Fig. 6 a strong lack of stability, this is explained by the fact that the face has a variable geometry. It should be noted that on the curve obtained, it is not the values of k that are on the low vertex that are selected, but rather the values of k for which clustering has given as a ratio $\frac{WSS}{TSS}$ a value in the vicinity of 0.2. The part of the curve above 0.2 and below 0.2 with a margin of error simply indicates that the corresponding k values do not allow a good partitioning. To determine the value of the number of clusters, we use the Silhouette index [24], which will allow us to measure the quality of the

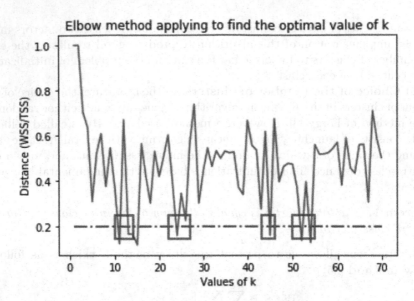

Fig. 6. Elbow method applied for determining the number of clusters

partitioning of one image. Thus, as we can see through Fig. 7, the partitioning quality is good for a face image when the number of clusters increases. Thus, the value $k = 51$ is chosen in the framework of our experiment.

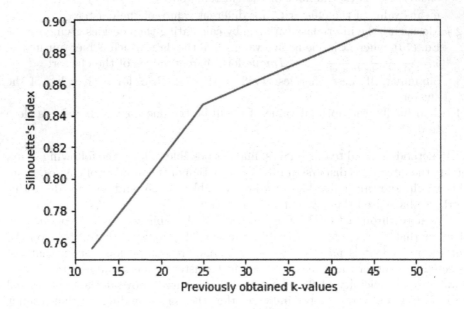

Fig. 7. Partitioning quality

With this **Silouhette index**, we observe remarkably how superb the partitioning quality becomes as a function of the number of clusters satisfying the conditions of Huygens' theorem.

(2) Initialization of the different centroids One of the recent versions of this algorithm was implemented in 2019, offering another way of initializing centroids [11]. The principle consists in choosing the initial centroids in each of the grid fragments of the image with the aim that the centers are uniformly distributed throughout the image. In the implementation of this algorithm, we put two convergence criteria:

(a.) We set the maximum number of iterations above which the algorithm stops;
(b.) If there is no more mobility between the different centroids, then there is convergence and we finish.

Fig. 8. Application of the $k-$means algorithm to some image of face

Figure 8 illustrates as well how the grouping of the different pixels of the image was carried out. Indeed, the different groups of pixels formed in the image of the face are such that one can always identify their respective layouts by assigning each pixel group a unique pixel value.

Once we have partitioned our images, what remains to be done is to associate with each partition a corresponding histogram, then from the histogram derive the Markov chains and so on, as shown in the Fig. 9:

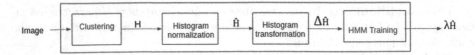

Fig. 9. Image model design approach by unsupervised learning

Table 2 present the results of the application of partitioning by unsupervised learning with k-means, for $k = 51$. The understanding of this Table 2 is the same as that of the Table 1.

5   Experimental Results

The image comparison methodology that we propose is given in Fig. 10:

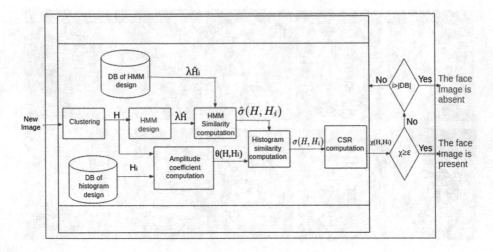

Fig. 10. Image comparison methodology

In a first step, which we call enrolment, templates of the images of the faces of the people who will be allowed to access the system are created and trained, and the system keeps two databases within it: a database that contains the different histograms of the clusters obtained from the images and a database of the trained models of these images. Thus, when a potential individual comes to the system, the following steps are taken by the system:

- Clustering of the captured facial image of the individual in question, resulting in the set of derived cluster histograms and the associated HMM and trained model;
- The system will, therefore, use its two databases, it will choose an image already enrolled in the system, i.e. choose a set of histograms and the corresponding trained model from the two respective databases;

- From this data chosen from the corresponding databases, the system evaluates the similarity between the model taken from the database and the model of the image it has just constructed, and it also evaluates the amplitude coefficient using the set of histograms;
- Evaluate the similarity between the histograms of the two images;
- The system then evaluates the rate of correspondence between the colors in the image using the similarity between the previously calculated histograms;
- Based on this rate of color matching between the two images, the system makes a decision: If this rate is above a certain threshold, then the individual who presented himself to the system will be allowed access to the image, otherwise, the system will repeat the process by selecting a new image from the database. If, in the end, the system does not find any image within the system such that the match rate is above the authorized threshold, then the system will deny access to the individual.

One of the peculiarities of this approach using HMMs is that the image base of enlisted persons is flexible, it is possible to add models of people's faces in the system. The results we obtained are therefore recorded in Table 3.

These results reveal all the interest of applying an unsupervised learning algorithm to the image in the partitioning phase, to proceed with the other steps. A result of 98.02% of true positives against 99.01% of false negatives also testifies that the method allows the recognition of what is real face and what is not.

Table 3. Comparison of the three methods.

Methods	TPR (in %)	FPR (in %)	TNR (in %)	FNR (in %)	Se (in %)	Sp (in %)
DMM	77.14	22.84	79.05	20.95	78.64	77.57
Grid + HMM	96.04	3.96	98.81	1.17	98.80	96.15
Grid + HMM (grayscale image)	83.81	16.19	86.67	13.33	86.27	84.26
Enhanced HMM	**98.02**	**1.98**	**99.01**	**0.98**	**99.02**	**98.04**
Enhanced HMM (grayscale image)	89.57	11.43	89.23	10.71	89.21	88.65

5.1   Synthesis of the Results of the Different Methods

When we look at the summary of the Table 4, we realize the diversity of the test image database proposed for FR. Despite the performances produced by each of these methods, we note the difficulty of being able to concretize the comparison of the different approaches. However, compared two approaches using statistics and linear algebra, stochastic approaches produce good performances, this is due to the information concerning the color of the image which is lost when switching from a color image to a grayscale image. This color information has been preserved in our approach using HMMs, but considering the results provided by neural networks, we understand that there is still much more information to

Table 4. Synthesis of the results of the different methods.

Approaches	Method	Dataset used	Accuracy (in %)
Statistics and linear algebra	PCA + LDA [8,16]	IFACE	92.64
	High-dim LBP [14]	LFW	95.17
	LG + PCA + LDA [26,27]	FERET	97.30
	EBGM [16]	LFW	95.25
*Neural networks	VGGface [20]	LFW, VGGface training set	98.95
	SphereFace [21]	LFW, CASIA-WebFace training set	99.42
	Arcface [22]	LFW, CASIA-WebFace training set	99.63
Stochastic approaches	DMM [12]	FERET	78.10
	Grid + HMM	**FERET**	**97.43**
	Enhanced HMM	**FERET**	**98.52**

take into account in our HMM associated with the image of the face. The texture of the image of the face as presented in Fig. 8, was the only characteristic extracted from the image. The *sensitivity* and *specificity* of a method allows an appreciation of the *intrinsic validity* of the latter.

5.2 Commentary on the Results

We have succinctly applied the method introduced by F. Samaria assigning to the face an HMM to five states including the forehead, eyes, nose, mouth, and chin. On the one hand, the fact that the image of the face is gray-scale is noticeable in the quality of the results. On the other hand, this method requires the face to be straight, which is not always realistic. All of these points help to understand the quality of the result because some of the information in the image is lost when the image is transformed into a grayscale image. Since the idea behind HMMs is to capture the statistical content of the image, and given the geometric variability of the face, the gridding process shows its limitations, especially when we look again at Fig. 5 which shows the stabilization of the values of the confusion matrix as a function of the size of the grid. The grid becomes stable when the image size in a frame is approximately 25×25 pixels. The result is all the better apprehended concerning the partitioning quality that we measure through the Silhouette index (see Fig. 7). However, to highlight the information lost when using grayscale images, Table 3 shows this drop in performance; TPR goes from 96.04% to 83.81% (for Grid + HMM); 98.02% to 89.57% (for Enhanced HMM); TNR goes from 98.81% to 86.67% (for Grid + HMM); 99.01% to 89.23% (for Enhanced HMM); FPR increases from 3.96% to 16.19% (for Grid + HMM); 1.98% to 11.43% (for Enhanced HMM), and FNR increases from 1.17% to 13.33% (for Grid + HMM); 0.98% to 10.71% (for Enhanced HMM). This observation allows us to understand that nearly 16.75% of information was lost during the conversion from color to grayscale image.

6   Conclusion and Perspectives

In this paper, we proposed to enhance the HMMs by initially integrating a clustering step by the k-means algorithm, instead of making a grid of the image which is a recent method of partitioning the image to lead to a better comparison. We have thereby shown to what extent the use of gray-level images certainly accelerates calculations, but is at the origin of a significant loss of information in the image. In particular, this work used the RGB color space, which made it possible to take into account almost all the information on the image in question. The image partitioning methods used were quite intuitive to highlight the major difference in the comparison of the images in the database. This allows us to point out the following perspectives in future work:

(*a.*) As we have seen in Fig. 10, the implementation of HMMs requires a lot of sequential steps, but a good part of these steps can be done in a parallel way such as the elaboration of the parameters A, B, and π of the initial model. A trick would be to evaluate these parameters in parallel to make the algorithm faster;

(*b.*) However, the main characteristic that we extracted from the image was its texture, to which we associated a descriptor that is the histogram to set up the associated HMM. This image descriptor is also the source of a loss of information in the image, the one providing information on the arrangement of the different pixels of the image. A perspective that we note for this work thus consists in combining texture characteristics based on a model [13], Gabor filters and co-occurrence matrices to better feed the HMM with much more information.

References

1. Thomas, L., Rauber, A.: Evaluation of feature extractors and psycho-acoustic transformations for music genre classification. In: ISMIR, pp. 34–41 (2005)
2. Samiria, F.: Face segmentation for identification using hidden Markov Modeles. In: British Machine Vision Conference, pp. 399–408. BMVA Press (1993)
3. Hamerly, G., Elkan, C.: Alternatives to the k-means algorithm that find better clusterings. In: Proceedings of the Eleventh International Conference on Information and Knowledge Management (CIKM) (2002)
4. Iloga, S., Romain, O., Tchuenté, M.: An accurate HMM-based similarity measure between finite sets of histograms. Pattern Anal. Appl. **22**, 1079–1104 (2019)
5. Xindong, W., Kumar, V.: The Top Ten Algorithms in Data Mining. Chapman and Hall/CRC, New York (2009)
6. Garnier, J., Perrier, V.: Introduction aux traitements mathématiques des images méthodes déterministes (2012–2015)
7. Arca, S., Campadelli, P., Lanzarotti, R.: A face recognition system based on automatically determined facial fiducial points. Pattern Recogn. **39**(3), 432–443 (2006)
8. Ahonen, T., Hadid, A., Pietikäinen, M.: Face recognition with local binary patterns. In: Pajdla, T., Matas, J. (eds.) ECCV 2004. LNCS, vol. 3021, pp. 469–481. Springer, Heidelberg (2004). https://doi.org/10.1007/978-3-540-24670-1_36

9. Arriaga, O., Plöger, P.G., Valdenegro, M.: Real-time convolutional neural networks for emotion and gender classification. arXiv:1710.07557v1 [cs.CV], 20 October 2017
10. Iloga, S.: Apprentissage à l'aide des modèles de Markov cachés et application. Note de cours, École de Mathématiques Africaine (EMA), Juillet 2019
11. Gupta, M., Chandra, P.: P-k-means: k-means using partition based cluster initialization method. In: 2019ICACM. Hosting by Elsevier SSRN, 06 April 2019
12. Samaria, F., Fallise, F.: Automated face identification using hidden Markov models. In: Proceedings of the International Conference on Advanced Mechatronics. The Japan Society of mechanical Engineers (1993)
13. Chaki, J., Dey, N.: Texture Feature Extraction Techniques for Image Recognition. Springer Briefs in Applied Sciences and Technology. Computational Intelligence. Springer, Singapore (2020). https://doi.org/10.1007/978-981-15-0853-0
14. Delac, K., Grgic, M., Grgic, S.: Independent comparative study of PCA, ICA, and LDA on the FERET data set. Technical report, University of Zagreb, FER, 27 February 2006
15. Turk, M., Pentland, A.: Eigenfaces for recognition. J. Cogn. Neurosci. 3(1), 71–86 (1991)
16. Changxing, D., Dacheng, T.: A comprehensive survey on pose-invariant face recognition. In: Centre for Computation and Intelligent Systems, Faculty of Engineering and Information Technology, University of Technology, Sydney 81–115 Broadway, Ultimo, NSW, Australia, 15 March 2016. https://doi.org/10.1145/2845089
17. Wang, M., Deng, W.: Deep face recognition: a survey. arXiv:1804.06655v9, 1 August 2020
18. Taigman, Y., Yang, M., Ranzato, M., Wolf, L.: DeepFace: closing the gap to human-level performance in face verification. In: Proceedings of the IEEE Conference on Computer Vision and Pattern Recognition, pp. 1701–1708 (2014)
19. Huang, G.B., Ramesh, M., Berg, T., Learned-Miller, E.: Labeled faces in the wild: a database for studying face recognition in unconstrained environments, Technical report 07–49, University of Massachusetts, Amherst. Technical report (2007)
20. Parkhi, O.M., Vedaldi, A., Zisseman, A.: Deep face recognition. In: BMVC, vol. 1, no. 3, p. 6 (2015)
21. Liu, W., Wen, Y., Yu, Z., Li, M., Raj, B., Song, L.: SphereFace: deep hypersphere embedding for face recognition. In: Proceedings of the IEEE Conference on Computer Vision and Pattern Recognition, pp. 212–220 (2017)
22. Deng, J., Guo, J., Xue, N., Zafeiriou, S.: ArcFace: additive angular margin loss for deep face recognition. In: Proceedings of the IEEE Conference on Computer Vision and Pattern Recognition, pp. 4690–4699 (2019)
23. Wilson, G., Cook, D.J.: A survey of unsupervised deep domain adaptation. Washington State University, USA. arXiv:1812.02849v3 [cs.LG], 6 February 2020
24. Starczewski, A., Krzyżak, A.: Performance evaluation of the silhouette index. In: Rutkowski, L., Korytkowski, M., Scherer, R., Tadeusiewicz, R., Zadeh, L.A., Zurada, J.M. (eds.) ICAISC 2015, Part II. LNCS (LNAI), vol. 9120, pp. 49–58. Springer, Cham (2015). https://doi.org/10.1007/978-3-319-19369-4_5
25. Marutho, D., Handaka, S.H., Wijakay, E., Muljono: The determination of cluster number at k-mean using elbow method and purity evaluation on headline news. In: 2018 International Seminar on Application for Technology of Information and Communication (iSemantic). IEEE (2018). https://doi.org/10.1109/ISEMANTIC.2018.8549751
26. Singh, C., Mogammed Sahan, A.: Face recognition using complex wavelet moments. Elsevier Ltd., 12 October 2012

27. Abrishami, S., Fazl Ersi, E., Abrishami, H.: Automatic person recognition by analyzing fiducial points. In: IKS SOCIETY (2005). ISBN 975-00132-0-4
28. Sahraeian, S.M.E., Yoon, B.-J.: A novel low-complexity HMM similarity measure. Signal Process Lett. **18**(2), 87–90 (2011)

Brain MRI Segmentation Using Autoencoders

Kishan Jackpersad[1] and Mandlenkosi Gwetu[2]([✉])(iD)

[1] University of KwaZulu-Natal, Private Bag X54001, Durban 4000, South Africa
[2] University of KwaZulu-Natal, Private Bag X01, Scottsville 3209, South Africa
gwetum@ukzn.ac.za

Abstract. Brain MRI segmentation is a popular area of research that has the potential to improve the efficiency and effectiveness of brain related diagnoses. In the past, experts in this field were required to manually segment brain MRIs. This grew to be a tedious, time consuming task that was prone to human error. Through technological advancements such as improved computational power and availability of libraries to manipulate MRI formats, automated segmentation became possible. This study investigates the effectiveness of a deep learning architecture called an autoencoder in the context of automated brain MRI segmentation. Focus is centred on two types of autoencoders: convolutional autoencoders and denoising autoencoders. The models are trained on unfiltered, min, max, average and gaussian filtered MRI scans to investigate the effect of these filtering schemes on segmentation. In addition, the MRI scans are passed in either as whole images or image patches, to determine the quantity of contextual image data that is necessary for effective segmentation. Ultimately the image patches obtained the best results when exposed to the convolutional autoenocoder and gaussian filtered brain MRI scans, with a dice similarity coefficient of 64.18%. This finding demonstrates the importance of contextual information during MRI segmentation by deep learning and paves the way for the use of lightweight autoencoders with less computational overhead and the potential for parallel execution.

Keywords: Brain MRI · Segmentation · Autoencoders · Filters · Image patches

1 Introduction

Brain imaging techniques have come a long way from the time they have been discovered. From Electroencephalography (EEG) to Magnetic Resonance Imagery (MRI), each of these has shown advancement in the way we obtain information about the human brain. This allows us to analyze and process data more efficiently to get a better understanding of the problem at hand. Efficient and

© ICST Institute for Computer Sciences, Social Informatics and Telecommunications Engineering 2022
Published by Springer Nature Switzerland AG 2022. All Rights Reserved
T. M. N. Ngatched and I. Woungang (Eds.): PAAISS 2021, LNICST 405, pp. 74–93, 2022.
https://doi.org/10.1007/978-3-030-93314-2_5

accurate segmentation of regions of interest within the brain aid neurologists in identifying brain diseases and disorders.

Manual segmentation has become a thing of the past. It is tedious and time-consuming. Hence automated segmentation has been introduced to enhance this process. This will improve diagnosis, and appropriate testing can take place within shorter spaces of time.

Brain MRI had taken the world by storm and is now the safest and most suggested brain imaging technique. It does not use radiation and can detect tumors or brain fractures that would not be picked up by an X-ray scan. Images from MRI scans are more detailed, and one can observe a greater range of soft-tissue structures. Segmentation of brain MRI scans are used to determine structural changes within the anatomy of the brain. These structural changes are used to detect brain diseases and disorders such as Alzheimer's. Automated segmentation methods have been widely explored and are still gaining popularity as new approaches in Deep Learning are allowing for advancement and more accurate segmentation.

Deep Learning methods have overcome the shortcomings of traditional Machine Learning techniques. They can generalize better by extracting a hierarchy of features from complex data due to their self-learning ability. The application of filters in image processing has also proved to play a significant role in obtaining better results, and hence, the effect of filtered slices for segmentation will be observed. These filtered slices could improve image data by making certain anatomical regions more visible and increase segmentation accuracy, or pixel values could be altered to a point where they affect the structure of brain anatomy and thus result in inaccurate or ineffective brain MRI segmentation.

The primary research question that this study will answer is: "Do filtered slices improve the effectiveness of brain MRI segmentation based on whole images and image patches?". Experiments will be conducted to investigate the effect that filtered slices have on segmentation, and further more, it will be determined if whole images or image patches improve the effectiveness of brain MRI segmentation.

This paper is structured in the following manner: Sect. 2 consists of the Literature Review which entails research on how Deep Learning models are being used for brain MRI segmentation. Section 3 is the Methodology that explains the implementation of this study. Section 4 is the Results and Discussion where the outcomes of this study are presented. Lastly, Sect. 5 is the Conclusion which summarizes the research findings and outlines future work.

2   Literature Review

Previously, Machine Learning algorithms were the go-to for many problems. These algorithms were applied to various scenarios and they asserted their dominance by proving to be very efficient. With the introduction of Deep Learning, things were taken a step further. Their application showed that there were new possibilities to obtain better results. When applied to brain MRIs, Deep Learning had opened numerous doors by achieving improved results in segmentation and classification tasks.

2.1 Convolutional Neural Networks

In terms of image processing, Convolutional Neural Networks (CNNs) work very well, as they are able to learn a hierarchy of complex features that can be used for image recognition, classification and are now being applied for image segmentation.

A journal article by Dolz et al. [9] reported the use of an ensemble of CNNs to segment infant T1 and T2-weighted brain MRIs. They found that segmentation of infant brain MRIs would pose a challenge as these scans have close contrast between white matter (WM) and grey matter (GM) tissue. The MICCAI iSEG-2017 Challenges public dataset was used to train the networks. Their main aim was to show how effective semi-dense 3D fully CNN, mixed with an ensemble learning strategy, could be and at the same time provide more robustness in infant brain MRI segmentation. Ensemble learning is the use of multiple models that are trained using different instances to improve performance accuracy and reduce variance for a problem. A set of models are used for prediction, and the outputs from these models are combined into a single prediction, usually generated by taking the most popular prediction of all the models. The basis behind using ensemble learning was to reduce random errors and increase generalization. The models used in ensemble learning varied by training data, where subsets from the overall training dataset were randomly chosen to train 10 CNNs. Majority voting was then used to choose the final prediction. For the activation function within the hidden layers, the authors used Parametric Rectified Linear Unit (PReLU), which increased model accuracy at a minor additional computation cost. Upon doing research, the authors found that using multiple input sources benefited the network and altered their model to allow for multi-sequence images (T1-weighted, T2-weighted, and Fractional Anisotropy - A type of brain MRI scan) as input. The CNN architecture composed of 13 layers made up of convolutional layers, fully-connected layers, and a classification layer. Batch normalization and a PReLU activation function is used before the convolutional filters. Input images were sent in as patches to reduce training time and increase the number of training examples. The average Dice Similarity Coefficient (DSC) for WM was 90%, GM was 92%, and cerebrospinal fluid (CSF) was 96%. The proposed architecture achieved excellent results as their metrics were able to rank first or second in most cases against twenty-one teams in the MICCAI iSEG-2017 Challenge.

A patch-based CNN approach was implemented by Yang et al. [8] which outperformed the two Artificial Neural Networks (ANNs) and three CNNs it was compared against. The proposed patchbased CNN contained seven main layers, made up of convolutional layers, two max-pooling layers, and a fully-connected layer. The architectures that it was compared against had various structures and differed by the number of feature maps and the input patch size. The proposed CNN employed a larger number of feature maps, which resulted in it having a higher performance than the other networks. The use of a larger patch size (32×32 compared to a patch size of 13×13) proved advantageous as the smaller patch size carried less information and made it harder for label learning. The proposed architecture achieved an average DSC of 95.19% for the segmentation of cerebral white matter, the lateral ventricle, and the thalamus proper. The dataset used in this article is the same as the one used in this study; the Schizbull2008 dataset from CANDI neuroimaging. The only pre-processing done in the article consisted of what was implemented in the original dataset, and the authors further implemented the generation of patches. This article shows that the use of patches used less memory and thus reducing the models' training time. The use of patches also mends the problem of having a limited dataset.

Label propagation entails assigning labels to unlabelled data points by propagating through the dataset. Liang et al. [19] implemented this method using a Deep Convolutional Neural Network (DCNN) to classify voxels into their respective labels. The model was trained to reduce the DSC loss between the final segmentation map and a one-hot encoded ground truth. Input images were fed into the network as mini-batches of $128 \times 128 \times 128$ patches. A combination of the ISBR and MICCAI 2012 dataset was used, and in total, 28 images were used as training, and 25 images were used for testing. Based on the discussion of the results, the implemented method obtained a DSC score of 84.5%.

2.2   U-Net Models

Lee et al. [18] implemented a U-net model that follows a patch-wise segmentation approach to segment brain MRIs into WM, GM, and CSF. A U-net architecture is similar to an autoencoder in the sense that it has an encoder and decoder layer and is an extension of a Fully Convolutional Network (FCN). A U-net architecture has a decoder, which is similar to the encoder to give it that U-shape. The authors used a combination of two datasets in their implementation: An Open Access Series of Imaging Studies (OASIS) and the International Segmentation Brain Repository (ISBR). They compared a patch-wise U-net architecture to a conventional U-net and a SegNet model. The results show that the proposed architecture achieved greater segmentation accuracy in terms of DSC and Jaccard Index (JI) values. An average DSC score of 93 was achieved, which beats the conventional U-net by 3% and the SegNet by 10%. Stochastic Gradient Descent (SGD) was used as the optimizer, and categorical cross-entropy was used as the loss function. An investigation of how patch sizes affect the DSC was conducted, and it was found that smaller patch sizes (32×32 was better than 128×128 and 64×64) resulted in a better DSC.

Zhao et al. [32] implemented convolutional layers in a U-net architecture to segment brain MRIs. Their implementation of a learning-based method for data augmentation and applied it to oneshot medical image segmentation. The segmentation labels were obtained from FreeSurfer, and the dataset was put together from 8 different databases. The brain images were of size $256 \times 256 \times 256$ and were then cropped to $160 \times 192 \times 224$. No intensity corrections were applied, and only skull stripping was applied as pre-processing. The model was trained to segment the brain images into 16 different labels, including WM, GM, and CSF. The implementation was evaluated against other learning-based methods and outperformed them. A DSC of 81.5% was achieved compared to the second-highest of 79.5% achieved from a model that used random augmentation.

2.3 Autoencoders

Atlason et al. [3] implemented a Convolutional Autoencoder to segment brain MRIs into brain lesions, WM, GM, and CSF in an unsupervised manner. The Convolutional Autoencoder architecture was created using fully convolutional layers. Noise was added to the inputs to ensure the model learns important features. The dataset used was obtained from the AGES-Reykjavik study. The Convolutional Autoencoder predictions were compared against a supervised method, a FreeSurfer segmentation, a patch-based Subject Specific Sparse Dictionary Learning (S3DL) segmentation, and a manual segmentation. The Convolutional Autoencoder performed the best against all these methods. The segmentation results for WM, GM, and CSF were not reported, although lesion segmentation achieved a DSC of 76.6%. The authors found that, at times, their model over-segmented due to image artifacts.

In 2018, a data scientist, Jigar Bandaria [5], implemented a Stacked Denoising Autoencoder (SDAE) to segment brain MRIs into WM, GM, and CSF. An Area Under the Curve evaluation of 83.16% was achieved on the OASIS dataset.

2.4 Review Summary

Brain MRI segmentation has come a long way and various Deep Learning methods (not limited to the ones mentioned above) have been applied to this problem in attempt to better previous state of- the-art results. These attempts do indeed beat previous results, be it in performance or metric. However, many of these attempts use different datasets (OASIS, ISBR, MICCAI, etc.) that have different properties, labels, etc. This does not create a level playing field and poses a challenge to actually determine which attempt is relatively better than the other. Certain attempts also focus on the entire brain while others focus on specific parts of the brain (WM, GM, CSF, tumors, etc.). However, they all appear to use DSC or JI as a metric to determine the accuracy of the model. Convolutional layers and batch normalization play an important role in obtaining good results and determining the right activation function for the architecture is key. Another common thing to note is that majority of the attempts that used image patches (size 32×32) showed to require less computational resources and at the same time, obtain as good or even better results. Even though the autoencoder implementations to segment brain MRIs did not achieve as high accuracy's as the other mentioned models as they can be lossy due to compression and decompression, the U-net model that uses patch-wise segmentation achieved results that are close to conventional CNNs.

3 Methodology

Autoencoders have been around for many years, but in the past, they were mainly used for dimensionality reduction and information retrieval as they did not produce better results than Principal Component Analysis (PCA). Since it was found that autoencoders can learn linear and nonlinear transformations, they proved to provide a more robust architecture [13] which makes them better at generalizing to problems.

Autoencoders are feed-forward neural networks that use self supervised or un-supervised learning to determine a hierarchy of important features within data. The aim is to learn an efficient encoding (representation) for a dataset and generate an output using that encoding. Using back-propagation to adjust weights within the network, an autoencoder will minimize reconstruction loss based on an output and a target. For the reconstruction of original data, the input becomes the target; otherwise, in terms of segmentation, the ground truth is used as the target.

There are three main components of an autoencoder: the encoder, the bottleneck (encoding), and the decoder. The encoders purpose is to reduce the dimensions of the data and train the network to learn meaningful representations along the way. The input into the encoder is the image to be segmented and the output from the encoder is fed into the bottleneck. The bottleneck is where the lowest point of the autoencoder lies. At this point, the dimensions of the data are at their lowest and contain very little information. The encoding is then fed into the decoder to decompress and generate an output (the segmented image). The bigger the size of the bottleneck, the more features are stored, and the more the reconstructed image will look like the original input. One should ensure not to keep the hidden layers too large, as the network would just learn to copy the data from input to output. The main idea of an autoencoder is to compress and decompress data. For this reason, autoencoders are known as lossy. The generated outputs often appear degraded when compared to the original inputs. More often than not, this is helpful when the transfer of data is more important than integrity or accuracy, e.g., live streaming concerts, game-plays, etc. Autoencoders are data specific and work best on data that they have been trained against. For example, an autoencoder that has been trained on compressing dogs would not be able to do a good job of compressing and reconstructing people.

Autoencoders have been implemented to segment images as in [30] for scene segmentation and in [25] for indoor and road scene segmentation. This goes to show that it is possible for an autoencoder to take in an image, compress it and then decompress it to generate a segmentation of the input. The process for segmenting brain MRIs is depicted in Fig. 1. The brain MRI scan is fed into the encoder to be compressed and is then fed into the bottleneck. The bottleneck then feeds the compressed image into the decoder to be decompressed, and as this occurs, the segmented image is being generated. The model output (segmented image) is then taken along with the corresponding ground truth, and a loss value is calculated. The network aims to minimize this loss value as it trains.

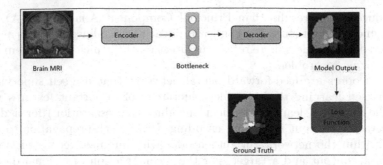

Fig. 1. Autoencoder image segmentation process.

3.1 Autoencoder Types

This study focuses on using two autoencoders for brain MRI segmentation: a Convolutional Autoencoder and a Denoising Autoencoder.

Convolutional Autoencoder. A Convolutional Autoencoder utilizes convolutional, pooling, and upsampling or transposed layers to compress and decompress data in an autoencoder architecture. The convolutional layers are used to extract features by applying filters to inputs and creating a feature map representing present information. This is where most of the network parameters are tweaked to obtain improved results. These parameters include the activation function, the number of kernels, the size of kernels, etc. Pooling layers perform the same task as convolutional layers by applying filters, although their primary purpose is to reduce data dimensionality within the network or, in other words, compress data [21]. Typical pooling layers consist of max-pooling (where the maximum pixel value within the neighborhood is taken) and average pooling (where the average of pixel values within a neighborhood is taken). Upsampling or transposed layers are then used for decompression. The final layer typically includes the use of a specific activation function based on the problem type. Convolutional Autoencoders are trained end-to-end to learn optimal filters to extract features that would help minimize the reconstruction error.

Convolutional Autoencoders have been used in areas such as segmentation of digital rock images [15], anomaly detection [28], and image classification paired with Particle Swarm Optimization (PSO) [27]. Figure 2 depicts the Convolutional Autoencoder architecture used in this study. The outcome of this model is the segmented brain MRI which needs to be as close to the ground truth as possible. The ConvolutionalAutoencoder contains convolutional layers (with LeakyRelu activation with $\alpha = 0.2$), batch normalization layers, maxpooling layers, upsampling layers, a layer normalization layer, and a final layer with a sigmoid activation.

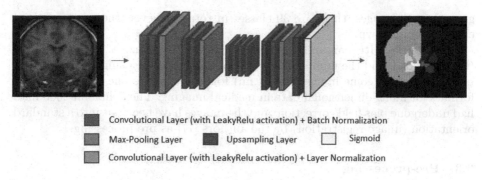

Convolutional Layer (with LeakyRelu activation) + Batch Normalization

Max-Pooling Layer   Upsampling Layer   Sigmoid

Convolutional Layer (with LeakyRelu activation) + Layer Normalization

Fig. 2. Convolutional Autoencoder architecture.

Denoising Autoencoder. Denoising Autoencoders are standard autoencoders that have been trained to denoise data or reconstruct corrupted data. Denoising autoencoders help reduce the problem of having the autoencoder merely copy the data from input to output throughout the network. It ensures that the purpose of the autoencoder is not rendered useless by reducing the risk of the network learning the "Identity Function" or "Null Function." Input data is stochastically corrupted on purpose and fed into the network. The loss function would then compare the output with the original, uncorrupted input. This would enhance the feature selection process and ensure useful features are extracted to help the network learn improved representations [29]. Typical noise that can be added to corrupt data include gaussian noise or salt-and-pepper noise.

Denoising autoencoders have been applied for speech enhancement [20], medical image denoising [12], fake twitter followers' detection [6]. The Denoising Autoencoder architecture used in this study has the same layers as the Convolutional Autoencoder, although the input is much noisier. This should allow the Denoising Autoencoder to learn important features that would improve segmentation accuracy.

3.2 Dataset

The dataset used for this study is obtained from the CANDIShare website, which was developed by The Child and Adolescent NeuroDevelopment Initiative (CANDI) at the University of Massachusetts Medical School. This dataset is more commonly known as Schizbull 2008 [17], the dataset contains linear, non-linear, and processed brain MRI scans, along with their corresponding ground truth segmentations. The ground truth images were manually generated by Jean A, Frazier et al. [17].

There are 103 subjects in the dataset that are between the ages of 4 and 17 years. Both male and female subjects are included and are from one of four diagnostic groups: Bipolar Disorder with Psychosis, Bipolar Disorder without Psychosis, Schizophrenia Spectrum, and Healthy Control. Considering all the ground truth images, there are 39 classes in total; however, the labels of these classes are unknown.

Each brain MRI scan and ground truth image has a size of $256 \times 256 \times 128$ (height, width, and the number of slices) and only contain a single channel. The brain MRI scans come in the NIfTI (.nii) format, which is one of the standard formats for multi-dimensional data in medical imaging. The Schizbull 2008 data had undergone bias field correction, and the images have been put into a standard orientation (image registration) by the authors [17] as pre-processing.

3.3   Pre-processing

Pre-processing refers to a technique that takes raw data and cleans or organizes it to allow the models to learn better. It makes the data more interpretable it is now easier for the model to parse. After obtaining brain MRIs, it is essential to pre-process these images to allow for a more efficient and accurate segmentation. Typical preprocessing methods in brain MRI segmentation include removing non-brain tissue, image registration [17,22], bias field correction [1,11,14,24] intensity normalization, and noise reduction. This study focused on the normalization and noise filtering preprocessing methods.

Intensity Normalization refers to the process of reducing intensity values to a standard or reference scale, e.g. [0, 1]. Intensity variations are caused when different scanners or different parameters were used to obtain MRI scans for the same or different patient at various times. One of the popular methods of intensity normalization includes the computing of z-scores. Yang et al. [26] used a histogram-based normalization technique as a pre-processing method, and they found that this greatly improved performance in image analyses and they were able to generate higher quality brain templates. Another popular method is the min-max normalization.

Min-max normalization was used as a pre-processing method in this implementation. Min-max normalization transforms the smallest value to zero and the largest value to one. When data points are very close together, normalization aids by making these datapoints sparse, this helps the model learn better and reduces training time. The formula for min-max normalization is given below.

$$norm(Img(i,j)) = \frac{Img(i,j) - min}{max - min} \tag{1}$$

In this case, $Img(i,j)$ is the brain MRI image pixel we wish to normalize, min refers to the minimum value found in the dataset, and max refers to the maximum value within the dataset.

Batch Normalization (BN) is a fundamental normalization technique that has shown significant improvement in the performance of a CNN [31]. BN solves the problem of preventing gradients from exploding. Since changing one weight affects successive layers (Internal Covariate Shift), BN reparametrizes the network to control the mean and magnitude of activations. This makes optimization easier. However, BN does have its kryptonite. Small batch sizes cause the estimates to be very noisy, which has a negative effect on training. Advantages of BN include: It accelerates the training of deep neural networks, implements regularization within the network, hence eliminating the need for dropout layers. It allows the use of much higher learning rates [2] and. Learning becomes more efficient with BN, and since it introduces regularization within the network, it reduces the chances of the model overfitting the data. BN works well with small training scales. As training scales increase, an evolution of BN called Synchronized Batch Normalization would be needed. BN was implemented after every convolution layer (as this is where the activation function lies) as [16] showed that BN performs and yields better results when placed after the activation function.

Layer Normalization (LN) works by normalizing across input features that are independent of each other, unlike Batch Normalization where normalization occurs across the batch. It is basically the transpose of Batch Normalization. LN helps speed up the training time of a network and address the drawbacks of Batch Normalization. [4] introduced the LN technique and found that this technique worked well with recurrent networks, but more research and tests would need to be conducted to make LN work well with Convolutional Networks.

3.4   Activation Function

Activation functions are a necessity in neural networks as nonlinear activation functions make back-propagation possible. It helps determine which features are important within the data, and they reduce the chances of the network learning irrelevant features. Basically put, activation functions classify data into useful and notso- useful. The activation function introduces non-linearity into the output of the neuron by determining whether or not a neuron should be activated. This is done by activation could better these results. This was done, and ultimately Leaky ReLU produced the best results. Leaky ReLU addresses the problems of ReLU as it rectifies the dying ReLU problem [10]. This allows the model to essentially continue learning and perform better. Unlike the traditional ReLU activation function where all values less than 0 are set to 0, Leaky ReLU sets these values to values that are slightly less than 0; hence the slight descend on the left of the graph. This is done by the following equation:

$$f(x) = \begin{cases} 0.01x, & \text{if } x < 0 \\ x, & \text{otherwise} \end{cases} \tag{2}$$

From the above equation, we can see that values less than zero are set much close to 0 (0.01x). If the values are not less than zero, they are not changed. This helps minimize the sensitivity to the dying ReLU problem.

The values in the dataset have been normalized to a range of 0 and 1. The network would need to predict a value within this range for each pixel. Hence, a Sigmoid activation function was used in the final layer of the network.

3.5 Loss Function

Mean Squared Error (MSE) is used as the loss function. This loss shows the squared difference between the ground truth and the output of the model. MSE is calculated as follows:

$$MSE = \frac{1}{N} \sum_{i=1}^{N} (y_i - \hat{y}_i)^2 \tag{3}$$

Where N is the number of pixels, y_i is the ground truth image, and $\hat{y}_i$ is the output from the model. The result of MSE is always positive, and when the ground truth and model output are identical, a value of zero is obtained. The models loss starts at a high value and converges to much smaller values that are close to zero. When the model makes big mistakes, the squaring penalizes the model. Smaller mistakes are not as heavily penalized.

Other common loss functions for image segmentation that can be applied are Cross-Entropy (CE) loss as in [29]. The authors in [29] tried both CE and MSE and found that the network learned different features depending on which loss function was implemented. Dice Loss is another loss function that can be implemented as applied in [19]. It is possible to create a custom loss function based on a combination of loss functions. These will depend on what features you wish the model to learn.

4   Results and Discussion

4.1 Evaluation Metrics

During medical imaging, in real-time, the ground truth for patients is not available, and only the segmentation is generated given a brain MRI. Hence, it is important to determine a metric to validate the loss of the model or algorithm that is going to be used to generate these segmentations. The evaluation can be based on unseen data that has the corresponding ground truth. These metrics will tell us how well the model should perform in real-time.

Dice Similarity Coefficient. One of the most common and well-known metrics to evaluate image segmentation is the Dice Similarity Coefficient (DSC) [7]. The DSC tells us how similar two images are. It calculates area of overlap between two images and divides that by the total size. This metric is calculated as follows:

$$DSC = \frac{2|X \cap Y|}{|X| + |Y|} \tag{4}$$

X is the predicted segmentation from the model, and Y is the corresponding ground truth. $|X|$ denotes the number of pixels in the predicted segmentation, and $|Y|$ denotes the number of pixels the corresponding ground truth. $|X \cap Y|$ is known as the area of overlap. This metric calculates the number of identical pixels at a corresponding point within two images. The DSC is within the range of 0 and 1. A DSC of 1 is achieved when both X and Y are identical, and a DSC of 0 is achieved when there is no overlap between the two images. This would mean that values closer to 1 are desired.

Jaccard Index. Another standard metric for image segmentation evaluation is the Jaccard Index (JI), also known as the Tanimoto Coefficient [7]. This metric also calculates the similarity between two images, just like the DSC. Although, it penalizes bad classifications. This metric is calculated as follows:

$$JI = \frac{|X \cap Y|}{|X| + |Y| - |X \cap Y|} \tag{5}$$

X is the predicted segmentation from the model, and Y is the corresponding ground truth. $|X|$ denotes the number of pixels in the predicted segmentation, and $|Y|$ denotes the number of pixels the corresponding ground truth. $|X \cap Y|$ is known as the area of overlap. The JI calculates the intersection divided by the union of two images. This is metric is also within the range of 0 and 1. A value of 0 means that the two images are entirely different, and a value of 1 means that the two images are identical. This would mean that a Jaccard Index closer to 1 would be desired.

4.2 Implementation

In this study, the use of filters on two autoencoder models are investigated. These filters include a min filter, a max filter, an average filter, and a gaussian filter. The autoencoder architectures implemented are a Convolutional Autoencoder and a Denoising Autoencoder. These architectures will take in whole images and images patches to determine which of these work best. Tests were run on these two autoencoders with the previously mentioned filters and the original unfiltered dataset. Their results will be discussed in the next section.

After the brain MRI scans were loaded, the filters are applied. For the min, max and average filtered scans, a combined image was created by taking 3 consecutive slices and the respective min, max or average filter was applied. For gaussian filtered scans, a gaussian filter with a sigma value of one was used. This gave the MRI scan a slight blur. The unfiltered MRI scans remained as so. The brain MRI scans and their corresponding ground truth are then reduced from 256×256 to 128×128. The reduction in size was done to decrease computational costs. Furthermore, the scans are cropped to 80×88 to reduce the large amount of background pixels.

The middle twenty slices from each brain MRI scan was used for training models on whole images. These slices were used as they contained less non-brain tissue. This gave us a total of 2060 scans, along with their corresponding ground truth images. For the image patches, three slices from the middle were used and overlapping patches of 40×44 were generated from each of the three slices. In total 7725 patches were generated from 309 scans, thus 25 overlapping patches from each images was generated. A batch size of 32 was used for all models, and they were trained for 250 epochs. RMSprop was used as the optimizer with the default learning rate of 0.001. The loss function implemented was Mean Squared Error. Early stopping with a patience of 10 was implemented to reduce the chances of the model overfitting. A random seed of 42 was used for reproducibility.

The images were split into training, validation, and testing sets. The dataset was split as follows: 60% of the data was used for training, 20% was used for validation, and the remaining 20% was used for testing. For the Denoising Autoencoder, gaussian noise was added to images before training.

The min, max, and average filters were applied by taking three consecutive slices, and their min, max, or average was computed to obtain a single image. The gaussian filter (with a sigma value of one) was applied to all unfiltered training images, which gave them a slight blur. Figure 3 depicts the original image and alongside it is what the image looks like with the filters applied. From left to right, the images are: the unfiltered image, the min filtered image, the max filtered image, the average filtered image, and the gaussian filtered image. These images were used as input to train the Convolutional Autoencoder.

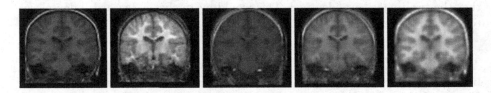

Fig. 3. Brain MRI scans with the applied filters.

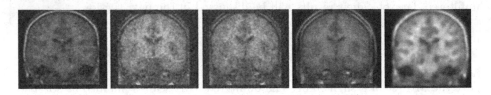

Fig. 4. Noisy brain MRI scans with the applied filters.

Figure 4 depicts the noisy images and alongside it is what the image looks like with the filters applied. From left to right, the images are: the unfiltered image, the min filtered image, the max filtered image, the average filtered image, and the gaussian filtered image. These images were used as input to train the Denoising Autoencoder.

It is apparent that compared to the unfiltered images, the other images vary in contrast. Certain regions of the brain appear in higher contrast to others. The min filter gives the center tissues of the brain a higher contrast, whereas the max filter makes it appear darker. The average filter image is basically a combination of the min and max filter. With the gaussian filter applied, the unfiltered image is now blurry and the center region of the brain is more defined.

4.3   Results

The results obtained from experimentation of various filters for each autoencoder on whole images and image patches are depicted below. These results are obtained from using the trained models to predict on the unseen test data. The filter that allowed an autoencoder model to obtain the highest result, for each table, is in bold. Table 1 shows the results obtained when various filters were applied to the whole images before being trained on the Convolutional Autoencoder. Based on the Dice Similarity Coefficient and Jaccard Index, the images that had an average filter applied to it has obtained the best results.

Table 1. Test results for Convolutional Autoencoder on whole images.

	Convolutional Autoencoder				
	Unfiltered	Min	Max	Average	Gaussian
DSC	44.47%	45.42%	45.07%	**45.86%**	45.30%
JI	29.42%	29.38%	29.09%	**29.75%**	29.33%

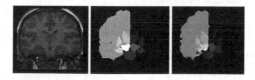

Fig. 5. Convolutional Autoencoder whole image segmentation.

Figure 5 depicts the segmentation of a brain MRI scan using the Convolutional Autoencoder. The first image shows the scan that is used as the input to be segmented. This is the average filtered image. The second image is the corresponding ground truth and this is what the predicted image from the Convolutional Autoencoder should look like. The third image is the predicted segmentation of the brain MRI scan. Table 2 shows the results obtained when various filters were applied to image data before being trained on the Denoising Autoencoder. The unfiltered whole images that were used as input obtained the best results.

Table 2. Test results for Denoising Autoencoder on whole images.

	Denoising Autoencoder				
	Unfiltered	Min	Max	Average	Gaussian
DSC	**44.59%**	44.27%	44.54%	44.28%	44.23%
JI	**28.67%**	28.43%	28.65%	28.43%	28.39%

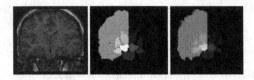

Fig. 6. Denoising Autoencoder whole image segmentation.

Figure 6 depicts the segmentation of a brain MRI scan using the Denoising Autoencoder. The first image shows the scan that is used as the input to be segmented. This is the unfiltered noisy image. The second image is the corresponding ground truth and this is what the predicted image from the Denoising Autoencoder should look like. The third image is the segmented brain MRI scan.

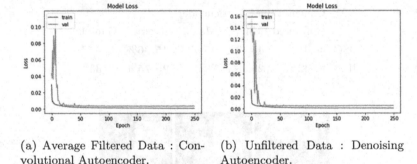

(a) Average Filtered Data : Convolutional Autoencoder.

(b) Unfiltered Data : Denoising Autoencoder.

Fig. 7. Loss graphs for the best performing models on whole images.

The graphs in Fig. 7 depict the loss curves for the models that were trained on average filtered whole images and unfiltered whole images respectively. These are best performing models for the Convolutional Autoencoder and Denoising Autoencoder. Table 3 shows the results obtained when various filters were applied to the input patches before being trained on the Convolutional Autoencoder. The gaussian filtered image patches that were used as input achieved the best results. Figure 8 depicts the segmentation of a brain MRI patch using the Convolutional Autoencoder. The first image shows the patch that is used as the input to be segmented. This is the gaussian filtered image patch. The second image is

Table 3. Test results for Convolutional Autoencoder on image patches.

	Convolutional Autoencoder				
	Unfiltered	Min	Max	Average	Gaussian
DSC	63.23%	63.84%	64.13%	63.44%	**64.18%**
JI	46.23%	46.88%	47.20%	46.45%	**47.26%**

Fig. 8. Convolutional Autoencoder image patch segmentation.

the corresponding ground truth and this is what the predicted patch from the Convolutional Autoencoder should look like. The third image is the predicted segmented patch from the model.

Table 4. Test results for Denoising Autoencoder on image patches.

	Denoising Autoencoder				
	Unfiltered	Min	Max	Average	Gaussian
DSC	62.49%	62.87%	62.80%	**63.41%**	63.25%
JI	45.45%	45.85%	45.77%	**46.42%**	46.25%

Table 4 shows the results obtained when various filters were applied to the input patches before being trained on the denoising autoencoder. The model that used average filtered image patches as input achieved best results. Figure 9 depicts the segmentation of a brain MRI patch using the Denoising Autoencoder. The first image is a noisy patch of an MRI scan that is used as the input to be segmented. This is an average filtered noisy image patch. The second image is the corresponding ground truth patch and this is what the prediction of the Denoising Autoencoder should look like. The third image is the predicted segmented patch from the model. The graphs in Fig. 10 depict the loss curves for the models that were trained on gaussian filtered image patches and average filtered image patches for the Convolutional Autoencoder and Denoising Autoencoder respectively.

4.4   Discussion

The results show that a simple autoencoder architecture can be used to segment brain MRIs. In two out of four cases (one being for the Convolutional Autoencoder on whole images and the other for the Denoising Autoencoder on image

Fig. 9. Denoising Autoencoder image patch segmentation.

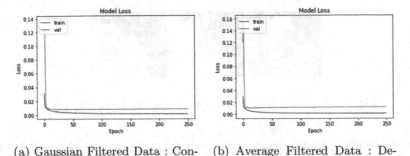

(a) Gaussian Filtered Data : Convolutional Autoencoder.

(b) Average Filtered Data : Denoising Autoencoder.

Fig. 10. Loss graphs for the best performing models on image patches.

patches), the average filtered data generated the best predictions and achieved the highest DSC and JI scores. The Convolutional Autoencoder achieved a DSC of 45.86% and JI of 29.75%, while the Denoising Autoencoder achieved a DSC of 63.41% and a JI of 46.42%. The model that achieved the best results on the Denoising Autoencoder using whole images had unfiltered MRI scans that were used as an input during training. It achieved a DSC of 44.59% and a JI of 28.67%. For the ConvolutionalAutoencoder that was trained on image patches, the gaussian filtered MRI scans achieved the best DSC and JI scores, this being 64.18% and 47.26% respectively. From all the experiments done, it is evident that the Convolutional Autoencoder which used gaussian filtered image patches as input achieved the best results.

The Convolutional Autoencoder achieved higher results than the Denoising Autoencoder when whole images and image patches were used for most filters applied. Although, the difference between their results is not very large. At most, there is a 2% difference. This shows that the autoencoder can work almost as well if given noisy data. The signal noise is reduced in the encoder as compression takes place. This will be advantages when noisy MRI scans are generated as the network is being trained to ignore this noise. This is main benefit of using a Denoising Autoencoder.

The use of filters has shown to increase segmentation accuracy in almost all models. This shows that their presence helps the network learn better. In three out of four cases, the min filter proved to be better than the max filter. When the filters were applied to image patches to train the model, they showed that they all had a greater effect as they achieved better results than the model that was trained on unfiltered image patches.

The use of image patches allowed the models to preform much better in every case as compared to those models that were trained on whole images. This showed a large ±20% improvement in both DSC and JI scores for the Convolutional Autoencoder and the Denoising Autoencoder. The models were able to focus more on the local features of the training data, which contributed to them performing better. The smaller the patch size, the more focus is given to local features. However, due the autoencoder architecture, one cannot make the patch size too small, as this would lead to a lot of information loss when the network compresses the data.

The lower the loss, the better a model is. The calculated loss is a representation of the errors made in the training and validation sets. Figure 7 depicts the loss graphs obtained from training the models on whole images. These models seem to be fitting the data very well as the training and validation loss curves are very close to each other. Both the curves have spikes in their early stages of training, but as training continues, the curves appear much smoother. Figure 10 depicts the loss graphs obtained from training the models on image patches. The graphs show that both models seem to be slightly overfitting as the training loss is decreasing while the validation loss seems to be increasing very slightly as each training epoch increases. If the overfitting begins to get worse, the early stopping will kick in.

Based on the graphs, the models seem to have learnt fairly well. At very early stages in training, the training and validation loss curves were closest to each other. In all four graphs, the validation loss either starts very high or goes very high for a small period of time and then decreases. The training curve starts off relatively low and continues decreasing as the model training occurs. Throughout training the loss curve is smooth and has no spikes.

Due to the large number of classes in the ground truth, the chances of a pixel being classified into one of the thirty-nine classes is slim; unlike other research experiments where pixels are classified into one of four classes (background, WM, GM, or CSF).

5 Conclusion

This study researched the application of autoencoders in image segmentation and whether or not filters improve its effectiveness. Based on the results and in response to the posed research question, it can be concluded that gaussian filtered images do improve segmentation quality. The use of whole images and image patches for training was also investigated. This investigation showed that image patches work much better than whole images. With a simple autoencoder architecture, we able to generate the segmentation of a brain MRI scan with fairly good results. However, the lossy nature of the autoencoder may prove to be a bit of a problem. More experiments need to be conducted to try and reduce this lossy nature.

Future work will focus on applying other types of autoencoders such as Stacked Autoencoders that worked well for brain MRI segmentation as in [5]. Transfer learning is another promising area of research that can prove beneficial to autoencoders as demonstrated in [23].

References

1. N4 bias field correction. https://simpleitk.readthedocs.io/en/master/link_N4BiasFieldCorrection_docs.html. Accessed 05 Sept 2021
2. Adaloglou, N.: In-layer normalization techniques for training very deep neural networks (2020). https://theaisummer.com/normalization/. Accessed 05 Sept 2021
3. Atlason, H.E., Love, A., Sigurdsson, S., Gudnason, V., Ellingsen, L.M.: Unsupervised brain lesion segmentation from MRI using a convolutional autoencoder. In: Medical Imaging 2019: Image Processing, vol. 10949, p. 109491H. International Society for Optics and Photonics (2019)
4. Ba, J.L., Kiros, J.R., Hinton, G.E.: Layer normalization. arXiv preprint arXiv:1607.06450 (2016)
5. Bandaria, J.: Brain MRI image segmentation using stacked denoising autoencoders. https://bit.ly/3dE0KFs (2017). Accessed 05 Sept 2021
6. Castellini, J., Poggioni, V., Sorbi, G.: Fake twitter followers detection by denoising autoencoder. In: Proceedings of the International Conference on Web Intelligence, pp. 195–202 (2017)
7. Crum, W.R., Camara, O., Hill, D.L.: Generalized overlap measures for evaluation and validation in medical image analysis. IEEE Trans. Med. Imaging **25**(11), 1451–1461 (2006)
8. Cui, Z., Yang, J., Qiao, Y.: Brain MRI segmentation with patch-based CNN approach. In: 2016 35th Chinese Control Conference (CCC), pp. 7026–7031. IEEE (2016)
9. Dolz, J., Desrosiers, C., Wang, L., Yuan, J., Shen, D., Ayed, I.B.: Deep CNN ensembles and suggestive annotations for infant brain MRI segmentation. Comput. Med. Imaging Graph. **79**, 101660 (2020)
10. Dubey, A.K., Jain, V.: Comparative study of convolution neural network's Relu and Leaky-Relu activation functions. In: Mishra, S., Sood, Y.R., Tomar, A. (eds.) Applications of Computing, Automation and Wireless Systems in Electrical Engineering. LNEE, vol. 553, pp. 873–880. Springer, Singapore (2019). https://doi.org/10.1007/978-981-13-6772-4_76
11. Fluck, O., Vetter, C., Wein, W., Kamen, A., Preim, B., Westermann, R.: A survey of medical image registration on graphics hardware. Comput. Methods Programs Biomed. **104**(3), e45–e57 (2011)
12. Gondara, L.: Medical image denoising using convolutional denoising autoencoders. In: 2016 IEEE 16th International Conference on Data Mining Workshops (ICDMW), pp. 241–246. IEEE (2016)
13. Goodfellow, I., Bengio, Y., Courville, A.: Deep Learning. MIT Press, Cambridge (2016)
14. Ivanovska, T., Wang, L., Laqua, R., Hegenscheid, K., Völzke, H., Liebscher, V.: A fast global variational bias field correction method for MR images. In: 2013 8th International Symposium on Image and Signal Processing and Analysis (ISPA), pp. 667–671. IEEE (2013)

15. Karimpouli, S., Tahmasebi, P.: Segmentation of digital rock images using deep convolutional autoencoder networks. Comput. Geosci. **126**, 142–150 (2019)
16. Kathuria, A.: Intro to optimization in deep learning: busting the myth about batch normalization (2018). https://bit.ly/2KXTA63. Accessed 05 Sept 2021
17. Kennedy, D.N., et al.: CANDIShare: a resource for pediatric neuroimaging data. Neuroinformatics **10**, 319–322 (2012)
18. Lee, B., Yamanakkanavar, N., Choi, J.Y.: Automatic segmentation of brain MRI using a novel patch-wise U-Net deep architecture. PLoS ONE **15**(8), e0236493 (2020)
19. Liang, Y., Song, W., Dym, J.P., Wang, K., He, L.: CompareNet: anatomical segmentation network with deep non-local label fusion. In: Shen, D., et al. (eds.) MICCAI 2019. LNCS, vol. 11766, pp. 292–300. Springer, Cham (2019). https://doi.org/10.1007/978-3-030-32248-9_33
20. Lu, X., Tsao, Y., Matsuda, S., Hori, C.: Speech enhancement based on deep denoising autoencoder. In: Interspeech, vol. 2013, pp. 436–440 (2013)
21. O'Shea, K., Nash, R.: An introduction to convolutional neural networks. arXiv preprint arXiv:1511.08458 (2015)
22. Subramanian, P., Faizal Leerar, K., Hafiz Ahammed, K.P., Sarun, K., Mohammed, Z.: Image registration methods. Int. J. Chem. Sci **14**, 825–828 (2016)
23. Rane, R.: Efficient pretraining techniques for brain-MRI datasets (2019). https://doi.org/10.13140/RG.2.2.11782.11843
24. Song, J., Zhang, Z.: Brain tissue segmentation and bias field correction of MR image based on spatially coherent FCM with nonlocal constraints. Comput. Math. Methods Med. **2019** (2019)
25. Spolti, A., et al.: Application of u-net and auto-encoder to the road/non-road classification of aerial imagery in urban environments. In: VISIGRAPP (4: VISAPP), pp. 607–614 (2020)
26. Sun, X., et al.: Histogram-based normalization technique on human brain magnetic resonance images from different acquisitions. Biomed. Eng. Online **14**(1), 1–17 (2015)
27. Sun, Y., Xue, B., Zhang, M., Yen, G.G.: A particle swarm optimization-based flexible convolutional autoencoder for image classification. IEEE Trans. Neural Netw. Learn. Syst. **30**(8), 2295–2309 (2018)
28. Tran, H.T., Hogg, D.: Anomaly detection using a convolutional winner-take-all autoencoder. In: Proceedings of the British Machine Vision Conference 2017. British Machine Vision Association (2017)
29. Vincent, P., Larochelle, H., Lajoie, I., Bengio, Y., Manzagol, P.A., Bottou, L.: Stacked denoising autoencoders: learning useful representations in a deep network with a local denoising criterion. J. Mach. Learn. Res. **11**(12) (2010)
30. Yusiong, J.P.T., Naval, P.C.: Multi-scale autoencoders in autoencoder for semantic image segmentation. In: Nguyen, N.T., Gaol, F.L., Hong, T.-P., Trawiński, B. (eds.) ACIIDS 2019. LNCS (LNAI), vol. 11431, pp. 587–599. Springer, Cham (2019). https://doi.org/10.1007/978-3-030-14799-0_51
31. Zhang, Q.: An overview of normalization methods in deep learning. https://zhangtemplar.github.io/normalization/. Accessed 05 Sept 2021
32. Zhao, A., Balakrishnan, G., Durand, F., Guttag, J.V., Dalca, A.V.: Data augmentation using learned transformations for one-shot medical image segmentation. In: Proceedings of the IEEE/CVF Conference on Computer Vision and Pattern Recognition, pp. 8543–8553 (2019)

Effective Feature Selection for Improved Prediction of Heart Disease

Ibomoiye Domor Mienye and Yanxia Sun[✉]

Department of Electrical and Electronic Engineering Science, University of Johannesburg,
Johannesburg 2006, South Africa
ysun@uj.ac.za

Abstract. Heart disease is among the most prevalent medical conditions globally, and early diagnosis is vital to reducing the number of deaths. Machine learning (ML) has been used to predict people at risk of heart disease. Meanwhile, feature selection and data resampling are crucial in obtaining a reduced feature set and balanced data to improve the performance of the classifiers. Estimating the optimum feature subset is a fundamental issue in most ML applications. This study employs the hybrid Synthetic Minority Oversampling Technique-Edited Nearest Neighbor (SMOTE-ENN) to balance the heart disease dataset. Secondly, the study aims to select the most relevant features for the prediction of heart disease. The feature selection is achieved using multiple base algorithms at the core of the recursive feature elimination (RFE) technique. The relevant features predicted by the various RFE implementations are then combined using set theory to obtain the optimum feature subset. The reduced feature set is used to build six ML models using logistic regression, decision tree, random forest, linear discriminant analysis, naïve Bayes, and extreme gradient boosting algorithms. We conduct experiments using the complete and reduced feature sets. The results show that the data resampling and feature selection leads to improved classifier performance. The XGBoost classifier achieved the best performance with an accuracy of 95.6%. Compared to some recently developed heart disease prediction methods, our approach obtains superior performance.

Keywords: Feature selection · Heart disease · Machine learning · SMOTE-ENN · XGBoost

1 Introduction

Cardiovascular diseases such as heart diseases are the leading cause of death worldwide. According to the world health organization (WHO), heart diseases amount to one-third of worldwide deaths [1]. Early detection of heart diseases is usually challenging, but it is essential to patient survival. Therefore, several machine learning methods have been developed to predict heart disease risk [2, 3]. Usually, medical data contains several features, and some could be noisy, which can negatively impact the model's performance. An efficient feature selection approach could select the most informative feature set,

T. M. N. Ngatched and I. Woungang (Eds.): PAAISS 2021, LNICST 405, pp. 94–107, 2022.
https://doi.org/10.1007/978-3-030-93314-2_6

reduce the computation cost of making predictions, and enhance the prediction performance [4]. Therefore, feature selection is an essential step in most ML applications, especially in medical diagnosis.

Feature selection refers to obtaining the most suitable features while discarding the redundant ones [5]. Feature selection is usually achieved using a wrapper, filter, or embedded method. Wrapper methods perform feature selection via a classifier's prediction, while filter-based techniques score each feature and select the highest scores [6]. Meanwhile, embedded methods combine both wrapper and filter-based methods [7]. Also, having too many attributes in a model increases its complexity and could lead to overfitting. On the other hand, fewer features lead to ML models that are more effective in predicting the class variable. Therefore, this research aims to use the recursive feature elimination technique to obtain the most relevant features for detecting heart disease.

Recursive feature elimination is a type of wrapper-based feature selection method. It is a greedy algorithm used to obtain an optimal feature set [8]. The RFE employs a different ML algorithm to rank the attributes and recursively eliminates the least important attributes whose removal will improve the generalization performance of the classifier. The iterative process of eliminating the weakest attributes goes on until the specified number of attributes is obtained. The RFE's performance relies on the classifier used as the estimator in its implementation. Therefore, it would be beneficial to use different classifiers and compare the predicted features to obtain a more reliable feature set.

Our research aims to develop a feature selection approach to obtain the most informative features to enhance the classification performance of the classifiers. This research uses three base algorithms separately in the RFE implementation to predict the most relevant features. The algorithms include gradient boosting, logistic regression, and decision tree. A feature selection rule based on set theory is applied to obtain the optimal feature set. Then, the optimum feature set serves as input to the logistic regression (LR), decision tree (DT), random forest (RF), linear discriminant analysis (LDA), naïve Bayes (NB), and extreme gradient boosting (XGBoost).

Meanwhile, the class imbalance problem is usually considered when dealing with medical datasets because the healthy (majority class) usually outnumber the sick (minority class) [9]. Most conventional machine learning algorithms tend to underperform when trained with imbalanced data, especially in classifying samples in the minority class. Furthermore, in medical data, samples in the minority class are of particular interest, and the cost of misclassifying them is higher than that of the majority class [10]. Hence, this study employs the hybrid synthetic Minority Oversampling Technique-Edited Nearest Neighbor (SMOTE-ENN) to resample the data and create a dataset with a balanced class distribution.

The contributions of this research include the development of an efficient approach to detect heart disease, implement effective data resampling, select the most relevant heart disease features from the dataset, and compare the performance of different ML algorithms. The rest of this paper is structured as follows: Sect. 2 reviews some related works in recent literature. Section 3 briefly discusses the proposed approach and the various algorithms used in the study. Section 4 describes the dataset and performance assessment metrics used in this paper. Section 5 presents the results and discussion, while Sect. 6 concludes the article and discusses future research directions.

2   Related Works

Many research works have presented different ML-based methods to predict heart disease accurately. For example, in [11], a new diagnostic system was developed to predict heart disease using a random search algorithm to select the relevant features and a random forest classifier to predict heart disease. The random search algorithm selected seven features as the most informative features from the famous Cleveland heart disease dataset, which initially contained 14 features. The experimental results showed that the proposed approach achieved a 3.3% increase in accuracy compared to the traditional random forest algorithm. The proposed approach also obtained superior performance compared to five other ML algorithms and eleven methods from previous literature.

In [12], a deep belief network (DBN) was optimized to prevent overfitting and underfitting in heart disease prediction. The authors employed the Ruzzo-Tompa method to eliminate irrelevant features. The study also developed a stacked genetic algorithm (GA) to find the optimal settings for the DBN. The experimental results achieved better performance compared to other ML techniques. Similarly, Ishaq et al. [13] used the random forest algorithm to select the optimal features for heart disease prediction. They employed nine ML algorithms for the prediction task, including adaptive boosting classifier (AdaBoost), gradient boosting machine (GBM), support vector machines (SVM), extra tree classifier (ETC), and logistic regression etc. The study also utilized the synthetic minority oversampling technique (SMOTE) to balance the data. The experimental results showed that the ETC achieved the best performance with an accuracy of 92.6%.

Ghosh et al. [1] proposed a machine learning approach for effective heart disease prediction by incorporating several techniques. The research combined well-known heart disease datasets such as the Cleveland, Hungarian, Long Beach, and Statlog datasets. The feature selection was achieved using the least absolute shrinkage and selection operator (LASSO) algorithm. From the results obtained, the hybrid random forest bagging method achieved the best performance. Meanwhile, Lakshmananao et al. [14] developed an ML approach to predict heart disease using sampling techniques to balance the data and feature selection to obtain the most relevant features. The preprocessed data were then employed to train an ensemble classifier. The sampling techniques include SMOTE, random oversampling, adaptive synthetic (ADASYN) sampling approach. The results show that the feature selection and sampling techniques enhanced the performance of the ensemble classifier, which obtained a prediction accuracy of 91%.

Furthermore, Haq et al. [15] applied feature selection to the Cleveland heart disease dataset to obtain the most relevant features to improve the classification performance and reduce the computational cost of a decision support system. The feature selection was achieved using the sequential backward selection technique, and the classification was performed using a k-nearest neighbor (KNN) classifier. The experimental results showed that the feature selection step improved the performance of the KNN classifier, and an accuracy of 90% was obtained.

Mienye et al. [2] proposed an improved ensemble learning method to detect heart disease. The study employed decision trees as based learners in building a homogenous ensemble classifier which achieved an accuracy of 93%. In [3], the authors presented a heart disease prediction approach that combined sparse autoencoder and an artificial neural network. The autoencoder performed unsupervised feature learning to enhance the classification performance of the neural network, and classification accuracy of 90% was obtained. Meanwhile, most of the heart disease prediction models in the literature achieved somewhat acceptable performance. Research has shown that datasets with balanced class distribution and optimal feature sets can significantly improve the prediction ability of machine learning classifiers [16, 17]. Therefore, this study aims to implement an efficient data resampling method and robust feature selection method to enhance heart disease prediction.

3 Methodology

This section briefly discusses the various methods utilized in the course of this research. Firstly, we discuss the hybrid SMOTE-ENN technique used to balance the heart disease data. Secondly, we provide an overview of the recursive feature elimination method and the proposed feature selection rule. Thirdly, the ML classifiers used in training the models are discussed.

3.1 Hybrid SMOTE-ENN

Resampling techniques are used to add or eliminate certain instances from the data, thereby creating balanced data for efficient machine learning. Conventional machine learning classifiers perform better with balanced training data. Oversampling techniques create new synthetic samples in the minority class, while undersampling techniques eliminate examples in the majority class [18]. Both techniques have achieved good performance in diverse tasks. However, previous research has shown that they perform excellent data resampling when both methods are combined [19].

This study aims to perform both oversampling and undersampling using the hybrid SMOTE-ENN method proposed by Batista et al. [20]. This hybrid method creates balanced data by applying both oversampling and undersampling. It combines the SMOTE ability to create synthetic samples in the minority class and the ENN ability to remove examples from both classes that have different class from its k-nearest neighbor majority class. The algorithm works by applying SMOTE to oversample the minority class until the data is balanced. The ENN is then used to remove the unwanted overlapping examples in both classes to maintain an even class distribution [21]. Several research works have shown that the SMOTE-ENN technique results in better performance than when the SMOTE or ENN is used alone [19, 22, 23].

3.2 Recursive Feature Elimination

Recursive feature elimination is a wrapper-based feature selection algorithm. Hence, a different ML algorithm is utilized at the core of the technique wrapped by the RFE. The algorithm iteratively constructs a model from the input features. The model coefficients are used to select the most relevant features until every feature in the dataset has been evaluated. During the iteration process, the least important features are removed. Firstly, the RFE uses the full feature set to calculate the performance of the estimator. Hence, every predictor is given a score. The features with the lowest scores are removed in every iteration, and the estimator's performance is recalculated based on the remaining feature set. Finally, the subset which produces the best performance is returned as the optimum feature set [24].

An essential part of the RFE technique is the choice of estimator used to select the features. Therefore, it could be inefficient to base the final selected features using a single algorithm. Combining two or more algorithms that complement each other could efficiently produce a more reliable feature subset. Therefore, in this research, we aim to use gradient boosting, decision tree, and logistic regression as estimators in the RFE. We introduce a feature selection rule to obtain the most relevant features from the three predicted feature sets. The rule is that a feature is selected if it was chosen by at least two of the three base algorithms used in the RFE implementation. Assuming the final feature set is represented by A and the optimal feature set selected by gradient boosting, logistic regression and decision tree is represented by the set X, Y, and Z, respectively. Then, we can use set theory to define the rule as:

$$A = (X \cap Y \cap Z) \cup (X \cap Y) \cup (Y \cap Z) \cup (X \cap Z) \tag{1}$$

3.3 Logistic Regression

Logistic regression is a statistical method that applies a logistic function to model a binary target variable. It is similar to linear regression but with a binary target variable. The logistic regression models the probability of an event based on individual attributes. Since probability is a ratio, it is the logarithm of the probability that is modelled:

$$\log\left(\frac{\pi}{1-\pi}\right) = \beta_0 + \beta_1 x_1 + \beta_2 x_2 + \ldots \beta_m x_m \tag{2}$$

where π represents the probability of an outcome (i.e., heart disease or no heart disease), β_i denotes the regression coefficients, and x_i represents the independent variables [25].

3.4 Decision Tree

Decision trees are popular ML algorithms that can be used for both classification and regression tasks. They utilize a tree-like model of decisions to develop their predictive models. There are different types of decision tree algorithms, but in this study, we use the classification and regression tree (CART) [26] algorithm to develop our decision tree model. CART uses the Gini index to compute the probability of an instance being wrongly classified when randomly selected. Assuming a set of samples has J classes, and $i \in \{1, 2, \ldots, J\}$, then Gini index is defined as:

$$Gini = 1 - \sum\nolimits_{i=1}^{J} p_i^2 \tag{3}$$

where p_i is the probability of a sample being classified to a particular class.

3.5 Random Forest

Random forest [27] is an ensemble learning algorithm that uses multiple decision tree models to classify data better. It is an extension of the bagging technique that generates random feature subsets to ensure a low correlation between the different trees. The algorithm builds several decision trees, and the bootstrap sample method is used to train the trees from the input data. In classification tasks, the input vector is applied to every tree in the random forest, and the trees vote for a class [28]. After that, the random forest classifier selects the class with the most votes. The difference between the random forest algorithm and decision tree is that it chooses a subset of the input feature, while decision trees consider all the possible feature splits. Different variants of the random forest algorithm [29–31] have been widely applied in diverse medical diagnosis applications with excellent performance.

3.6 Linear Discriminant Analysis

Linear discriminant analysis is a generalization of Fisher's linear discriminant, a statistical method used to compute a linear combination of features that separates two or more target variables. The calculated combination can then be utilized either as a linear classifier or for dimensionality reduction and then classification. LDA aims to find a linear function:

$$y = a_1 x_{i_1} + a_2 x_{i_2} + a_3 x_{i_3} + \cdots + a_m x_{i_m} \tag{4}$$

where $a^T = [\{a_1, a_2, \ldots, a_m\}]$ is a vector of coefficients to be calculated, whereas $x_i = [x_{i_1}, x_{i_2}, \ldots, x_{i_m}]$ are the input variables [32].

3.7 Naïve Bayes

Naïve Bayes classifiers are probabilistic classifiers based on Bayes' Theorem. They are called naïve because they assume the attributes utilized for training the model are independent of each other [33]. Assuming X is a sample with n attributes, represented by $X = (x_1, \ldots, x_n)$. To compute the class C_k that X belongs to, the algorithm employs a probability model using Bayes theorem:

$$P(C_k | X) = \frac{P(X | C_k) P(C_k)}{P(X)} \tag{5}$$

The class that X belongs to is assigned using a decision rule:

$$y = argmax P(C_k) \Pi_{i=1}^{n} P(X_i | C_k) \tag{6}$$

where y represents the predicted class. The naïve Bayes algorithm is a simple method for building classifiers. There are numerous algorithms based on the naïve Bayes principle, and all of these algorithms assume that the value of a given attribute is independent of the value of the other attributes, given the class variable. In this study, we employ the Gaussian naïve Bayes algorithm, which assumes that the continuous values related to each class are distributed based on a Gaussian (i.e. normal) distribution.

3.8 Extreme Gradient Boosting

Extreme gradient boosting (XGBoost) is an implementation of the gradient boosting machine. It is based on decision trees and can be used for both regression and classification problems. The primary computation process of the XGBoost is the collection of repeated results:

$$\hat{y}_i^{(T)} = \hat{y}_i^{(0)} + \sum_{t=1}^{T} f_t(x_i) \tag{7}$$

where $f_0(x_i) = \hat{y}_i^{(0)} = 0$ and $f_t(x_i) = \omega_{q(x_i)}$. T represents the number of decision trees, $\hat{y}_i^{(T)}$ denotes the predicted value of the i_{th} instance, ω represents a weight vector associated with the leaf node, and $q(x_i)$ represents a function of the feature vector x_i that is mapped to the leaf node [34]. In the XGBoost implementation, the trees are added one after the other to make up the ensemble and trained to correct the misclassifications made by the previous models.

3.9 The Architecture of the Proposed Heart Disease Prediction Model

The flowchart of the proposed heart disease prediction method is shown in Fig. 1. Firstly, the heart disease dataset is resampled using the SMOTE-ENN method to create a dataset with a balanced class distribution. Secondly, the proposed feature selection method is used to select the optimal feature set, which is then split into training and testing sets. The training set is used to train the various classifiers, while the testing set is used to evaluate the classifiers' performance.

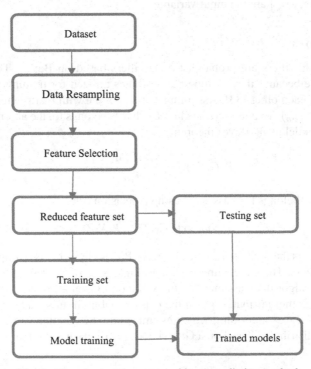

Fig. 1. Flowchart of the proposed heart prediction method

4 Dataset and Performance Metrics

The heart disease dataset used in this study contains 303 samples obtained from medical records of patients above 40 years old. The dataset was compiled at the Faisalabad Institute of Cardiology in Punjab, Pakistan [35]. It comprises 12 attributes and a target variable, including binary attributes such as anaemia, gender, diabetes, smoking, high blood pressure (HBP). Furthermore, the attributes include creatinine phosphokinase (CPK), which is the level of the CPK enzyme in the blood. Other features include ejection fraction, the amount of blood leaving the heart at every contraction, platelets, serum creatinine, etc. The full features are shown in Table 1.

Table 1. Features of the heart disease dataset.

S/N	Features	Code
1	Age	F1
2	Anaemia	F2
3	HBP	F3
4	Creatinine phosphokinase	F4
5	Diabetes	F5
6	Ejection fraction	F6
7	Gender	F7
8	Platelets	F8
9	Serum creatinine	F9
10	Serum sodium	F10
11	Smoking	F11
12	Time	F12
13	Death event (target variable)	F13

Meanwhile, the dataset is not balanced, as there are more samples in the majority class than the minority class. Hence, the need to efficiently balance the data to enhance the classification performance. Furthermore, this research utilizes performance metrics such as accuracy, precision, sensitivity, and F-measure. Their mathematical representations are shown below:

$$Accuracy = \frac{TP + TN}{TP + TN + FP + FN} \tag{8}$$

$$Precision = \frac{TP}{TP + FP} \tag{9}$$

$$Sensitivity = \frac{TP}{TP + FN} \tag{10}$$

$$Fmeasure = \frac{2 \times precision \times recall}{precision + recall} \qquad (11)$$

where TN, TP, FN, and FP represent true negative, true positive, false negative, and false positive, respectively. Also, we utilize the receiver operating characteristic (ROC) curve and area under the ROC curve (AUC) to evaluate the performance of the various ML models.

5   Results and Discussion

This section presents the results obtained from the experiments. Firstly, the heart disease data is resampled using the SMOTE-ENN to create a dataset with a balanced class distribution. Secondly, the feature selection is performed using the proposed RFE technique. Though all the features are associated with heart disease, research has shown that reduced feature sets usually improve classification performance [36, 37]. The optimal feature set obtained by the RFE with gradient boosting estimator comprises the following: F1, F3, F5, F7, F8, F9, F10, F11, and F12.

The logistic regression estimator selected the following features: F1, F2, F3, F5, F7, F8, F9, F10, and F12, whereas the decision tree estimator selected F1, F2, F3, F5, F6, F7, F8, F9, F12. Therefore, applying the proposed feature selection rule gives the following features: F1, F2, F3, F5, F7, F8, F9, F10, F12, which is the final feature set. The selected features are used to build ML models. Tables 2 shows the performance of the classifiers when trained with the complete feature set. In contrast, Table 3 shows the performance when the algorithms are trained after the data has been resampled and the feature selection applied.

Table 2. Performance of the algorithms without feature selection and data resampling.

Algorithm	Accuracy	Sensitivity	Precision	F-measure	AUC
LR	0.822	0.746	0.765	0.755	0.857
DT	0.775	0.655	0.686	0.670	0.741
RF	0.830	0.753	0.770	0.761	0.880
LDA	0.810	0.686	0.703	0.694	0.867
NB	0.791	0.694	0.717	0.705	0.854
XGBoost	0.824	0.762	0.776	0.769	0.885

Table 3 shows that the reduced feature set enhanced the performance of the classifiers, and the XGBoost obtained the best performance with an accuracy, sensitivity, precision, F-measure, and AUC of 0.956, 0.981, 0.932, 0.955, and 0.970, respectively. Furthermore, the ROC curves of the various classifiers trained with the reduced feature set are shown in Fig. 2. The ROC curve further validates the superior performance of the XGBoost model trained with the reduced feature set.

Table 3. Performance of the algorithms after feature selection and data resampling.

Algorithm	Accuracy	Sensitivity	Precision	F-measure	AUC
LR	0.929	0.967	0.898	0.931	0.940
DT	0.877	0.913	0.887	0.900	0.870
RF	0.930	0.942	0.942	0.942	0.950
LDA	0.925	0.968	0.896	0.931	0.940
NB	0.904	0.928	0.914	0.921	0.900
XGBoost	0.956	0.981	0.932	0.955	0.970

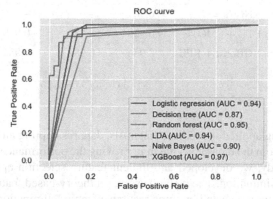

Fig. 2. ROC curves of the classifiers trained with the reduced feature set

Furthermore, we used the XGBoost model to conduct a comparative study with other recently developed research works, shown in Table 4. The comparative analysis is conducted to further validate the performance of our approach. We compare the XGBoost performance with recently developed methods, including an SVM and LASSO based feature selection method [38], XGBoost model [39], a hybrid random forest [40], a deep neural network (DNN) [41], a sparse autoencoder based neural network [3], an enhanced ensemble learning method [2], an improved KNN model [42], and an extra tree classifier with SMOTE based data resampling [13].

Table 4 further shows the robustness of our approach, as the XGBoost model trained with the reduced feature set outperformed the methods developed in the other literature. Furthermore, this research has also shown the importance of data resampling and efficient feature selection in machine learning.

Table 4. Performance comparison with other studies.

Reference	Algorithm	Accuracy	Sensitivity	Precision	F-measure
Li et al. [38]	SVM + LASSO	0.923	0.980	–	–
Tasnim and Habiba [39]	XGBoost	0.835	0.830	0.820	–
Pahwa and Kumar [40]	Hybrid RF	0.8415	–	–	–
Le et al. [41]	DNN	0.8382	0.9166	0.8627	0.8888
Mienye et al. [3]	Sparse autoencoder	0.900	0.910	0.890	0.900
Mienye et al. [2]	Ensemble classifier	0.930	0.910	0.960	0.930
Shah et al. [42]	KNN (k = 7)	0.907	–	–	–
Ishaq et al. [13]	ETC + SMOTE	0.926	0.930	0.930	0.930
This paper	XGBoost + RFE	0.956	0.981	0.932	0.955

6 Conclusion

In machine learning applied to medical diagnosis, data resampling and the selection of relevant features from the dataset is vital in improving the performance of the prediction model. In this study, we developed an efficient feature selection approach based on recursive feature elimination. The method uses a set theory-based feature selection rule to combine the features selected by three recursive feature elimination estimators. The reduced feature set then served as input to six machine learning algorithms, where the XGBoost classifier obtained the best performance. Our approach also showed superior performance compared to eight other methods in recent literature.

Meanwhile, the limitation of this work is that the proposed approach was tested on a single disease dataset. Future research would apply the proposed approach for the prediction of other diseases. Furthermore, future research could utilize evolutionary optimization methods such as a genetic algorithm to select the optimal feature set for training the machine learning algorithms, which could be compared with the method proposed in this work and tested on other disease datasets.

Acknowledgment. This work was supported in part by the South African National Research Foundation under Grant 120106 and Grant 132797 and in part by the South African National Research Foundation Incentive under Grant 132159.

References

1. Ghosh, P., et al.: Efficient prediction of cardiovascular disease using machine learning algorithms with relief and LASSO feature selection techniques. IEEE Access **9**, 19304–19326 (2021). https://doi.org/10.1109/ACCESS.2021.3053759

2. Mienye, I.D., Sun, Y., Wang, Z.: An improved ensemble learning approach for the prediction of heart disease risk. Inf. Med. Unlock. **20**, 100402 (2020). https://doi.org/10.1016/j.imu.2020.100402

3. Mienye, I.D., Sun, Y., Wang, Z.: Improved sparse autoencoder based artificial neural network approach for prediction of heart disease. Inf. Med. Unlock. **18**, 100307 (2020). https://doi.org/10.1016/j.imu.2020.100307

4. Saha, P., Patikar, S., Neogy, S.: A correlation - sequential forward selection based feature selection method for healthcare data analysis. In: 2020 IEEE International Conference on Computing, Power and Communication Technologies (GUCON), pp. 69–72 (2020). https://doi.org/10.1109/GUCON48875.2020.9231205

5. Kumar, S.S., Shaikh, T.: Empirical evaluation of the performance of feature selection approaches on random forest. In: 2017 International Conference on Computer and Applications (ICCA), pp. 227–231 (2017). https://doi.org/10.1109/COMAPP.2017.8079769

6. Hussain, S.F., Babar, H.Z.-U.-D., Khalil, A., Jillani, R.M., Hanif, M., Khurshid, K.: A fast non-redundant feature selection technique for text data. IEEE Access **8**, 181763–181781 (2020). https://doi.org/10.1109/ACCESS.2020.3028469

7. Pasha, S.J., Mohamed, E.S.: Novel Feature Reduction (NFR) model with machine learning and data mining algorithms for effective disease risk prediction. IEEE Access **8**, 184087–184108 (2020). https://doi.org/10.1109/ACCESS.2020.3028714

8. Zhang, W., Yin, Z.: EEG feature selection for emotion recognition based on cross-subject recursive feature elimination. In: 2020 39th Chinese Control Conference (CCC), pp. 6256–6261 (2020). https://doi.org/10.23919/CCC50068.2020.9188573

9. Mienye, I.D., Sun, Y.: Performance analysis of cost-sensitive learning methods with application to imbalanced medical data. Inf. Med. Unlock. **25**, 100690 (2021). https://doi.org/10.1016/j.imu.2021.100690

10. Guan, H., Zhang, Y., Xian, M., Cheng, H.D., Tang, X.: SMOTE-WENN: solving class imbalance and small sample problems by oversampling and distance scaling. Appl. Intell. **51**(3), 1394–1409 (2020). https://doi.org/10.1007/s10489-020-01852-8

11. Javeed, A., Zhou, S., Yongjian, L., Qasim, I., Noor, A., Nour, R.: An intelligent learning system based on random search algorithm and optimized random forest model for improved heart disease detection. IEEE Access **7**, 180235–180243 (2019). https://doi.org/10.1109/ACCESS.2019.2952107

12. Ali, S.A., et al.: An optimally configured and improved deep belief network (OCI-DBN) approach for heart disease prediction based on ruzzo-tompa and stacked genetic algorithm. IEEE Access **8**, 65947–65958 (2020). https://doi.org/10.1109/ACCESS.2020.2985646

13. Ishaq, A., et al.: Improving the prediction of heart failure patients' survival using SMOTE and effective data mining techniques. IEEE Access **9**, 39707–39716 (2021). https://doi.org/10.1109/ACCESS.2021.3064084

14. Lakshmanarao, A., Srisaila, A., Kiran., T.S.R.: Heart disease prediction using feature selection and ensemble learning techniques. In: 2021 Third International Conference on Intelligent Communication Technologies and Virtual Mobile Networks (ICICV), pp. 994–998 (2021). https://doi.org/10.1109/ICICV50876.2021.9388482

15. Haq, A.U., Li, J., Memon, M.H., Hunain Memon, M., Khan, J., Marium, S.M.: Heart disease prediction system using model of machine learning and sequential backward selection algorithm for features selection. In: 2019 IEEE 5th International Conference for Convergence in Technology (I2CT), pp. 1–4 (2019). https://doi.org/10.1109/I2CT45611.2019.9033683

16. Kasongo, S.M., Sun, Y.: Performance analysis of intrusion detection systems using a feature selection method on the UNSW-NB15 dataset. J. Big Data **7**(1), 1–20 (2020). https://doi.org/10.1186/s40537-020-00379-6

17. Kasongo, S.M., Sun, Y.: A deep learning method with filter based feature engineering for wireless intrusion detection system. IEEE Access **7**, 38597–38607 (2019). https://doi.org/10.1109/ACCESS.2019.2905633

18. Hasanin, T., Khoshgoftaar, T.M., Leevy, J.L., Bauder, R.A.: Severely imbalanced Big Data challenges: investigating data sampling approaches. J. Big Data **6**(1), 1–25 (2019). https://doi.org/10.1186/s40537-019-0274-4

19. Xu, Z., Shen, D., Nie, T., Kou, Y.: A hybrid sampling algorithm combining M-SMOTE and ENN based on Random forest for medical imbalanced data. J. Biomed. Inform. **107**, 103465 (2020). https://doi.org/10.1016/j.jbi.2020.103465

20. Batista, G.E.A.P.A., Prati, R.C., Monard, M.C.: A study of the behavior of several methods for balancing machine learning training data. SIGKDD Explor. Newsl. **6**(1), 20–29 (2004). https://doi.org/10.1145/1007730.1007735

21. Fitriyani, N.L., Syafrudin, M., Alfian, G., Rhee, J.: HDPM: an effective heart disease prediction model for a clinical decision support system. IEEE Access **8**, 133034–133050 (2020). https://doi.org/10.1109/ACCESS.2020.3010511

22. Le, T., Vo, M.T., Vo, B., Lee, M.Y., Baik, S.W.: A Hybrid approach using oversampling technique and cost-sensitive learning for bankruptcy prediction. Complexity **2019**, e8460934 (2019). https://doi.org/10.1155/2019/8460934

23. Dogo, E.M., Nwulu, N.I., Twala, B., Aigbavboa, C.: Accessing imbalance learning using dynamic selection approach in water quality anomaly detection. Symmetry **13**(5), Art. no. 5 (2021). https://doi.org/10.3390/sym13050818

24. Koul, N., Manvi, S.S.: Ensemble feature selection from cancer gene expression data using mutual information and recursive feature elimination. In: 2020 Third International Conference on Advances in Electronics, Computers and Communications (ICAECC), pp. 1–6 (2020). https://doi.org/10.1109/ICAECC50550.2020.9339518

25. Sperandei, S.: Understanding logistic regression analysis. Biochem. Med. (Zagreb) **24**(1), 12–18 (2014). https://doi.org/10.11613/BM.2014.003

26. Breiman, L., Friedman, J.H., Olshen, R.A., Stone, C.J.: Classification and regression trees. Wadsworth & Brooks, Monterey (1983). /paper/Classification-and-Regression-Trees-Breiman-Friedman/8017699564136f93af21575810d557dba1ee6fc6. Accessed on 05 Aug 2020

27. Breiman, L.: Random forests. Mach. Learn. **45**(1), 5–32 (2001). https://doi.org/10.1023/A:1010933404324

28. Mushtaq, M.-S., Mellouk, A.: 2 - Methodologies for subjective video streaming QoE assessment. In: Mushtaq, M.-S., Mellouk, A. (eds.) Quality of Experience Paradigm in Multimedia Services, pp. 27–57 Elsevier (2017). https://doi.org/10.1016/B978-1-78548-109-3.50002-3

29. Ke, F., Liu, H., Zhou, M., Yang, R., Cao, H.-M.: Diagnostic biomarker exploration of autistic patients with different ages and different verbal intelligence quotients based on random forest model. IEEE Access **9**, 1 (2021). https://doi.org/10.1109/ACCESS.2021.3071118

30. Cui, H., Wang, Y., Li, G., Huang, Y., Hu, Y.: Exploration of cervical myelopathy location from somatosensory evoked potentials using random forests classification. IEEE Trans. Neural Syst. Rehabil. Eng. **27**(11), 2254–2262 (2019). https://doi.org/10.1109/TNSRE.2019.2945634

31. Guo, C., Zhang, J., Liu, Y., Xie, Y., Han, Z., Yu, J.: Recursion enhanced random forest with an improved linear model (RERF-ILM) for heart disease detection on the internet of medical things platform. IEEE Access **8**, 59247–59256 (2020). https://doi.org/10.1109/ACCESS.2020.2981159

32. Ricciardi, C., et al.: Linear discriminant analysis and principal component analysis to predict coronary artery disease. Health Inf. J. **26**(3), 2181–2192 (2020). https://doi.org/10.1177/1460458219899210

33. Chen, S., Webb, G.I., Liu, L., Ma, X.: A novel selective naïve Bayes algorithm. Knowl.-Based Syst. **192**, 105361 (2020). https://doi.org/10.1016/j.knosys.2019.105361
34. Cui, L., Chen, P., Wang, L., Li, J., Ling, H.: Application of extreme gradient boosting based on grey relation analysis for prediction of compressive strength of concrete. Adv. Civil Eng. **2021**, e8878396 (2021). https://doi.org/10.1155/2021/8878396
35. Ahmad, T., Munir, A., Bhatti, S.H., Aftab, M., Raza, M.A.: Survival analysis of heart failure patients: a case study. PLoS ONE **12**(7), e0181001 (2017). https://doi.org/10.1371/journal.pone.0181001
36. Miao, J., Niu, L.: A survey on feature selection. Proc. Comput. Sci. **91**, 919–926 (2016). https://doi.org/10.1016/j.procs.2016.07.111
37. Mienye, I.D., Kenneth Ainah, P., Emmanuel, I.D., Esenogho, E.: Sparse noise minimization in image classification using Genetic Algorithm and DenseNet. In: 2021 Conference on Information Communications Technology and Society (ICTAS), pp. 103–108 (2021). https://doi.org/10.1109/ICTAS50802.2021.9395014
38. Li, J.P., Haq, A.U., Din, S.U., Khan, J., Khan, A., Saboor, A.: Heart disease identification method using machine learning classification in e-healthcare. IEEE Access **8**, 107562–107582 (2020). https://doi.org/10.1109/ACCESS.2020.3001149
39. Tasnim, F., Habiba, S.U.: A comparative study on heart disease prediction using data mining techniques and feature selection. In: 2021 2nd International Conference on Robotics, Electrical and Signal Processing Techniques (ICREST), pp. 338–341 (2021). https://doi.org/10.1109/ICREST51555.2021.9331158
40. Pahwa, K., Kumar, R.: Prediction of heart disease using hybrid technique for selecting features. In: 2017 4th IEEE Uttar Pradesh Section International Conference on Electrical, Computer and Electronics (UPCON), pp. 500–504 (2017). https://doi.org/10.1109/UPCON.2017.8251100
41. Le, M.T., Thanh Vo, M., Mai, L., Dao, S.V.T.: Predicting heart failure using deep neural network. In: 2020 International Conference on Advanced Technologies for Communications (ATC), pp. 221–225 (2020). https://doi.org/10.1109/ATC50776.2020.9255445
42. Shah, D., Patel, S., Bharti, S.K.: Heart disease prediction using machine learning techniques. SN Comput. Sci. **1**(6), 1–6 (2020). https://doi.org/10.1007/s42979-020-00365-y

Convolutional Neural Network Feature Extraction for EEG Signal Classification

Liresh Kaulasar and Mandlenkosi Gwetu[✉][ID]

University of KwaZulu-Natal, Private Bag X01, Scottsville 3209, South Africa
gwetum@ukzn.ac.za

Abstract. This study explores a possible improvement to automated eye state prediction using an electroencephalogram (EEG). A Convolutional Neural Network (CNN) is used for EEG signal transformation in order to determine whether this improves the reliability of eye state predictions made using 42 different machine learning algorithms. Previous work based on raw EEG signal readings managed to automatically predict eye states with an error rate of only 2.7%. The K-Star algorithm was highlighted as being the most effective in this domain, from a group of 42 WEKA machine learning algorithms. This study demonstrates that by using a CNN to extract new EEG signal features, it is possible to predict a subject's eye state with 100% accuracy. Moreover, this improvement is demonstrated in the context of five different machine learning algorithms. The deployment of soft computing technologies in clinical environments normally requires absolute accuracy due to the critical nature of these contexts. This work demonstrates the fulfillment of this requirement, thus indicating the applicability of the proposed artificial intelligence techniques in smart systems for EEG classification.

Keywords: EEG · Preprocessing · Feature extraction · CNN · Machine learning algorithms

1 Introduction

Electroencephalogram (EEG) signals can be analyzed to reveal patterns that may indicate the current physical state of a patient. Example applications include automatic deduction of a patient's current eye state or the sleep level of an individual. These applications are essential for improving the overall quality of life for patients with brain disabilities or sleep disorders. The overall accuracy of manually analyzing and interpreting these signals leaves room for human error, which can result in misdiagnoses. Reliable automated EEG signal classification could significantly improve this process. Since CNN models have been successfully used in the area of image and classification [10], they could play a vital role in this study if EEGs can be represented as images.

© ICST Institute for Computer Sciences, Social Informatics and Telecommunications Engineering 2022
Published by Springer Nature Switzerland AG 2022. All Rights Reserved
T. M. N. Ngatched and I. Woungang (Eds.): PAAISS 2021, LNICST 405, pp. 108–119, 2022.
https://doi.org/10.1007/978-3-030-93314-2_7

This study aims to use Convolutional Neural Networks (CNNs) for transforming EEG signals, then determine whether this improves the reliability of the EEG sleep state predictions by legacy machine learning algorithms. CNNs incorporate four kinds of layers, specifically one or more convolutional layers, REctified Linear Unit (RELU) layers, pooling layers, and possibly a fully connected layer. The functioning of a CNN is similar to the way that the visual cortex in the human brain functions. The fact that EEG signals are susceptible to noise when they are recorded indicates that this study may have to remove this noise for better signal processing [2]. However, this does not necessarily mean that only noise will be removed, as critical diagnostic information may also be lost, resulting in a double-edged sword scenario. The objective of this study is to determine whether using CNN feature extraction will prove to be more effective at classification than using raw or preprocessed EEG signals. The research question for this study is: are CNN selected features more effective than raw EEG traces as input to legacy supervised machine learning models? When applying a filter to remove EEG signal noise, valuable information may be mistakenly interpreted as noise, thus compromising the overall accuracy of the CNN.

This study incorporates all 14980 instances of a publicly available dataset; this differs from the number of instances used in the study by Roesler and Suendermann [16] where only 14977 instances were used and the exact three instances removed are not specified. It is understood that this difference may have a bearing on study result disparities, albeit to a small extent. This study focuses on the central concept of improving the reliability of how EEG signals are classified. The machine learning algorithms are an essential part of what determines the success of this project - hence only existing implementations of legacy supervised machine learning models are used. The assumptions made are that the EEG signals are readily available, and this study does not focus on how the EEG signals are taken. Alternatively, the focal point is actually to process these signals in a manner that will improve the reliability of the adopted classification methods.

The remainder of this paper is structured as follows. Section 2 introduces EEG technology and highlights its common applications. Section 3 outlines some previous work related to EEGs and deep learning. Section 4 presents the methods and techniques used in this study. Section 5 presents the results of this study in comparison to previous work. Section 6 concludes this paper and highlights possible extensions to this study.

2   Electroencephalograms

The fluctuations in the electrical activity of the brain are clearly visible in an EEG. These impulses represent the communication that occurs between brain cells and organs. In order to categorise these patterns it is neccessary to understand what the different fluctuations depict. Figure 1 presents a case where these fluctuations appear as spike waves, indicating that the patient is suffering from absence epilepsy.

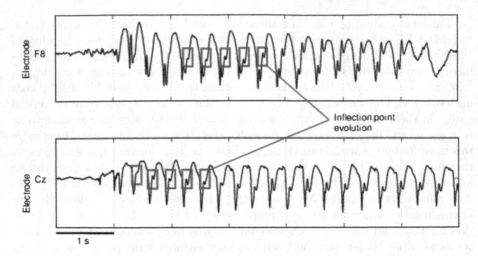

Fig. 1. Scalp EEG showing childhood absence epilepsy [9].

EEG readings are taken by technicians using a headset, which is worn by the patient. The headset consists of electrodes (these are conductors through which electricity enters and leaves) which supply the readings to a machine that records this data and creates an EEG. Abnormal EEGs can be used to detect brain tumors, brain damage, brain inflammations, strokes, comas, sleep disorders and any other generalized brain dysfunctions. Figure 2 represents an overview of how the sensors were placed on the scalp in order to extract the relevant readings. The sensors that are encased in blue circles represent a maximum increase, and those that are red represent a minimum decrease when opening eyes. The measured electrical current is the transfer of electrical impulses between neurons in the brain, and ultimately various muscles in body. It is through these readings that the state of the patient can be determined.

Electroencephalography originated with the study of electrical activity in exposed cerebral hemispheres of rabbits and monkeys [6]. By as early as 1890, the electrical activity of the brain was analyzed while animals were subjected to flashes of powerful light [4]. Electrodes that were positioned precisely on the brain's surface to examine neural stimulation led to observations of the changes in brain activity and the discovery of brain waves. The first animal EEG was recorded in 1912, by Ukrainian physiologist Vladimir Vladimirovich Pravdich-Neminsky [14]. Napoleon Cybulski and Jelenska-Macieszyna photographed EEGs of experimentally induced seizures. The first human EEG was recorded in 1924, by a German physiologist and psychiatrist, Hans Berger, who incidentally was the same person who invented the EEG [6]. In more recent times, an experiment was conducted on thought sharing, in which the brains of three people were connected. From the five groups of three people that participated in this experiment, the success rate was noted to be 81% [12,13].

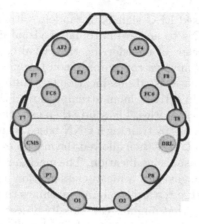

Fig. 2. Indication of the sensor positions and the behaviour groups that they correspond to. Blue indicates a maximum increase and red indicates a minimum decrease when opening eyes [16]

Brain diseases that alter the function or structure of the brain are known as encephalopathies [15]. The structure of the neurons that compose the brain consist of three parts: axons, dendrites and the body that contains the nucleus. It is through an electrochemical process known as a synapse that neurons transfer and receive information. Paroxysmal activity is a sudden and unrestrained change in the electrical charge distribution within the neurons in the brain. A paroxysm is represented on an EEG, as section of the EEG with a high amplitude, unlike the rest of the EEG reading. An example of paroxysmal activity is an EEG of a patient who has absence epilepsy. The spike waves are clearly visible in Fig. 1, and the amplitude of these waves is abnormal when compared to the earlier waves in the EEG. These paroxysmal waves are used to identify encephalopathies. Brain-Health is a device designed by Q. Zhang et al., and it is a portable wireless system that is capable of continuously recording and detecting encephalopathies [19]. This device has the capability of being used daily and functions with reasonably good accuracy and sensitivity.

3   Previous Work

Electroencephalography is one of the most popular techniques to measure brain activity. As a result of its popularity, many studies involving EEG analysis have applied deep learning to this field for optimum results. A study by Antoniades et al. used CNNs to detect Interictal EEG Discharges (IEDs) [1]. It involved 18 subjects and used leave-subject-out training methods and two-fold validation. This study successfully proved that IED detection using a trained Multi-model CNN achieved a more significant average than any other method used in this study. The average accuracy for the Multi-model CNN was 89.01%.

Spampinato et al. used EEG signals in tandem with Recurrent Neural Networks (RNNs) and CNNs to achieve automated visual classification [17]. This study explored the concept of transferring the visual capabilities that humans possess to methods that involve computer vision through the use of RNNs and CNNs. It aimed to automate visual classification by training RNNs to identify and make distinctions of brain activity in an attempt to read the way that the human mind responds to visual categories. The study then used the capabilities that were learned to emulate machines by training a CNN-based regressor to project images onto the learned manifold. This then allowed the machines to adopt human-based features for automated visual classification. The machines used in this study were able to classify these images with a mean classification accuracy of 89.7%. This study was a successful step towards training machines to perform visual classification similar to the way that humans can classify objects visually.

Chambayil et al. focused on how to track eye blinking from EEG signals [3]. In this study, an Artificial Neural Network (ANN) was trained for this task. Two supervised algorithms were used to train the ANN: Feed-Forward BackPropagation (FFBP) and Cascade Forward BackPropagation (CFBP). High training accuracies with values of 0.96687 and 0.99832 were recorded for the FFBP, and the CFBP approaches, respectively. The overall test accuracies were however relatively low, with values of 0.71678 and 0.54784 for FFBP and CFBP, respectively. The overall regression for FFBP and CFBP was determined to be 0.84990 and 0.90856, respectively. This study then concluded that CFBP had the best performance.

A study by Roesler and Suendermann [16], focused on how to track eye blinking. This study used a dataset of 14977 instances with 8255 instances that corresponded to the open eye state and 6722 of these instances corresponding to the closed eye state. It was mentioned in this study that there were originally 14980 instances. However, three instances were removed but no specific details are given as to which three instances were removed. The classification error rate of 42 different machine learning algorithms was then tested for overall eye state prediction on a single subject. Each of the instances was classified using 10-fold cross-validation.

From the above studies, it is evident that there has been work conducted on EEG classification using advanced deep learning methods. It is also evident that there is still room for improvement from the studies that have been conducted concerning EEG signal classification, as the performance does not yet match the accuracy levels required for clinical deployment.

4   Methods an Techniques

4.1   Convolutional Neural Networks

In numerous image classification studies, the use of two dimensional CNNs has shown positive outcomes. In the study by Jaswal et al., multiple image datasets were used to classify images, and excellent results were recorded [10], even though the dataset used, did not contain colour information. Although the current study uses a 2-Dimensional (2D) dataset, as an initial attempt, it was believed that a

1-Dimensional (1D) CNN could be ideal, since such CNNs can effectively generalize two-dimensional input [5]. The current study uses the same dataset used in [16]. The dataset was obtained from the Emotiv Epoc Headset worn by the subject. Each sensor position is highlighted in Fig. 2. The dataset consists of 14980 instances, each with 15 values in which 14 of these represent sensor values in the order AF3, F7, F3, FC5, T7, P7, O1, O2, P8, T8, FC6, F4, F8, AF4. These 14 values represent readings from 14 strategically placed sensors on the head as shown in Fig. 2. The output of the headset is therefore a 14 channel signal which is used to create a dataset where the fifteen value indicates the eye state of the subject, which is either open or closed. Since the data is in 2D form, it is possible to process these signals through a 1D CNN. The process of how a 1D CNN functions is indicated in Fig. 3. The process shown in Fig. 3 is similar to how a 2D CNN would work on images, except the input data is 2D. Therefore the window or kernel would slide over one dimension rather than two dimensions. After the 2D input data is fed into the 1D CNN, the steps in Fig. 3 are performed to successfully preprocess the signal. This study aims to determine whether the preprocessed signals perform better than the raw EEG signals. It may seem that this should be the case, however, preprocessing the signals could remove noise and also misinterpret vital information from the EEG signals as being noise.

INPUT SIGNAL ➡ CONVOLUTION LAYER ➡ POOLING LAYER

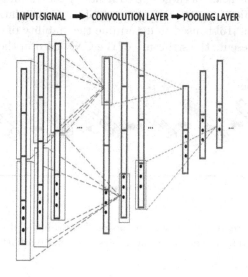

Fig. 3. This diagram represents a one dimensional convolutional neural network consisting of an input layer, convolutional layer and pooling layer. This diagram was adapted from [18].

The initial preprocessing phase involved applying zero mean and unit variance to the data. This step was used to normalize the data to minimize the risk of the CNN being biased towards any particular features. This normalization step was applied using the Weka software [7]. After many attempts, the initial 1D CNN approach did not prove viable since the model's training accuracy was low. This issue led to a shift in emphasis towards using a 2D CNN since these CNNs have a history of excellent image classification. However, since the dataset used in this study is 2D, and a 2D Keras [11] CNN requires 3-Dimensional (3D) input, the data had to be transformed accordingly. The shape of the dataset would now be 14980 instances of $1 \times 1 \times 14$ features. The CNN had 2 output nodes and was trained using the cross entropy loss function. It was noted that the 2D CNN's training accuracy was low on the original dataset. However, after normalizing the data, the training accuracy exceeded 97%.

The CNN's primary purpose in this study is not particularly for classification but rather for creating a reduced set of five features replacing the 14 sensor values in this study. The CNN used consisted of six convolutional layers, each with 1×1 filters to process the 14 features and remove any noise present, resulting in five new features. These new features in addition to a sixth feature representing the eye state of the subject are supplied as an .arff file extension to Weka and used as input to the same 42 supervised machine learning algorithms used in [16]. The explanation of these 42 algorithms is beyond the scope of this paper, the reader is referred to [7,8] for details in this regard. In the rest of this paper, these classifiers are each referred to using their standard name or acronym in Weka. The default hyper parameters of each of the 42 classifiers within Weka, were retained to allow for easy replication of these experiments. After training, these algorithms then predict the subject's eye state using ten-fold cross-validation. A comparison against the results of [16] is used to determine the viability of our proposed approach. Figure 4 represents the structure of the CNN used in the current study.

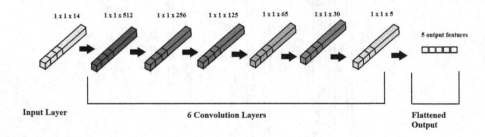

Fig. 4. This diagram represents a two dimensional convolutional neural network consisting of an input layer, six convolutional layers and finally a flattened output.

4.2 Experimental Evaluation

For effective comparison between these results and the results from [16], the same evaluation and validation metrics are used i.e. accuracy and/or classification error. The relationship between accuracy (ACC) and classification error (ERR) is shown below:

$$ERR = 1 - ACC. \tag{1}$$

This study's success depends on how well the preprocessed EEG signals perform against the raw EEG signals. Ten-fold cross validation was also carried out on each of the supervised machine learning algorithms used in [16]. The programming platform used in this study is Python 3.6. Since this study requires CNNs to preprocess the EEG signals, the Keras library was used. The Weka Toolkit was used in this study for the legacy supervised machine learning algorithms. To enable the reproducibility of these experiments, the default hyper-parameters for each Weka machine learning algorithm were adopted. The hardware specifications of the machine that was used to create this software comprised of a Windows 10 version 1909 operating system, 16 GB RAM, a Intel Core i5-9400F 2.9 GHz, six cores, six logical processors and a 1TB hardrive with a 225 GB SSD.

5   Results and Discussion

This study aimed to produce at least one result similar to that in Fig. 5. Since [16] used only 14977 instances of the dataset, it is expected that results may differ to a small extent in this study. By achieving a superior result it would prove that for those EEG signals in which noise is present, it can be differentiated and removed by the CNN.

Table 1. The accuracy (%) of 42 machine learning algorithms with respect to eye state prediction.

Machine learning algorithm	Acc	Machine learning algorithm	Acc
CVParameterSelection	51.4686	AttributeSelectedClassifier	99.9933
InputMappedClassifier	51.4686	Bagging	99.9933
MultiScheme	51.4686	ClassificationViaRegression	99.9933
NaiveBayesMultinomialText	51.4686	DecisionStump	99.9933
SGDText	51.4686	DecisionTable	99.9933
Stacking	51.4686	FilteredClassifier	99.9933
Vote	51.4686	J48	99.9933
ZeroR	51.4686	JRip	99.9933
NaiveBayesMultinomial	98.1509	LogitBoost	99.9933
NaiveBayesMultinomialUpdateable	98.1509	OneR	99.9933
NaiveBayes	99.8064	PART	99.9933
NaiveBayesUpdateable	99.8064	RandomComittee	99.9933
VotedPerceptron	99.8465	RandomForest	99.9933
SMO	99.9266	RandomSubSpace	99.9933
MultilayerPerceptron	99.9733	RandomTree	99.9933
MultiClassClassifierUpdateable	99.98	REPTree	99.9933
SGD	99.98	BayesNet	100
KStar	99.9866	Ibk(IB1)	100
Logistic	99.9866	LMT	100
MultiClassClassifier	99.9866	LWL	100
AdaBoostM1	99.9933	SimpleLogistic	100

In this study, it is proven that it is possible to predict the eye state of a subject with 0% classification error rate or 100% accuracy. In this study, the top-performing algorithms were BayesNet, Ibk (IB1), LMT, LWL, and SimpleLogistic. All of these algorithms achieved 100% prediction accuracy and 0% classification error rate. The majority of the machine learning algorithms used in this study achieved classification accuracies of less than 100% but above 99% and classification error rates of less than or equal to 0.1936%. It was noted that the top performer in [16], namely the KStar algorithm achieved a classification accuracy of 99.9866%, and a classification error rate of 0.0134% which is higher than the 97.3% accuracy and 2.7% classification error rate that was previously attained.

Classifiers such as NaiveBayes and SMO that performed poorly in [16], performed rather well in this study since SMO achieved an accuracy of 99.9266% and a classification error rate of 0.0734%, and NaiveBayes achieved an accuracy of 99.9064% and a classification error rate of 0.1936%. These results completely outperform those achieved in [16]. A total of eight algorithms performed poorly in this study. All these algorithms had a classification error rate of 48.5314% and a prediction accuracy of 51,4686%. These algorithms were CVParameterSelection, InputMappedClassifier, MultiScheme, NaiveBayesMultinomialText, SGDText, Stacking, Vote, and ZeroR. Although there were a total of eight classifiers that performed poorly, a total of 34 machine learning algorithms performed exceptionally, clearly, indicating that this study was a success. This provides an answer to the research question posed in this study - CNN feature extraction is indeed much more effective than using raw input to legacy supervised machine learning models.

It is also evident that in Fig. 5 that the classifiers, CVParameterSelection, InputMappedClassifier, MultiScheme, NaiveBayesMultinomialText, SGDText, Stacking, Vote, and ZeroR are all seen to have low classification error rates. This study supports that deduction since all of the abovementioned classifiers constitutes the eight worst performers in our results. However, noticeably the NaiveBayes classifier is the worst performer in [16]. In this study, the NaiveBayes classifier achieves an excellent accuracy and classification error rate contradicting its placement in [16]. Since the NaiveBayes classifier is proven to have a high classification performance [5], it is justified that this classifier should achieve exceptional accuracy and an impressive classification error rate. In this study, it manages to accomplish both. Table 1 presents the performance of all of the 42 distinct machine learning algorithms used in this study. Each machine learning algorithm is represented with its corresponding classification accuracy.

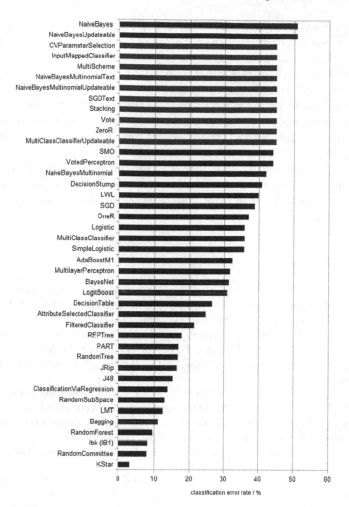

classification error rate / %

Fig. 5. Performance of all classifiers with default settings on raw EEG data. Classifiers which use majority vote are shown in red [16]. (Color figure online)

6   Conclusion and Future Work

This study concluded that it was possible to predict the eye state of a single subject with 100% accuracy or 0% classification error rate. It is clearly evident that the use of CNN feature extraction proved much more effective than simply using raw EEG signals which yielded training accuracy of approximately 97%, after normalization. Since this study only involved the signal readings for one individual the question is still questionable whether these results are generalizable. To address this limitation, future work in this field could explore the creation of larger EEG datasets to cater for temporal and individual variations in EEG recordings. This study could prove to be very useful in eliminating human error in EEG signal analysis. By successfully removing the noise from the EEG signals and successfully predicting the outcome of the eye state of the subject. This study has achieved its goal and provides promising results for future work in this area. Future work in this study area could involve identifying epilepsy in patients using EEG signal classifications.

This study could be extended to include sleep monitoring for patients that suffer from sleep disorders. It could also be beneficial in eliminating noise from EEGs to diagnose epilepsy and other medical-related studies better. In the medical sector, brain dysfunctions can be identified with better accuracy if noise interference with the actual EEG signal is removed. In everyday applications, a device could be built to monitor an individual's sleep level in high-risk jobs, such that it would be easy to determine whether the individual is tired or they were sleeping on the job.

References

1. Antoniades, A., et al.: Detection of interictal discharges with convolutional neural networks using discrete ordered multichannel intracranial EEG. IEEE Trans. Neural Syst. Rehabil. Eng. **25**(12), 2285–2294 (2017)
2. Casson, A.J., Abdulaal, M., Dulabh, M., Kohli, S., Krachunov, S., Trimble, E.: Electroencephalogram. In: Tamura, T., Chen, W. (eds.) Seamless Healthcare Monitoring, pp. 45–81. Springer, Cham (2018). https://doi.org/10.1007/978-3-319-69362-0_2
3. Chambayil, B., Singla, R., Jha, R.: EEG eye blink classification using neural network. In: Proceedings of the World Congress on Engineering, vol. 1, pp. 2–5 (2010)
4. Coenen, A., Fine, E., Zayachkivska, O.: Adolf beck: a forgotten pioneer in electroencephalography. J. Hist. Neurosci. **23**(3), 276–286 (2014)
5. Friedman, N., Geiger, D., Goldszmidt, M.: Bayesian network classifiers. Mach. Learn. **29**(2), 131–163 (1997)
6. Haas, L.F.: Hans Berger (1873–1941), Richard Caton (1842–1926), and electroencephalography. J. Neurol. Neurosurg. Psychiatry **74**(1), 9 (2003)
7. Hall, M., Frank, E., Holmes, G., Pfahringer, B., Reutemann, P., Witten, I.H.: The WEKA data mining software: an update. ACM SIGKDD Explor. Newsl. **11**(1), 10–18 (2009)
8. Holmes, G., Donkin, A., Witten, I.H.: WEKA: a machine learning workbench. In: Proceedings of ANZIIS 1994-Australian New Zealand Intelligent Information Systems Conference, pp. 357–361. IEEE (1994)
9. Jasper, H., Kershman, J.: Electroencephalographic classification of the epilepsies. Arch. Neurol. Psychiatry **45**(6), 903–943 (1941)
10. Jaswal, D., Vishvanathan, S., Kp, S.: Image classification using convolutional neural networks. Int. J. Sci. Eng. Res. **5**(6), 1661–1668 (2014)
11. Ketkar, N.: Introduction to keras. In: Ketkar, N. (ed.) Deep Learning with Python, pp. 97–111. Springer, Berkeley (2017). https://doi.org/10.1007/978-1-4842-2766-4
12. NASA: Beckman instruments supplying medical flight monitoring equipment. Space News Roundup **4**(10), 4–5 (1965)
13. Nield, D.: Scientists have connected the brains of 3 people, enabling them to share thoughts. ScienceAlert (2018)

14. Pravdich-Neminsky, W.: An attempt to register electrical brain symptoms. Zentralbl Physiol. **27**, 951–960 (1912)

15. Reyes, L.M.S., Reséndiz, J.R., Ramírez, G.N.A.: Trends of clinical EEG systems: a review. In: 2018 IEEE-EMBS Conference on Biomedical Engineering and Sciences (IECBES), pp. 571–576. IEEE (2018)

16. Rösler, O., Suendermann, D.: A first step towards eye state prediction using EEG. In: Proceedings of the AIHLS (2013)

17. Spampinato, C., Palazzo, S., Kavasidis, I., Giordano, D., Souly, N., Shah, M.: Deep learning human mind for automated visual classification. In: Proceedings of the IEEE Conference on Computer Vision and Pattern Recognition, pp. 6809–6817 (2017)

18. Yang, K., Huang, Z., Wang, X., Li, X.: A blind spectrum sensing method based on deep learning. Sensors **19**(10), 2270 (2019)

19. Zhang, Q., et al.: A real-time wireless wearable electroencephalography system based on support vector machine for encephalopathy daily monitoring. Int. J. Distrib. Sens. Netw. **14**(5), 1550147718779562 (2018)

Race Recognition Using Enhanced Local Binary Pattern

Eone Etoua Oscar Vianney[1(✉)], Tapamo Kenfack Hippolyte Michel[1,2],
Mboule Ebele Brice Auguste[1], Mbietieu Amos Mbietieu[1],
and Essuthi Essoh Serge Leonel[1]

[1] LIRIMA, Team IDASCO, Faculty of Science, Department of Computer Science,
B.P. 812, Yaoundé, Cameroon
{oscar.eone,hippolyte.tapamo,brice.mboule,amos.mbietieu,
leonel.essuthi}@facsciences-uy1.cm
[2] IRD UMI 209 UMMISCO, University of Yaoundé I, B.P. 337, Yaoundé, Cameroon

Abstract. Automatic race classification is a subtask of facial recognition
that improves facial recognition by reducing the number of images captured by a surveillance camera to find any criminal whose race is known.
Facial recognition is particularly useful for airports, border gates and
other social areas. Convolutional Neural Network (CNN), while producing very good results for race classification, are very expensive, in terms of
computation, for practical applications. Local binary patterns as initially
proposed have very good results but their local histograms are quite large
(256 levels of gray), after concatenation generates very large histograms
that must then be reduced with algorithms such as Principal Component
Analysis (PCA) which are just as time consuming. Thus, in this paper
we study Central Symmetric Local Binary Pattern (CSLBP) a variant of
LBP which generates histograms with 16 levels of gray, and we propose
a new variant of Local Binary Pattern (LBP) called Diagonal Symmetric
Local Binary Pattern (DSLBP) which generates histograms with 8 levels of gray. These two methods are used in the feature extraction phase
to improve the performance of race classification. We find that the size of
the image blocks and the contiguity of the blocks influence the size of the
feature vectors and the classification performance. For the experiment we
use 765 images of FERET dataset as a dataset, which is constituted in 3
classes (Negroid, Caucasoid, Mongoloid) and a Support Vector Machine
(SVM) for the classification. We report accuracies of more than 90% with
reduced vector sizes (between 200 and 500 features). When using large
feature vectors (13456, 2704 and 6728 features) we achieve an accuracy of
99.47% with $CSLBP_{(8,1)}$ and 98.43% with $DSLBP_{(8,1)}$.

Keywords: Race recognition · Local binary pattern · Feature
extraction

Supported by Ummisco, University of Yaoundé 1.

T. M. N. Ngatched and I. Woungang (Eds.): PAAISS 2021, LNICST 405, pp. 120–136, 2022.
https://doi.org/10.1007/978-3-030-93134-2_8

1   Introduction

Faces carry a plethora of social indications including race, expression, identity, age, and gender, all of which have increasingly attracted the attention of multidisciplinary research, such as psychology, neuroscience, and computer science, to name a few. Recent advances in computer vision, computer graphics, and machine learning have made machine learning-based racial face analysis particularly popular due to its significant potential and broader impacts in broad real-world applications, such as security and defense, surveillance, human-computer interface, biometric identification, among others. Face processing and facial recognition are based on biometric technologies and have a wide range of potential applications related to marketing, security and safety. Current research efforts in this area consist in developing more accurate, robust and less complex methods and algorithms for face recognition [20], gender recognition [4,13], race [8,17], age [13], facial expression [15]. The information obtained from race classification can improve the performance of face recognition. Obviously, race information could be used to reduce the search space when matching unknown faces to a set of known faces, but also to optimize face recognition algorithms using face categories. The flexibility and ease with which the LBP method adapts to the different problems related to face classification raised questions that challenged us and piqued our interest in the classification of race from faces and the method to be used.

Since real world applications do not all have the same demands in terms of time and precision, we propose in this paper a method of description of face which will reduce the histograms without using the methods of dimensionality reduction while maintaining acceptable performances and by a block method we will choose to increase the characteristics of the characteristic vectors to increase the accuracy.

In this work, our goal is to improve the race classification in terms of prediction accuracy and/or prediction time (with small feature vectors). This is why we use $CSLBP_{(8,1)}$ proposed by Heikkila [5] (Center symmetric local binary pattern with 8 neighbors and radius 1, an operator that represents the image with 16 patterns) which to our knowledge has not yet been used for the classification of races and we also provide a method that we call diagonal symmetric local binary pattern (DSLBP), an operator that represents the image with 8 patterns ($DSLBP_{(8,1)}$) and we use it for the classification of races. The main steps taken to provide a solution to the problem are given by Ghulam [9] and are illustrated in Fig. 1.

Fig. 1. Main steps involved in race classification [9].

Figure 1 shows 3 steps from image reading to decision: preprocessing to normalize all images, feature extraction to retrieve features that will be used for classification, classification to categorize the different faces in the dataset. In order to contribute to the resolution of this problem we decided to study the division of images into blocks ($10 \times 10, 15 \times 15, 20 \times 20, 25 \times 25, 30 \times 30, 40 \times 40, 50 \times 50, 100 \times 100$) as well as the contiguity of these blocks. The objective of this work is to study the local binary patterns and improve the classification performances while showing the relevance of local features from $CSLBP_{8,1}$ and $DSLBP_{8,1}$.

In this work, we show the influence of the contiguity of the blocks of an image on the classification performance, we use CSLBP for race classification purposes, we propose DSLBP a new variant of LBP, which allows to reduce the number of features to represent an image while keeping a good representation of the image and we will use it in the feature extraction phase in a race classification.

The rest of the paper is organized as follows: in Sect. 2 we present related works, in Sect. 3 we present the local and global methods of feature extraction, our approach for the representation of the image in the feature extraction phase is presented in Sect. 4, in Sect. 5 we describe you the dataset that we use in this work, Our experimental protocol is described in Sect. 5, the results of our work are presented in Sect. 6 and we conclude our work in Sect. 7.

2   Related Works

A lot of research has been done to contribute to the solution of the race classification problem using different methods and approaches. Among these works we present some in this section. In this section. LBP have been used to provide solutions to the problem of race classification. Zhiguang and Haizhou [22] used LBP histograms and Haar wavelets for feature extraction; Adaboost and Chi-square distance as classifiers for a two-class problem (Asians and non-Asians) from FERET image base, they obtained error rates of 2.98% and 3.01% for Haar and LBP wavelets respectively. Zhang and Wang [19] improve the error rate to 0.42% on the FRCG V.2 image base, using LBP histograms in the feature extraction phase in block split images and Adaboost to build a classifier; their problem was also a two-class problem(Asians and Caucasians); but this excellent result has a cost because each image produces a vector of 81540 features and they resorted to feature selection to reduce the dimensionality of the feature vectors and feature selection is and feature selection is very time consuming as shown in [19]. Since two-class problems are somewhat easier, Muhammad et al. [9] move to a five-class problem (East Asian, Central Asian, Hispanic, Caucasian, African American), so they study LBP and Weber Local Descriptor (WLD) separately, then they combine the LBP and WLD histograms for the feature extraction part, all this is followed by a feature selection using the Kruskal wallis method to reduce the dimensionality of the feature vectors; experiments conducted on face images from the FERET image base report an accuracy of 99% with 3265 features per image; the classifier used is the City-block distance. But the fact that the features were selected to reduce the dimensionality of the feature vectors is time consuming, so Salah et al. [14] use a scheme that merges local uniform binary block-based patterns and a Haar wavelet transform to combine local and global features; they conducted the experiments on 746 face images from the EGA database labeled into 3 classes: Caucasian, Asian, and African; they use principal component analysis (PCA) to reduce the dimensionality and they go from 536 features to 15 features, for a prediction accuracy of 96.3%; certainly the features are reduced but PCA like any dimensionality reduction method will consume a lot of time during the feature extraction phase, not to mention that global methods like Haar wavelets are not robust to occlusion. Wady and Ahmed [18], propose an approach for race classification by merging a local descriptor and global descriptor; in this approach, local uniform binary patterns (ULBP or LBP^{riu2}) were used to extract local features while discrete cosine transformation (DCT) was used to extract global features from facial images. The classification of the selected feature vector is performed using the selected is performed using the k-nearest neighbor (KNN) classifier with City-block distance; they used 1000 images from the image databases such as FERET dataset, GUFD face dataset, the YALE face dataset, etc.; their classification problem is to classify three races (Caucasian, Asian and African-American); a maximum classification accuracy of 98% is observed in the observed during the experiments.

Although the approaches integrating LBP have obtained good results, other approaches have also been proposed in order to improve the performance of race classification such as approaches integrating geometric features of the face. Thus Becerra-Riera et al. [3], propose an approach in which they combine local appearance and geometric features to describe face images, and exploit race information from different parts of the face by means of a component-based method; they analyze the impact of using color, texture and anthropometric features, combine them using two different classifiers: Support Vector Machine (SVM) and Random Forest (RF); the classification problem here amounts to classifying five races (Caucasian, Asian, African, Indian, and Latin) from 2345 images from the EGA image base; they obtained an overall accuracy of 93.7%. Wang et al. [19], show the distinctiveness of three ethnic groups and seek to find the common features in some local regions for the three ethnic groups (Chinese Uyghurs, Tibetans and Koreans); for this purpose, they first use the STASM facial landmark detector to find prominent landmarks in a face image, and then use the well-known data mining technique, mRMR algorithm, to select the salient geometric length features based on all possible lines connected by two landmark points; thus the distance between each pair of landmark points is used to form a feature vector, and 2,926 length features are produced for ethnicity description, then 199 features are selected after mRMR feature selection, then based on these selected salient features they construct three "T" regions in a facial image for ethnic feature representation and prove that they are effective areas for ethnicity recognition ethnicity. An overall accuracy of 90% is reported. But it should be noted that the feature extraction method used is used is sensitive to non-frontal face images. We can see that the approaches integrating LBP outperform those integrating geometric features.

Approaches using neural networks have been very successful in the field of machine learning and have also been used to provide a solution to the problem of race classification. Anwar and Islam [2], present an approach to extract ethnicity from a facial image; they proposed a method that uses a pre-trained convolutional neural network (CNN) to extract the features, then the support vector machine (SVM) with linear kernel is used as the classifier; Here they consider race classification as a three-class problem (Asian, African American, and Caucasian); they use images from several image databases like FERET; an overall average accuracy of 94% is reported. Vo et al. [17] studied the use of a deep learning model; in this work they propose two independent models, the first one is race recognition using a convolutional neural network (RR-CNN), the second one is race recognition using Visual Geometry Group(RR-VGG), the images used are from VNFaces(Images collected on Vietnamese Facebook pages) divided into two classes(Vietnamese and non-Vietnamese), the RR-CNN model reported an accuracy of 88.64% and RR-VGG an accuracy of 88.84%. The proposed models reach overall accuracies of more than 90% in the extended experiments on other datasets. Masood et al. [8] addressed the problem of predicting the race of humans based on their facial features, three main races were considered for this work: Mongoloid, Caucasian and Black. A total of 447 image samples were collected from the FERET database. Several geometric features and color attributes were extracted from the image and then used for the classification problem. The accuracy of the model obtained using a MLP (Multi Layer Perceptron) approach was 82.4% while the accuracy obtained using a convolutional neural network was 98.6%. We note here the use of many features, which will require a lot of computing time. The approaches based on CNN-based approaches yield good results, but they are computationally expensive for practical applications.

It can be seen that approaches based on CNNs like those of Masood et al. [8] report good results but in [2,17] the results could be improved by adding more images because CNNs need a lot of data to provide very good results. Approaches using anthropometric and geometric features [3,19] are sensitive to the occlusion of the face. Because we will not have all these elements on the image. Approaches using LBP have very good results but the local histograms generated are often large (256 features for basic LBP) and are merged with global descriptors [18,22] or other local descriptors [9] but in all cases we have very large feature vectors (e.g. 81540 features in [21]) that will have to be reduced with methods such as PCA, Wallis which are very expensive in time. It is for all these reasons that we have decided to use CSLBP with a neighborhood of 8 pixels a variant of LBP for the classification of races and then to propose a new variant of LBP that we called DSLBP for the race classification, these two descriptors both provide small local histograms (size 16 for CSLBP and size 8 for DSLBP) for DSLBP), these local histograms which will then be concatenated to form global histograms relevant for a classification of the races.

3   Feature Extraction Methods

For face analysis, feature extraction is required to represent high dimensional image data into low dimensional feature vectors. Such features will provide good classification accuracies. In this section, we study CSLBP and present the proposed DSLBP.

3.1   Center Symmetric Local Binary Pattern (CSLBP)

CSLBP is a variant of LBP [10]. It is a texture descriptor proposed by Heikkilä et al. [5] that allows to describe the areas of interest in an image. CSLBP has the power of LBP and SIFT (Scale-invariant feature transform [6]) and surpasses them in describing areas of interest in an image [5].

The CSLBP image is calculated as follows: each pixel has a neighborhood of P pixels regularly spaced on a radius R centered in it, so we calculate the difference between a neighboring pixel and its symmetrical with respect to the central pixel if the difference is less than a fixed threshold it gives 0 otherwise we have 1, we get a binary number that we will convert into decimal to obtain the CSLBP value of the central pixel, the process is repeated over the entire image, Fig. 2 gives the calculation of the CSLBP code for a central pixel: with 8 neighbors and a threshold of 0:

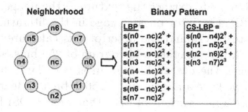

Fig. 2. Calculation of the LBP and CSLBP code for a pixel with a neighborhood of 8 pixels [5]

The formula for computing the CSLBP code of a pixel with P neighbors on a radius R as proposed by Heikkilä et al. [5] is:

$$CSLBP_{P,R}(x_c, y_c) = \sum_{i=0}^{\frac{P}{2}-1} s(n_i - n_{i+\frac{P}{2}}).2^i. \tag{1}$$

For CSLBP with P neighbors we have $2^{\frac{P}{2}}$ possible patterns. The coordinates of the neighboring pixels are given by the Eq. 3 and the thresholding function is given

$$s(x) = \begin{cases} 1 & \text{if } x \geq h \\ 0 & \text{otherwise.} \end{cases} \tag{2}$$

where h is a threshold.

Figure 3 shows an image $CSLBP_{8,1}$.

Fig. 3. On the left original image (source: FERET dataset [11]), on the right image $CSLBP_{8,1}$

4   Proposed Method: Diagonal Symmetric Local Binary Pattern (DSLBP)

To our knowledge, there is no feature extraction technique in the literature that makes pairwise comparisons between pixels that are symmetrical with respect to the south west-north east diagonal direction. The proposed method mimics the compass gradient mask which allows to extract the diagonal contours and the LBP which will allow to extract the texture of the image.

To apply the LBP descriptor on an image in the literature authors usually divide the image into blocks and the descriptor is calculated on each block so for LBP basic a block will generate a histogram of 256 bins, so when the blocks multiply in the image, the overall histogram is very large for example for an image of 100 blocks we have a histogram of 25600 bins, so feature vectors of size 25600. So we propose a new variant of LBP that we call DSLBP. Just like basic LBP, DSLBP only applies in connection with our work on grayscale images. So before any calculation of the DSLBP image, transform it into a grayscale. Considering the size of the local histograms generated by basic LBP (256 bins), we propose for this, with 8 pixels around the central pixel to go to 8 bins. Thus we propose to choose the diagonal of direction south west - north east as axis of symmetry. Thus for each pixel above the diagonal we will threshold it by its symmetrical with respect to the diagonal. So if we consider this the pixel n_c of Table 1

Table 1. Neighborhood of 8 pixels around the central pixel

n_1	n_0	n_7
n_2	n_c	n_6
n_3	n_4	n_5

The calculation of n_c is given by:

$$DSLBP(n_c) = s\,(n_0 - n_6)\,.2^0 + s\,(n_1 - n_5)\,.2^1 + s\,(n_2 - n_4)\,.2^2.$$

Example of calculating the DSLBP code of the central pixel in the Table 1

The mathematical formula to generalize the DSLBP operator with P neighbors on a radius R is the formula 6:

$$DSLBP_{P,R}(x_c, y_c) = \sum_{i=0}^{\frac{P}{2}-2} s(n_i - n_{P-(i+2)})\,.2^i. \tag{3}$$

With this method we have $2^{\frac{P}{2}-1}$ possible patterns, so a feature vector more reduced than the one of CSLBP. Example of calculation of the DSLBP code of the central pixel in the Table 2

Table 2. Neighborhood of 8 pixels around a central pixel for the calculation of the DSLBP value of the central pixel

145	148	143
141	141	143
140	142	144

$$DSLBP = s\,(148 - 143)\,.2^0 + s\,(145 - 144)\,.2^1 + s\,(141 - 142)\,.2^2$$
$$= 1 \times 2^0 + 1 \times 2^1 + 0 \times 2^2 = 3.$$

Figure 4 shows an image $DSLBP_{8,1}$.

Fig. 4. Left original image (source: FERET dataset [11]), right DSLBP image

5 Experiments

The experiments are conducted on 765 frontal face images from FERET dataset [11]. The image size is 512×768. The face images collected in this dataset, have different facial expressions, are of different ages and gender, have variations in brightness and are frontal. The images are divided into 3 classes (Caucasoid, Mongoloid and Negroid). The dataset is separated as follows: 75% of the images for training and 25% for testing. Table 3 gives the distribution of the images.

Table 3. Distribution of the images of the data set.

	Caucasoid	Mongoloid	Negroid	Total
Training	253	215	105	573
Test	90	60	42	192
Totals	343	275	147	765

Some images found in our dataset (Faig. 5):

(a)   (b)   (c)

Fig. 5. (a) negroid, (b) mongoloid, (c) caucasoid (source: FERET dataset [11])

The race classification approach adopted in this work is illustrated in Fig. 6

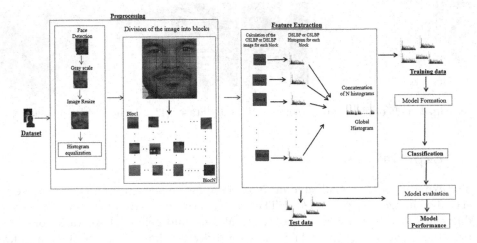

Fig. 6. Race classification process

The phases of this classification process are as follows:

Preprocessing. This is the first step of the classification process, it is divided into sub-steps: Face detection, Resizing of the image in size 100×100, Passage of the image in level of gray because LBP are calculated on the images in level of gray, Equalization of histogram. Just after all these we will divide the image into blocks before the phase of feature extraction.

Feature Extraction. In this phase the image divided into N *blocks* of the same size then the $DSLBP$ (or $CSLBP$) are computed for each block and histograms are extracted from them and for each image a global histogram is built from the concatenation of the block histograms. It should be noted that in our approach, when dividing the image into blocks, we took into account the overlapping of the blocks introduced; thus we study in this work 3 blocks contiguity:

- $1 - contiguity$: The M + 1 block directly follows the block M
- $\frac{1}{2} - contiguity$: The block M + 1 starts halfway through block M
- $\frac{1}{4} - contiguity$: The M + 1 block starts at the quarter of the M block

Classification. For the classification step, the SVM classifier proposed by Vapnik [16] is used in our work. The linear kernel SVM used for the classification. We use for this purpose the SVM proposed by the scikit-learn library [1] for our race classification.

5.1 Experiment 1

This experiment is conducted with $CSLBP_{(8,1)}$, so for a block we have a feature vector of size 16, then for an image that we divide into M blocks, we have a feature vector of size $16 \times M$.

5.2 Experiment 2

The feature extraction is performed on $DSLBP_{(8,1)}$ images, so for a block we have a feature vector of size 8, then for an image that we divide into M blocks, we have a feature vector of size $8 \times M$.

The results of the two experiments are presented in Sect. 6.

6 Results and Discussions

We did a preliminary experiment before the block adjacency experiments. In this experiment we take the image as a single block, to show that the 8 and 16 features rendered by $DSLBP_{(8,1)}$ and $CSLBP_{(8,1)}$ respectively are quite discriminating. In this experiment DSLBP and CSLBP report respective accuracies of 57.81% and 61.45% for 8 and 16 features. The results obtained by the two operators are acceptable from the point of view of the number of features provided and the accuracy report. But these accuracies have been improved which allows us to present you the results of experiment 1 and experiment 2 after having the number of features.

6.1   Experiment 1 Results

– 1-contiguity case

Table 4. Experiment 1 results: 1-contiguity with $CSLBP_{(8,1)}$

Block size	10 × 10	15 × 15	20 × 20	25 × 25	30 × 30	40 × 40	50 × 50
Blocks	100	**36**	25	16	9	4	4
Feature size	1600	**576**	400	256	144	64	64
Testing accuracy (%)	95.31	**95.83**	90.10	88.54	83.85	76.04	74.47
Macro average precision (%)	95	**96**	90	89	86	75	74
Macro average recall (%)	96	**96**	89	88	83	76	72
Testing runtime (s)	0.116	2.9×10^{-2}	1.5×10^{-2}	9.5×10^{-3}	5×10^{-3}	4×10^{-3}	2.8×10^{-3}

With the blocks 10 × 10 and 15 × 15 we reach good performances of about 95% in reasonable time.(see Table 4)

Table 5. Experiment 1 results: $\frac{1}{2}$-contiguity with $CSLBP_{(8,1)}$

Block size	10 × 10	15 × 15	20 × 20	25 × 25	30 × 30	40 × 40	50 × 50
Blocks in image	361	**169**	81	49	25	16	9
Feature size	5776	**2704**	1296	784	400	256	144
Testing accuracy (%)	97.39	**98.43**	97.91	94.79	92.18	89.06	81.77
Macro average precision (%)	97	**98**	98	95	93	89	82
Macro average recall (%)	98	**99**	98	94	92	87	82
Testing runtime (s)	0.36	**0.15**	6×10^{-2}	3.2×10^{-2}	1.5×10^{-2}	9×10^{-3}	8×10^{-3}

– $\frac{1}{2}$-contiguity case

The performances in this case are quite good, because with the blocks 15 × 15 we obtain a good accuracy of 98.43% because we have quite well supplied vectors of features necessary and sufficient enough to represent the faces. (see Table 5)

– $\frac{1}{4}$-contiguity case

Table 6. Experiment 1 results: $\frac{1}{4}$-contiguity with $CSLBP_{(8,1)}$

Block size	10×10	15×15	20×20	25×25	30×30	40×40	50×50
Blocks	2116	**841**	289	169	121	49	25
Feature size	33856	**13456**	4624	2704	1936	784	400
Testing accuracy (%)	97.39	**99.47**	97.39	96.87	96.87	94.79	91.14
Macro average precision (%)	97	**99**	97	97	97	95	91
Macro average recall (%)	98	**99.9**	98	97	97	94	91
Testing runtime (s)	2.39	**0.72**	0.22	0.14	0.09	0.033	0.021

All the performances in this case are very good because the image is completely covered for all blocks and the discriminating local features are features are also extracted (see Table 6).

6.2 Experiment 2 Results

– 1-contiguity case

The best performance is obtained with the 10×10 blocks with an accuracy of 89.59% in a rather short time. The other performances, not good enough but still acceptable, are due to the reduced number of features of the vectors which do not have enough discriminatory information (see Table 7).

– $\frac{1}{2}$-contiguity case

The accuracies obtained with the blocks 10×10 and 15×15 are of the order of 96% thus good, moreover they are obtained with rather reduced vectors respectively 2888 features and 1352 features (see Table 8).

Table 7. Experiment 2 results: 1-contiguity with $DSLBP_{(8,1)}$

Block size	10×10	15×15	20×20	25×25	30×30	40×40	50×50
Blocks	**100**	36	25	16	9	4	4
Feature size	**800**	288	200	128	72	32	32
Testing accuracy (%)	**89.58**	88.54	87.5	81.77	76.56	70.83	76.04
Macro average precision (%)	89	88	88	82	77	70	75
Macro average recall (%)	**88**	88	87	80	76	70	73
Testing runtime (s)	5×10^{-2}	10^{-2}	7×10^{-3}	4×10^{-3}	2.5×10^{-3}	1.5×10^{-3}	1.6×10^{-3}

Table 8. Experiment 2 results: $\frac{1}{2}$-contiguity with $DSLBP_{(8,1)}$

Block size	10×10	15×15	20×20	25×25	30×30	40×40	50×50
Blocks	361	**169**	81	49	25	16	9
Feature size	2888	**1352**	648	392	200	128	72
Testing accuracy (%)	95.83	**96.35**	94.27	93.22	90.1	83.33	80.2
Macro average precision (%)	95	**96**	94	94	90	84	79
Macro average recall (%)	96	**96**	94	93	89	83	79
Testing runtime (s)	0.19	6×10^{-2}	3×10^{-2}	1.2×10^{-2}	1.2×10^{-2}	5×10^{-3}	2.4×10^{-3}

– $\frac{1}{4}$-**contiguity case**

Table 9. Experiment 2 results: $\frac{1}{4}$-contiguity with $DSLBP_{(8,1)}$

Block size	10×10	15×15	20×20	25×25	30×30	40×40	50×50
Blocks	2116	**841**	289	169	121	49	25
Feature size	16928	**6728**	2312	1352	968	392	200
Testing accuracy (%)	97.39	**98.43**	95.31	93.22	95.83	89.58	82.81
Macro average precision (%)	98	**99**	95	93	95	89	82
Macro average recall (%)	97	**98**	96	93	96	90	83
Testing runtime (s)	0.97	**0.32**	0.12	7×10^{-2}	3.3×10^{-2}	1.6×10^{-2}	7×10^{-3}

The best result in term of accuracy is obtained by using the blocks 15×15, 98.43% for 6728 features (see Table 9).

Figure 7 present the influence of block size and contiguity on the accuracy. We can also see that for the same block size and for the same operator, the deeper the contiguity (the $\frac{1}{4}$-contiguity is deeper than the $\frac{1}{2}$-contiguity which is deeper than the 1-contiguity) better is the accuracy.

6.3 Robustness Testing of DSLBP

The aim here is to demonstrate that the features provided by the DSLBP operator can be learned by other machine learning algorithms in the same way as they were learned by SVM. Thus, we tested the features provided by DSLBP on four algorithms: K-nearest neighbors (KNN), Random forest (RF), Logistic regression (LR) and Multi Layer Perceptron (MLP). The observation that can be made on the results recorded in Table 10 and Table 11 is that despite the fact that these results are not equal to those obtained by SVM, they approach them because all the results exceed the 80% on all the metrics, moreover we can note

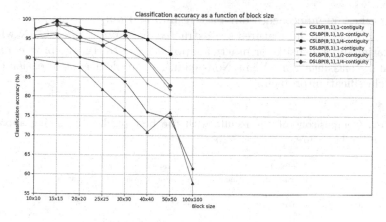

Fig. 7. Evolution of accuracy as a function of block size

the results of MLP which exceed the 90% and those of RL which exceed the 97%. All these results prove that DSLBP features are as well learned by SVM as by other supervised learning algorithms.

Table 10. Results obtained with 15×15 block sizes with $\frac{1}{2}$-contiguity

Classifier	Accuracy	Macro average recall	Macro average precision
KNN	89.06%	90%	89%
Random Forest	81.77%	84%	82%
Logistic regression	97.39%	97%	97%
MLP	94.27%	94%	94%

Table 11. Results obtained with 15×15 block sizes with $\frac{1}{4}$-contiguity

Classifier	Accuracy	Macro average recall	Macro average precision
KNN	86.45%	88%	86%
Random Forest	83.33%	84%	83%
Logistic regression	97.91%	98%	98%
MLP	91.14%	91%	91%

6.4 Discussions

In Table 12, we make comparisons with the best results obtained in the literature. The results presented are those obtained mostly on the basis of FERET dataset images. The results show that our approach outperforms the majority of approaches. [2] approaches our best results and outperforms some of them due to the fact that its features are extracted by a pre-trained CNN which is computationally expensive for practical applications. In [12] the problem is that of a binary classification (Asian/Non-Asian), a problem a little easier than a 3-class classification problem.

Table 12. Comparisons of our results with the best results of existing approaches existing in the literature.

Authors	Approach		Accuracy of each race			Datasets
	Feature	Classifier	Mongoloid (%)	Negroid (%)	Caucasoid (%)	
Wady and Hamed [18]	ULBP+DCT	KNN	99.55	95.5	99.05	FERET, Yale face, others
Muhammed et al. [9]	LBP+WLD	KNN	99.47	98.99	100	FERET
Anwar et Islam [2]	CNN	SVM	97.21	100	100	FERET, others
Roomi et al. [12]	Skin	Adaboost	79.13	90	90.9	FERET, Yale
Manesh et al. [7]	Gabor features	SVM	96	N/A	N/A	FERET, PEAL
Salah et al. [14]	ULBP+Harr	KNN	95.53	97.84	97.38	GUFD, others
Becerra-Riera et al. [3]	skin + geometric feature	Random Forest + SVM	68.6	93.9	98.5	FERET
Our*	DSLBP	SVM	83.33	88.23	95.34	FERET
Our**	CSLBP	SVM	95.08	95.34	96.59	FERET
Our***	DSLBP	SVM	95.16	97.56	96.62	FERET
Our***	CSLBP	SVM	96.77	97.67	100	FERET
Our#	DSLBP	SVM	98.33	100	97.8	FERET
Our#	CSLBP	SVM	98.36	100	100	FERET

(*) means that in this case we used the $10x10$ blocks with the 1-contiguity, (**) the 15×15 blocks with the 1-contiguity, (***) the 15×15 blocks with the $\frac{1}{2}$-contiguity and (#) the $15x15$ blocks with the $\frac{1}{4}$-contiguity

7   Conclusion

Several methods and approaches have been proposed by research teams to solve the problem of race classification, this problem is addressed using either local methods, global methods, neural networks. The aim of this work was to find a better representation of the face to bring a solution to the problem of the classification of the races.

We chose to study the $CSLBP_{8,1}$ operator and used it for race classification. We also proposed an operator for describing points of interest $DSLBP$ and we used it for the classification of races. We have seen that the choice of blocks is very important because the choice of features depends on it, we have shown that the choice of the contiguity of these blocks also influences the performances. We have seen that $DSLBP_{8,1}$ with small feature vectors could reach more than 90% accuracy. The high discriminating power of $CSLBP_{8,1}$ and $DSLBP_{8,1}$ has been demonstrated with their respective accuracies of 99.47% and 98.43%, moreover we can note the accuracies of 87.5% and 83.85% obtained respectively with $DSLBP_{8,1}$ (200 features) $CSLBP_{8,1}$ (144 features), encouraging performances.

Our work is limited by the small size of the dataset, the evaluation of our operators by a single algorithm, the exclusive use of frontal face images, the exclusive use of $CSLBP$ and $DSLBP$ with radius 1 and a neighborhood of 8 pixels, the study of a limited number of block sizes, the study of only 3 contiguous blocks Our work could be extended to a larger dataset, improving DSLBP and CSLBP by searching for their uniform patterns and extending their radius and neighborhood, studying a larger number of blocks and more adjacencies; by applying a feature selection method such as Kruskal Wallis feature selection or PCA, we can reduce the size of the feature vectors while keeping the current results or in the best case improve them.

References

1. Pedregosa, F., et al.: Scikit-learn: machine learning in python. J. Mach. Learn. Res. **12**, 2825–2830 (2011)
2. Anwar, I., Islam, N.U.: Learned features are better for ethnicity classification. Cybern. Inf. Technol. **17**(3), 152–164 (2017)
3. Becerra-Riera, F., Llanes, N.M., Morales-González, A., Vazquez, H.M., Tistarelli, M.: On combining face local appearance and geometrical features for race classification. In: CIARP (2018)
4. Dhomne, A., Kumar, R.S., Bhan, V.: Gender recognition through face using deep learning. Procedia Comput. Sci. **132**, 2–10 (2018)
5. Heikkilä, M., Pietikäinen, M., Schmid, C.: Description of interest regions with center-symmetric local binary patterns. In: Kalra, P.K., Peleg, S. (eds.) ICVGIP 2006. LNCS, vol. 4338, pp. 58–69. Springer, Heidelberg (2006). https://doi.org/10.1007/11949619_6
6. Lowe, D.G.: Distinctive image features from scale invariant keypoints. Int. J. Comput. Vis. **60**, 91–110 (2004). https://doi.org/10.1023/B:VISI.0000029664.99615.94
7. Manesh, F., Ghahramani, M., Tan, Y.: Facial part displacement effect on template-based gender and ethnicity classification. 11th International Conference on Control Automation Robotics & Vision (ICARCV), pp. 1644–1649 (2010)
8. Masood, S., Gupta, S., Wajid, A., Gupta, S., Ahmed, M.: Prediction of human ethnicity from facial images using neural networks. In: Satapathy, S.C., Bhateja, V., Raju, K.S., Janakiramaiah, B. (eds.) Data Engineering and Intelligent Computing. AISC, vol. 542, pp. 217–226. Springer, Singapore (2018). https://doi.org/10.1007/978-981-10-3223-3_20
9. Muhammad, G., Hussain, M., Alenezy, F.: Race classification from face images using local descriptors. Int. J. Artif. Intell. Tools **21**(5), 1–24 (2012)
10. Ojala, T., Pietikäinen, M., Harwood, D.: A comparative study of texture measures with classification based on featured distribution. Pattern Recogn. **29**, 51–59 (1996)
11. Phillips, J., Moon, H., Risvi, S.A., Rauss, P.J.: The FERET evaluation methodology for face recognition algorithms. IEEE Trans Pattern Anal. Mach. Intell. **22**, 1090–1104 (2000)
12. Roomi, S.M.M., Virasundarii, S.L., Selvamegala, S., Jeevanandham, S., Hariharasudhan, D.: Race classification based on facial features. In: 2011 Third National Conference on Computer Vision, Pattern Recognition, Image Processing and Graphics, pp. 54–57 (2011)

13. Rothe, R., Timofte, R., Gool, L.V.: DEX: deep expectation of apparent age from a single image. In: 2015 IEEE International Conference on Computer Vision Workshop (ICCVW), pp. 252–257 (2015)
14. Salah, S.H., Du, H., Al-Jawad, N.: Fusing local binary patterns with wavelet features for ethnicity identification. Proc IEEE Int. Conf. Signal Image Process. **21**(5), 416–422 (2013)
15. Toudjeu, I., Tapamo, J.R.: Circular derivative local binary pattern feature description for facial expression recognition. Adv. Electr. Comput. Eng. **19**, 51–56 (2019). https://doi.org/10.4316/AECE.2019.01007
16. Vapnik, V.N.: Statistical Learning Theory. Wiley, Chichester (1998)
17. Vo, T., Nguyen, T., Le, C.: Race recognition using deep convolutional neural networks. Symmetry (2018). https://doi.org/10.3390/sym10110564
18. Wady, S.H., Ahmed, H.O.: Ethnicity identification based on fusion strategy of local and global features extraction. Int. J. Multidiscip. Curr. Rese. **4**, 200–205 (2016)
19. Wang, C., Zhang, Q., Liu, W., Liu, Y., Miao, L.: Facial feature discovery for ethnicity recognition. WIREs Data Min. Knowl. Discov. **9**(2), e1278 (2019)
20. Zangeneh, E., Rahmati, M., Mohsenzadeh, Y.: Low resolution face recognition using a two-branch deep convolutional neural network architecture. Expert Syst. Appl. **139**, 112854 (2020)
21. Zhang, G., Wang, Y.: Multimodal 2D and 3D facial ethnicity classification. In: Fifth International Conference on Image and Graphics (ICIG), pp. 928–932 (2009)
22. Yang, Z., Ai, H.: Demographic classification with local binary patterns. In: Lee, S.-W., Li, S.Z. (eds.) ICB 2007. LNCS, vol. 4642, pp. 464–473. Springer, Heidelberg (2007). https://doi.org/10.1007/978-3-540-74549-5_49

Detection and Classification of Coffee Plant Diseases by Image Processing and Machine Learning

Serge Leonel Essuthi Essoh[1(✉)], Hippolyte Michel Tapamo Kenfack[1,2],
Brice Auguste Mboule Ebele[1], Amos Mbietieu Mbietieu[1],
and Oscar Vianney Eone Etoua[1]

[1] University of Yaoundé I, B.P. 337, Yaoundé, Cameroon
{serge.essuthi,hippolyte.tapamo,brice.mboule,amos.mbietieu,
oscar.eone}@facsciences-uy1.cm
[2] UMMISCO, Bondy, France

Abstract. With the expansion of the population, agriculture has become a major economic source. But its productivity and the quality of the resulting products are threatened by many diseases that attack plants. Thus, the detection and classification of these diseases remains a major problem in agriculture principally when the cultivated space becomes too large. The use of image processing and machine learning can be a digital contribution to resolve this problem. Methods based on pixels values processing and texture analysis of plant leaf image can extract the disease area and provide necessary information to classify the disease. In this paper, we propose a method to improve the detection of diseased areas. We also use a large number of texture descriptors extracted by the 3D-GLCM (three-dimensional Gray-level Co-occurrence Matrix) on color images to classify the diseases. The detection is done by k-means. PCA (Principal Component Analysis) selects the necessary texture descriptors for classifying the diseases. The classification is done by multi-class SVM (Support Vectors Machine) and KNN (K-Nearest Neighbors) is used for comparison of classification results. Experiments were carried out on leaves images of Arabica coffee plant. The best performances show an accuracy of 96% and a mean F1-score of 96.75%. From those results we observed a considerable gain compared to the literature.

Keywords: Texture · Machine learning · 3D-GLCM · k-means · SVM · KNN · PCA

1 Introduction

Agriculture, which initially was only intended for consumption, is now a major economic source in the world. Despite various resolutions taken, this field still

Supported by University of Yaoundé 1.

T. M. N. Ngatched and I. Woungang (Eds.): PAAISS 2021, LNICST 405, pp. 137–149, 2022.
https://doi.org/10.1007/978-3-030-93314-2_9

suffers from many difficulties such as diseases that regularly attack plants [2,4]. Coffee farmers are not left out of this situation and generally call upon agricultural engineers to help them in their fight. Coffee is an industrial crop cultivated in several countries (from Armenia Coffee Corporation, n.d.) and is among the major economic sources for some of them [1]. The presence of diseases on coffee leaves allows plant disease specialists to distinguish between healthy and diseased plants, for the diseased ones to specify the type of disease and finally to suggest treatments. This work is very tedious when the cultivated area becomes increasingly vast. It is imprecise because of human imperfection. And it is also financially costly for the farmers. Initially, two major damages result from a deficient accomplishment of this task which are poor and/or lost productivity and high unnecessary expenses that are vectors towards serious health problems and economic drop. Intelligent computerization of this process would greatly reduce (if not eliminate) these damages and this heavy human dependence.

Machine Learning (ML) and Image Processing (IP) are two computational fields currently widely used in agriculture, specifically in the detection and classification of plant diseases [14,18]. When the disease is present on a plant leaf, IP can be used to process an image of that leaf and gather its texture properties. ML will then be used to model a system capable of adapting according to these properties. This system will then predict the health status of a new leaf. In imaging, texture is the repetition of set of pixels or patterns on an image [13]. Gray-level Co-occurrence Matrix (GLCM) is a method widely used to analyze and characterize the texture of an image [4]. These later technologies will help us in designing a digital solution to this problem of detection and classification of plant diseases present on their leaves, particularly those of coffee. Numerically it can be interpreted as the detection and classification of the colors of these diseases on leaves images.

In general, the steps (based on ML and IP) followed to solve these problems are: image acquisition, image preprocessing, segmentation of the diseased area (disease detection), feature extraction, feature selection and disease classification [4,6,16,20]. In addition, the most commonly used images are gray-scale. Therefore, two-dimensional co-occurrence matrix (2-GLCM) is the one used to extract a very restricted number of texture descriptors. In this study, we work with color images. We propose a method of thresholding the image to improve the segmentation. Then we extract a very large number of texture descriptors using three-dimensional co-occurrence matrix (3-GLCM) by taking as axes, the channels of our color space. Hence, the main goal of this work is to show that a large number of texture properties for volumetric data extracted on color images, are also exploitable to detect and classify plant diseases, especially that of coffee.

This paper is structured as follows: Sect. 1 presents the introduction, Sect. 2 lists some related works, Sect. 3 succinctly and clearly generalizes our approach, our experiments are presented in Sect. 4, the results and discussions constitute Sect. 5 and finally we conclude this work in Sect. 6.

2   Releted Works

Here we present some articles concerning the detection and classification of plant illnesses.

A. Mengistu et al. [16] propose (in 2016) an imaging and ML-based app-roach to recognize diseases of Ethiopian Arabica coffee. They study three types of diseases: coffee leaf rust, coffee berry disease and coffee wilt disease. They use grayscale images and 2D-GLCM to extract texture characteristics. They use PCA and genetic algorithm (GA) to select properties. The work is concluded with classification using artificial neural network (ANN), KNN, and the combi-nation of self-organizing map (SOM) and radial basis function (RBF).

V. Singh et al. (in 2017) [20] combine thresholding and genetic algorithm to perform segmentation in RGB space. Image is transformed into HSV space and the texture attributes needed for classification (contrast, energy, local homogene-ity and entropy, cluster hue and cluster dominance) are extracted only in the H band. Several classification algorithms are employed including SVM to recognize diseases of various plants. The work is performed on a set of 106 images with 60 images for training and 46 images for testing. The set consists of images of rose with bacterial disease, bean leaves with bacterial disease and fungal disease, lemon leaves with sun disease, banana leaves with early blight disease.

G. Dhingra et al. develop (in 2018) [4], perform a survey of the causes of dis-eases that attack plants and the main steps employed in the literature to address the problems of detection and classification of these diseases using image pro-cessing techniques and machine learning algorithms. In addition, they present reviews of papers on some image processing and ML methods.

N. Farooqui et al. [6] (in 2019) identify and detect wheat plant diseases. The image is segmented in L*a*b* color space by k-means. At the end of the seg-mentation, they directly distinguish the diseased leaves from the healthy ones. Only the leaves considered infected after the later step are used for classifica-tion. Three supervised algorithms used for the classification are: KNN, SVM and advanced neural network (ANN). The authors use 14308 images of healthy and infected leaves (by black straw, brown rust, powdery mildew and yellow rust diseases) and reserve 75% of them for model training and 25% for testing.

J. Esgario et al. (2020) [5] use deep learning (DL) through convolutional neu-ral networks (CNN) to classify and estimate the severity of biotic stresses that affect Arabica coffee leaves. The biotic stresses they analyze are miner, yellow rust, phoma and cercospora. There is no segmentation and features extraction phases, the image is just preprocessed and sent to the CNN for recognition and estimation of the severity of these diseases. The image is converted to HSV for pre-processing and back to RGB for classification. The different CNN architec-tures employed by J. Esgario et al. are: AlexNet, GoogLeNet, VGG16, ResNet50, MobileNetV2. They use two data augmentation techniques namely standard aug-mentation and Mixup method. 1747 images were collected of which 372 contained more than one disease on a leaf and among these 372, 62 presented stresses with the same severity. The 62 were removed from the batch and the rest were sub-divided into three subsets: training (70%), validation (15%) and test (15%).

3   Proposed Approach of Detection and Classification of Coffee Plant Diseases

Figure 1 illustrates our approach. It is organized in two parts: detection and classification. Detection consists of preprocessing and segmentation phases. While classification consists of feature extraction, feature selection and classification itself.

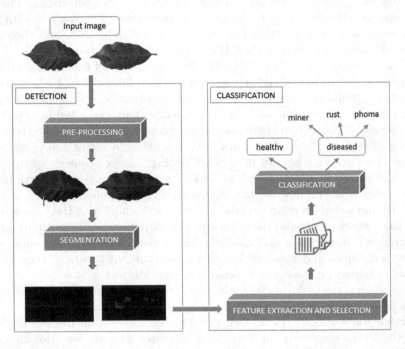

Fig. 1. Detection and classification process of (coffee) plant leaf diseases. (Color figure online)

3.1   Preprocessing

This phase aims to enhance the quality of our images. We perform preprocessing on our images as follows:

1. **Image resizing:** when the size of an infected leaf image is very small, it is difficult to perceive low severity infections. A minimum size T_{min} is therefore set. Any image whose size is smaller than T_{min} is resized to T_{min} using bilinear interpolation.
2. **Color space conversion:** *HSV* (Hue, Saturation, Value) is an adequate color space for contrast enhancement and segmentation of a color image [10, 12]. Our images are then converted from *RGB* (Red, Green, Blue) color space to *HSV*.

3. **Histogram equalization:** it is used to improve the contrast of our images. We recall that equalizing the histogram of a monochromatic image is finding a transformation that uniformizes the histogram of its intensity values. It is possible to equalize the histogram of a color image by applying the method on each band of a color system considered. However, this operation results in erroneous colors [10]. So, we apply this operation on the component V of our space HSV.

4. **Thresholding:** This method is added to ameliorate and/or facilitate the segmentation phase. A green leaf may have disease whose symptom color is close to green. The dissociation of these two colors can lead to undesirable effects. A healthy part can be considered as unhealthy and vice versa. To solve this problem we mask the green (healthy) part of our image by using a green level threshold in the H-band of our color space.

   Explicitly, let I be the image to threshold, h_{th} be the green level threshold in the H channel, max_g be the maximum green level value in H, $A = [h_{th}, max_g] \subset H$ be a subset of H representing the healthy part on I, (p_h, p_s) be the coordinates of a pixel p of I in the sub-space HS of HSV. The threshold is done as follows.

$$\forall p \in I, \text{ if } p_h \in A \text{ then } p_h = h', p_s = s'.$$

The values h' and s' are chosen so that the resulting color is both different from the colors of the symptoms and from the background color of the image. Assuming we have the same background color for all the images.

3.2   Segmentation

Its role is to extract from the image, the diseased area of the leaf using *k-means* method. The pixels of the thresholded image are the points to be clustered. Since all the color information is contained in the H and S channels and for reason of temporal complexity reduction, the V channel is omitted during the clustering. The pixels are thus labeled according to their colors. Therefore, these k groups produce k different images.

K-means Principle: The simplest unsupervised clustering algorithm, it groups a training data set of points into k clusters (groups) of similar or close points. To each group it assigns a class number and computes its average point called *center*. The algorithm alternates between two steps: after having randomly placed the k centers, it assigns to each point the class of the closest center then it redefines the value of each center as the average value of the points that have been assigned to it. The algorithm stops when the values of the centers no longer vary. The class of a new point corresponds to that of the center to which it is closer. [17]

3.3   Feature Extraction

In most cases, the categorization of an object is based on a significant set of features. Thus, we extract texture properties from the image resulting from the segmentation using 3D-GLCM. We compute 13 3D-GLCMs for each of the 13 directions in the space formed by the bands H, S, V. Then for each of these 3D-GLCMs we compute the 14 Haralick texture properties.

3D Gray Level Co-occurrence Matrix: Define for monochromatic images, GLCM has been introduced for the first time by Haralick in 1973 to compute 14 texture properties (*Contrast, Correlation, Variance, Inverse moment, Mean sum, Variance sum, Entropy, Entropy sum, Variance difference, Entropy difference, Correlation measure 1, Correlation measure 2, Maximum correlation coefficient*). 3D-GLCM is a square matrix G of size N which contains the occurrences of intensity pairs of neighboring pixels in an image. N being the number of distinct intensities of this image. The value at row i and column j of G noted $G(i,j)$, is equal to the number of times that a pixel of intensity i is neighbor of another pixel of intensity j. Neighborhood defined according to an integer *distance* d (relative to the image size) and an *orientation or direction* θ. The parameters d and θ can be redefined as a displacement vector $D = (d_x, d_y, d_z)$ where d_x represents the number of pixels traveled on the x axis, d_y the number of pixels traveled on the y axis and d_z the number of pixels traveled on the z axis (considering the image projected in a three-dimensional space) [11,13,19].

3.4   Feature Selection

A classification operation including vectors of 182 attributes (13 directions × 14 properties) is very time consuming. Moreover, among these 182 attributes, some are redundant and others have almost no influence on the classification process. We select our features with the dimensionality reduction method, PCA.

PCA Principle: PCA is one of the simplest unsupervised learning algorithm used for dimensionality reduction. This method is used to rotate a set of possibly correlated data attributes into another set of statistically non-correlated attributes (i.e., the axes on which they are projected are orthogonal) called principal components (PCs). The PCs are organized in decreasing order of variation. Dimensionality reduction is done by removing the PCs (axes) on which we observe less variations [7,17,21].

3.5   Classification

Feature extraction and selection transform each image into a vector of its texture properties. The vector is then used to classify the image. The idea here is to better distinguish healthy from diseased leaves and then to categorize the type of disease. We mainly use the Gaussian kernel SVM with a non-strict or light margin. The choice of this algorithm is due to the fact that our training set is not very large. Then because the points representing our images are non-linearly separable (for the kernel). And finally because SVM is widely used in the literature. The use of KNN here is just to show the efficiency of SVM compared to other classification algorithms (of ML).

SVM Principle: It is a binary classification algorithm which consists of determining a separator between 2 sets of points (examples) from 2 classes but with a maximum margin on either side of this separator. The margin is defined with respect to the support vectors, which are the closest points to the hyperplane (Fig. 2-(a)). *Kernel* is a concept used to solve the *non-linearity* problem in SVMs. A problem is said to be *non-linearly separable* when the separator is non-linear. Kernel is then used to transform a non-linear problem into a linear problem by changing the initial space of the points and projecting them into a new space where they will be linearly separable (Fig. 2-(b) and (c)). The Eqs. (1), (2), (3) formulate the kernels commonly used between two input points x and y. It is sometimes difficult to find a perfect margin between two classes, hence the intervention of the concept of *soft margin* which corresponds to accepting the presence of a certain number of points inside this margin while penalizing this presence. The classification of a new example is done on the basis of these support vectors [8, 9, 21].

- *polynomial* kernel of degree d

$$\mathbf{K}\left(x, y\right) = \left(1 + x^T y\right)^d.$$ (1)

It is called linear kernel if $d = 1$.

- *Radial-based function (RBF)* kernel or Gaussian kernel with parameter σ.

$$\mathbf{K}\left(x, y\right) = exp\left(-\left(x - y\right)^2 / 2\sigma\right).$$ (2)

- *Sigmoid function* kernel with parameters κ and δ.

$$\mathbf{K}\left(x, y\right) = tanh\left(\kappa x^T y - \delta\right).$$ (3)

KNN Principle: It is a supervised classification algorithm that has almost no learning phase. It stores in memory all the training examples and their respective labels. When we want to predict the class of a new example, we compare it to those stored using a *similarity measure* and we retain only the k most similar examples denoted *k-nearest neighbors*. The number of k neighbors and the similarity measure are the main parameters of this algorithm. The choice of k is not trivial: for a very small value, the nearest neighbors are exposed to noise and for a very large value, the accuracy decreases. There is a variety of similarity measures such as the *Euclidean distance* and the *Manhattan distance* [7].

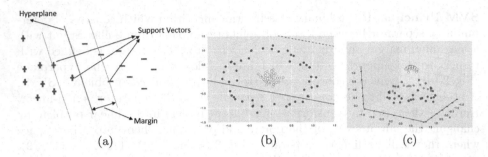

Fig. 2. SVM algorithm illustration. (a): Soft margin and hyperplane. (b): non-linearly separable problem [3]. (c): kernel application result [3].

4   Experiments

4.1   Dataset Description

We experimented 3 coffee diseases namely, miner, phoma and yellow rust (Fig. 3). The images utilized come from the dataset proposed by Esgario et al. [5]. We chose images with a perfectly white background (more appropriate for segmentation [15]). Our dataset is composed of 1113 color images in total including 252 for healthy, 316 for miner, 204 for phoma and 341 for yellow rust. Each image is of size 1024 × 2048 pixels. We split the dataset into 70%, 15%, 15% respectively for training, validation and testing.

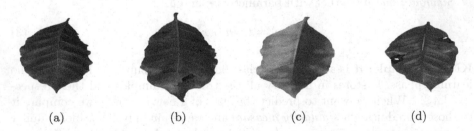

Fig. 3. Healthy and unhealthy coffee leaves images.(a): healthy (b): miner (c): yellow rust (d): phoma. (Color figure online)

4.2   Detection of Diseased Area

The minimum image size taken is $T_{min} = 500 \times 500$ pixels. With respect to the thresholding, the trade-off of choosing the green level threshold is higher with the presence of a yellow symptom (yellow rust). If we take a threshold close to green, a healthy portion of the leaf can be considered as infected. On the other hand, a threshold close to yellow is likely to make an infected part be considered healthy. The choice of our threshold can be done in the interval [35, 50] on a

360 scale. With 50 favoring the detection of a disease in its early stages. And 35 favoring its detection at an advanced level. The chosen threshold $h_{th} = 40$ is the one that best classifies healthy leaves. To mask the green (healthy) part of our image we chose $h' = 150$ and $s' = 50$ producing a purple color. The preprocessing phase is highlighted by Fig. 4.

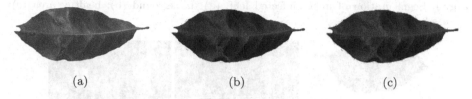

(a)   (b)   (c)

Fig. 4. Preprocessing illustration. (a): initial image in RGB space (b): conversion to HSV space and histogram equalization. (c): masking of healthy area. (Color figure online)

Concerning the segmentation, we do a 3-clustering (k = 3 for k-means) with Euclidean distance as metric. This metric is computed in the subspace HS. The initial image is then separated into 3 other images: the background, the healthy part and the infected or empty (for healthy leaves) area. Figures 5, 6, 7 and 8 elucidate respectively the segmentation of healthy, miner, rust and phoma leaves.

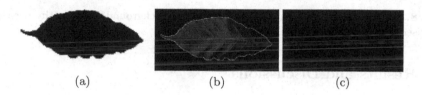

(a)   (b)   (c)

Fig. 5. Segmentation of healthy leaf. (a): background (b): healthy area (c): empty area.

4.3   Diseases Classification

The background images (examples Figs. 5-a, 6-a, 7-a and 8-a) and those of the healthy area (examples Figs. 5-b, 6-b, 7-b, and 8-b) from the segmentation are omitted during feature extraction. The last sub-images (examples Figs. 5-c, 6-c, 7-c and 8-c) are the ones used to extract 182 texture properties by the 3D-GLCM method with a distance $d = 1$. After selecting the features by PCA, we obtain 57 useful texture properties. Those features are subsequently normalized individually over the interval $[0, 1]$ according to their minimum and maximum values (to reduce execution time costs) and then used for classification. The classifications are made by the two supervised learning algorithms (SVM, KNN) by considering 4 classes: class 0 for healthy, class 1 for miner, class 2 for yellow rust and class 3 for phoma. The best results are achieved with the RBF kernel for SVM and with $K = 3$ for KNN.

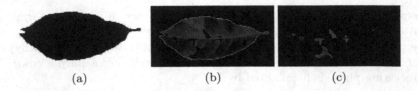

(a)   (b)   (c)

Fig. 6. Segmentation of miner infected leaf. (a): background (b): healthy area (c): diseased area.

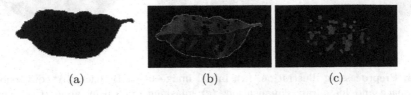

(a)   (b)   (c)

Fig. 7. Segmentation of yellow rust infected leaf. (a): background (b): healthy area (c): diseased area.

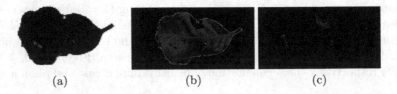

(a)   (b)   (c)

Fig. 8. Segmentation of phoma infected leaf. (a): background (b): healthy area (c): diseased area.

5   Results and Discussions

5.1   Results

Table 1 displays the performance of each of the 4 classes studied with the SVM associated with the PCA. We notice for example that a healthy leaf can be predicted correctly with a precision of 97% and a recall of 100%.

Table 1. Individual results for each class.

	Precision (%)	Recall (%)	F1-score (%)
Healthy	97	100	99
Miner	98	93	95
Rust	97	94	96
Phoma	94	100	97

Tables 2 and 3 respectively present the results obtained with SVM and KNN when the dimensionality is reduced and when it is not.

Table 2. Results obtained by SVM and KNN with dimensionality reduction.

	SVM + PCA (%)	KNN + PCA (%)
Precision	96, 50	90, 25
Recall	96, 75	89, 50
F1-score	96, 75	89, 25
Accuracy	96, 42	89, 28

Table 3. Results obtained by SVM and KNN without dimensionality reduction.

	SVM (%)	KNN (%)
Precision	94, 75	88
Recall	94, 75	89, 25
F1-score	94, 50	88, 25
Accuracy	94, 64	88, 09

5.2 Discussions

In this study we proposed a thresholding method to improve the segmentation of diseased areas in a leaf. Then we exploited a very large number of texture properties computed by 3D-GLCM on color images to classify these diseases. We simulated our approach on a dataset composed of 1113 color images of healthy and diseased coffee leaves. We experimented 3 types of diseases, namely miner, yellow rust and phoma. The best classification results are obtained by the SVM+PCA configuration. We got precisions of 97%, 98%, 97% and 94% and recalls of 100%, 93%, 94% and 100% respectively for healthy, miner, yellow rust and phoma diseases (classes).

Table 4. Summary of the results obtained by the proposed approach to some benchmark approaches found in the literature.

Approach	Plant	Year	Accuracy (%)
Ours	coffee	2021	96.42
J. Esgario et al. [5]	coffee	2020	97.07
A. Mengistu et al. [16]	coffee	2016	90.07

We notice that for healthy class we have both highest precision and recall. This highly depends on the threshold value chosen. Another observation made is that in each case (with and without dimensionality reduction) SVM classify better than KNN. This is because it is more likely to find a delimiter to separate (SVM) classes compared to finding nearest neighbors (KNN), especially when the projected points are close. Also we observe that we have better performances when the dimensionality is reduced (features selection) compared to when it is not. This is due to the fact that there are properties that are insignificant (or almost insignificant) for the classification and also that some of these properties are correlated. We are not interested in these superfluous attributes because they are automatically eliminated by PCA. Finally, we can see that the best classification configuration is SVM+PCA. For both practice and research, the results obtained here show that our contribution is useful to detect and classify (coffee) plants diseases as compare to those of the literature. A potential limit of this work is the a homogeneous and perfectly white background of our images. But this issue has already been addressed by Esgario et al. [5].

Moreover, we can see that the size of our dataset is small. But we are using SVM for classification, which doens't demande a larger dataset to generalize well. Hence, our propose approach has a good generalization capability.

Furthermore, Table 4 compares the results obtained by the proposed approach to some benchmark approaches found in the literature. We notice that our approach produces a better performance than the majority of these approaches. Exception is made on the approach based on the CNN which is practically very computationally time and training data consuming. Also, as compared to the ML approaches we have a high time complexity, this is due to the large number of properties employed (extraction and classification).

6   Conclusion

Plant disease detection and classification remains a major concern in agriculture. A plethora of relevant ML and IP based approaches have been proposed to solve this problem [4,6,16,20]. In this paper we have proved that texture descriptors of volumetric data obtained on color images by 3D-GLCM are also exploitable to solve this problem when diseases are present on plant leaves. Generally, the results obtained from the experiments on healthy and diseased coffee leaves (miner, yellow rust and phoma diseases) show an accuracy of 96%, a mean precision of 96.50%, a mean recall of 96.75% and a mean F1-score of 96.75%. These results reveal that our approach is a relevant digital contribution to the resolution of this problem. However we can denote some limits of the evaluated model. Firstly, we don't have full control on the properties used. Also the model can only be used with one disease on a leaf. In the future, we envisage the possibility of detecting more than one disease on a leaf and identifying all the diseases present on an image of a large cultivated area. In addition, we will also experiment other dimensionality reduction algorithms that are more powerful than the simple PCA.

References

1. coup d'œil sur les produits de edition spéciale sur le café en Afrique de l'Ouest et du Centre. United Nations (2018)
2. Brauman, F., et al.: Solutions for a cultivated planet. Nature **478**, 337–342 (2011)
3. Cleary, M.: Python Data Science, vol. 53 (2019)
4. Dhingra, G., Kumar, V., Joshi, H.D.: Study of digital image processing techniques for leaf disease detection and classification. Multimedia Tools Appl. **77**(15), 19951–20000 (2017). https://doi.org/10.1007/s11042-017-5445-8
5. Esgario, J.G., Krohling, R.A., Ventura, J.A.: Deep learning for classification and severity estimation of coffee leaf biotic stress. Comput. Electron. Agric. **169**, 105162 (2020). https://doi.org/10.1016/j.compag.2019.105162
6. Farooqui, N.A., Ritika, R.: An identification and detection process for leaves disease of wheat using advance machine learning techniques. Biosci. Biotechnol. Res. Commun. **12**(4), 1081–1091 (2019). https://doi.org/10.21786/bbrc/12.4/31
7. Géron, A.: Hands-On Machine Learning with Scikit-Learn and TensorFlow: Concepts, Tools, and Techniques to Build Intelligent Systems. O'Reilly Media Inc., Newton (2017)
8. Ghodsi, P.A.: Hard margin support vector machine, October 2015
9. Ghodsi, P.A.: Soft margin support vector machine, October 2015
10. Gonzalez, R.C., Woods, R.E.: Digital Image Processing, 3rd edn. Pearson, London (2007)
11. Haralick, R., Shanmugam, K., Dinstein, I.: Textural features for image classification. IEEE Trans. Syst. Man Cybern. **SMC-3**, 610–621 (1973)
12. Jyoti Bora, D.: Importance of image enhancement techniques in color image segmentation: a comprehensive and comparative study. Indian J. Sci. Res **15**(1), 115–131 (2017)
13. Kurani, A.S., Xu, D.H., Furst, J., Raicu, D.S.: Co-occurrence matrices for volumetric data. In: Proceedings of the Seventh IASTED International Conference on Computer Graphics and Imaging, pp. 447–452 (2004)
14. Liakos, K.G., Busato, P., Moshou, D., Pearson, S., Bochtis, D.: Machine learning in agriculture: a review. Sensors **18**(8), 1–29 (2018). https://doi.org/10.3390/s18082674. (Switzerland)
15. Manso, G.L., Knidel, H., Krohling, R.A.: A smartphone application to detection and classification of coffee leaf miner and coffee leaf rust (2019)
16. Mengistu, A.D., Alemayehu, D.M., Mengistu, S.G.: Ethiopian coffee plant diseases recognition based on imaging and machine learning techniques. Int. J. Database Theory Appl. **9**(4), 79–88 (2016). https://doi.org/10.14257/ijdta.2016.9.4.07
17. Müller, A.C., Guido, S.: Introduction to Machine Learning with Python (2017)
18. Pandurng, J.A., Lomte, S.S.: Digital image processing applications in agriculture: a survey. Int. J. Adv. Res. Comput. Sci. Softw. Eng. **5**(3), 622–624 (2015)
19. Poonam, D.S.: Image texture: Algorithms and models (2018)
20. Singh, V., Misra, A.K.: Detection of plant leaf diseases using image segmentation and soft computing techniques. Inf. Process. Agric. **4**(1), 41–49 (2017). https://doi.org/10.1016/j.inpa.2016.10.005
21. Stephen, M.: Machine Learning An Algorithmic Perspective, 2nd edn. Chapman and Hall/CRC, Boca Raton (2014)

Plant Diseases Detection and Classification Using Transfer Learning

Emma Genders and Serestina Viriri[✉]

School of Mathematics, Statistics and Computer Science,
University of KwaZulu-Natal, Durban, South Africa
viriris@ukzn.ac.za

Abstract. Plant disease detection and identification have been ongoing global concerns, especially towards food security and ensuring sustainable crop yield. To overcome these issues, Artificial Intelligent techniques have been implemented and achieved some great success in this field. However, improvements can still be made, as many approaches still suffer from prolonged training/testing time. In this paper, a relatively new efficient deep neural network, EfficientNets was implemented for the classification of plant diseases. Specifically, the EfficientNets models B0 to B5 were implemented on the PlantVillage dataset. Furthermore, Transfer learning techniques were included in the proposed model to minimize the training time. The two phases of Transfer learning are performed: first using an Imaganet pre-trained model as a feature extraction, where all layers are frozen except the classification layer. Then fine-tuning was performed on the model, where all layers are retrained. The proposed model achieved a classification accuracy of 99.43% on the EfficientNets B0. The proposed model can classify plant diseases accurately in real-time, and can be deployed on mobile devices with limited computation resources.

Keywords: Plant diseases · Classification · Deep learning · EfficientNets · Transfer learning

1 Introduction

Plant disease recognition is seen to be a critical process in agricultural practice. Early detection of crop diseases is necessary to help monitor and control diseases, prevent loss of production and maximize crop yield. Traditional methods involve farmers manually observing the plants with the naked eye, which can be time-consuming and inaccurate. The advancement in technology such as mobile cameras and the growth of online information about plant diseases have facilitated application of technology in this area. The capacity of automatic plant disease diagnosis has furthermore expanded due to the growth in deep machine learning technologies.

T. M. N. Ngatched and I. Woungang (Eds.): PAAISS 2021, LNICST 405, pp. 150–166, 2022.
https://doi.org/10.1007/978-3-030-93314-2_10

Deep Convolutional Neural Networks (CNN) have provided remarkable achievements in areas of image classification problems and machine learning [1]. A challenge faced in current CNN models is that they are computationally expensive and require a large amount of time for identification. Thus, there is a need to research fast and efficient CNN models, providing real-time results with low complexity. This paper proposes to utilize EfficientNets, a relatively new family of smaller CNNs that have proven to be effective and efficient.

Traditionally, CNNs are trained in isolation to solve a specific task. However, training a CNN model from scratch can be time-consuming and requires an extensively large dataset. To combat this drawback, transfer learning can be utilized. This paper explores transfer learning techniques at feature extraction, and parameter optimization levels.

The paper is structured as follows, Sect. 2 presents a literature review on plant disease classification using Deep learning and transfer learning techniques; Sect. 3 describes the methods and techniques implemented; Sect. 4 describes the design and implementation process; Sect. 5 discusses the experimental results obtained and evaluates the model's performances. Finally, Sect. 6 provides a conclusion and recommendation of possible future work.

2 Literature Review

2.1 Plant Disease Classification using Deep Learning

Numerous Deep learning (DL) architectures together with visualization techniques have been used for the classification of plant diseases over the years. Improvements have been made in this field by the evolution of state-of the-art DL models, especially using CNNs. AlexNet is one of the most popular architectures, followed by GoogLeNet, VGG-16, and ResNet-50 [2]. More recently, smaller DL models were introduced such as MobileNet and reduced MobileNet, getting a similar accuracy with fewer parameters compared to the other models.

Brahimi, et al. [3], proposed a study on the identification of apple leaf diseases utilizing Deep Convolutional Neural Networks with end-to-end learning. The AlexNet model achieved an overall accuracy of 97.62%. The study showed that using data augmentation techniques such as image processing technologies, direction disturbance, brightness, adjustment and Principal Component Analysis (PCA) jittering reduced overfitting and diversified the training set for better generalisation. Concluding that although a robust model was built, in order for a more real time classification, other faster DL models and approaches would need to be considered.

A study on Deep learning for tomato diseases did a comparison in the performance between deep models and shallow models with hand-crafted features [4]. As pre-processing and feature engineering techniques can be very time-consuming and difficult, the study proposed using CNNs (namely AlexNet and GoogLeNet) as an automated feature extraction for the classification of diseases. The raw images can be used directly, and features are established and learnt from the data in the training phase. The Deep models obtained an accuracy of 99%

outperforming shallow models obtaining an accuracy of 95%. Thus, the results showed how deep models can be used as good feature extractors without human expert involvement.

2.2 Transfer Learning Approach

The issue with using CNNs is that it requires an extensively large amount of data to be trained on, which can be infeasible to collect. Thus, many authors have applied the concept of transfer learning in their studies [5–12], which has significantly reduced the demand for massive datasets and increases the model's accuracy.

This study paved the way for smartphone assistance in disease classification [5]. The results show that transfer learning using fine-tuning outperforms learning from scratch on the PlantVillage dataset. Obtaining an accuracy of 99.34% on GoogleNet using transfer learning. A comparison between Colour, Gray scale and Leaf Segmented versions of the dataset was done. The results showed that the model performed best using the coloured version with an 80:20 training and validation split. While the model yielded a good accuracy on the PlantVillage dataset, however, when the model was tested on images collected from online sources, the accuracy dropped to 31%. Showing the issues concerning the limitation of the PlantVillage dataset. These concerns were further found in [6].

A comparison between four different transfer learning approaches on a deep neural network for plant classification was preformed [7]. The five classification models were designed for the study, comparing the different transfer learning approaches. The results showed that transfer learning outperforms end-to-end training from scratch in terms of classification accuracy. Furthermore, deep features and using fine-tuning provided a better accuracy than the other transfer learning approaches such as cross-dataset fine-tuning. However, this study showed that not a lot of comprehensive research has been done on evaluating different transfer learning approaches, extended to plant disease detection.

Lee et al. [8], presented a comparison of different transfer learning techniques based on different pre-training task domains. One pre-trained model used a specialized plant domain, whereas another pre-trained model used a generalized object domain (ImageNet). The experiment showed that pre-training with a plant specialized domain reduced overfitting for the Inception model. However, using the ImageNet domain on the VGG16 model gave a better generalization ability towards new data. In [9], the authors proposed a model to identify plant diseases using a nine-layer CNN on the PlantVillage dataset. In the study, it was observed that using data augmentation increased the performance of the model. Different training epochs, batch sizes and dropout rates were compared with a transfer learning approach. The proposed model achieved 96.46%.

Too et al. [10], presented a study to compare fine-tune numerous Deep learning models using the PlantVillage dataset. The DenseNet architecture obtained the highest accuracy of 99.75%, having the lowest computational training time

with the fewest parameters compared to the other model. However, it was con
cluded that further research should be done to improve the computational time
for plants disease identification tasks.

Chen et al. [11], proposed a new model called MobileNet-Beta (a modified
Mobile-NetV2 model with a classification Activation Map) for the identification
of plant diseases. Transfer learning was performed in 2 phases; first the convolutional layers are kept frozen with the initialized parameters from ImageNet, while
the new extended layers are trained on with the target dataset. The second phase
involved retraining all the parameter with the target dataset on the pre-trained
model from the first phase. Yielding an optimum model with a classification
accuracy of 99.85%. The transfer learning technique here is very similar to the
one proposed in this project. Furthermore, a new scaling method was proposed,
consequently producing a new family of models called EfficientNets [13]. Achieving state-of-the-art accuracy of 84.4% being 8.4× smaller and 6.1× faster on an
ImageNet dataset with fewer parameters. The model was also shown to transfer
well, achieving state-of-the-art accuracy on 5 out of the 8 transfer datasets used.
Thus, it can be seen that further research can be done on EfficientNets models,
extending it to plant diseases dataset.

3   Methods and Techniques

3.1   Dataset

The well-known PlantVillage dataset taken from TensorFlow [14] was used in
this work, containing 54,303 diseased and healthy leaf images classified into 38
classes, with 26 diseases and 14 crop species. The dataset was split into its
training, validation and testing set by 80%, 16% and 4% containing 43442, 8689,
2172 image samples respectively.

3.2   Pre-processing

Minimal pre-processing was done to the data, the idea being putting the raw
data in to the CNN models. However, to prepare the data, all the plant images
are reshaped to 224 × 224 pixels for the EfficientNets model. Furthermore, data
augmentation was preformed on the training dataset.

Data Augmentation. Image augmentation techniques involve increasing the
amount of data by adding slight modifications to it. This can be done by randomly rotating images at different angles, scaling, cropping, adding noise, vertical and horizontal flipping and colour manipulation. It diversifies the dataset
and helps prevent overfitting (which reduces the classification accuracy). Figure 1
shows the data augmentation technique used in this project, which involves randomly rotating the images by 15°, flipping, changing contrast and translating
the images.

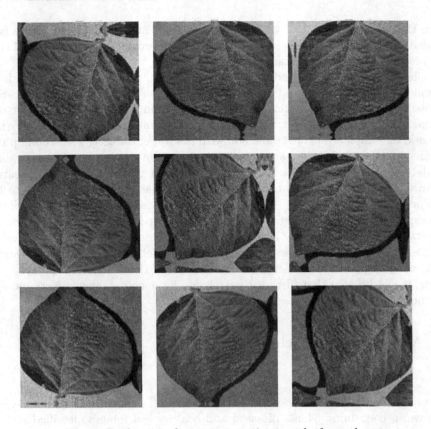

Fig. 1. Preforming data augmentation on a leaf sample.

3.3   Deep Learning

Deep learning is a type of machine learning method, based on Artificial Neural Networks. Mimicking the functioning of a human brain, consisting of a web of interconnecting neurons. Each connection has an assigned weight, corresponding to the importance of that neuron when multiplied by the value of its input. The weighted sum of the inputs are also adjusted by the bias. The input signal then goes through an activation function, producing the output of the neuron.

The learning processes can be described by training the neural network, learning the parameters (weights and biases) though an iterative process. This is done through forwardpropagation and backpropagation. Forwardpropagation involves the entire network being exposed to the training data to calculate its prediction labels. Then a loss function is used to estimate the loss, which compares the prediction results to its true labels (since this is in a supervised learning environment). Thereafter, backpropagation is performed, where the loss for each neuron is propagated back to it. The propagated information is then used to adjust the parameters to try to increase the model's predictive performance. This process is usually iterated in batches of data through much training iteration (epochs) until the loss (error) is minimized and good predictions are obtained.

Convolutional Neural Networks. A Convolutional Neural Network is an evolved type of feed-forward Neural Network, which is commonly applied to image recognition problems. This is due to its ability to capture spatial and temporal dependencies in images with a lower number of parameters compared to other neural networks.

A CNN consisting of three different types of layers, a convolutional, pooling and a fully-connected layer. The convolutional layer involves kernels being applied to the input data to extract important features from the image. It then creates a feature map by summing up the results to give a one-depth, convoluted output. The Pooling layer is responsible for down sampling each feature map independently. Reducing the spatial size of the feature map. These two layers perform feature extraction, which involves a hierarchy of learning visual features at various levels of abstraction and detail at different layers (such as learning detectors like shape, colour and edges to more specialized features). The fully-connected layers are added on top of these features to classify the image. Where every neuron in one layer is connected to every other neuron in the next layer. Then, for classification, the output of the last fully-connected layer is fed through a Softmax classifier. Figure 2 shows a simplified architecture of a CNN, describing the different layers mentioned above.

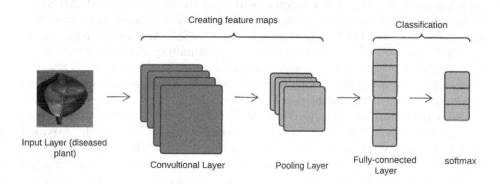

Fig. 2. A typical simplified CNN architecture.

A CNN can be described by the following dimensions; **width** being the amount of feature maps at each layer; **depth** being the number of layers and **resolution**, being the size of a feature map. These parameters have a huge effect on how well the model performs. Thus, scaling up methods can be used to help achieve better performances on CNNs. This is done by increasing the depth, width and resolution of the network. Where the extension of each dimension is beneficial in increasing the accuracy. Increasing the resolution or width helps in capturing fine-grained patterns, while increasing the depth helps capture more complex features. However, the optimal way of scaling up CNNs has proven to be difficult and usually involves scaling up in only one of these dimensions, which have its limitations [13].

3.4 EfficientNets

In a recent study proposed by Tan et al., [13] it was seen that in order to achieve better accuracy and efficiency when scaling up CNNs, all dimensions of the CNN must be balanced. Thus, proposing a new effective scaling method that uses a compound coefficient to uniformly scale each dimension.

The compound scaling method uses a user defined compound co-efficient ϕ to scale the model's dimensions. Equation 1 defines the formula for scaling the depth, width, and resolution as follows:

$$depth : d = \alpha^{\phi}; \qquad width : w = \beta^{\phi}; \qquad resolution : r = \gamma^{\phi};$$
$$such that : \alpha \cdot \beta^2 \cdot \gamma^2 \approx 2\alpha \geq 1, \beta \geq 1, \gamma \geq 1. \tag{1}$$

Where α, β, γ are constants obtained by the grid search under the fixed constraints, finding the optimal values responsible for determining how the resources are assigned to the dimensions. The compound coefficient ϕ defines how many resources are available for scaling of the model.

The computational cost in a convolution network is largely due to its convolution process. In general, the floating point operations per second (FLOPS) for a convolution process are proportional to d, w^2, r^2. So by scaling the network as shown in Eq. 1 the FLOPS will increase by $(\alpha \cdot \beta^2 \cdot \gamma^2)^{\phi}$. And due to the following constraint, $\alpha \cdot \beta^2 \cdot \gamma^2 \approx 2$ it will therefore approximately increase only by 2^{ϕ}.

The EfficientNets Network also aims to reduce the number of FLOPs and parameters, by using the mobile inverted bottleneck convolution baseline network (which was first introduced in MobileNetV2 [15]). EfficientNets also utilizes Swish activation function rather than the common ReLU activation function.

EfficientNets contains 8 models ranging from B0 to B7. The models are scaled first by starting with the baseline network, EfficientNetB0. With the assumption that there are twice as many resources available, ϕ is set to 1 and using Eq. 1, a grid search is performed. Finding the optimal values to be $\alpha = 1.2, \beta = 1.1, \gamma = 1.15$. Then to obtain EfficientNetB1 to B7 α, β, γ were fixed to these values and were scaled up using Eq. 1 with increasing ϕ values.

3.5 Softmax Classifier

A Softmax function is commonly used in deep learning for classification tasks. It is a generalization of the binary form of Logistic Regression, that can classify multiple classes. Where the output is the normalized class probability scores for each class label. The mapping function is defined as follows,

$$f(x_i; W) = W x_i \tag{2}$$

Where the mapping function f takes x, the set of input data, and maps it to the output their class labels. This is done via a dot product between x and W (the weighted matrix) similar to other common losses. However, the scores are then interpreted as unnormalized log probabilities for each class label using cross-entropy loss, that can be defined as:

$$L_i = -\log\left(\frac{e^{f_{y_i}}}{\sum_j e^{f_j}}\right) \tag{3}$$

Where f_j is the j-th element of the class scores vector. The equation inside the log function ($\frac{e^{f_{y_i}}}{\sum_j e^{f_j}}$) is known as the Softmax function. Which takes the exponents of each output and normalizes it by the sum of all the exponents, so that it sums up to one. Thus enables the cross-entropy loss to be applied.

Now looking at the cross-entropy between the true distribution p (the true set of labels) and an estimated distribution q can be described as follows,

$$H(p, q) = -\sum_x p(x) \log q(x) \tag{4}$$

Thus shows how the Softmax classifier aims to minimize the cross-entropy between the q, the estimated class probabilities which is defined by the Softmax function and p, the true distribution (encoded as one-hot labels).

3.6 Transfer Learning

Transfer learning is a newer machine learning technique that involves reusing or transferring knowledge acquired from one task domain to solve a similar task. In practice, transfer learning involves exploiting pre-trained models having previously learned visual knowledge and already initialized weights for training a new model. Compared with training a model from scratch in isolation, it has the advantage of saving time and achieving higher accuracies. The formal definition of transfer learning can be described as follows [2],

Definition 1. *Given a source domain D_S and learning task T_S, a target domain D_T and learning task T_T, transfer learning aims to help improve the learning of the target predictive function $f_T(\cdot)$ in D_T using the knowledge in D_S and T_S, where $D_S \neq D_T$, or $T_S \neq T_T$.*

Feature Extraction. Using transfer learning as a feature extractor involves utilizing pre-trained models to extract meaningful features from new samples. Allowing the knowledge from the source domain task, in this case ImageNet, to be used to extract important features for the new domain task, the PlantVillage dataset. The fully-connected layers are replaced with new layers to accommodate the specific disease's classification task. During training, all layers are frozen except the classifier layer (i.e. only its weights get updated). Thus, the set of extracted features from the base convolutional layers are used by the classifier to provide the probabilities of that image (the plant image) belonging to each class (the type of disease).

Fine-Tuning. Fine-tuning is another, more involved in transfer learning techniques. Where previous layers can be selectively retrained as well. When considering Deep neural networks, the initial layers of the architecture capture and learn more generic features (e.g. edge detectors or colour segment detectors), whereas the higher ones learn more task specific features. Thus, consider retraining parts or all of the layers of the network could be a useful technique to improve the network's performance [16].

Proposed Transfer Learning Models. Figure 3 illustrates the models used in this research work. In case (a) the pre-trained EfficientNets model having already initialized weights from ImageNet is used as a feature extractor for model (b). In model (b) the final layer is replaced and the softmax classifier layer is retrained, leaving all other layers frozen. Thereafter, we go back and fine-tune all the layers from model (b) which is shown in model (c), where all layers are set to trainable.

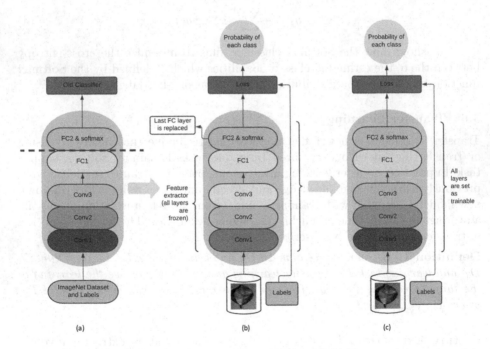

Fig. 3. Proposed models: a) Pre-trained ImageNet model. b) Feature extractor model. c) Fine-tune model.

4   Design And Implementation

4.1   System Design and Experimental Setup

This agriculture follows a general transfer learning work flow and is consistent
for all the EfficientNets models (B0–B5) used in this project. Figure 4 shows a
graphical representation of the work flow.

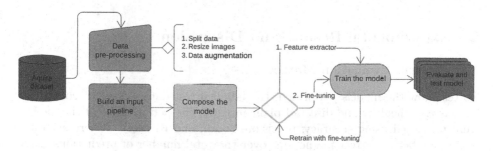

Fig. 4. System flow diagram

Acquire Dataset, requires downloading the PlantVillage dataset from tensorFlow. **Data pre-processing** is performed, where the dataset is **split** randomly into its training, validation and testing set with a 80:16:4 split respectively.
The training and validation dataset are used to train and fit the model, whereas
the test set (unseen sample) is used to evaluate the classification performance of
the model. The images are **resized** to 224×224 pixels; the input size needed to
support EfficientNets. **Data augmentation** is performed, which involves randomly rotating the images by $15°$, flipping, changing contrast and translating
the images.

Building an input pipeline, prepares the data before feeding it into the
model. The labels are put into a one-hot category encoding (a vector of size 38
(number of classes), where all values are set to 0 except for the value of the
i-th position of its corresponding class label which is set to 1). Then the data
was batched to size 64, this defines the number of samples that will propagate
through the network.

Composing the model, the EfficientNets base model is initiated with pre-
trained weights from the ImageNet dataset, which has over 1 million images
and 1000 class categories. The fully-connected layer is then replaced, and the
output is changed to 38, according to the number of classes in this classification
problem. Softmax was selected as the activation function in the last layer, and
the loss function is set to categorical cross-entropy. The dropout rate was set to
0.2. Dropout is a regularization technique that prevents the model becoming too
specialized to the training data by randomly selecting neurons to be dropped-out.
The Adam optimization method was utilized, as it was the same optimization
method used by the pre-trained EfficientNets model.

Training the model, for the first step, transfer learning as a feature extractor is implemented. Involving all layers to be frozen and only the top layer is trained on. The learning rate is set to 0,01 (relatively high). The model was trained using 20 epochs, as that's when all the models were seen to converge. The second step involves fine-tuning the model, to try to increase its accuracy. All layers of the base model were unfrozen and set to trainable. The whole model was then retained with a lower learning rate of 0,0001, to avoid overfitting and train for 60 epochs.

5   Experimental Results and Discussion

5.1   System Evaluation Matrix

To test how the models performed, the labelled test data was used, containing 38 classes of healthy and diseased plant images. The performance of the models were measured using accuracy, precision, recall, and F1 score. Where accuracy is the number of correct predictions over the total number of predictions made by the model. Precision is the number of correctly predicted plant leaves (true positive) over all positive predictions (correct and misclassified positives). Recall is the number of correctly predicted plant leaves (true positive) over all relevant samples (true positive and false negative). F1 portrays the number of plant leaves that are classified correctly, and is calculated as the harmonic average between precision and recall.

The evaluation metrics described above are defined respectively as follows, taken from [17] to accommodate for multi-class classification:

Where TP = True Positive, TN = True Negatives, FP = False Positives and FN = False Negatives.

$$Accuracy = \frac{TP + TN}{TP + TN + FP + FN} \tag{5}$$

$$Precision = \frac{TP}{TP + FP} \tag{6}$$

$$Recall = \frac{TP}{TP + FN} \tag{7}$$

$$F1 = 2 \times \frac{Precisonn \times Recall}{Precision + Recall} \tag{8}$$

5.2   Results obtained

In this section, the results obtained by all the experiments will be compared and evaluated for the classification of plant diseases. Examining the success of utilizing the EfficientNets models (B0-B5) with 2 phases of transfer learning being performed.

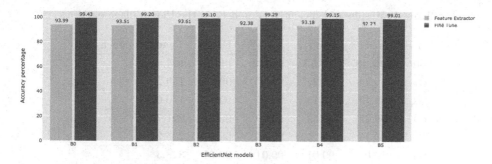

Fig. 5. Feature extractor vs fine-tuning accuracy results.

Firstly, the impact of using transfer learning as a deep feature extractor compared to fine-tuning the model will be compared. The bar chart in Fig. 5 shows the comparison of the classification accuracy of the EfficientNets models after using transfer learning as a feature extractor, then going back and fine-tuning the model. Fine-tuning greatly increased the accuracy by almost 6% on all the models. However, it can be noted that by just implementing feature extraction (no retraining of the layers) still gave fairly high accuracies, all above 92%. This could be due to the fact that the large Imagenet dataset contained closely related images/features to this problem domain. Thus, the visual knowledge transferred was extremely useful in automatically finding the best features in the PlantVillage dataset, to reduce loss.

The results show that the smaller EfficientNets models (B0–B3) achieved higher accuracies compared to the bigger models. With EfficientNets B0 achieving the highest classification accuracy of 93.99% and EfficientNets B5 achieving the lowest classification accuracy of 92.23%. A possible reason for this could be that the smaller models are less complex with fewer layers, as a result perform better on the PlantVillage dataset when using transfer learning as a feature extractor. However, further research would be needed to investigate this.

The results obtained after fine-tuning the models are explored further using; accuracy, recall, precision and F1 scores which are presented in Table 1. For further comparison purposes, the average time per epoch was also calculated, by taking the total time to train the models and dividing it by the number of the total number of epochs. This is just to get an idea of how long each model took to train, evaluating the feasibility of the model's training time.

Table 1 shows that EfficientNets B0 outperformed all the other models over all the evaluation results. Achieving a classification accuracy of 99.43%, precision of 99.53%, recall of 99.43% and f1 score of 99.48%. Including having the lowest training time as it is the smallest model. These results were fairly surprising, as it could be assumed that the higher models would perform better. However, as a whole, the results were on very similar margins. With EfficientNets B3 performing the second best, having an accuracy and F1 score of 99.29%. Followed by EfficientNets B1, EfficientNets B4 and EfficientNets B2 with accuracies of

Table 1. Results of EfficientNets models on the PlantVillage dataset.

Model	Acc (%)	Pre (%)	Rec (%)	F1 (%)	Time per epoch (*sec*)
B0	**99.43**	**99.53**	**99.43**	**99.48**	124.46
B1	99.20	99.29	99.10	99.19	159.2
B2	99.10	99.15	99.05	99.10	170.63
B3	99.29	99.29	99.29	99.29	221.77
B4	99.15	99.15	99.15	99.15	285.22
B5	99.01	99.01	99.01	99.01	328.3

99.20%, 99.15% and 99.10%, respectively. EfficientNets B5 performed the worst with an accuracy of 99.01% and took approximately 2.6 times longer to train than EfficientNets B0.

These results were obtained from the smaller test dataset. To further explore the performance of the models, the training and validation accuracy graphs per epoch are compared in Fig. 6 and Fig. 7.

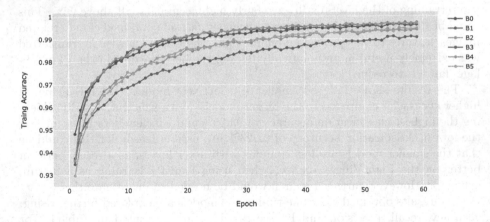

Fig. 6. EfficientNets model's training accuracy per epoch.

Furthermore, these results are obtained while fine-tuning the model, meaning after training the model by just performing feature extraction. That is why each of the models start at different training and validation accuracies. This could explain why EfficientNets B0 (starting with an increasingly higher accuracy margin) had the overall highest classification accuracy. Furthermore, by looking at the training accuracy graphs it can be seen that EfficientNets B3 and EfficientNets B4 models converged the fastest, closely followed by EfficientNets B1. EfficientNets B2 and EfficientNets B5 converged at the same rate with each other, but slower than the other 3 models. EfficientNets B1 converged the slowest with a noticeably lower training accuracy.

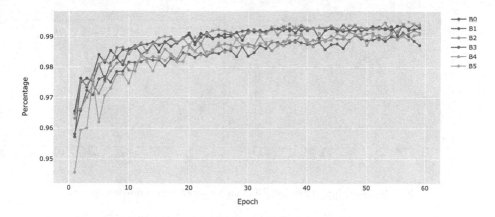

Fig. 7. EfficientNets model's validation accuracy per epoch.

The model's validation accuracy corresponds with the training accuracy; with EfficientNets B0, B3 and B4 ending with the highest validation accuracy. Followed by B2 and B5 and with B1 having the lowest validation accuracy. Most of these results correspond with the results obtained from the test set. Except for EfficientNets B1, which performed a lot better on the test set.

The learning curves for EfficientNets B0 are shown in Fig. 8 and Fig. 9. The learning curves help give an understanding of a model's learning performance (by looking at the training curve) and its ability to generalize (by looking at the validation curve). Diagnosing whether the model fits well or if the dataset is a suitable representation of the problem domain.

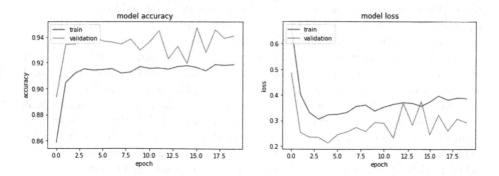

Fig. 8. Learning curve for EfficientNets B0 with transfer learning as a feature extractor.

Figure 8 shows the learning curves for the feature extraction model. It can be seen that it converges almost after the second epoch. There is also a large gap between the training and the validation curves. This is normally found when an unrepresentative dataset is used. With the validation curve having a much higher

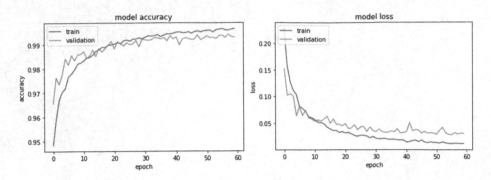

Fig. 9. Learning curve for EfficientNets B0 with fine-tuning.

Table 2. Comparing results presented in literature on the PlantVillage dataset.

Study	Model	Dataset	Acc (%)	Pre (%)	F1 (%)
[5] [2016]	GoogleNet	Original dataset	99.35	99.35	99.35
[4] [2017]	GoogleNet	Tomato diseases	99.18	99.35	99.35
[10] [2018]	DenseNet	Original dataset	99.75	–	–
[9] [2019]	9-Layer CNN	Augmented dataset	96.46	96.47	98.15
[11] [2020]	MobileNet	Original dataset	99.85	–	–
Proposed	**EfficientNets B0**	**Augmented dataset**	**99.43**	**99.53**	**99.48**

accuracy and lower loss compared to the training curve. Meaning, it was easier for the model to predict the validation dataset than the larger training dataset. The validation curve is also very noisy and jumps up and down a lot. Thus, the validation dataset does not provide sufficient information on the ability of the model to generalize. These results could be explained as knowledge transferred from the large ImageNet dataset was utilized, where no retraining is done to specialize it to the new problem (plant diseases) domain.

On Fig. 9, the learning curves of the model after fine-tuning, it can be seen as a relatively good fit. The plot of both the training and validation loss and accuracy seems to converge to a point of stability (with minor fluctuations). The final loss of the training dataset is lower than that of the validation dataset (this is known as the generalization gap). For an optimal model, this gap is kept to a minimum; whereas here, a noticeably small gap is present. Thus, it can be evident that slight overfitting occurred. Which is definitely found more in the other models, where the validation loss started increasing. Overfitting occurs when the model becomes too specialized to the training dataset and is less able to generalize to new data. Possible ways to avoid this phenomenon would be potentially lowering the learning rate, earlier stopping, increasing the dropout rate or increasing the dataset.

Many studies in the literature utilized the PlantVillage dataset for the classifying plant disease. Table 2 compares the latest results presented in literature throughout the years compared to the EfficientNets B0 model, the best preformed model proposed in this project. EfficientNets B0 preformed better than [4,5,9] in terms of accuracy, precision and F1 scores. It did not preform better than the DenseNet model in [10] with a 99.75% accuracy. However, DenseNet containing 121 layers and 7.1M parameters, compared to EfficientNets B0 with only 18 layers and 5.3M parameters. The Enhanced MobileNet-V2 in [11] also still preformed better in terms of classification accuracy. Nonetheless, the results obtain by the EfficientNets models on the PlantVillage dataset still performed exceptionally well and are up there with the other state-of-the-art accuracies.

6   Conclusion

In this paper, the deep learning EfficientNets models are used for the classification of plant diseases images from the PlantVillage dataset, containing 38 classes. Two phases for transfer learning were performed, feature extraction and fine-tuning. It is concluded that performing feature extraction on the pre-trained EfficientNets models (B0-B5) with the Imagenet dataset achieved a classification accuracy all above 92%. Therefore, parameter fine-tuning greatly increase the accuracy by almost 6%. EfficientNets B0 performed the best, achieving a classification accuracy of 99.43% and a F1 score of 99.48% on the test dataset. Compared with literature to other state-of-the-art deep learning architectures, the EfficientNets architecture with the use of transfer learning proved to be an efficient and effective approach, achieving an optimum accuracy for the detection and classification of plant diseases.

For future work, it could be considered to explore the models using an extended plant disease dataset, allowing for more accurate classifications in different environments. Furthermore, to make the model deployable on mobile devices, thereby allowing farmers to have an automated system for real time plant disease diagnosis.

References

1. Guo, Y., Liu, Y., Oerlemans, A., Lao, S., Wu, S., Lew, M.S.: Deep learning for visual understanding: a review. Neurocomputing **187**, 27–48 (2016). Recent Developments on Deep Big Vision
2. Pan, S.J., Yang, Q.: A survey on transfer learning. IEEE Trans. Knowl. Data Eng. **22**(10), 1345–1359 (2010)
3. Liu, B., Zhang, Y., He, D.J., Li, Y.: Identification of apple leaf diseases based on deep convolutional neural networks. Symmetry **10**(1), 11 (2018)
4. Brahimi, M., Boukhalfa, K., Moussaoui, A.: Deep learning for tomato diseases: classification and symptoms visualization. Appl. Artif. Intell. **31**(4), 299–315 (2017)
5. Mohanty, S.P., Hughes, D.P., Salathé, M.: Using deep learning for image-based plant disease detection. Front. Plant Sci. **7**, 1419 (2016)
6. Ferentinos, K.P.: Deep learning models for plant disease detection and diagnosis. Comput. Electron. Agric. **145**, 311–318 (2018)
7. Kaya, A., Keceli, A.S., Catal, C., Yalic, H.Y., Temucin, H., Tekinerdoganm, B.: Analysis of transfer learning for deep neural network based plant classification models. Comput. Electron. Agric. **158**, 20–29 (2019)

8. Lee, S.H., Goëau, H., Bonnet, P., Joly, A.: New perspectives on plant disease characterization based on deep learning. Comput. Electron. Agric. **170**, 105220 (2020)
9. Geetharamani, G., Pandian, A.: Identification of plant leaf diseases using a nine-layer deep convolutional neural network. Comput. Electr. Eng. **76**, 323–338 (2019)
10. Too, E.C., Yujian, L., Njuki, S., Yingchun, L.: A comparative study of fine-tuning deep learning models for plant disease identification. Comput. Electron. Agric. **161**, 272–279 (2019)
11. Chen, J., Zhang, D., Nanehkaran, Y.A.: Identifying plant diseases using deep transfer learning and enhanced lightweight network. Multimed. Tools Appl. **79**(41), 31497–31515 (2020). https://doi.org/10.1007/s11042-020-09669-w
12. Aravind, K.R., Raja, P., Aniirudh, R., Mukesh, K.V., Ashiwin, R., Vikas, G.: Grape crop disease classification using transfer learning approach. In: Pandian, D., Fernando, X., Baig, Z., Shi, F. (eds.) ISMAC 2018. LNCVB, vol. 30, pp. 1623–1633. Springer, Cham (2019). https://doi.org/10.1007/978-3-030-00665-5_150
13. Tan, M., Le, Q.V.: EfficientNet: rethinking model scaling for convolutional neural networks. arXiv preprint arXiv:1905.11946 (2019)
14. Hughes, D.P., Salathé, M.: An open access repository of images on plant health to enable the development of mobile disease diagnostics through machine learning and crowdsourcing. CoRR, abs/1511.08060 (2015)
15. Sandler, M., Howard, A., Zhu, M., Zhmoginov, A., Chen, L.-C.: MobileNetV2: inverted residuals and linear bottlenecks. In: Proceedings of the IEEE Conference on Computer Vision and Pattern Recognition, pp. 4510–4520 (2018)
16. Yosinski, J., Clune, J., Bengio, Y., Lipson, H.: How transferable are features in deep neural networks? In: Advances in Neural Information Processing Systems, pp. 3320–3328 (2014)
17. Sokolova, M., Japkowicz, N., Szpakowicz, S.: Beyond accuracy, F-score and ROC: a family of discriminant measures for performance evaluation. In: Sattar, A., Kang, B. (eds.) AI 2006. LNCS (LNAI), vol. 4304, pp. 1015–1021. Springer, Heidelberg (2006). https://doi.org/10.1007/11941439_114

Neural Networks and Support Vector Machines

Hybridised Loss Functions for Improved Neural Network Generalisation

Matthew C. Dickson[1], Anna S. Bosman[1]([✉]) [iD], and Katherine M. Malan[2] [iD]

[1] Department of Computer Science, University of Pretoria, Pretoria, South Africa
anna.bosman@up.ac.za
[2] Department of Decision Sciences, University of South Africa, Pretoria, South Africa
malankm@unisa.ac.za

Abstract. Loss functions play an important role in the training of artificial neural networks (ANNs), and can affect the generalisation ability of the ANN model, among other properties. Specifically, it has been shown that the cross entropy and sum squared error loss functions result in different training dynamics, and exhibit different properties that are complementary to one another. It has previously been suggested that a hybrid of the entropy and sum squared error loss functions could combine the advantages of the two functions, while limiting their disadvantages. The effectiveness of such hybrid loss functions is investigated in this study. It is shown that hybridisation of the two loss functions improves the generalisation ability of the ANNs on all problems considered. The hybrid loss function that starts training with the sum squared error loss function and later switches to the cross entropy error loss function is shown to either perform the best on average, or to not be significantly different than the best loss function tested for all problems considered. This study shows that the minima discovered by the sum squared error loss function can be further exploited by switching to cross entropy error loss function. It can thus be concluded that hybridisation of the two loss functions could lead to better performance in ANNs.

Keywords: Neural network loss function · Hybrid loss function · Squared error function · Quadratic loss function · Cross entropy error

1 Introduction

Loss functions in artificial neural networks (ANNs) are used to quantify the error produced by the model on a given dataset. ANNs are trained via the minimisation of a given loss function. Therefore, loss function properties can directly affect the properties of the resulting ANN model [1, 4]. One such property that is of a specific interest is the ability of the ANN to generalise, i.e. correctly predict the outputs for data patterns not seen during training. It was previously

This research was funded by the National Research Foundation of South Africa (Grant Number: 120837).

T. M. N. Ngatched and I. Woungang (Eds.): PAAISS 2021, LNICST 405, pp. 169–181, 2022.
https://doi.org/10.1007/978-3-030-93314-2_11

shown that choosing an appropriate loss function for a problem is a fundamental task in ANN design, as it has a direct correlation to model performance during evaluation [1].

Techniques that deal with training an ANN in order to develop better performing models usually involve tuning hyper-parameters and selecting an architecture that best suits the problem being solved in any given instance [7]. However, another factor that could potentially improve the performance of ANNs is choosing the correct loss function for a problem, as there is no single universal loss function that performs the best on all problems [1]. It is therefore suggested that adapting existing loss functions that have complementary properties and combining them to form a new hybrid error metric may improve or mitigate faults of existing loss functions, and thus create adaptable general loss functions [1,4]. These hybrid loss functions can then be used on a range of problems with varying degrees of difficulty and ultimately produce better ANN models.

This study investigates a number of different hybrid loss functions that combine the entropic and the quadratic loss functions. Hybrid variants investigated include static combinations of the two loss functions with different proportions, combinations that gradually adapt from one function to the other, and hybrids that switch from one function to the other based on stagnation/deterioration. The proposed hybrids are tested on a selection of classification problems and benchmarked against the constituent entropic and quadratic loss functions. Results show that the hybrid loss functions generalised better or on a par with the baseline loss functions on all problems considered. It is also shown that the hybrid which starts training using the quadratic loss, and later switches over to the entropic loss, performed the best overall. Contrary to the results of Golik et al. [4], who found that the quadratic loss did not perform well with randomised weights, but performed well when used to fine-tune the solution that the entropic loss function produced, this study shows that the minima discovered by quadratic loss can be further exploited by switching to entropic loss.

The rest of the paper is organised as follows. Section 2 defines the loss functions hybridised in this study. Section 3 proposes three types of hybrid losses. Section 4 details the experimental setup. Section 5 provides the empirical results, and Sect. 6 discusses them. Finally, Sect. 7 concludes the paper.

2   Loss Functions in ANNs

In order for an ANN to solve a particular problem, a loss function must be defined. Loss functions are used to measure the error of a model. Two commonly used error metrics for determining the effectiveness of a classification model are the sum squared error (SE), also known as quadratic error, and the cross entropy error (CE) loss functions [1,11]. SE and CE are formally defined below in Sects. 2.1 and 2.2, respectively. Section 2.3 discusses the effect that the loss functions can have on ANN performance.

2.1   Sum Squared Error

The SE function is defined as:

$$E_{se} = \sum_{p=1}^{P} \sum_{k=1}^{K} (t_{k,p} - o_{k,p})^2. \tag{1}$$

For Eqs. 1 and 2, P is the total number of training patterns, K is the total number of output units, $t_{k,p}$ is the k-th target value for pattern p, and $o_{k,p}$ is the k-th output obtained for pattern p. The SE function, also known as the quadratic loss, calculates the sum of the squared errors produced by an ANN during training. The minimisation of the SE lowers the total error produced by an ANN.

2.2   Cross Entropy

The CE function is defined as:

$$E_{ce} = \sum_{p=1}^{P} \sum_{k=1}^{K} \left(t_{k,p} \log o_{k,p} + (t_{k,p} - 1) \log(o_{k,p} - 1) \right). \tag{2}$$

The CE function, also known as the entropic loss, measures the difference between two distributions, namely the distribution of the target outputs of the ANN and the distribution of the actual outputs of the observations in the dataset. The entropic loss can only be used if the outputs of an ANN can be interpreted as probabilities. The minimisation of the CE results in the convergence of the two distributions.

2.3   The Effect of Loss Functions on Performance

Bosman et al. [1] have shown that a loss function directly impacts the performance of an ANN for a given problem, and therefore is a major factor to consider when implementing an ANN model. It has been observed that the true posterior probability for both the CE and SE loss functions is a global minimum and as such, in theory an ANN can be equally trained by minimising either of the two criteria as long as it is able to approximate the true posterior distribution within an arbitrary close range [2, 4]. However, in practice this is not the case, as the SE and CE loss functions exhibit different properties from one another, leading to different results in accuracy values during both training and testing [4].

   It has also been found that the SE loss function is more resilient to overfitting than the CE loss function, due to the fact that the SE loss function is bounded when modelling a distribution, therefore minimisation is more robust to outliers compared to the minimisation of the CE loss function [4]. Resilience to overfitting indicates that SE may exhibit superior generalisation properties compared to CE. However, the entropic loss exhibits stronger gradients than the quadratic loss, therefore convergence is faster for the entropic loss [1]. It has also been argued [1,4] that the entropic loss provides a more searchable loss landscape due to larger gradients, as compared to the quadratic loss, and thus should be more favourable to gradient-based optimisation techniques such as stochastic gradient descent.

In terms of the generalisation behaviour, it has been suggested in the literature that wide minima generalises better than narrow minima [3,5]. Bosman *et al.* [1] showed that SE exhibits more local minima than CE, thus making CE less susceptible to local minima trapping. However, the stronger gradients of CE suggest that CE is more likely to converge to sharp (narrow) minima with inferior generalisation performance.

3   Hybrid Loss Functions

A number of hybrid variants of the entropic and quadratic loss functions are proposed in this section to investigate whether such hybrids could combine the advantages while limiting the disadvantages of the two loss functions. With the hybrid approach, a new error metric can be developed and used for the purpose of training and evaluating ANNs. This hybrid metric may result in better generalisation and improved loss landscape properties, leading to loss functions that yield better ANN models.

It was observed [4] that, if started with good initial ANN weights, the SE loss function could on average further improve the minimisation of the error value found by the CE loss function in different system setups. This observation once again indicates that a hybrid approach to loss functions in ANN training could have merit.

This study provides an empirical investigation into different ways of combining the SE and CE loss functions. Nine different hybrid variants of loss functions were tested, summarised in Table 1. Variants 1 and 5 are the basic CE and SE loss functions, respectively, which were included as baselines for comparison against the different hybrids. The remaining hybrids are described below.

For the purpose of this study, three different approaches to hybridise the two loss functions were experimented with, which will be described as static (Sect. 3.1), adaptive (Sect. 3.2), and reactive (Sect. 3.3).

3.1   Static Approach

In the static approach, the loss is defined as a weighted sum of the quadratic (SE) and entropic (CE) loss functions. The error values from Eqs. 1 and 2 are not normalised and the range of values are problem dependent. Therefore, to avoid an imbalance in the sum, the error values from the individual loss functions are first normalised using an estimate of the maximum value for the loss on that problem.

The hybrid loss function used is defined as follows:

$$E_{he} = s_1 \frac{E_{se}}{max_{se}} + s_2 \frac{E_{ce}}{max_{ce}} \tag{3}$$

Table 1. Nine variants of the loss functions used in the experimentation

Variant	Label	Description
1. CE only	$CE_{100}SE_0$	Equation 3 with $s_1 = 0$, $s_2 = 1$
2. Static hybrid 1	$CE_{75}SE_{25}$	Equation 3 with $s_1 = 0.25$, $s_2 = 0.75$
3. Static hybrid 2	$CE_{50}SE_{50}$	Equation 3 with $s_1 = 0.5$, $s_2 = 0.5$
4. Static hybrid 3	$CE_{25}SE_{75}$	Equation 3 with $s_1 = 0.75$, $s_2 = 0.25$
5. SE only	CE_0SE_{100}	Equation 3 with $s_1 = 1$, $s_2 = 0$
6. Adaptive hybrid 1	$CE_{to}SE$	Starting with 100% CE and moving over to 100% SE in steps of 1%
7. Adaptive hybrid 2	$SE_{to}CE$	Starting with 100% SE and moving over to 100% CE in steps of 1%
8. Reactive hybrid 1	$CE_{>>}SE$	Starting with CE and switching to SE on stagnation/deterioration
9. Reactive hybrid 2	$SE_{>>}CE$	Starting with SE and switching to CE on stagnation/deterioration

where E_{se} is the sum square error loss function, E_{ce} is cross entropy loss function as defined in Eqs. (1) and (2) respectively, s_1 and s_2 are scalar values that are the proportions given to the loss functions where $s_1 + s_2 = 1$. The values max_{se} and max_{ce} are the approximate maximum values produced by the individual loss functions over the problem before training.

The proportions that were used for this analysis are defined in Table 1, where each static hybrid is assigned a unique label. The proportions for the static hybrid loss functions were chosen based on linearly subdividing the range, producing three static hybrid loss functions that could be tested.

3.2 Adaptive Approach

In the adaptive approach, the same loss function as defined in Eq. (3) was used, but instead of assigning a static proportion to each component of the hybrid at the beginning of training, either SE or CE was chosen to contribute 100% to the loss function at the start (either s_1 or s_2 set to 1). The proportion of that component was gradually decreased by a factor of one percent for each epoch until that component had no weight associated with it, while the proportion of the other component was increased by the same factor until the last epoch.

In the experiments, training was executed for one hundred epochs, so the adaptation was spread over the full length of the training. This approach produced two hybrids, $CE_{to}SE$ and $SE_{to}CE$, where the $CE_{to}SE$ hybrid gradually changed from CE to SE, and the $SE_{to}CE$ hybrid gradually changed from SE to CE.

3.3 Reactive Approach

Two reactive hybrids are proposed that switch from one loss function to the other based on the training error. At the beginning of training, only SE or CE was used for the training of the ANN, then after twenty epochs of training a condition was checked to see if any stagnation or deterioration occurred in the accuracy of the ANN. If no improvement occurred after three sequential epochs, then a switch was performed from one baseline function to the other depending on which loss function was deployed at the beginning of training. This approach yielded two hybrid loss functions, $CE_{>>}SE$ and $SE_{>>}CE$, where the hybrid $CE_{>>}SE$ loss function began training with CE, and the hybrid $SE_{>>}CE$ loss function began training with SE.

4 Experimental Setup

This section details the experimental setup of the study. Section 4.1 lists the datasets used in the experiments, and Sect. 4.2 discusses the hyper-parameters chosen for the ANNs.

4.1 Datasets

The following five classification datasets were used in this study:

1. **Cancer:** Consists of 699 observations each containing a tumor. Depending on the values of 30 features, the observations are classified into tumors either being benign or malignant [10].
2. **Glass:** Consists of 214 observations of glass shards. Each glass shard belongs to one of six classes, depending on nine features that capture the chemical components of the glass shards. The classes include float processed or non-float process building windows, vehicle windows, containers, table-ware, or head lamps [10].
3. **Diabetes:** Consists of 768 observation of Pima Indian patients. Depending on the values of eight features, observations are classified as either being diabetic or not [10].
4. **MNIST:** Consists of 70 000 observations of handwritten digits, where each digit is a 28 by 28 pixel image of a digit between 0 and 9 [13].
5. **Fashion-MNIST:** Consists of 70 000 observations that include ten categories of clothing, where each item is a 28 by 28 gray-scale pixel image [12].

The inputs values for all problems were standardised using the Z-score normalisation. All labels were binary encoded for each problem that contained two output classes, and one-hot encoded for problems that contained more than two output classes.

Table 2. ANN architectures and hyper-parameter values used for each problem (function: output layer activation function).

Problem	Input	Hidden	Output	Dimension	Learning rate	Batch size	Function
Cancer [10]	30	10	1	321	0.0005	32	Sigmoid
Glass [10]	9	9	6	150	0.005	32	Softmax
Diabetes [10]	8	8	1	81	0.0005	32	Sigmoid
MNIST [13]	784	10	10	7960	0.001	128	Softmax
Fashion-MNIST [12]	784	10	10	7960	0.0005	128	Softmax

4.2 ANN Hyper-parameters

The ANN architecture that was adopted for each problem is given in Table 2. The table summarises the ANN architecture used for each dataset, the source from which each dataset and/or ANN architectures was adopted, the total dimensionality of the weight space and the corresponding hyper-parameter sets. The hyper-parameters for each architecture was chosen based on the best performance for the given architecture in terms of accuracy and training time. The network size for each problem was chosen to be as minimal as possible based on the principle of parsimony, this was to ensure that the ANN captured the general characteristics of the datasets and that no ANN was over-parameterised.

All experiments conducted used 10-fold cross validation, and each test was run 30 independent times for 100 epochs. The optimiser used for all experiments was Adam, as it is considered to be robust against suboptimal hyper-parameter choices, providing more leeway in parameter tuning [6]. The learning rates tested for Adam for each problem were $0.0005, 0.001$, and 0.005. The best-performing learning rate was then chosen based on the generalisation performance across all loss functions for a problem. The activation function that was used for all experiments in the hidden layer was the Relu activation function, as it is considered the standard activation function to use in practice for neural networks at the time of writing [9].

5 Results

Figure 1 shows the average test accuracy with standard deviation bars on the five datasets. The bars in each plot represent the accuracy for the nine variants of loss functions in the same order as they appear in Table 1: (1) $CE_{100}SE_0$, (2) $CE_{75}SE_{25}$, (3) $CE_{50}SE_{50}$, (4) $CE_{25}SE_{75}$, (5) CE_0SE_{100}, (6) $CE_{to}SE$, (7) $SE_{to}CE$, (8) $CE_{>>}SE$, and (9) $SE_{>>}CE$.

For example, Fig. 1d shows that the lowest accuracy values were achieved for the first and fifth variants which correspond to the CE only and SE only loss functions. This shows that in the case of the MNIST dataset, any of the hybrids performed better than either of the constituent loss functions on their own. Although the last variant resulted in slightly higher accuracy values than the other hybrids, there is not much difference in the performance.

The standard deviation bars in Fig. 1 show that some variants resulted in higher deviations in performance than other variants. For example, Fig. 1e shows that on the Fashion-MNIST dataset, the first (CE only), second (static hybrid with 75% CE) and sixth (adaptive hybrid starting with 100% CE) variants had wider deviations in accuracy values than the other variants. This indicates that the use of the CE loss function results in more volatile performance on the Fashion-MNIST dataset.

The mean test accuracy values are presented in Table 3 with standard deviation values given in parentheses below each mean. The Mann-Whitney U test [8] was carried out in order to compare the average test accuracy results of all loss functions to one another to establish if the difference was statistically significant. The null hypothesis $H_0 : \mu_1 = \mu_2$, where μ_1 and μ_2 are the means of the two samples being compared, was evaluated at a significance level of 95%. The alternative hypothesis was defined as $H_1 : \mu_1 \neq \mu_2$. Any p-value < 0.05 corresponded to rejection of the null hypothesis, and indicated statistical significance.

Mean values plotted in red indicate the worst performance on that dataset and values plotted in green indicate the best performing hybrid. Results that were not statistically significantly different shared the best or worst result. For example, on the Cancer dataset, all of the variants performed equally well except for the fifth (SE only) and seventh (adaptive hybrid starting with 100% SE) variants, that performed equally poorly. This result is confirmed in Fig. 1a, where the fifth and seventh bars are clearly lower than the others, even though the standard deviations are very large across all variants. From the results in Table 3, it can be seen that for all datasets except Cancer, a loss function using only CE ($CE_{100}SE_0$) was the worst performing option. In addition, for two of the datasets, a loss function using only SE (CE_0SE_{100}) was the worst performing option. It can also be seen that for all datasets, $SE_{>>}CE$ (reactive hybrid that started with SE and switched to CE on stagnation/deterioration) was the best performing loss function variant.

6   Discussion

Results showed that on the datasets studied, hybrid loss functions generalise better than the baseline loss functions CE and SE. This provides evidence to the claim made by Bosman *et al.* [1] that the SE and CE loss functions should be combined in one way or another, as their error landscapes were shown to exhibit different yet complementary properties. In [1], the CE loss function was shown to be more searchable, and the SE loss function was shown to be more robust against overfitting.

Of all the hybrid functions, the best performing variant overall was the $SE_{>>}CE$ function (either the best performing or not statistically significantly different from the best performing variant). This variant starts with the SE function, and switches to CE once stagnation or deterioration in accuracy is detected. This is contrary to work done by Golik *et al.* [4] who analysed that starting with CE loss function and later switching over to the SE loss function

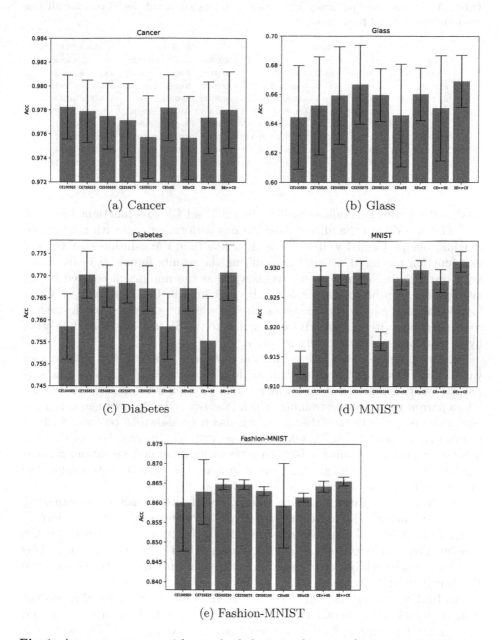

Fig. 1. Average accuracy with standard deviation bars on the test set for the five classification problems when using the nine loss function variants. Each bar represents a variant plotted in order from left to right (1) $CE_{100}SE_0$, (2) $CE_{75}SE_{25}$, (3) $CE_{50}SE_{50}$, (4) $CE_{25}SE_{75}$, (5) CE_0SE_{100}, (6) $CE_{to}SE$, (7) $SE_{to}CE$, (8) $CE_{>>}SE$, and (9) $SE_{>>}CE$.

Table 3. Average test accuracy with corresponding standard deviations for all loss function variants and problems

	Cancer	Glass	Diabetes	MNIST	Fashion-MNIST
$CE_{100}SE_0$	0.9782 (±0.0027)	0.6443 (±0.0353)	0.7585 (±0.0074)	0.9140 (±0.0020)	0.8600 (±0.0123)
$CE_{75}SE_{25}$	0.9779 (±0.0026)	0.6523 (±0.0335)	0.7702 (±0.0053)	0.9286 (±0.0017)	0.8628 (±0.0082)
$CE_{50}SE_{50}$	0.9775 (±0.0027)	0.6593 (±0.0334)	0.7677 (±0.0048)	0.9289 (±0.0019)	0.8647 (±0.0014)
$CE_{25}SE_{75}$	0.9771 (±0.0031)	0.6666 (±0.0270)	0.7684 (±0.0045)	0.09292 (±0.0019)	0.8647 (±0.0012)
CE_0SE_{100}	0.9757 (±0.0034)	0.6594 (±0.0181)	0.7671 (±0.0051)	0.9177 (±0.0016)	0.8630 (±0.0012)
$CE_{to}SE$	0.9782 (±0.0028)	0.6456 (±0.0351)	0.7585 (±0.0074)	0.9282 (±0.0019)	0.8594 (±0.0107)
$SE_{to}CE$	0.9757 (±0.0035)	0.6601 (±0.0180)	0.7672 (±0.0052)	0.9296 (±0.0016)	0.8614 (±0.0011)
$CE_{>>}SE$	0.9774 (±0.0030)	0.6506 (±0.0360)	0.7553 (±0.00101)	0.9278 (±0.0019)	0.8642 (±0.0014)
$SE_{>>}CE$	0.9780 (±0.0032)	0.6689 (±0.0179)	0.7708 (±0.0063)	0.9310 (±0.0017)	0.8655 (±0.0011)

produced superior generalised models than SE and CE loss functions individually. This was due to the SE loss function not performing well with randomised weights, but performed well when used to fine tune the solution that the CE loss function produced, this study confirms the results found by Golik. However, during experimentation it was shown that the minima discovered by SE loss function can be further exploited by switching to CE loss function. Golik found that tuning hyper-parameters such as the learning rate and batch size had some effect on switching the CE loss function to the SE loss function while other hyper-parameters were not very sensitive.

The landscapes of the CE loss function have been shown to contain narrower valleys, but fewer local optima than SE loss landscapes [1]. Thus, a gradient-based algorithm starting at an initial random position is more likely to descend into a narrow valley during training, which is associated with poor generalisation performance [3,5]. On the other hand, SE has been shown to be more resilient to overfitting than CE [1]. Therefore, starting with SE, the search algorithm has a better chance of reaching a better region in terms of generalisation. Switching then to CE, the stronger gradients can assist the algorithm to exploit the discovered minimum.

In other words, during training, the SE loss function focuses on exploring an area in the fitness landscape until it finds itself stuck at some arbitrary point. Once it is stuck the switch to the CE loss function occurs where the CE loss function then exploits the solution obtained by the SE loss function. This process seems to exhibit a generalisation ability that is superior to the base line loss functions and all other hybrid loss functions tested.

To further analyse the behaviour of the $SE_{>>}CE$ variant, Fig. 2 shows the distribution of neural network weights before the switch (blue) and at the end of training (light green) for the five problems. For example, Fig. 2a shows that before the switch (when SE was being utilised as the loss function), most of the weights had values around zero, but there were a few weights with values above 1.

The histograms in Fig. 2 show that the weights exhibited a negative skew, indicating that a larger proportion of weights were set to negative values at the end of training. The hidden layer activation function used in this study

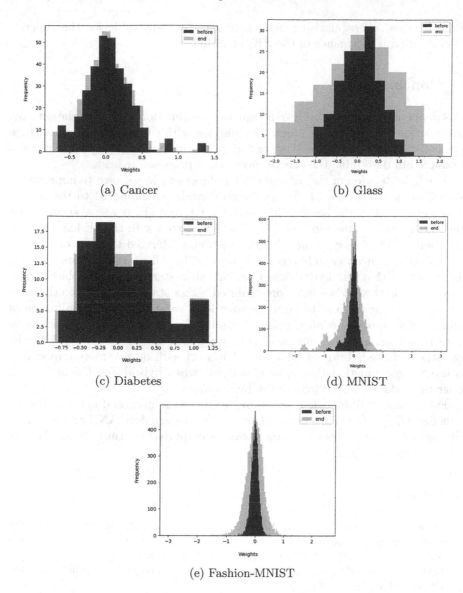

(a) Cancer

(b) Glass

(c) Diabetes

(d) MNIST

(e) Fashion-MNIST

Fig. 2. Histograms showing the distribution of neural network weights for the $SE_{>>}CE$ loss function variant before the switch (blue) and after training (light green). (Color figure online)

was the Relu function, which outputs a zero for negative input. Thus, a large number of negative weights indicates that more neurons were effectively switched off (e.g. output set to zero) as the training progressed. Disabling unnecessary neurons can be seen as a form of self-regularisation exhibited by the ANN during training. This self-regularising behaviour may be responsible for the superior generalisation performance of the $SE_{>>}CE$ hybrid.

7   Conclusion

This paper proposed to hybridise the squared loss function (SE) with the entropic loss function (CE) to create a new loss function with superior properties. Three types of hybrids were proposed: static, adaptive, and reactive. Experiments were conducted to determine the effectiveness of the proposed hybrids.

The hybridisation of the SE and CE loss functions was shown to improve the generalisation ability for all five problems considered compared to the performance exhibited by the baseline loss function CE and SE. It was also concluded that the hybrid loss function $SE_{>>}CE$, which started with the SE loss function and then switched over to the CE loss function, performed the best on average or was not significantly different from the best for all problems tested. It was also observed that the hybrid loss functions that started with or placed more importance on the CE loss function exhibited higher standard deviation throughout training, showing CE to be more volatile in regards to the initialisation of weights. The opposite configuration of baseline loss functions was shown to be more robust against the initialisation of weights in the model. Therefore, the robustness of the hybrid loss functions that start with or give more importance to the SE loss function should be considered when hybridising CE and SE in order to produce optimal hybrid loss functions.

Future work will include a scalability study of the proposed hybrids. Performance of $SE_{>>}CE$ can be evaluated on various modern deep ANN architectures. Fitness landscape analysis techniques can be employed to study the landscapes of the proposed hybrids.

References

1. Bosman, A.S., Engelbrecht, A., Helbig, M.: Visualising basins of attraction for the cross-entropy and the squared error neural network loss functions. Neurocomputing **400**, 113–136 (2020). https://doi.org/10.1016/j.neucom.2020.02.113
2. Bourlard, H.A., Morgan, N.: Connectionist Speech Recognition. Springer, Boston (1994). https://doi.org/10.1007/978-1-4615-3210-1
3. Chaudhari, P., et al.: Entropy-SGD: biasing gradient descent into wide valleys. J. Stat. Mech: Theory Exp. **2019**(12), 124018 (2019)
4. Golik, P., Doetsch, P., Ney, H.: Cross-entropy vs. squared error training: a theoretical and experimental comparison. In: 14th Annual Conference of the International Speech Communication Association, pp. 1756–1760. ISCA (2013)
5. Keskar, N.S., Mudigere, D., Nocedal, J., Smelyanskiy, M., Tang, P.T.P.: On large-batch training for deep learning: generalization gap and sharp minima. arXiv preprint arXiv:1609.04836 (2016)
6. Kingma, D., Ba, J.: Adam: a method for stochastic optimization. In: International Conference on Learning Representations (2015)

7. Li, H., Xu, Z., Taylor, G., Studer, C., Goldstein, T.: Visualizing the loss landscape of neural nets. In: Proceedings of the 32nd Conference on Neural Information Processing Systems, pp. 6391–6401 (2018)
8. Mann, H.B., Whitney, D.R.: On a test of whether one of two random variables is stochastically larger than the other. Ann. Math. Stat. **18**(1), 50–60 (1947)
9. Nwankpa, C., Ijomah, W., Gachagan, A., Marshall, S.: Activation functions: comparison of trends in practice and research for deep learning. ArXiv abs/1811.03378 (2018)
10. Prechelt, L.: PROBEN1 - a set of neural network benchmark problems and benchmarking rules. Technical report 21/94, July 1995
11. Solla, S.A., Levin, E., Fleisher, M.: Accelerated learning in layered neural networks. Complex Syst. **2**, 625–640 (1988)
12. Xiao, H., Rasul, K., Vollgraf, R.: Fashion-MNIST: a novel image dataset for benchmarking machine learning algorithms. ArXiv abs/1708.07747 (2017)
13. LeCun, Y., Cortes, C., Burges, C.J.C.: MNIST handwritten digit database. http://yann.lecun.com/exdb/mnist/

Diverging Hybrid and Deep Learning Models into Predicting Students' Performance in Smart Learning Environments – A Review

Elliot Mbunge[1]([✉]) [iD], Stephen Fashoto[1] [iD], Racheal Mafumbate[2] [iD],
and Sanelisiwe Nxumalo[1]

[1] Department of Computer Science, Faculty of Science and Engineering,
University of Eswatini, Kwaluseni Campus, Private Bag 4, Kwaluseni, Eswatini
mbungeelliot@gmail.com
[2] Department of Educational Foundations and Management, University of Eswatini,
Kwaluseni, Eswatini

Abstract. COVID-19 continues to overwhelm the education sectors globally posing threats to progress made towards inclusive and equity education in the previous years. Before COVID-19, continuous evaluation methods were systematically done manually in many learning institutions, now it is difficult to timely identify underperforming students, and students who are at risk of dropping out and provision of timely remedial and appropriate actions tailored for individual's needs. To alleviate this situation, early prediction of students' performance using deep learning techniques and data generated from smart learning environments becomes imperative. Therefore, this study aimed at providing a pioneering comprehensive review of hybrid and deep learning models to predict students' performance in online learning environments. The study revealed that deep learning techniques extract hidden data to predict students' performance, identify students at risk of dropping out, monitor students' cognitive learning styles and unusual learning behaviours, emotional state of students to facilitate pedagogical content knowledge, instructional designs and appropriate action promptly. These models use various performance predictors such as course attributes, study time and duration, internal assessments, socio-economic, students' legacy and learning environment. Furthermore, the study revealed that the psychological state of students was not taken into consideration, yet it impacts learning outcomes. However, the varying context of implementation could be the leading cause of differences in perspective to determine performance predictors that are reliable to predict student performance. Predicting students' performance should be done prior, during and at the end of the course to ensure effective implementation of educational interventions.

Keywords: Deep learning · Students' academic performance · Smart online learning

1 Introduction

The outbreak of coronavirus disease 2019 (COVID-19) came as a stellar explosion that tremendously affects all aspects of life, education without exception. As of April 30

T. M. N. Ngatched and I. Woungang (Eds.): PAAISS 2021, LNICST 405, pp. 182–202, 2022.
https://doi.org/10.1007/978-3-030-93314-2_12

2020, after World Health Organisation (WHO) declared COVID 19 a global pandemic, over 100, 000 schools, universities and college were closed, and an estimated 1.52 billion learners were affected globally [1]. This has been exacerbated by the stringent COVID-19 measures imposed by governments and WHO to reduce the spread of the virus. Such measures include quarantine, self-isolation [2], contact-tracing [3], blanket lockdown [4], face masking [5], a temporary ban of international travelling, and maintaining social distancing among others. Although these measures reduce the transmission rate, they present unprecedented challenges and opportunities to redesign pedagogical methods and assessment policy [6]. However, as many higher institutions drastically adopted online learning, reopening of universities in higher education is imminent [7] and transition towards hybrid learning approaches is inevitable. This requires a sudden change of pedagogical policies which is yet to come. Many institutions accepted the imposed digital checkmate and alternatively resorted to distance education and adopted hybrid learning models to manage and cope, with the crisis and to ensure that teaching and learning continues. Digital technologies such as mobile learning, learning management systems (LMS), student response systems or interactive games, Massive Open Online Courses (MOOC), virtual reality, mass media communication (especially radio and television) and video conferencing tools have been adopted to facilitate online learning during the pandemic.

However, students in resource-constrained areas, especially those with limited internet access and financial constraints have been severely affected. This threatens the realization of inclusive education and equitable quality for all where equity, excellence and students' well-being are prioritised to reduce learning disparities [8]. The situation is quite disconcerting for students with fragile socio-economic background, and mental health issues and disabilities [9], as teaching and learning are now conducted completely online, on an untested and unprecedented scale replacing face-to-face classes. Such drastic transformation presents new challenges and uncertainties to parents, students, instructors, and higher institutions of learning. Teaching and learning during the COVID-19 pandemic have been a difficult process coupled with many challenges which subsequently lead to drop-out and some learners fail to complete their levels in record time. This is exacerbated by several factors including lack of conducive learning environment, insufficient financial support, mental health issues, abuse of substances, poor time management, physical and emotional abuse, information overload, assignment scheduling, lack of assertiveness training, lack of proper guidance, and counselling services [10], lack of robust and resilience support systems and policies. Also, huge costs of technology infrastructure, lack of digital skills, digital divide [11], poor network connectivity, high internet cost and unavailability of computing devices impedes the successful use of learning platforms in universities and subsequently impact students' academic performance, especially in distance learning. Also, the drastic change of teaching methods to embrace innovative pedagogical methods such as online course design, change of assessment methods, course delivery method affects students' cognitive learning styles and outcomes. This is orchestrated by the lack of training of students and lecturers on how to conduct online classes as well as designing course materials that incorporate learning principles in technology-mediated environments [12, 13]. Also, emerging challenges such as mental health issues (anxiety, stress, depression) due to lack of psycho-social support, abuse of substances, and teenage pregnancies have resurfaced among university students during the COVID-19 pandemic [14].

Prior to COVID-19, assessing students' performance was systematically done manually in many higher learning institutions [15]. Notably, assessments, teaching and learning are now conducted online, posing tremendous challenges in real-time analysing students' performance, behaviour, cognitive learning styles, and other metacognitive patterns of learning online to build a strategy for instructional design, further development and future remedial actions on real-time [16]. Knowledge speaks volumes in education; performance analysis provides an image of what students know, what they need to know and what can be done to fulfil their academic goals. Educators can make informed decisions that have a positive effect on student results with excellent assessment and analysis of data. Therefore, analysing students' performance requires deep learning computational models that combine computational dexterity, knowledge inference, and visual presentation of results. Students' data amassed since the advent of learning management systems and databases can be processed quickly by using educational data mining techniques and learning analytics tools. The goal of these computational models is to extract hidden insights and subsequently improve education by modelling students' data, predicting students' performance, modelling student behaviour and predicting dropouts and recommend vulnerable students for psychosocial and counselling services and other remedial actions.

1.1 Contribution of the Study

The study aimed at providing a comprehensive analysis of deep learning models applied to predict students' academic performance in online learning environments to provide timely intervention, identifying students at-risk and provide suitable pedagogical support. Before COVID-19, several scholars including [17–21] conducted reviews focusing on the application of educational data mining (EDM) models to achieve the same goal. More specifically, [17] conducted a review of EDM models to predict students' performance based on predictor attributes in the classroom environment. Also, [22] also conducted a survey on EDM and determining factors affecting students' academic performance in the hybrid learning environment (face-to-face and online learning). Most recently, [19] conducted a survey on student performance analysis and prediction models in the classroom learning environment. Also, [23] also conducted a review with a set of guidelines to assist novice on the application of educational data mining techniques to predict student success. Although the researchers have applied educational data mining techniques in both traditional and computer-based online education, the application in conventional education is comparatively less than the other alternatives available [19]. Also, previous reviews focus primarily on the performance predictors in classroom-based education and EDM prediction model efficiency, while excluding the temporal aspects, the mental health of students as well as student learning cognitive styles in online learning environments. Also, some scholars developed drop-out prediction models (fixed-term and temporal) using learning analytics, especially in MOOC to address the challenge of monitoring and identifying the large-scale at-risk students of potentially dropping out [24]. Such drop-out prediction models have tremendous implementation challenges in online learning environments. For instance, fixed-term dropout prediction models can identify all students at risk once after a fixed-term. So, decision-makers cannot provide effective and timely educational interventions tailored for individuals needs given many dropout students in online learning environments. Although temporal drop-out prediction models address that, they do not offer personalized educational interventions due to limited log data collected when students interact in online learning environments [24]. Thus, determining students' learning behaviour and their various learning patterns, predicting students at-risk of dropouts based on their interactions with the various virtual learning environments and mental health as well as provision of remedial actions is becoming a daunting task especially with traditional educational data mining models and learning analytics due to veracity, velocity, voluminous, variety and variability of students' data generated from various online learning environments. However, despite the successfully implementation of deep learning techniques in various disciplines, few studies applied deep learning models to predict students' performance in online learning environments. Deploying deep learning techniques to predict successful and at-risk students is rather a new area of research [16]. Therefore, this review focuses on the following research objectives:

- To analyse deep learning models used to predict students' academic performance in smart learning environments and their respective performance and limitations.
- To identify attributes relevant to predict students' academic performance in online learning environments using deep learning techniques.
- To analyse influential factors relevant to predict students' academic performance in smart learning environments.

In this paper, we present a pioneering review on the application of deep learning models applied to predict students' performance in smart learning environments, with specific reference to COVID-19 as an accelerator for online learning. However, the review is not restricted to traditional deep learning techniques only rather it also considers all hybrid deep learning transfer models. Based on our knowledge, none of the published reviews analysed hybrid and deep learning transfer techniques to predict students' performance in online learning environments.

The following section elaborates the methodology adopted to extract and synthesize the literature covering 2015 – May 2021. Section 3 presents hybrid and deep learning models applied to predict students' academic performance and their respective performance as well as limitations. This section also presents both attributes and influential factors relevant for predicting students' academic performance in online learning environments. Finally, Sect. 4 presents the concluding remarks and future work.

2 Method

The study adopted the Preferred Reporting Items for Systematic Reviews and Meta-Analyses (PRISMA) model proposed by [25]. The PRISMA model illustrates the steps required to conduct a systematic literature review. It is predominantly used in healthcare studies [26], therefore, some elements are not applicable in educational settings [27]. This review follows PRISMA steps namely, identification, screening, eligibility and synthesizing of literature included in the study.

2.1 Search Strategy

In conducting a review, a well-planned search strategy is paramount to guide the literature search and to ensure that all relevant studies are included in the search results [19]. We constructed the search terms by identifying the educational attribute as well as hybrid and deep learning models. Therefore, search strings used in this study are: *"deep learning techniques"* OR *"hybrid learning classifier"* OR *"deep transfer learning"* OR *"deep neural networks"* AND *"predict student performance"* OR *"online learning environments."* We searched the literature in the following electronic databases as they were relevant to the subject area: Google Scholar, IEEE Xplore, Science Direct, Springer Link and ACM digital Library. We further performed a citation chain for additional studies for each retrieved article to make sure that all relevant articles are considered for screening.

2.2 Inclusion and Exclusion Criteria

The search identified 257 papers. We excluded opinion pieces, non-peer-reviewed articles, incomplete articles, and studies in other languages with no English translation. We excluded studies that modelled students' performance using data from the traditional face-to-face classroom or in physical classroom-based education. We also discard those studies which are not well-presented, contains unclear methodology, dataset, and contribution.

2.3 Eligibility Criteria

All authors double-screened all articles for quality assessment and eligibility. At the initial phase, we selected studies by reading the titles and abstracts relevant to the topic. After that, irrelevant studies were removed from the list of selected studies. We then created a list of eligible articles that initially passed the initial phase. In the second eligibility phase, we removed all duplicates. To further check the eligibility of literature, we read the full text and to determine whether the contribution of the study is relevant to the objectives of this study. This assist to further eliminate studies that were not related to the application of deep learning models to predict students' performance in online learning environments. The degree of accuracy and reliability of quality assessment of articles was measured using Cohen Kappa statistic [28], therefore, the substantial agreement of authors was 94.7%, with Cohen's k: 0.63809.

3   Results

We included 40 papers from online electronic databases. From the selected articles, it was possible to identify that hybrid and deep learning models for predicting students' performance that met the eligibility criteria were mostly published between 2020–2021 (May), most of them in the year 2020 (n = 15, 37.5%). The data of interest on hybrid and deep learning models to predict students' academic performance in smart learning environments are organized in the following format:

- Deep neural networks for predicting students' academic performance.

- Hybrid deep learning models for predicting students' performance.
- Deep Long short-term memory network for predicting students' performance.
- Influential factors (attribute) for predicting students' academic performance in smart learning environments.

The attributes used for each model as well as performance accuracy and limitations are explained in the following sections. Also, influential factors relevant to predict students' academic performance in online learning environments are explained in Sect. 3.5.

3.1 Predicting Students' Academic Performance Using Deep Learning Techniques

Deep learning techniques have been employed in the field of educational data mining to analyze students' data from various learning management systems, massive open online courses, course management systems, intelligent tutoring systems, virtual learning environments, among others. Since the COVID-19 outbreak, many students have been learning online, generating overwhelming volumes of data that exceeds the human capacity and traditional techniques to manage, predict and analyze students' data [29]. To counter this, deep learning and educational data mining models offer unprecedented opportunities to predict students' academic performance in educational settings to assess the prospective behaviour of learners, analyzing activities of successful and at-risk students, providing corrective strategies based on learner's performances [16], consequently assisting instructors in improving the pedagogical methods. Also, these techniques utilize students' data to cluster students based on their performance, personalized recommendations and support educators and metacognitive triggers to learners especially during the pandemic [30]. Based on the available information, deep learning and educational data mining techniques such as classification, clustering and association rule mining enable institutions to use their present reporting trends to unmask hidden interesting patterns and identify data relationships [31].

Deep learning is a subset of machine learning, which also a subset of artificial intelligence, as shown in Fig. 1. Thus, deep learning refers to artificial neural networks with complex multilayers [32]. Deep learning models are defined as deep neural networks with more neurons, more hidden layers, and more connected layers functioning as a computational algorithm that trains and learns features automatically [33]. These models are classified based on training methods such as supervised, unsupervised, and hybrid [34, 35].

In education, deep learning techniques are applied to solve various problems including prediction, identification, detection, and classification [33, 37]. They utilize various characteristics of students data such as demographics, personal, educational background, psychological, academic progress, financial support [38] and other course variables which might be difficult to analyze using conventional techniques, which heavily depend on the choice of data representation [17].

The distinction between deep learning and artificial neural networks (ANN) lies in their characteristics. Deep neural networks have more complex ways of connecting layers, also have more neurons count in the hidden layers than neural networks (see Fig. 2) to express complex models, more also with more processing power to train

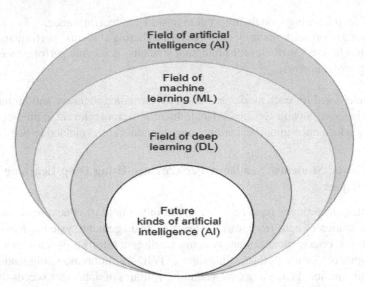

Fig. 1. Evolution of deep learning [36]

and further has automatic extraction of the feature [36]. Therefore, deep learning is defined as neural networks with broad variables and layers with a single basic network architecture of convolutional neural networks, recursive neural networks, and recurrent neural networks. In contrast with neural networks, deep learning neural networks perform automatic feature extraction without any human intervention while extracting relevant features necessary to solve the problem. Thus, deep learning performs optimum model tuning and selection on its own, which saves a lot of human effort and time.

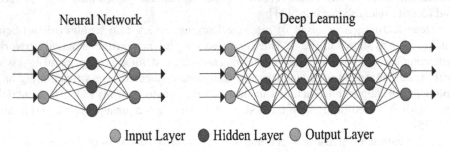

Fig. 2. Structure of neural network and deep learning [24].

3.2 Deep Neural Networks for Predicting Students' Academic Performance

Deep neural networks are inspired by artificial neural networks, which mimic the biological neurons. ANNs are building block of deep neural networks, which consists of an interrelated set of artificial neurons, interconnected together to process information using a connectionist form to computation [39]. The artificial neuron consists of inputs, weights, linear collector, bias value, activation function and output value, as shown in Fig. 3.

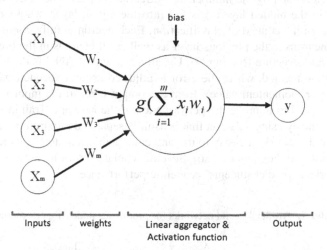

Fig. 3. Structure of an artificial neuron [40]

The collector value is calculated by multiplying inputs and weight values in the input layer and then the output can be limited in a specific range by using an activation function. The general structure of artificial neural networks is made up of an input layer, hidden layer (s) and an output layer as shown in Fig. 4.

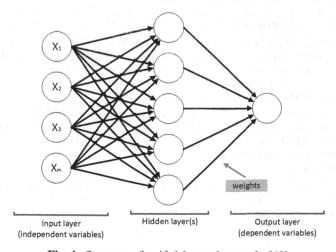

Fig. 4. Structure of artificial neural networks [40].

Independent variables and their respective weights are defined in the input layer. The weight value determines the strength and direction (inhibitory or excitatory) of each neuron input. The output of the input layer is then used as the input of the preceding layer, called the hidden layer [41]. The hidden layer is an interlayer created by multiplying the values in the variables found in the input layer with weights. The depth of the neural network is determined by the number of hidden layers [42]. The computed output of each neuron in the hidden layer(s) is fed into the output layer, whose purpose is to classify labels in the context of classification. Each neuron is fully connected with all predecessor neurons in the previous layer as well as all neurons in the preceding layer in a feedforward structure (see Fig. 3). Usually, training of ANN is done by using the backpropagation method, where the error is adjusted using associated weights values (learning rate or momentum value), from the output layer to the input layer. Weights values are adjusted to improve the performance of the network. Training of the ANN is generally done by using a dataset that is usually separated into training and test data. Artificial neural networks are easy to use and can obtain accurate results from complex natural systems with large inputs [36]. Several scholars shown in Table 1 applied deep neural networks to predict students' academic performance.

Table 1. Artificial neural networks for predicting students' performance.

Ref	Attributes used	Accuracy	Limitations
[40]	The study used a dataset that consists of variables such as gender, content score, time spent on the content, number of entries to content, homework score, number of attendances to live sessions, total time spent in live sessions, number of attendances to archived courses, and total time spent in archived courses	The ANN model achieved 80.47% prediction accuracy	The study excludes other important variables such as the lecturer's role, course feedbacks and additional-curricular classes
[43]	The study used variables such as courses viewed, courses viewed, discussions viewed, course module instance list viewed and assessment submissions	The model achieved 78.2% prediction accuracy	The study did not consider student's activity frequency measures
[44]	A dataset used by the study consists of socio-economic background and national university entrance examination of the students	The model achieved 84.8% prediction accuracy	The model performs poorly to classify students based on their gender
[45]	Course design and activity log attributes were used to predict the students' performance	80.36% accuracy	The dataset used was limited to few records

Table 1 shows that artificial neural networks promise to yield promising results in predicting students' success. These networks utilize course data, web log data, socio-economic data to predict students' success. For instance, [45] used course data, and achieved 80.36% prediction accuracy, though the ANN was trained with limited data.

Also, [40] applied socio-economic data and course data, and achieved 80.47% prediction accuracy. However, artificial neural networks experience challenges including over-fitting [40], and the time needed for neural network training [46].

3.3 Hybrid Deep Learning Models for Predicting Students' Performance

To alleviate some challenges of ANNs, several authors (see Table 2) applied hybrid deep learning models, which combine EDM and deep learning techniques to predict students' academic performance.

Hybrid deep learning models shown in Table 2 use data generated from online learning environments such as MOOC, learning management systems (like Moodle, Blackboard) and custom-made e-learning platforms. Due to their wider and deeper structure, hybrid deep learning models generally outperform ANNs in predicting students' success [23]. For example, [16] applied hybrid deep neural networks to predict students' performance and achieved a classification accuracy of 84%–93% and outperformed baseline LR and SVM. Logistic regression achieved 79.82%–85.60% and SVM 79.95%–89.14% classification accuracy. However, the modest GritNet deep earning model achieved 58.06% prediction accuracy, probably because of the limited dataset used. Also, a hybrid deep learning model called SPPN, achieved 77.2% accuracy while Naive Bayes and SVM achieved 20.7% and 48.4% prediction accuracy, respectively, though the model was not optimized and trained with the limited dataset. Thus, predicting students' academic performance using hybrid deep learning models require massive data, which is not always available in many smart (online) learning environments, especially before the semester ends. This is a major setback in implementing hybrid deep learning models in this context.

3.4 Deep Long Short-term Memory Network for Predicting Students' Performance

Long short-term memory network (LSTM) is a hierarchal representational deep learning model which consists of several non-linear layers that contribute to learning the representations from the input data [50]. It is now mostly utilized in deep learning and learning analytics to analyze students' data in education. LSTM analyses students log data created in form of time series. LSTM was introduced by Hochreiter and Schmidhuber [51] as an extension of recurrent neural network (RNN). RNNs are not efficient to learn a pattern from long-term dependency because of the gradient vanishing and the exploding gradient problems [52]. Therefore, LSTM was introduced to address these limitations of recurrent neural networks by adding additional interactions per module (or cell). Cells are memory blocks of LSTM that have two states transferred to the next cell state (C_t); the hidden state and cell state (C_{t-1}), as shown in Fig. 5. Long Short-term memory networks process a complete sequence of data at once by capturing information temporarily but cannot remember the full input context [53]. Most recently, the bidirectional Long Short-term Memory network (Bi-LSTM), which is an extension of LSTM has been utilized to train two LSTM models namely: forward LSTM and reverse LSTM [54]. Long Short-term memory network is organized in form of a chain structure, with each repeating cell having a different structure (see Fig. 5).

Table 2. Hybrid deep learning models, variables used, accuracy and limitations.

Model and Ref	Description and attributes used	Prediction accuracy	Limitations
MOOCVERSITY [47]	The model used data from the massive open online course to predict dropouts and student's dropout probability	The model shows that there is a strong correlation between clickstream actions and successful learner's outcomes	The model did not consider the learning cognitive style and mental thinking process of the students
GritNet [23]	Unsupervised deep learning model called GritNet was developed to students' outcomes on massive open online	The GritNet deep earning model achieved 58.06% prediction accuracy	The model was tested using a small dataset which affects its performance
Transfer Learning from Deep Neural Networks [48]	The study predicted students' performance using attributes such as forums, assignments, submitted assignments, student grades, and the total number of times a student accessed the resource	The model achieved 77.68% after 100 epochs	The model needs to be validated with larger datasets from different courses
Deep Multi-source Behavior Sequential Network [46]	The study integrated bi-LSTM and other models to represent to predict students' performance using attributes such as students' internet access activity and online learning activity	The SPSN performed better than the traditional machine learning models	The study excluded the mental state of the students
Deep artificial neural network [16]	The study used data from OULA dataset with variables such as students' demographics, student interaction with the VLE, assessment marks and courses information	The model achieved a classification accuracy of 84%–93% and outperformed baseline LR and SVM. Logistic regression achieved 79.82%–85.60% and SVM 79.95%–89.14% classification accuracy	The study states that legacy data and assessment-related data improves the performance of the model. However, such variables were not considered

(continued)

Table 2. (*continued*)

Model and Ref	Description and attributes used	Prediction accuracy	Limitations
Students' Performance Prediction Network (SPPN) [49]	The model used students' demographic data, previous results, school assessment data, course data and personal data	The SPPN model achieved 77.2% accuracy while Naive Bayes and SVM achieved 20.7% and 48.4% prediction accuracy, respectively	The SPPN model was not optimized and trained with a limited dataset

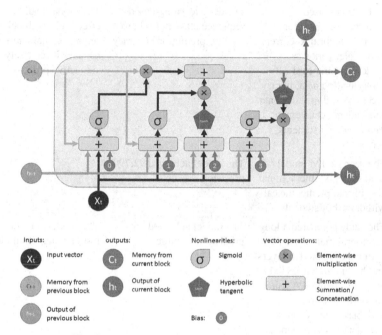

Fig. 5. Structure of long short-term memory [55]

The procedure of developing a Long short-term memory network is to remove irrelevant information and will be omitted from the cell in that step. The sigmoid function (σ) plays an important role in removing and excluding irrelevant information, which takes the output of the last LSTM unit (h_{t-1}) at time $t - 1$ and the current input (X_t) at time t, as shown in Fig. 3. Additionally, the sigmoid function determines which part from the old output should be eliminated [55]. LSTM has been applied to predict students' academic performance as shown in Table 3.

Table 3. Predicting students' using deep long short-term memory network

Ref	Description and attributes used	Learning environment and accuracy	Limitations
[56]	The model combines LSTM and recurrent neural networks to predict student success based on the flowing variables; the number of times a student access Moodle each week and course-level features	The study extracted data from Moodle VLE. The results were evaluated using Random Forests, and LSTM outperformed it by 13.3% of the variance of the model, as opposed to 8.1%	The study predicted student success using a limited dataset, therefore, generalizability issues and poor prediction results were reported
[57]	A sequence-based performance classifier based on Hybrid Recurrent Neural Network was modelled using card data, books lending data, library access data, dormitory data, and student achievement data to predict students' performance	The deep learning-based sequence classifier achieved 86.90% prediction accuracy	The model could not deal effectively with behavioural sequence characteristics because it relatively subjective process
[58]	The deep LSTM model used students' interactional activities to predict the early withdrawal of students	The model achieved 92.79% precision	
[59]	The study compared a long short-term memory network with multiple hidden layers and bi-directional LSTM to predict student GPA using data extracted from variables such as course attendance, assessments, and semester grade point averages	The model achieved 76% prediction accuracy	The model was trained and tested using simulation data
[58]	The study predicted students' performance using the final grade of a student	The LSTM achieved 92.6% prediction accuracy	The study used a small dataset with eleven rows of data

3.5 Influential Factors for Predicting Students' Academic Performance in Smart Learning Environments

Findings in this study revealed that various influential factors are contributing to students' academic performance in online learning environments. These influential factors are categorized into the following emerging themes: availability of course content; nature of assessment; study time and duration; socio-economic background; student participation; psychological support and interest; and learning environment. Predictors of students' academic performance in smart (online) learning environments differ with context, platform, and availability of students' data (see Table 4). The study classified students' academic performance predictors as follows; course attributes, e-learning activity, internal assessments, students' legacy data, access to online resources and psychological attributes. The findings of the study revealed that internal assessments and students' legacy data are major attributes that have been widely used. Internal assessments include quizzes, forums, discussions, assessments submission and peer-reviewed assignments, lab work, class test and attendance. These course progress evaluation assessments contribute significantly towards semester grade point average, cumulative grade point average [17]. CGPA is one of the key factors in predicting students' success.

The findings of the study revealed that socio-economic information such as family economic data (expenditure, income student's personal data, family characteristics, occupation, and size) and demographic data (gender, age, disability, race/ethnicity, parents' education, and religion) are important predictors of predicting students' success. Also, [55] state that demographic data such as gender (males/females), race religion and disability influence students' cognitive thinking process which subsequently affect students' performance. In comparison to male students, [23] discovered that most female students had different constructive learning styles and behaviours. As a result, it has been established that gender is one of the most important factors affecting student's success. A study conducted by [50] posits that performance predictors such as the number of student attendance to live class sessions and archived courses as well as the time spent in the content are also relevant to predict students' academic performance.

Availability of course content involves factors such as courses viewed, courses module viewed, discussions viewed, course module instance list viewed, and assessment submissions. Another important aspect to enhance students' performance in online learning environments is the teachers' preparedness in the pedagogical content knowledge as well as being fully equipped with the relevant technical skills which address their instructional needs. Thus, teachers and lecturers also need to be sufficiently trained, accommodating for their level of comfort and experience with technology. Local technology champions who can share best practices with colleagues are invaluable in this regard. However, it was revealed in this study that during the lockdown, lectures who should be the focus of all learning activities had shifted all the obligation to parents who now had exclusive access to their children while teachers and lectures were redundant physically.

The nature of assessments is a paramount predictor in predicting students' performance in smart learning environments. Nature of assessments influence assessment score, completion of assigned tasks, and how often the course materials are accessed online. Scholars such as [16, 24, 63] applied quizzes, forums, discussions, assessments submission and peer-reviewed assignments as predictors of students' performance. This

Table 4. Attributes relevant for predicting students' performance.

Attribute category	Attributes involved	Used in Ref
Couse Attributes	Course organization, course materials, forums, workload, homework score, courses viewed, courses viewed, discussions viewed, course attendance, course features and course module instance list viewed	[23, 60, 61]
e-learning activity	Study time and duration, student access to online resources in each week and course-level features, time spent on the content, number of entries to content, number of attendances to live sessions, total time spent in live sessions, number of attendances to archived courses, and total time spent in archived courses	[45, 51, 62]
Internal assessments	Quizzes, forums, discussions, assessments submission and peer-reviewed assignments (homework, tests)	[16, 24, 63]
Socio-economic data	Family economic data (expenditure, income student's data, family characteristics, occupation, and size), Demographic data (gender, age, disability, race/ethnicity, parents' education, residential place and religion), distance travelled access to learning resources	[24, 64]
Students' legacy data	Past performances in previous assessments (semester Grade point average, cumulative Grade Point Average, individual course letter marks, and individual assessment grades) and entry test, Pre-university data: high school background (i.e., high school results), pre-admission data (e.g., admission test results)	[16, 23, 65, 68]
Online resources	Internet access, pedagogical approach, card data, books lending data, number of times a student access online LMS, library access data and dormitory data	[63, 67]
Psychological attributes	Stress, anxiety, attitude towards study, student interests and counselling sessions	[23, 67]

influence students' GPA as alluded by [59], who applied these assessments methods to predict students' performance and achieved 76% prediction accuracy. Therefore, the nature of assessments becomes an influential predictor when predicting students' performance in smart learning environments.

Among the reviewed papers, the study revealed that student participation is imperative in predicting students' success. Scholars such as [45, 51, 62] used log data, the number of discussion posts viewed, the number of content pages viewed, and the time spent viewing discussion pages to predict students' success. Also, [56, 57, 59] applied LSTM to predict students' performance using student e-learning activity consists of student access to online resources in each week and course-level features, time spent on the content, number of entries to content, number of attendances to live sessions, total time spent in live sessions, number of attendances to archived courses, and total time spent in archived courses. However, the study revealed that psychological support and interest, access to counselling services, rehabilitation, stress and anxiety, student interest behaviour and motivation towards study, preoccupation and motivation are rarely used to predict students' academic performance, yet they are paramount to detect and monitor students' cognitive learning style and unusual learning behaviours.

4 Conclusion

The application of hybrid and deep learning models into predicting students' performance in smart learning environments is inevitable due to the increasing demand to model data generated in online learning platforms. Processing such data using the convectional method becomes a daunting and challenging task [58]. Deep learning techniques extract hidden data to predict students' performance, identify students at risk of dropping out, monitor students' cognitive learning styles and unusual learning behaviours, emotional state of students to facilitate pedagogical and instructional designs and appropriate action promptly. These models use various performance predictors such as course attributes, study time and duration, internal assessments, socio-economic data, students' legacy data and learning environment. However, predicting student' academic performance in smart learning encounter several impediments such as:

- Timing of data gathering process: the ultimate goals of predicting students' academic performance include the provision of timely interventions, identifying students at-risk, provision of suitable pedagogical support and educational interventions to facilitate student achievement. However, many studies utilize data generated from the online learning environment at the end of each course, thus making students' performance prediction models inapplicable in real academic setup [45]. Some authors including propose that predicting students' performance should be done prior, during and at the end of the course to ensure effective implementation of educational interventions. Also, to alleviate this issue, [68] developed an early warning system based on weekly student's activity data using classification and regression tree (CART), supplemented by AdaBoost to identify students at-risk early before the end of the course. Thus, based on student engagement and participation, [69] highlighted that students' academic performance can be predicted as early as the sixth week of the course. Early detection of students at risk, along with preventive measures, can drastically improve their success.
- Use of students' activity frequency measures: several studies shown in Table 1 use students' activity frequency measures of one form or another, as reliable predictors to predict students' academic performance. For instance, [60] applied course item frequencies and students' activity frequencies on course resources, forums, videos, quizzes, and peer-reviewed assignments to predict student performance. In contrast,

a study conducted by [70] states that such predictors have limited value in predicting students' performance to provide timely interventions, especially in the blended learning environment. Thus, the varying context of implementation could be the leading cause of differences in perspective to determine whether students' activity frequency measures are reliable predictors of student performance.

To effectively implement hybrid and deep learning models into predicting students' performance in smart learning environments, educators and students must use online learning platforms whenever they are engaged in teaching and learning activities. Students in need of computing devices and internet access should be assisted to avoid learning disparities among learners. It is recommended that future work should include psycho-social support as well as student's interest, access to counselling services, rehabilitation, stress and anxiety, student interest, behaviour towards study, preoccupation and motivation when predicting students' academic performance.

References

1. Ferrel, M.N., Ryan, J.J.: The Impact of COVID-19 on medical education. Cureus. (2020). https://doi.org/10.7759/cureus.7492
2. Mbunge, E., Fashoto, S.G., Akinnuwesi, B., Metfula, A., Simelane, S., Ndumiso, N.: Ethics for integrating emerging technologies to contain COVID-19 in Zimbabwe. Hum. Behav. Emerg. Technol. **3**, 876–890 (2021). https://doi.org/10.1002/HBE2.277
3. Mbunge, E.: Effects of COVID-19 in South African health system and society: an explanatory study. Diabetes Metab. Syndr. Clin. Res. Rev. **14**, 1809–1814 (2020). https://doi.org/10.1016/J.DSX.2020.09.016
4. Monaghesh, E., Hajizadeh, A.: The role of telehealth during COVID-19 outbreak: a systematic review based on current evidence, BMC Public Health **20** (2020). https://doi.org/10.1186/s12889-020-09301-4
5. Mbunge, E., et al.: Framework for ethical and acceptable use of social distancing tools and smart devices during COVID-19 pandemic in Zimbabwe. Sustain. Oper. Comput. **2**, 190–199 (2021). https://doi.org/10.1016/J.SUSOC.2021.07.003
6. Shahzad, A., Hassan, R., Aremu, A.Y., Hussain, A., Lodhi, R.N.: Effects of COVID-19 in E-learning on higher education institution students: the group comparison between male and female. Qual. Quant. **55**(3), 805–826 (2020). https://doi.org/10.1007/s11135-020-01028-z
7. Mbunge, E.: Integrating emerging technologies into COVID-19 contact tracing: opportunities, challenges and pitfalls. Diabetes Metab. Syndr. Clin. Res. Rev. **14**, 1631–1636 (2020). https://doi.org/10.1016/J.DSX.2020.08.029
8. Azorín, C.: Beyond COVID-19 supernova. Is another education coming (2020). https://doi.org/10.1108/JPCC-05-2020-0019
9. Leal Filho, W., Brandli, L.L., Lange Salvia, A., Rayman-Bacchus, L., Platje, J.: COVID-19 and the UN sustainable development goals: threat to solidarity or an opportunity? Sustainability **12**, 5343 (2020). https://doi.org/10.3390/su12135343
10. Melese, W., Fenta, G.: Trend and causes of female students dropout from teacher education institutions of Ethiopia: The case of Jimma University. Ethiop. J. Educ. Sci. **5**, (2010). https://doi.org/10.4314/ejesc.v5i1.56309
11. Khetsiwe Eunice, M.-K., Cosmas, M.: An analysis of factors affecting utilisation of moodle learning management system by open and distance learning students at the University of Eswatini. Am. J. Soc. Sci. Humanit. **5**, 17–32 (2020). https://doi.org/10.20448/801.51.17.32

12. Gurajena, C., Mbunge, E., Fashoto, S.G.: Teaching and learning in the new normal: opportunities and challenges of distance learning amid COVID-19 pandemic. SSRN Electron. J. (2021). https://doi.org/10.2139/ssrn.3765509
13. Adedoyin, O.B., Soykan, E.: Covid-19 pandemic and online learning: the challenges and opportunities. J. Comput. High Educ. 1–18 (2020). https://doi.org/10.1080/10494820.2020. 1813180
14. Al-Balas, M., et al.: Distance learning in clinical medical education amid COVID-19 pandemic in Jordan: current situation, challenges, and perspectives. BMC Med. Educ. (2020). https:// doi.org/10.1186/s12909-020-02257-4
15. Zhai, X., Yin, Y., Pellegrino, J.W., Haudek, K.C., Shi, L.: Applying machine learning in science assessment: a systematic review. Stud. Sci. Educ. 56, 111–151 (2020). https://doi. org/10.1080/03057267.2020.1735757
16. Waheed, H., Hassan, S.U., Aljohani, N.R., Hardman, J., Alelyani, S., Nawaz, R.: Predicting academic performance of students from VLE big data using deep learning models. Comput. Human Behav. 104, 106189 (2020). https://doi.org/10.1016/j.chb.2019.106189
17. Shahiri, A.M., Husain, W., Rashid, N.A.: A Review on predicting student's performance using data mining techniques. Procedia Comput. Sci. 72, 414–422 (2015). https://doi.org/10.1016/ j.procs.2015.12.157
18. Dutt, A., Ismail, M.A., Herawan, T.: A systematic review on educational data mining, IEEE Access 5, 15991–16005 (2017). https://doi.org/10.1109/ACCESS.2017.2654247
19. Khan, A., Ghosh, S.K.: Student performance analysis and prediction in classroom learning: a review of educational data mining studies. Educ. Inf. Technol. 26(1), 205–240 (2020). https:// doi.org/10.1007/s10639-020-10230-3
20. Baker, R.S.J.D., Yacef, K.: The state of educational data mining in 2009: a review and future visions. J. Educ. Data Mining1(1), 3–17 (2009). https://doi.org/10.5281/ZENODO.3554657
21. Romero, C., Ventura, S.: Educational data mining: a review of the state of the art. IEEE Trans. Syst. Man Cybern. Part C 40, 601–618 (2010). https://doi.org/10.1109/TSMCC.2010. 2053532
22. Khanna, L., Singh, S.N., Alam, M.: Educational data mining and its role in determining factors affecting students academic performance: a systematic review. In: Proceedings of the India International Conference on Information Processing, IICIP 2016, Institute of Electrical and Electronics Engineers Inc. (2017). https://doi.org/10.1109/IICIP.2016.7975354
23. Alyahyan, E., Düştegör, D.: Predicting academic success in higher education: literature review and best practices. Int. J. Educ. Technol. High. Educ. 17(1), 1–21 (2020). https://doi.org/10. 1186/s41239-020-0177-7
24. Xing, W., Du, D.: Dropout prediction in MOOCs: using deep learning for personalized intervention. J. Educ. Comput. Res. 57, 547–570 (2019). https://doi.org/10.1177/073563311875 7015
25. Moher, D., Liberati, A., Tetzlaff, J., Altman, D.G.: Preferred reporting items for systematic reviews and meta-analyses: the PRISMA statement. PLoS Med. 6, e1000097 (2009). https:// doi.org/10.1371/journal.pmed.1000097
26. Moher, D., et al.: Preferred reporting items for systematic review and meta-analysis protocols (PRISMA-P) 2015 statement. Rev. Esp. Nutr. Humana y Diet. 20, 148–160 (2016). https:// doi.org/10.1186/2046-4053-4-1
27. Nogues, C.P., Dorneles, B.V.: Systematic review on the precursors of initial mathematical performance. Int. J. Educ. Res. Open. 2, 100035 (2021). https://doi.org/10.1016/j.ijedro.2021. 100035
28. McHugh, M.L.: Interrater reliability: the kappa statistic. Medicinska naklada 22(3), 276–282 (2012)

29. Fidalgo-Blanco, Á., Sein-Echaluce, M.L., García-Peñalvo, F.J., Conde, M.Á.: Using learning analytics to improve teamwork assessment. Comput. Hum. Behav. **47**, 149–156 (2015). https://doi.org/10.1016/j.chb.2014.11.050
30. Dias, S.B., Hadjileontiadou, S.J., Diniz, J., Hadjileontiadis, L.J.: DeepLMS: a deep learning predictive model for supporting online learning in the Covid-19 era. Sci. Rep. **10**, 1–17 (2020). https://doi.org/10.1038/s41598-020-76740-9
31. Križanić, S.: Educational data mining using cluster analysis and decision tree technique: a case study. Int. J. Eng. Bus. Manag. **12**, 184797902090867 (2020). https://doi.org/10.1177/1847979020908675
32. Albawi, S., Mohammed, T.A., Al-Zawi, S.: Understanding of a convolutional neural network. In: Proceedings of 2017 International Conference on Engineering and Technology, ICET 2017, pp. 1–6. Institute of Electrical and Electronics Engineers Inc. (2018). https://doi.org/10.1109/ICEngTechnol.2017.8308186
33. Yunita, A., Santoso, H.B., Hasibuan, Z.A.: Deep learning for predicting students' academic performance. In: Proceedings of 2019 4th International Conference on Informatics and Computing, ICIC 2019. Institute of Electrical and Electronics Engineers Inc. (2019). https://doi.org/10.1109/ICIC47613.2019.8985721
34. Mbunge, E., Makuyana, R., Chirara, N., Chingosho, A.: Fraud detection in E-transactions using deep neural networks-a case of financial institutions in Zimbabwe. Int. J. Sci. Res. **6**, 2319–7064 (2015). https://doi.org/10.21275/ART20176804
35. Rastrollo-Guerrero, J.L., Gómez-Pulido, J.A., Durán-Domínguez, A.: Analyzing and predicting students' performance by means of machine learning: a review. Appl. Sci. **10**, 1042 (2020). https://doi.org/10.3390/app10031042
36. Abiodun, O.I., et al.: State-of-the-art in artificial neural network applications: a survey. Heliyon **4**, e00938 (2018). https://doi.org/10.1016/j.heliyon.2018.e00938
37. Gbenga Fashoto, S., Mbunge, E., Ogunleye, G., Van Den Burg, J.: Implementation of machine learning for predicting maize crop yields using multiple linear regression and backward elimination. Malaysian J. Comput. **6**, 679–697 (2021)
38. Namoun, A., Alshanqiti, A.: Predicting student performance using data mining and learning analytics techniques: a systematic literature review. Appl. Sci. **11**, 237 (2020). https://doi.org/10.3390/app11010237
39. Fashoto, S.G., Owolabi, O., Mbunge, E., Metfula, A.S.: Evaluating the performance of two hybrid feature selection model of machine learning for credit card fraud detection on classification and prediction methods. Adv. Appl. Sci. Technol. **2**, 70–87 (2019)
40. Aydoğdu, Ş: Predicting student final performance using artificial neural networks in online learning environments. Educ. Inf. Technol. **25**(3), 1913–1927 (2019). https://doi.org/10.1007/s10639-019-10053-x
41. Elujide, I., Fashoto, S.G., Fashoto, B., Mbunge, E., Folorunso, S.O., Olamijuwon, J.O.: Application of deep and machine learning techniques for multi-label classification performance on psychotic disorder diseases. Inform. Med. Unlocked. **23**, 100545 (2021). https://doi.org/10.1016/j.imu.2021.100545
42. Bimha, H., Mbunge, E., Fashoto, S.: Prediction of box-office success: a review of trends and machine learning computational models. Int. J. Bus. Intell. Data Min. **1**, 1 (2021). https://doi.org/10.1504/ijbidm.2021.10032162
43. Rivas, A., González-Briones, A., Hernández, G., Prieto, J., Chamoso, P.: Artificial neural network analysis of the academic performance of students in virtual learning environments. Neurocomputing **423**, 713–720 (2021). https://doi.org/10.1016/j.neucom.2020.02.125
44. Lau, E.T., Sun, L., Yang, Q.: Modelling, prediction and classification of student academic performance using artificial neural networks. SN Appl. Sci. **1**(9), 1 (2019). https://doi.org/10.1007/s42452-019-0884-7

45. Raga, R., Raga, J.: Early prediction of student performance in blended learning courses using deep neural networks. In: Proceedings - 2019 International Symposium on Educational Technology, ISET 2019. pp. 39–43. Institute of Electrical and Electronics Engineers Inc. (2019). https://doi.org/10.1109/ISET.2019.00018

46. Li, X., Zhu, X., Zhu, X., Ji, Y., Tang, X.: Student academic performance prediction using deep multi-source behavior sequential network. In: Lauw, H.W., Wong, R.-W., Ntoulas, A., Lim, E.-P., Ng, S.-K., Pan, S.J. (eds.) PAKDD 2020. LNCS (LNAI), vol. 12084, pp. 567–579. Springer, Cham (2020). https://doi.org/10.1007/978-3-030-47426-3_44

47. Muthukumar, V., Bhalaji, N.: MOOCVERSITY-deep learning based dropout prediction in MOOCs over weeks. J. Soft Comput. Paradig 2, 140–152 (2020). https://doi.org/10.36548/jscp.2020.3.001

48. Tsiakmaki, M., Kostopoulos, G., Kotsiantis, S., Ragos, O.: Transfer learning from deep neural networks for predicting student performance. Appl. Sci. 10, 2145 (2020). https://doi.org/10.3390/app10062145

49. Guo, B., Zhang, R., Xu, G., Shi, C., Yang, L.: Predicting students performance in educational data mining. In: Proceedings - 2015 International Symposium on Educational Technology, ISET 2015, pp. 125–128. Institute of Electrical and Electronics Engineers Inc. (2016). https://doi.org/10.1109/ISET.2015.33

50. Mubarak, A.A., Cao, H., Ahmed, S.A.M.: Predictive learning analytics using deep learning model in MOOCs' courses videos. Educ. Inf. Technol. 26(1), 371–392 (2020). https://doi.org/10.1007/s10639-020-10273-6

51. Hochreiter, S., Schmidhuber, J.: Long short-term memory. Neural Comput. 9, 1735–1780 (1997). https://doi.org/10.1162/neco.1997.9.8.1735

52. Bengio, Y., Simard, P., Frasconi, P.: Learning long-term dependencies with gradient descent is difficult. IEEE Trans. Neural Netw. 5, 157–166 (1994). https://doi.org/10.1109/72.279181

53. Ali, A.M., Joshua Thomas, J., Nair, G.: Academic and uncertainty attributes in predicting student performance. In: Vasant, P., Zelinka, I., Weber, G.-W. (eds.) ICO 2020. AISC, vol. 1324, pp. 838–847. Springer, Cham (2021). https://doi.org/10.1007/978-3-030-68154-8_72

54. Dong, H.A.: The Application of Artificial Neural Network, Long short-term Memory Network and Bidirectional Long short-term Memory Network in the Grades Prediction. http://users.cecs.anu.edu.au/~Tom.Gedeon/conf/ABCs2020/paper/ABCs2020_paper_v2_138.pdf

55. Le, Ho, Lee, J.: Application of long short-term memory (LSTM) neural network for flood forecasting. Water 11, 1387 (2019). https://doi.org/10.3390/w11071387

56. Corrigan, O., Smeaton, A.F.: A course agnostic approach to predicting student success from VLE log data using recurrent neural networks. In: Lavoué, É., Drachsler, H., Verbert, K., Broisin, J., Pérez-Sanagustín, M. (eds.) EC-TEL 2017. LNCS, vol. 10474, pp. 545–548. Springer, Cham (2017). https://doi.org/10.1007/978-3-319-66610-5_59

57. Wang, X., Yu, X., Guo, L., Liu, F., Xu, L.: Student performance prediction with short-term sequential campus behaviors. Information 11, 201 (2020). https://doi.org/10.3390/info11040201

58. Hassan, S., Waheed, H., Aljohani, N.R., Ali, M., Ventura, S., Herrera, F.: Virtual learning environment to predict withdrawal by leveraging deep learning. Int. J. Intell. Syst. 34, 1935–1952 (2019). https://doi.org/10.1002/int.22129

59. Patil, A.P., Ganesan, K., Kanavalli, A.: Effective deep learning model to predict student grade point averages. In: 2017 IEEE International Conference on Computational Intelligence and Computing Research, ICCIC 2017. Institute of Electrical and Electronics Engineers Inc. (2018). https://doi.org/10.1109/ICCIC.2017.8524317

60. Conijn, R., Van den Beemt, A., Cuijpers, P.: Predicting student performance in a blended MOOC. J. Comput. Assist. Learn. 34, 615–628 (2018). https://doi.org/10.1111/jcal.12270

61. Hussain, S., Gaftandzhieva, S., Maniruzzaman, M., Doneva, R., Muhsin, Z.F.: Regression analysis of student academic performance using deep learning. Educ. Inf. Technol. **26**(1), 783–798 (2020). https://doi.org/10.1007/s10639-020-10241-0

62. Hussain, S., Gaftandzhieva, S., Maniruzzaman, M., et al.: Regression analysis of student academic performance using deep learning. Edu. Infor. Tech. **26**, 783–798 (2021). https://doi.org/10.1007/s10639-020-10241-0

63. Hussain, S., Muhsin, Z.F., Salal, Y.K., Theodorou, P., Kurtoğlu, F., Hazarika, G.C.: Prediction model on student performance based on internal assessment using deep learning. Int. J. Emerg. Technol. Learn. **14**(08), 4 (2019). https://doi.org/10.3991/ijet.v14i08.10001

64. Daud, A., Lytras, M.D., Aljohani, N.R., Abbas, F., Abbasi, R.A., Alowibdi, J.S.: Predicting student performance using advanced learning analytics. In: 26th International World Wide Web Conference 2017, WWW 2017 Companion, pp. 415–421. International World Wide Web Conferences Steering Committee, New York (2017). https://doi.org/10.1145/3041021.3054164

65. Aluko, R.O., Daniel, E.I., Shamsideen Oshodi, O., Aigbavboa, C.O., Abisuga, A.O.: Towards reliable prediction of academic performance of architecture students using data mining techniques. J. Eng. Des. Technol. **16**, 385–397 (2018). https://doi.org/10.1108/JEDT-08-2017-0081

66. Adekitan, A.I., Salau, O.: The impact of engineering students' performance in the first three years on their graduation result using educational data mining. Heliyon. **5**, e01250 (2019). https://doi.org/10.1016/j.heliyon.2019.e01250

67. Hernández-Blanco, A., Herrera-Flores, B., Tomás, D., Navarro-Colorado, B.: A systematic review of deep learning approaches to educational data mining, Complexity **2019** (2019). https://doi.org/10.1155/2019/1306039

68. Hu, Y.H., Lo, C.L., Shih, S.P.: Developing early warning systems to predict students' online learning performance. Comput. Human Behav. **36**, 469–478 (2014). https://doi.org/10.1016/j.chb.2014.04.002

69. Lu, O.H.T., Huang, A.Y.Q., Huang, J.C.H., Lin, A.J.Q., Ogata, H.S.J.H.: Applying learning analytics for the early prediction of students' academic performance in blended learning. Educ. Technol. Soc. **21**, 220–232 (2018)

70. Conijn, R., Snijders, C., Kleingeld, A., Matzat, U.: Predicting student performance from LMS data: a comparison of 17 blended courses using moodle LMS. IEEE Trans. Learn. Technol. **10**, 17–29 (2017). https://doi.org/10.1109/TLT.2016.2616312

Combining Multi-Layer Perceptron and Local Binary Patterns for Thermite Weld Defects Classification

Mohale Emmanuel Molefe[1,2](✉) [iD] and Jules-Raymond Tapamo[1] [iD]

[1] University of KwaZulu-Natal, Durban, South Africa
tapamoj@ukzn.ac.za
[2] Transnet Freight Rail, Johannesburg, South Africa

Abstract. During the new or existing rail network installation, sections of rails are welded together to produce a continuously welded railway. Thermite welding is the widely used welding method to permanently joint rail sections, and Non-Destructive Testing methods such as radiography are used to inspect the formed weld joint for quality assurance. Conventionally, the process of detecting and classifying defects in the generated radiography images is conducted manually by trained experts. However, the conventional process is lengthy, costly and has a high false alarm rate even if experts conduct it. This work proposes a method based on computer vision algorithms for automatic detection and classification of defects. The proposed method uses Local Binary Patterns as a feature descriptor and Multi-Layer Perceptron as a classifier. The results obtained indicated that the proposed method outperforms the state-of-the-art method found in the literature.

Keywords: Radiography · Local binary patterns descriptor · Multi-Layer Perceptron · Classification

1 Introduction

During the installation of the new or existing rail network, sections of rails are usually welded together using the thermite welding process to produce continuously welded rails. However, the thermite welding process produces unwanted defects on the welded joints. Therefore, Non-Destructive Testing (NDT) methods such as Radiography Testing (RT) are used as a tool to inspect the joint for possible welding defects. The radiography images produced from RT are usually given to the trained radiography experts. The prominent role of the experts is to visually detect and classify defects on radiography images and accept or reject the weld joint based on the type of defects detected.

Despite being conducted by trained experts, the process of detecting and classifying welding defects using human expertise is not acceptable due to a

Supported by Transnet Freight Rail.

T. M. N. Ngatched and I. Woungang (Eds.): PAAISS 2021, LNICST 405, pp. 203–216, 2022.
https://doi.org/10.1007/978-3-030-93314-2_13

high false alarm rate, long turnaround time and high maintenance costs. In many railway industries, the process takes up to two months to complete due to a lack of qualified radiography experts. Thus, the weld joint is left exposed to a possible rail break, leading to train derailment and loss of lives and revenue. Furthermore, radiography images generally consist of poor contrast; thus, certain defects are left undetected or misclassified as they are not visible to the human eye.

To address the shortcomings of the manual process, this work proposes an automated defect detection and classification method based on computer vision algorithms. The use of computer vision algorithms allow thermite weld defects to be detected and classified in a fast, reliable and objective manner. Furthermore, an automated defect classification method will significantly improve the railroad condition monitoring and maintenance planning since defects will be classified more objectively and immediately after performing RT on the weld joints. Generally, defect detection and classification using computer vision involves detecting defects using feature extraction algorithms and classifying the defects using machine learning classifiers.

Computer vision methods have been applied for infrastructure condition monitoring in the railway industry for rail defects; however, most methods are for the automatic detection and classification of defects on the surface of rails [7,12]. To the best of the authors' knowledge, limited research work is available on the topic of detecting and classifying rail welding defects using computer vision methods. The method proposed in [8] is the only method available in the literature. The authors made use of the Local Binary Patterns (LBP) descriptor to extract features in the weld joint images and the K-Nearest Neighbours (K-NN) to classify thermite weld defects. Indeed, it was proven that the LBP cell size parameter and the K value in the K-NN classifier have a significant impact on the classification accuracy.

Therefore, the method proposed in this work uses the dataset and the LBP algorithm (with the same LBP cell size parameters) similar to the method proposed in [8] for feature extraction. However, the Multi-Layer Perceptron (MLP) algorithm is used as a classifier to compare its performance in terms of the classification accuracy against the K-NN classifier used in [8]. The LBP descriptor is used as a feature extractor in this work; it allows for a fast and reliable way of extracting features from an image. The LBP descriptor is a local feature extractor, and it is invariant to illumination changes and image rotation.

Local feature extractors generally outperform global feature extractors because global feature extractors are not invariant to significant image transformation such as scale, rotation, and illumination changes [5]. Other local feature extractors such as the Speeded Up Robust Features (SURF) and the Scale Invariant Feature Transform (SIFT) are available; however, they produce many feature vectors representing a single image. Thus, mid-level image representation is usually applied to form a single feature vector for every image. The advantage of the LBP descriptor over the SIFT and SURF descriptors is that a single feature vector can represent an image without relying on mid-level image representation methods.

2   Materials and Methods

The proposed method has four steps; first, the Contrast Limited Histogram Equalisation (CLAHE) technique is applied to improve image quality. After that, the Geodesic Active Contour Model (ACM) is applied to segment the image, and the weld joint is extracted as the Region of Interest (RoI). Then, the LBP descriptor is applied to the extracted weld joint images to extract features and represent every image as a feature vector. Finally, the extracted features are fed into the MLP classifier for training and validation purposes. The trained MLP classifier is then used to classify a given feature vector into one of the following classes: defect-less, wormholes, inclusions and shrinkage cavities.

2.1   Weld Joint Segmentation and Extraction

It is recommended to eliminate the RoI from the image background in computer vision tasks before performing feature extraction. This helps to eliminate noisy background regions and to reduce computational costs. In detecting and classifying thermite weld defects, the RoI is the weld joint where potential defects could be found (see Fig. 1(b)).

(a)   (b)

Fig. 1. Thermite weld image: (a) Original image and (b) Weld joint image

Image segmentation methods are initially applied to identify the region, coordinates and position of the weld joint before extracting the weld joint as the RoI from the image background. In this work, the main requirement of the segmentation technique is to segment the irregularly shaped weld joint from the complex image background. Image segmentation techniques such as Thresholding, Hough transform and ACM have been used for segmenting radiography images [1,4,10]. Thresholding techniques are simple and fast to compute; however, their application is limited only to images with bimodal histogram. The Hough transform segmentation techniques allows for the segmentation of images with various known shapes such as circles and ellipses. However, they are not effective for segmenting image regions with irregular shapes.

Image segmentation using ACM is one of the successful and widely used segmentation techniques for a variety of tasks in image processing [2,3]. ACM provides an efficient way of using an energy function to drive the contour towards the object's boundaries to segment, thus allowing irregularly shaped image regions to be segmented. Two mathematical approaches for segmenting images using ACM exist: parameterised approaches and level set approaches. A representation of the parameterised ACM is the snake model proposed by Kass et al. [6]. Snake model segments the image by first defining a snake-like contour around the RoI. The contour is then driven towards the object by the energy function, and it stops at the boundaries of the RoI. However, the snake model requires the contour to be placed near the RoI to minimise the computation cost.

Level set approaches represents the contour implicitly using a level set function: $\phi(x, y)$, where (x, y) is the point in the image domain Ω. The pixels in Ω, where $\phi(x, y) = 0$, defines the contour C and this is expressed as: $C = \{(x, y) \in \Omega : \phi(x, y) = 0\}$. This work uses a level set method based on the Geodesic ACM, which was proposed to derive the level set equation for the snake model. Given that the contour, C moves with speed F in the normal direction, then, $\phi(x, y)$ must satisfy the following level set equation.

$$\frac{\partial \phi(x, y)}{\partial t} = F |\nabla \phi(x, y)| \tag{1}$$

In Geodesic ACM, the gradient descent equation providing speed F is derived in terms of the contour C and then implemented using the level set equation. The energy function which must be minimised is defined as:

$$E(C) = \int g(C) dC \tag{2}$$

The above equation is minimum at the edges of the object and g is an edge indicator function defined as:

$$g(I(x, y)) = \frac{1}{1 + |\nabla I_\sigma(x, y)|} \tag{3}$$

Where $I_\sigma(x, y)$ is the smoothed version of image $I(x, y)$. The gradient descent equation providing the speed of the contour in the normal direction is given as:

$$\frac{dC}{dt} = g\kappa n + (n \times \nabla g)n \tag{4}$$

Where κ is the local curvature of C and n is the outer normal. Implementing Eq. 4 in terms of Eq. 1 gives the level set equation for Geodesic ACM defined as:

$$\frac{\partial \phi(x, y)}{\partial t} = g(I(x, y))|\nabla \phi(x, y)| div \left(\frac{\nabla \phi(x, y)}{|\nabla \phi(x, y)|} \right) + \nabla g(I(x, y))\nabla \phi(x, y) \tag{5}$$

Algorithm 1 presents the steps used to segment and extract the weld joint as the RoI using the Geodesic ACM.

Algorithm 1. Weld joint segmentation and RoI extraction

Require: Enhanced thermite weld images

Output: Weld joint images

1: **for** each image I in the dataset **do**
2:    Apply CLAHE technique.
3:    Initialise ϕ.
4:    Define n number of iterations.
5:    **while** C is not at weld joint edges **do**
6:        Compute edges using Eq. 3.
7:        Evolve ϕ^{n+1} using Eq. 5.
8:    **end while**
9:    Segment the image and obtain the weld joint coordinates.
10:    Apply the coordinates to the original image.
11:    Apply the bounding box across the coordinates.
12:    Crop the region inside the bounding box.
13:    Save the cropped image region as weld joint.
14: **end for**

2.2 Feature Extraction

After extracting the weld joint as the RoI, the LBP descriptor was applied on weld joint images to extract features and represent every weld joint image as a feature vector. Feature extraction using the LBP descriptor can be summarised in three steps. First, the image is divided into non-overlapping cells of equal size. Then, the LBP code of any pixel in a cell is computed by using the same pixel as a threshold against the pixels in the 3×3 neighbourhood region. Pixels greater than the threshold are assigned a value of 1; otherwise, pixels are assigned a value of 0. The obtained binary number is converted to a decimal number which is the LBP code of the pixel used as a threshold. The LBP code of any pixel q in a cell, with P neighbouring pixels placed on a circle of radius R from c is calculated as:

$$LBP_{(R,P)}(q) = \sum_{i=0}^{P-1} S(g_i - g_q) \times 2^i \tag{6}$$

where g_q is the grey intensity value of pixel q and g_i is the grey intensity value of neighbourhood pixels. The function S allows the LBP descriptor to be invariant to illumination change; it is computed as:

$$S(x) = \begin{cases} 1, & \text{if } x \geq 0 \\ 0, & \text{if } x < 0 \end{cases} \tag{7}$$

The notable disadvantage of the original LBP descriptor is that the 3×3 neighbourhood region is unable to capture large scale image features. Therefore, the original LBP descriptor was modified for use with neighbourhood regions of different sizes. Furthermore, the LBP descriptor of Eq. 6 produces the feature vector of length 2^P for every LBP cell size. For instance, 8 neighbourhood pixels will produce a vector length of 256, while 12 neighbourhood pixels will produce a vector length of 4096. This indicates that there is an exponential increase in the feature vector length with a small increase in the P neighbourhood pixels. The extended LBP descriptor [9] uses uniform patterns to reduce the feature dimensionality produced from the original LBP descriptor. Compared to non-uniform patterns, uniform patterns have been experimentally found to occur more on texture images [9]. A pattern is considered uniform if it contains at most two spatial transitions (from 0 to 1 or vice versa), otherwise, a pattern is non-uniform.

To separate the uniform patterns from the non-uniform patterns, the uniformity measure U was defined. Patterns where $U < 2$ are termed uniform patterns, otherwise patterns are termed non-uniform. U is defined as:

$$U(LBP_{(R,P)}) = |S(g_{i-1} - g_q) - S(g_0 - g_q)| + \sum_{i=0}^{P-1} |S(g_{i-1} - g_i) - S(g_{i-1} - g_i)| \quad (8)$$

The uniform LBP descriptor, taking into account the uniformity measure, is then defined as:

$$LBP_{(R,P)}^{un} = \begin{cases} \sum_{i=0}^{P-1} S(g_i - g_q) \times 2^i, & \text{if } U(LBP_{(R,P)}) \geq 2 \\ P+1, & \text{Otherwise} \end{cases} \quad (9)$$

To illustrate the advantages of the uniform LBP descriptor, consider using 8 neighbourhood pixels for assigning the LBP code to a centre pixel. This combination gives a total of $2^8 = 256$ patterns, and according to the uniformity measure equation, 58 of these patterns are uniform, while 198 patterns are non-uniform. Then, the uniform LBP descriptor dedicates a single histogram bin to accumulate non-uniform patterns. Subsequently, the remaining bins are used for each uniform pattern. Thus, a total of 59 patterns are generated for every LBP cell size, compared to the 258 patterns produced by the LBP descriptor without uniform patterns. Thus, the uniform LBP descriptor was used in this work as a feature extractor. Algorithm 2 [8], shows the steps used to extract features using the uniform LBP descriptor.

Algorithm 2. Feature extraction using the uniform LBP descriptor

---

Require: Weld joint images from training and validation dataset
Output: Concatenated feature vector v per image

1: **for** each image I in the dataset **do**
2:     Divide into cells.
3:     **for** each cell **do**
4:         Compute the uniform patterns using Eq. 9.
5:         Calculate and normalise the histogram.
6:     **end for**
7:     Concatenate cells histograms and form feature vector v.
8: **end for**

2.3 Feature Classification

Due to their ability to derive meaningful patterns from complicated data, Multi-Layer Perceptrons (MLPs) are the simplest and widely used Neural Networks algorithms [11]. MLPs are supervised learning algorithms; during training, they receive, as input, feature vectors with a corresponding class label. Based on the predicted output, the loss is computed and used to adjust the weight parameters such that the predicted output is closer to the actual output during the next iteration. As depicted in Fig. 2, a Multi-Layer Perceptron is a fully connected network that comprises three layers, namely: the input layer, the hidden layer and the output layer.

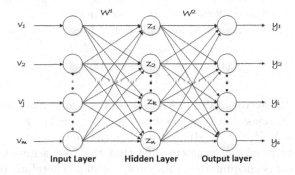

Fig. 2. Multi-layer perceptron, with m neurons in the input layer and c neurons in the output layer.

Neurons in the input layer acts as a buffer to distribute input feature vectors $V = \{v_1, v_2, v_3, ..., v_m\}$. The hidden layer acts as the intermediate intersection between the input layer and the output layer. The size of the output layer is determined by the number of classes to predict, and each neuron is the probability that the given input vector belongs to a particular class. The input layer consists of weight parameters $W^1 = \{w_1^1, w_2^1, ..., w_m^1\}$ for transforming input layer to the neurons in the hidden layer. The weight parameters $W^2 = \{w_1^2, w_2^2, ..., w_n^2\}$ transform the neurons in the hidden layer to the output layer. The value of any neuron z_k in the hidden layer is the sum of products of all the input vectors and the corresponding weight parameter plus the bias term. This is mathematically defined as:

$$z_i = (w_{0,i}^1 + \sum_{j=1}^{m} v_j w_{j,i}^1) \tag{10}$$

Subsequently, the output y_i of neuron i in the output layer is calculated as:

$$y_i = g(w_{0,i}^2 + \sum_{j=1}^{n} z_j w_{j,i}^2) \tag{11}$$

The function g in Eq. 11 is the activation function, and its purpose is to introduce a non-linear decision boundary in the MLP network. This work uses a sigmoid function as the non-linear activation function. The sigmoid function takes any real number as input and produces a bounded output between 0 and 1. The sigmoid function is defined as: $g(z) = \frac{1}{1+e^{-z}}$.

Training the Multi-layer Perceptron Algorithm. During training, the MLP algorithm is given the training feature vectors as inputs. For each input feature vector, it produces the predicted output in the form of a score vector that is a probability of the given input vector belonging to each class. Then the predicted output is compared to the actual output to measure the network error (loss). The loss defines how accurate the MLP network is performing. The lower the loss, the better the performance. The loss function used in this work is the Mean Squared Error (MSE) loss, and it is defined as:

$$E(W) = \frac{1}{m} \sum_{j=1}^{m} (y_i - y_i(W, v_j))^2 \tag{12}$$

where $E(W)$ is the average MSE loss across all the training feature vectors, y_j is the actual output (class label) of the input vector v_j, $y_j(W, v_j)$ is the predicted output and $W = \{W^1, W^2, \ldots, W^k\}$. Based on the measured loss, the MLP algorithm adjusts its weight parameters such that the loss is minimised when the same input vector is encountered in future iterations. Therefore, optimisation in MLP involves finding a set of weight parameters that achieve the lowest possible loss across the training dataset. The optimisation is achieved by computing the gradient of the loss with respect to the wight parameters, then moving to the direction opposite to the gradient until convergence is reached. This procedure is called gradient descent optimisation. The updated weight parameters are calculated as:

$$W_n = W - u\frac{\partial E}{\partial W} \tag{13}$$

where w_n is the newly updated weight parameters. The parameter, u is the learning rate, and it determines the step size taken during each iteration. The gradient, $\frac{\partial E}{\partial W}$ is calculated using the backpropagation algorithm, which indicates how the small change in any weight parameter affect the final loss. Backpropagation is calculated using the chain rule. For instance, computing the gradient with respect to any weight parameter w_j^2 between the hidden layer and the output layer can be computed by taking the gradient of the loss function with respect to the output y multiplied by the gradient of y with respect to w_j^2. This is mathematically defined as:

$$\frac{\partial W}{\partial w_j^2} = \frac{\partial W}{\partial y} \times \frac{\partial y}{\partial w_j^2} \tag{14}$$

Equation 14 is repeated for every weight parameter in the network using the gradients from previous layers. Algorithm 3 shows the steps used in this work to classify weld joint images using the MLP algorithm.

Algorithm 3. Feature classification using MLP

Require: Training and validation feature vectors
output: Class label for validation feature vectors
 1: Training phase:
 2: Randomly initialise weight parameters.
 3: **while** convergence is not achieved **do**
 4:   **for** each input feature vector **do**
 5:      Compute the inputs to the hidden layer using Eq. 10.
 6:      Compute the predicted output using Eq. 11.
 7:      Compute MSE using Eq. 12.
 8:      Compute the gradient using Eq. 14.
 9:      Update the weights using Eq. 13.
10:   **end for**
11:   Return weight parameters.
12: **end while**
13: Classification phase:
14: **for** each validation feature vector **do**
15:   Feed into the classifier and obtain the class label.
16: **end for**

---

3 Experimental Results and Discussion

The dataset used to conduct the experiments comprises 300 thermite weld images obtained from the Transnet Freight Rail (TFR) welding department. The dataset represents a defect-less class, and classes of three welding defects types, namely: the wormholes, the shrinkage cavities and the inclusions defects. Each class consist of 75 images, a five fold cross-validation method was employed, and in each fold, 240 feature vectors (60 per class) were used to train the MLP classifier, and 60 feature vectors (15 per class) were used for validation. Figure 3 depicts the sample thermite weld image for each class.

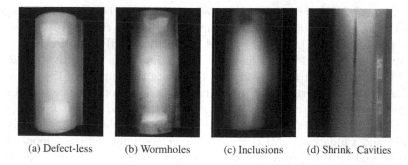

(a) Defect-less   (b) Wormholes   (c) Inclusions   (d) Shrink. Cavities

Fig. 3. Sample image per each class

3.1 Weld Joint Extraction

The CLAHE technique was first applied to the collected thermite weld images to improve image quality and defect visibility. Thereafter, the Geodesic ACM was applied to each image to segment and extract the weld joint according to Algorithm 1. With reference to Fig. 4, the Geodesic ACM was applied on each image to drive the contour towards the edges of the weld joint region (see Fig. 4(a)). As depicted in Fig. 4(b), the contour was then segmented to distinguish the weld joint (white region) from the image background (black region). The coordinates of the segmented weld joint were then superimposed to the original image, thereafter, the rectangular bounding box was placed across the coordinates (see Fig. 4(c)). The region inside the bounding box was cropped (see Fig. 4(d)) and saved as the weld joint RoI.

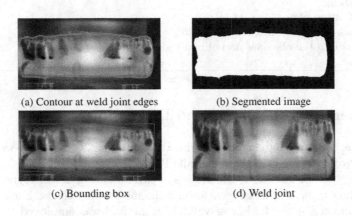

(a) Contour at weld joint edges   (b) Segmented image

(c) Bounding box   (d) Weld joint

Fig. 4. Weld joint segmentation and RoI extraction

3.2 Defect Classification

The uniform LBP descriptor was applied to the extracted weld joint images to extract features according to Algorithm 2. Similar to the approach proposed in [8], the LBP descriptor was applied at different LBP cell size parameters, namely 6×14 (6 and 14 pixels in the x and y directions respectively), 12×28, 30×70, and 60×140; this was done to evaluate the impact of the cell size on the classification performance. Furthermore, the neighbouring pixels and radius parameters were kept at 8 and 1, respectively to avoid a long feature vector length. Features extracted at each LBP cell size were then independently used to train and validate the MLP classifier for classifying the considered classes. The proposed MLP network consist of the input layer, output layer and a single hidden layer. The learning rate parameter u and the size of the hidden layer were fine tuned for optimal performance in terms of the classification accuracy. A five fold cross-validation method was proposed, in each fold 60 feature vectors (per class) were used for training and 15 (per class) were used for validation.

Table 1 to 4 shows the average classification accuracies at varying hidden layer size and learning rate parameter in each LBP cell size.

Table 1. Classification accuracies (%) for features extracted at 6×14 cell size

Hidden layer	Learning rate, u				
Size	0.0001	0.001	0.01	0.1	0.3
10	83.3	81.7	70.0	52.0	54.0
15	81.7	76.7	81.3	66.0	64.0
20	55.0	83.3	78.3	75.3	62.7
25	**86.7**	70.0	73.3	64.0	61.3

Table 2. Classification accuracies (%) for features extracted at 12×28 cell size

Hidden layer	Learning rate, u				
Size	0.0001	0.001	0.01	0.1	0.3
15	80.0	83.3	**91.7**	69.3	67.7
20	90.0	80.0	83.3	66.0	65.3
25	88.0	78.3	90.0	71.7	61.0
30	86.7	78.3	81.3	62.7	55.0

Table 3. Classification accuracies (%) for features extracted at 30×70 cell size

Hidden layer	Learning rate, u				
Size	0.0001	0.001	0.01	0.1	0.3
15	88.3	85.7	83.3	71.3	66.0
20	93.7	90.0	86.7	69.7	55.7
25	**96.3**	86.7	81.3	55.0	55.7
30	91.7	90.0	85.3	61.7	61.3

Table 4. Classification accuracies (%) for features extracted at 60×140 cell size

Hidden layer	Learning rate, u				
Size	0.0001	0.001	0.01	0.1	0.3
15	86.7	90.0	88.6	55.7	55.0
20	90.3	85.0	85.3	61.3	53.7
25	90.3	83.3	85.0	60.3	67.7
30	**91.7**	88.0	85.0	66.7	51.3

It can be observed from Table 3 that the highest classification accuracy obtained by the proposed method is 96.3%, and it was obtained at the LBP cell size parameter of 30 × 70. In the MLP classifier, the optimal learning rate parameter and number of neurons in the hidden layer were found to be 0.0001 and 25, respectively. It can also be observed that in each cell size, the classification accuracy decreases with an increase in the learning rate parameter. This is because the learning rate determines the step size at each iteration while moving towards the direction that minimises the loss. Therefore a higher learning rate generally reaches convergence quickly at the expense of the optimal weight parameters that minimise the loss. Furthermore, the number of neurons in the hidden layer does not have a significant impact on the classification accuracies as observed from the obtained results.

3.3   Methods Comparison

The highest classification accuracy obtained from the proposed method has been compared to the method proposed in [8] for the same objective of classifying the thermite weld defects. Both methods used a similar dataset and a similar LBP feature descriptor. However, the method in [8] used the K-NN classifier, while the method proposed in this work used the MLP classifier. Table 5 shows that the proposed MLP classifier outperforms the K-NN classifier in [8] for classifying thermite weld images based on features extracted by the LBP descriptor on a similar dataset. Furthermore, the MLP classifier is able to classify the LBP features at a much higher cell size parameter. Thus, the feature vector length of only 5 900 histograms is obtained for each weld joint image. On the other hand, the K-NN classifier only achieved the best classification accuracy at a smaller LBP cell size, thus resulting to a feature vector length of 147 500 histograms. The feature vector length of 147 500 requires much time to compute compared to the feature vector length of 5 900. Therefore, the method proposed in this work outperforms the method in [8] in terms of classification accuracy and computational cost for feature extraction.

Table 5. Comparison of the methods

Method	Optimal parameters		Feature length	Accuracy(%)
LBP + K-NN [8]	Cell size: 6 × 14	K = 5	147 500	94.0
LBP + MLP	**Cell size: 30×70**	$u = 0.0001$	**5 900**	**96.3**

4   Conclusion

This work has proposed a method to detect and classify thermite weld defects automatically using the LBP descriptor and the MLP classifier. The Geodesic ACM was first applied to the radiography images to extract the weld joint from the image background. Feature extraction on the weld joint images was achieved using LBP as a feature descriptor at different cell size parameters. Extracted features were then used to train and validate the MLP classifier. The proposed method achieved a classification accuracy of 96.3%. The results obtained in this work outperforms the state of the art method found in the literature for classifying thermite weld defects based on a similar dataset. It should be noted that the proposed method only classify three types of thermite weld defects due to a limited dataset. Therefore, future work will involve collecting more dataset and comparing the results obtained by the proposed method to other feature extraction and classification algorithms, including deep learning approaches.

References

1. Al-Hameed, W., Mayali, Y., Picton, P.: Segmentation of radiographic images of weld defects. J. Glob. Res. Comput. Sci. **4**, 28–34 (2013)
2. Cai, L., Wang, Y.: A phase-based active contour model for segmentation of breast ultrasound images. In: 2013 6th International Conference on Biomedical Engineering and Informatics, pp. 91–95 (2013). https://doi.org/10.1109/BMEI.2013.6746913
3. Chen, X., Williams, B.M., Vallabhaneni, S.R., Czanner, G., Williams, R., Zheng, Y.: Learning active contour models for medical image segmentation. In: 2019 IEEE/CVF Conference on Computer Vision and Pattern Recognition (CVPR), pp. 11624–11632 (2019). https://doi.org/10.1109/CVPR.2019.01190
4. Gharsallah, M.B., Braiek, E.B.: Weld inspection based on radiography image segmentation with level set active contour guided off-center saliency map. Adv. Mater. Sci. Eng. **2015**, 1–10 (2015)
5. Ibrahim, A.S., Youssef, A.E., Abbott, A.L.: Global vs. local features for gender identification using Arabic and English handwriting. In: 2014 IEEE International Symposium on Signal Processing and Information Technology (ISSPIT), pp. 000155–000160 (2014). https://doi.org/10.1109/ISSPIT.2014.7300580
6. Kass, M., Witkin, A., Terzopoulos, D.: Snakes: active contour models. Int. J. Comput. Vis. **04**, 321–331 (1988)
7. Liu, Y., Fan, L., Zhang, S.: Exploration of rail defects detection system. In: 2018 5th International Conference on Information Science and Control Engineering (ICISCE), pp. 1118–1122 (2018). https://doi.org/10.1109/ICISCE.2018.00230
8. Molefe, M.E., Tapamo, J.R.: Classification of thermite welding defects using local binary patterns and k nearest neighbors. In: 2021 Conference on Information Communications Technology and Society (ICTAS), pp. 91–96 (2021). https://doi.org/10.1109/ICTAS50802.2021.9395030
9. Ojala, T., Pietikainen, M., Maenpaa, T.: Multiresolution gray-scale and rotation invariant texture classification with local binary patterns. IEEE Trans. Pattern Anal. Mach. Intell. **24**(7), 971–987 (2002). https://doi.org/10.1109/TPAMI.2002.1017623
10. Sridevi, V., Jianmin, G., Nirmala, A.: Inspection of welding images using image segmentation techniques. Int. J. Eng. Res. Technol. (IJERT) **2**, 28–34 (2013)

11. Vahid, A., Hoorieh, M., Fatemeh, D., Mohsen, H., Mehrdad, P.: Multilayer percep-
    tron neural network with supervised training method for diagnosis and predicting
    blood disorder and cancer. In: 2009 IEEE International Symposium on Indus-
    trial Electronics, pp. 2075–2080, August 2009. https://doi.org/10.1109/ISIE.2009.
    5213591
12. Yongzhi, M., Benyu, X., Jianwu, D., Biao, Y., Tiandong, C.: Real time detection
    system for rail surface defects based on machine vision. EURASIP J. Image Video
    Process. **2018**, 3 (2018). https://doi.org/10.1186/s13640-017-0241-y

Smart Systems

An Elliptic Curve Biometric Based User Authentication Protocol for Smart Homes Using Smartphone

Amir Mohammadi Bagha[1]($\boxtimes$), Isaac Woungang[1], Sanjay Kumar Dhurandher[2], and Issa Traore[3]

[1] Department of Computer Science, Ryerson University, Ontario, Toronto, Canada
{amir.mohammadi,iwoungan}@ryerson.ca
[2] Department of Information Technology, Netaji Subhas University of Technology, University of Delhi, Delhi, India
[3] Department of Electrical and Computer Engineering, University of Victoria, Victoria, B.C, Canada
itraore@ece.uvic.ca

Abstract. The Internet of Things (IoT) is one of the most prominent technologies which establishes the foundation of smart homes and cities by creating a communication method for physical objects over the Internet. In smart homes, devices (objects) are not fundamentally homogeneous in security protocols, computational power, topology, or communication. This heterogeneous nature of these objects leads to incompatibilities with common authentication methods and the security requirements of IoT standards. This paper proposes an enhanced version of the RSA-Biometric-based user Authentication Scheme for Smart Homes using smartphone (denoted RSA-B-ASH-S) by utilizing the Elliptic-curve Diffie–Hellman (ECDH) protocol to optimize the computational power. The formal security analysis of the proposed scheme is presented using the Burrows-Abadi-Needham (BAN) logic, demonstrating how the proposed scheme achieves a perfect forward secrecy (PFS) by taking advantage of a unique encryption key for each session. An informal security analysis of the proposed scheme is also presented, highlighting its computational time, communication overhead, and storage requirements. A proof of concept of the proposed scheme is also presented.

Keywords: Internet of Things · Elliptic curve · Diffie-Hellman · One time password · DoS attack · Man-in-the-middle attack · Burrows-Abadi-Needham logic · Two-factor remoted user authentication · Smart home · Smartphone · Perfect forward secrecy · Advanced encryption standard

1 Introduction

Internet of Things (IoT) can be considered as a leading technology that makes the communication and interaction of physical objects possible over the Internet [1]. These

T. M. N. Ngatched and I. Woungang (Eds.): PAAISS 2021, LNICST 405, pp. 219–236, 2022.
https://doi.org/10.1007/978-3-030-93314-2_14

devices or objects can observe, and collect data about their surrounding physical environment by utilizing a variety of sensors and detectors, and then share the data by the communication systems they have in place. To share the collected data, these objects are required to authenticate each other through an IoT-based local communication protocol, or a cloud method. However, the security protocols used by these systems are considered to be incompatible with the IoT security requirements, considering that the majority of them rely on single-factor authentication protocols [2]. Several IoT-based authentication schemes have been presented in the literature, including the RSA-Biometric-based User Authentication Scheme proposed in [3], known as RSA-B-ASH-S. The proposed scheme in this paper is based on RSA-ASH-SC [4], and substituted the use of smartphones, as opposed to smart cards, which was an improvement over the previous scheme. It was shown that it satisfies Perfect Forward Secrecy (PFS) property while supporting all the security features inherited from the RSA-ASH-SC scheme. However, to satisfy PFS, RSA-B-ASH-S takes advantage of the Diffie–Hellman key exchange, which is considered to be computationally expensive. In the proposed scheme, the use of Diffie–Hellman key exchange is substituted with the Elliptic-curve Diffie–Hellman (ECDH) which requires shorter encryption keys, leading to lower computation and memory requirements. The ECDH protocol exponentially outperforms other protocols when more security is required. ECDH exhibits the same cryptographic strength as an RSA-based system with much smaller key sizes. For instance, a 256-bit ECDH key corresponds to RSA 3072-bit keys which are 50% longer than the 2048-bit keys commonly used today.

The remainder of the paper is structured in the following way. In Sect. 2, some related works, along with their security performance summaries are presented. In Sect. 3, the proposed scheme is described in depth. Section 4, presents the formal security analysis using the Burrows-Abadi-Needham (BAN) logic [5] and performance evaluation of the scheme. Moreover, Sect. 5 presents an informal security analysis of the proposed scheme. In Sect. 6, a proof-of-concept of the scheme is detailed. Finally, Sect. 7 concludes the paper.

2   Related Work

In this section, some related work on user authentication for smart homes are reviewed and evaluated in terms of their security protocols.

In [3] Mohammadi Bagha proposed an authentication protocol for smart homes, which satisfied PFS by taking advantage of Diffie–Hellman key exchange. This method also took advantage of smart phones as an additional layer of biometric authentication. In this scheme, RSA keys are generated in the first step as per the method described in RSA-ASH-SC. Then, the user and the server exchange a biometric impression and password, and an ID and a one-time-token, respectively, in a secure manner. This concludes the registration phase. In the next phase, user login and authentication takes place. In this phase, a Diffie–Hellman key exchange takes place, which allows the scheme to generate a new key for each session, therefore PFS is satisfied. To satisfy PFS, this scheme uses the Diffie–Hellman key exchange, which is computationally expensive.

In [6], Liu et al. proposed a remote user authentication protocol for smart homes, which relies on the establishment of a relationship at the registration phase to check the legitimacy of the user at login time. Upon receipt of a login request from a user at the registration phase, the server checks the validity of ID_i and calculates $CID_i = f(ID_i \oplus d)$ so that when the server receives a login request, it checks the validity of ID_i and if successful, it calculates $CID'_i = f(ID_i \oplus d)$; where f is a collision free one-way hash function and d is the private key component of RSA. If $CID'_i = CID_i$, the user gets authenticated.

In [4], Raniyal et al. proposed the RSA-ASH-SC scheme, in which the Rebalanced-Multi-Power RSA protocol [7] is used as underlying RSA algorithm. In their scheme, the user generates the values: $x = (f(((f(PW) \oplus ID))^e \oplus f(T))) \bmod N$, $HXOTT = f(x \oplus OTT)$ and $y = (OTT \| T \| S_i \| f(OTT \| T \| S_i \| HXOTT) \| HXOTT)$, where OTT is the user's one-time-token, then sends the value (OTT, C) to the server, where $C = y^e \bmod (N)$. Next, the server validates OTT and T, then computes $x = ((HPWID)^e \oplus f(T)) \bmod N$ and $Z = f(x \oplus OTT)$. If Z and $HXOTTi$, the extracted value from the decrypted message, are equal, the user gets authenticated.

In [8], Wazid et al. proposed a secure remote user authentication scheme for smart homes which utilizes bitwise XOR operations, one-way hash functions and symmetric encryptions and decryptions to achieve mutual authentications between the user and HGN, HGN and smart device, and user and smart device. In their scheme, each user has a smartphone capable of reading their credential information (identity, password, biometric). The user's request for authentication is handled by the HGN, which forwards it to the smart card. The response is sent back to the HGN, which passes it to the user. A registration authority is also involved, which securely registers the HGN and each smart device offline prior to the authentication step. In this process, a user who wishes to access the smart device must first register at the registration authority by providing its credential information. After registration, the following steps are carried: (i) user's authentication and agreement, (ii) user's biometric and password update, and (iii) verification using a fuzzy extractor.

In [9] Bae and Kwak proposed a user authentication protocol in IoT environment using smart card, which is made of three phases: (1) Registration phase – where the user and IoT server request for registration to a authentication server, which in response sends a smart card to the user and the secret information that it has stored (i.e. encrypted password *(EncPass_i)*, *h(EncPass_i)*), which will be needed for login and authentication. In the Login and authentication phase, the server verifies the identity of the user upon request for login, then issue a session key if the user and server are confirmed as legitimate entities. Only then, the mutual authentication between the server and the user is performed, which involves the value generated by the user and the *h(x)* value contained in the smart card. A password change phase is also implemented to account for the situation where the user wishes to change his/her password.

In [10], Dammak et al. proposed a user authentication scheme for IoT environment, which consists of offline smart device, home gateway registration, user registration, and token distribution between the home gateway and smart devices. Upon completion of these steps, the user logs in the system to trigger the authentication step. Similarly, in [11], Dhillon and Kalra proposed another user authentication scheme for IoT environments based on password, biometrics and smart device. Their scheme consists of: a registration step – where the user and home gateway node (HGN) must register; a login step – if successful, this step gives access to a IoT node and its resources to the user; and a mutual authentication step – where the user and the IoT node generate an encrypted session key based on parameters generated by the HGN, which enables a secure communication between the user and the IoT node; and a password change step – where the user's password is updated if necessary.

Like RSA-B-ASH-S, the proposed scheme uses a fresh shared key for each session; thus, even if the private key of the server is compromised, the attacker cannot access to any of the previous sessions' plaintext data. This proposed scheme uses the Elliptic-curve Diffie–Hellman (ECDH) for the key exchange, which requires shorter encryption keys compare to RSA-B-ASH-S, resulting in lower computation cost requirements.

3 Proposed EC-B-ASH-S Scheme

For the sake of clarity, the notations in Table 1 are considered.

Table 1. Notations.

Notation	Definition
$\phi(N)$	Euler's totient
n	Input security parameter for the key generation algorithm
E_P	Elliptic curve
F_P	Finite field
g	Base point of E_P
k	Distinct prime numbers in RSA key generation
s	Size of prime numbers in RSA key generation (Rebalanced)
p, q	Prime numbers used in the RSA key generation
e, d	RSA encryption and decryption exponents
$mod()$	Modulus operation
$gcd()$	Greatest common divisor
$\oplus$	XOR operator
$h()$	One-way hash function
ΔT	Threshold time used to prevent replay attack
$\{\}_x$	Symmetric-key encryption/decryption, where x is a symmetric key
U_i	i^{th} user
ID_i	ID of U_i
PW_i	Password of U_i
B_i	Biometric impression of U_i
OTT_i	One-time-token of U_i
Θ	Predetermined threshold for biometric verification

(continued)

Table 1. (*continued*)

Notation	Definition
$\sigma()$	Symmetric parametric function for biometric factor comparison
p_{ec}	Large prime for the Elliptic Curve Diffie Hellman key exchange algorithm
n_{ec}	Size of p_{ec} (in bits)
a_i	Session independent random exponent chosen by U_i
b_i	Session independent random exponent chosen by the server to communicate with U_i
sk_i	Session key for communication between U_i and the server
tsk_i	Session independent temporary key chosen randomly by U_i to encrypt the communication with the server

The proposed EC-B-ASH-S scheme consists of four steps:

3.1 Initialization Phase

The RSA keys are generated as per the method described in RSA-ASH-SC [4]. The key generation algorithm takes two security parameters as inputs: n and k. First, it generates two prime numbers p and q of $\frac{n}{k}$ bits long such that $gcd((p-1), (q-1)) = 2$. Second, it calculates $N = p^{(k-1)}.q$. Third, it generates two random numbers $r1$ and $r2$ such that $gcd(r1, (p-1)) = 1$, $gcd(r2, (q-1)) = 1$ and $r1 = r2 \ mod(2)$. Fourth, it finds the integer d such that $d = r1 \ mod(p-1)$ and $d = r2 \ mod(q-1)$. Finally, it calculates e such that $e = d^{-1} mod(\phi(N))$. Here, the public key is (e, N) and the private key is $(p, q, r1, r2)$, which is kept secret at the server side. The server also generates n_{ec} bits long prime P_{ec}. The equation for the elliptic curve on a prime field is given as:

$$ y^2 mod p_{ec} = \left(x^3 + ax + b \right) mod p_{ec} $$

Where $\left(4a^3 + 27b^2\right) mod p_{ec}$ is not equal to 0. Then we choose long prime g as the starting point of EC.

3.2 Registration Phase

The user (U_i) submits a request in a secure manner to the server by sharing his/her biometric impression B_i and the hash of his/her password $(h(PW_i), B_i)$ where PW_i is the chosen password. Upon receiving this request, the server creates a random and unique ID_i for U_i. It also creates a random one-time-token OTT_i to keep for future authentication requests. Then, it calculates $CR_i = h(h(PW_i), ID_i)$ and stores this value and OTT_i in the database along with B_i and ID_i, which is protected by the server's private key. Next, the server submits the following information $(ID_i, OTT_i, g, e, N, h, \Delta T, E_P, F_P)$ to the smartphone over a secure channel.

3.3 Login and Authentication Phase

First, U_i opens the authenticator software, imprints his/her biometric B_i^* at the sensor, then inputs his/her password. The software then performs the following steps. First, it generates a random number a_i and keeps it secure as the private key, then computes the EC public key $PK_{user}^{ec} = a_i g \ mod \ (p_{ec})$. Next, tsk_i, a session independent temporary key is created randomly by the user application. For the server-side application to be able to encrypt the response of the initial request asymmetrically, the tsk_i variable is needed. It should be noted that this value does not function as session key, but it is used to prevent the server's EC public parameter to be communicated without encryption. Finally, the user generates $P_1 = (PK_{user}^{ec}, T, tsk_i)$, where T is the current timestamp. Next, the software encrypts P_1 with the server's RSA public key $C_1 = (P_1)^e \ mod \ (N)$, then sends the following message (OTT_i, C_1) to the server. Upon receipt, the server compares OTT_i against the entries in the database. If there is a match, the server extracts (ID_i, B_i, CR_i) from the database corresponding to the OTT_i, decrypts C_1 and retrieves P_1. To decrypt C_1, it computes $M_1 = C_1^{r1} mod \ (p)$ and $M_2 = C_1^{r2} mod \ (q)$. Using CRT (Chinese Remainder Theorem), it calculates $P_1 \in Z_N$ such that $P_1 = M_1 mod \ (p)$ and $P_1 = M_2 mod \ (q)$. Then, it checks whether the timestamp is recent, i.e. $(T^s - T) < \Delta T$, where T_s is the current timestamp of the server and ΔT is the acceptable difference. If that is true, the server obtains U_i's EC public key along with tsk_i. After that, it creates a random number b_i and keeps it secure, then computes the server's EC public key $PK_{server}^{ec} = b_i g \ mod \ (p_{ec})$ and the session key $sk_i = b_i PK_{user}^{ec} mod \ (p_{ec})$. Next, the server creates a new random token OTT_i^{new}, but it does not update U_i's token before authentication. Finally, the server computes $P_2 = h(ID_i, sk_i, P_{1,})$ and $C_2 = \{OTT_i^{new}, T, PK_{server}^{ec}, P_2\}_{tsk_i}$ where T is the current timestamp, then sends C_2 back to U_i. Hence, only the server can decrypt C_1, thus P_2 is used as a challenge and the user can authenticate the integrity of the message and its sender. Upon receipt of C_2, the client-side application decrypts it using tsk_i, therefore gains access to OTT_i^{new}, T, P_2 and the server's EC public key PK_{server}^{ec}, and finally obtains the sk_i value by computing $sk_i = a_i PK_{server}^{ec} mod \ (p_{ec})$. The client-side application verifies the freshness of the received message by comparing the current and received timestamps. Next, U_i confirms the integrity of the message by calculating $P_2^* = h(ID_i, sk_i, P_1)$ and checking $P_2^* = P_2$. If the message was genuine, U_i creates $P_3 = h(OTT_i^{new}, OTT_i, h(h(PW_i), ID_i))$, encrypts it along with B_i^* and the current timestamp T, producing $C_3 = \{P_3, B_i^*, T\}_{sk_i}$. Eventually, U_i sends C_3 back to the server as the last step of authentication. The server then decrypts C_3 with sk_i, confirms if the message is fresh i.e. $T_s - T < \Delta T$ and then computes $P_3^* = h(OTT_i^{new}, OTT_i, h(h(PW_i), ID_i))$ from the database entries, then checks if it is identical to P_3. If this is valid, a biometric verification phase is trigger, which compares the imprinted biometric impression B_i^* with the stored B_i value. If B_i^* is validated ($\sigma(B_i^*, B_i) \leq \Theta$), then the two values are matched successfully and the authentication phase successfully finishes, otherwise the software generates the decline message and terminates the process. Then the server authenticates the user and updates his/her OTT_i^{new} in the database. Then the user replaces his/her one-time token with OTT_i^{new}.

3.4 Password/Biometric Change Phase

To update the password or the biometric impression, the user needs to be authenticated in advance. The user enters the new password and imprints his/her biometric impression at the sensor B_i^{new} and calculates $y = h(PW_i^{new})$ then sends a password/biometric update command to the server as $CMD = (pass_{update}, \{T, y, B_i^{new}\}_{sk_i})$ where $pass_{update}$ is a known command to the server, and T is the current timestamp. After receiving the command, the server decrypts the message using sk_i and validates the timestamp T. If validated, the server computes $CR_i^{new} = h(y, ID_i)$, then updates the database corresponding to the user ID_i.

4 Security Analysis and Performance Evaluation of the Proposed EC-B-ASH-S Scheme

4.1 Formal Security Analysis Using BAN Logic

BAN Logic [5] was introduced in 1989 as a model to evaluate the validity of an authentication protocol; in this case, between the user U equipped with a smartphone and the server S. The following notations are considered:

$U| \equiv X$: U believes the statement X.
$\#(X)$: X is fresh.
$U \Rightarrow X$: U has jurisdiction over the statement X.
$U \lhd X$: U sees the statement X.
$U| \sim X$: U once said the statement X.
(X, Y): X or Y is one part of the expression (X, Y).
$\{X\}_Y$: X encrypted with Y.
$U \overset{sk}{\leftrightarrow} S$: sk is a secret parameter shared (or to be shared) between U and S.
$\overset{X}{\rightarrow} S$: X is public key of S. The private key associated with X is denoted with X^{-1}.

The following BAN logic rules are used to prove that the proposed EC-B-ASH-S scheme key agreement is fulfilled successfully.

R1. Random Number Freshness: When an entity creates a random value, it believes the value is fresh.

$$\frac{U \ creates \ random \ X}{U| \equiv \#(X)}$$

R2. The Rule For $\overset{k}{\leftrightarrow}$ Introduction: With X indicating the essential elements for a key. Formally, it is required that U believes that S also participates in the protocol. Informally, the rule means that to believe a new session key, U must believe that the key is fresh and U must also believe that S believes in X, so S can generate the key.

$$\frac{U| \equiv \#(K), U| \equiv S| \equiv X}{U| \equiv U \overset{K}{\leftrightarrow} S}$$

R3. Message Meaning

I.   If U perceives X as an encrypted value with K, and believes K is a shared secret key with S, then U believes S once said X:

$$\frac{U| \equiv U \overset{K}{\leftrightarrow} S, U \triangleleft \{X\}_K}{U| \equiv S| \sim X}$$

II. If U perceives X as an encrypted value with K^{-1} and believes K is S public key, then U believes S once said X:

$$\frac{U| \overset{K}{\equiv\rightarrow} S, U \triangleleft \{X\}_{K^{-1}}}{U| \equiv S| \sim X}$$

R4. Message Freshness. If U believes X is fresh and U believes S once said X, then U believes S believes X:

$$\frac{U| \equiv \#(X), U| \equiv S| \sim X}{U| \equiv S| \equiv X}$$

R5. Hash Function. If U believes S once said $H(X)$ and U sees X, then U believes S once said X:

$$\frac{U| \equiv S| \sim H(X), U \triangleleft X}{U| \equiv S| \sim X}$$

R6. Jurisdiction. If U believes S has full control over X and U believes S believes X, then U believes X:

$$\frac{U| \equiv S \Rightarrow X, U| \equiv S| \equiv X}{U| \equiv X}$$

R7. Freshness Propagation. If one parameter of an expression is fresh, then the entire expression is fresh:

$$\frac{U| \equiv \#(X)}{U| \equiv \#(X, Y)}$$

R8. Belief. If U believes X and Y, then U believes X:

$$\frac{U| \equiv (X, Y)}{U| \equiv X}$$

R9. Observation. If U perceives X and Y, then U perceives X:

$$\frac{U \triangleleft (X, Y)}{U \triangleleft X}$$

The core objectives of our authentication scheme analysis are described as follows:

G1. U believes S believes sk is a secure shared parameter between U and S.

$$U| \equiv S| \equiv U \overset{sk}{\leftrightarrow} S$$

G2. U believes sk is a secure shared parameter between U and S.

$$U| \equiv U \overset{sk}{\leftrightarrow} S$$

G3. S believes U believes sk is a secure shared parameter between U and S.

$$S| \equiv U| \equiv U \overset{sk}{\leftrightarrow} S$$

G4. S believes sk is a secure shared parameter between U and S.

$$S| \equiv U \overset{sk}{\leftrightarrow} S$$

The assumptions about the initial state of the proposed scheme are as follows:

A1. $S| \overset{K_S}{\equiv \rightarrow} S$: The server believes K_S as its public key.

A2. $U| \overset{K_S}{\equiv \rightarrow} S$: The user believes K_S as the server's public key.

A3. $S| \equiv U \overset{ID}{\leftrightarrow} S$: The server believes ID is a secret parameter between the server and user.

A4. $U| \equiv U \overset{ID}{\leftrightarrow} S$: The user believes ID is a secret parameter between the server and user.

A5. $U| \equiv U \overset{h(PW)}{\leftrightarrow} S$: The user believes $h(PW)$ is a secret parameter between the server and user.

A6. $S| \equiv U \overset{h(PW)}{\leftrightarrow} S$: The server believes $h(PW)$ is a secret parameter between the server and user.

A7. $S| \equiv U \Rightarrow B$: The server believes that only user has jurisdiction over his/her biometric.

A8. $S| \equiv U \Rightarrow PW$: The server believes that only user has jurisdiction over his/her password.

The analysis of our authentication scheme is as follows, where D_i represents the ith deduction and M_i represents the ith message.

D1: $\frac{U \ creates \ random \ a}{U| \equiv \#(a)}$: Based on R1.

D2: $\frac{U \ read \ current \ timestamp \ T_1}{U| \equiv \#(T_1)}$

D3: $\frac{U \ creates \ random \ tsk}{U| \equiv \#(tsk)}$: Based on R1.

M1: $U \rightarrow S : \langle OTT, \{ag \ mod \ (p_{ec}), T_1, tsk\}_{K_s} \rangle$: The user initiates the authentication procedure by sending this message to the server.

D4: $U| \equiv U \overset{tsk}{\leftrightarrow} S$: Based on M1 is encrypted with the public key of the server, and based on A1 and A2, the user believes tsk is a secret parameter between U and S.

D5: $S \lhd (ag \ mod \ (p_{ec}), T_1, tsk)$: Based on the fact that M1 is encrypted with the public key of the server, and based on R3.II, A1 and A2, the server decrypts the received message (M1) and sees $(ag \ mod \ (p_{ec}), T_1, tsk)$.

D6: $S| \equiv U| \sim (ag\ mod(p_{ec}), T_1, tsk)$: Based on D4, D5, A1 and A2.

D7: $\dfrac{S| \equiv \#(T_1)}{S| \equiv \#(ag\ mod(p_{ec}), T_1, tsk)}$: Based on R7.

D8: $\dfrac{S| \equiv \#(ag\ mod(p_{ec}), T_1, tsk), S| \equiv U| \sim (ag\ mod(p_{ec}), T_1, tsk)}{S| \equiv U| \equiv (ag\ mod(p_{ec}), T_1, tsk)}$: Based on R4, D6 and D7.

D9: $\dfrac{S| \equiv U| \equiv (ag\ mod(p_{ec}), T_1, tsk)}{S| \equiv U| \equiv (ag\ mod(p_{ec}))}$: Based on R8 and D8.

D10: $\dfrac{S\ creates\ random\ b}{S| \equiv \#(b)}$: Based on R1.

D11: $\dfrac{S| \equiv \#(b)}{S| \equiv \#(bg\ mod(p_{ec}))}$: Based on R7.

D12: $sk := b(ag\ mod(p_{ec}))mod(p_{ec})$: The server generates the session key.

D13: $\dfrac{S| \equiv \#(b)}{S| \equiv \#(b(ag\ mod(p_{ec}))mod(p_{ec}))}$: Based on R7 and D10.

D14: $\dfrac{S\ read\ current\ timestamp\ T_2}{S| \equiv \#(T_2)}$

D15: $\dfrac{S| \equiv \#(sk), S| \equiv U| \equiv (ag\ mod(p_{ec}))}{S| \equiv U \overset{sk}{\leftrightarrow} S}$: Based on D9, R2 and D13, (G4) is achieved.

D16: $\dfrac{S\ creates\ random\ NOTT}{S| \equiv \#(NOTT)}$: Based on R1.

M2: $S \rightarrow U$: $\langle \{bg\ mod(p_{ec}), h(ID, sk, (ag\ mod(p_{ec}), T_1, tsk)), NOTT, T_2\}_{tsk} \rangle$:
Server sends the response of the initial request encrypted with tsk to the server.

D17: $U \lhd (bg\ mod(p_{ec}), h(ID, sk, (ag\ mod(p_{ec}), T_1, tsk)), NOTT, T_2)$: Based on the fact that M2 is encrypted with tsk, and based on R3.II, A1 and A2, the user decrypts the received message (M2) and gets $(bg\ mod(p_{ec}), h(ID, sk, (ag\ mod(p_{ec}), T_1, tsk)), NOTT, T_2)$.

D18: $\dfrac{U| \equiv U \overset{tsk}{\leftrightarrow} S, U \lhd \{bg\ mod(p_{ec}), h(ID, sk, (ag\ mod(p_{ec}), T_1, tsk)), NOTT, T_2\}_{tsk}}{U| \equiv S| \sim (bg\ mod(p_{ec}), h(ID, sk, (ag\ mod(p_{ec}), T_1, tsk)), NOTT, T_2)}$: Based on R3.I.

D19: $\dfrac{U| \equiv S| \sim (bg\ mod(p_{ec}), h(ID, sk, (ag\ mod(p_{ec}), T_1, tsk)), NOTT, T_2)}{U| \equiv S| \sim (bg\ mod(p_{ec}))}$: Based on R8.

D20: $U \lhd bg\ mod(p_{ec})$: Based on D17 and R8.

D21: $sk := a(bg\ mod(p_{ec}))mod(p_{ec})$: The user generates the session key.

D22: $\dfrac{U| \equiv \#(T_2)}{U| \equiv \#(bg\ mod(p_{ec}), h(ID, sk, (ag\ mod(p_{ec}), T_1, tsk)), NOTT, T_2)}$: Based on R7.

D23:

$$\dfrac{U| \equiv \#(bg\ mod(p_{ec}), h(ID, sk, (ag\ mod(p_{ec}), T_1, tsk)), NOTT, T_2), U| \equiv S| \sim (bg\ mod(p_{ec}), h(ID, sk, (ag\ mod(p_{ec}), T_1, tsk)), NOTT, T_2)}{U| \equiv S| \equiv (bg\ mod(p_{ec}), h(ID, sk, (ag\ mod(p_{ec}), T_1, tsk)), NOTT, T_2)}$$

: Based on R4, D22 and D18.

D24: $\dfrac{U| \equiv S| \equiv (bg\ mod(p_{ec}), h(ID, sk, (ag\ mod(p_{ec}), T_1, tsk)), NOTT, T_2)}{U| \equiv S| \equiv h(ID, sk, (ag\ mod(p_{ec}), T_1, tsk))}$: Based on R8 and D23.

D25: $\dfrac{U| \equiv S| \equiv h(ID, sk, (ag\ mod(p_{ec}), T_1, tsk))}{U| \equiv S| \equiv U \overset{sk}{\leftrightarrow} S}$: Based on D24 and R8, (G1) is achieved.

D26: $\dfrac{S| \equiv \#(a)}{S| \equiv \#(a(bg\ mod(p_{ec}))mod(p_{ec}))}$: Based on R7 and D1.

D27: $\dfrac{U| \equiv S| \equiv (bg\ mod(p_{ec}), h(ID, sk, (ag\ mod(p_{ec}), T_1, tsk)), NOTT, T_2)}{U| \equiv S| \equiv bg\ mod(p_{ec})}$: Based on R8 and D23.

D28: $\dfrac{U| \equiv \#(sk), U| \equiv S| \equiv bg\ mod(p_{ec})}{U| \equiv U \overset{sk}{\leftrightarrow} S}$: Based on R2, D27 and D26, (G2) is achieved.

D29: $\dfrac{S\ read\ current\ timestamp\ T_3}{S| \equiv \#(T_3)}$

M3: $U \rightarrow S$: $\{B, T_3, h(NOTT, OTT, h(ID, h(PW)))\}_{sk}$

D30: $\dfrac{S| \equiv U \overset{sk}{\leftrightarrow} S, S \lhd \{M3\}_{sk}}{S| \equiv U| \sim M3}$: Based on R3.I and D15.

D31: $\dfrac{S| \equiv \#(T_3)}{S| \equiv \#(B, T_3, h(NOTT, OTT, h(ID, h(PW))))}$: Based on R7.

D32: $\dfrac{S| \equiv \#(M_3), S| \equiv U| \sim M3}{S| \equiv U| \equiv U \overset{sk}{\leftrightarrow} S}$: Based on R4, D31 and D30 (G3) is achieved.

4.2 Comparison of Computational Performance of Authentication Schemes

We have considered the following notations: T_{exp}: Time taken by modular exponent operation, T_{ec}: Time taken by elliptic curve operation to calculate multiplication of two points, T_d: Time taken by the modular decryption exponent (d) operation, T_e: Time taken by the modular encryption exponent (e) operation, T_s: Time taken to encrypt/decrypt using the symmetric key, T_h: Time taken by the hash function operation, T_{mul}: Time taken by the modular multiplication operation, T_{xor}: Time taken by the XOR operation.

In the above authentication phase, steps 1 and 3 are completed over the client-side while steps 2 and 4 are completed over to the server-side. Table 2 summarizes the computation time taken by each of these steps.

Table 2. Total computation time needed for each step.

Step	Server-side	Client-side	Total Time
1	–	$T_{ec} + T_e$	$T_{ec} + T_e$
2	$2T_{ec} + T_d + T_h + T_s$	–	$2T_{ec} + T_d + T_h + T_s$
3	–	$T_{ec} + 4T_h + 2T_s$	$T_{ec} + 4T_h + 2T_s$
4	$T_{bio} + 3T_h + 2T_s$	–	$T_{bio} + 3T_h + T_s$
Total	$2T_{ec} + T_d + T_{bio} + 4T_h + 3T_s$	$2T_{ec} + 4T_h + 2T_s + T_e$	$4T_{ec} + T_d + 8T_h + T_e + T_{bio} + 5T_s$

Based on the entries given in Table 2, the proposed scheme is compared against selected RSA variants in terms of computational time. The results are given in Table 3.

Table 3. Comparison of selected RSA variants in terms of computational time.

	Login phase	Authentication phase	Total time
Yang et al. [12]	$2T_{exp} + 3T_{mul} + T_h$	$T_e + T_{exp} + T_{mul} + T_h$	$4T_{mul} + 3T_{exp} + T_e + 2T_h$
Fan et al. [13]	$2T_{exp} + 3T_{mul} + T_h$	$T_e + T_{exp} + T_{mul} + T_h$	$4T_{mul} + 3T_{exp} + T_e + 2T_h$
Yang et al. [14]	$2T_{exp} + 3T_{mul}$	$T_e + 2T_{exp} + T_{mul}$	$4T_{mul} + 4T_{exp} + T_e$
Om et al. [7]	$T_e + T_{exp} + T_h + T_{xor}$	T_d	$T_{xor} + T_{exp} + T_d + T_h + T_e$
Om et al. [15]	$T_e + T_{exp} + 2T_h + T_{xor}$	$T_d + T_{exp} + T_h + T_{xor}$	$2T_{xor} + 2T_{exp} + T_d + 3T_h + T_e$
Shen et al. [16]	$T_e + 2T_{exp} + 3T_{mul} + 2T_h$	$T_d + 2T_h + T_{xor}$	$T_{xor} + 2T_{exp} + T_d + 4T_h + T_e + 3T_{mul}$
Liu et al. [6]	$T_d + T_e + T_{exp} + T_{mul} + 2T_h + 2T_{xor}$	$T_e + 2T_h + T_{xor} + 3T_{mul} + 2T_{exp}$	$3T_{xor} + 3T_{exp} + T_d + 4T_h + 2T_e + 4T_{mul}$
Chien et al. [17]	$2T_h + 2T_{xor}$	$3T_h + 3T_{xor}$	$5T_{xor} + 5T_h$

(continued)

Table 3. (*continued*)

	Login phase	Authentication phase	Total time
Raniyal et al. [4]	$2T_e + T_s + 6T_h + 2T_{xor}$	$T_d + T_e + 2T_h + 2T_{xor} + T_s$	$4T_{xor} + T_d + 8T_h + 3T_e + 2T_s$
Bagha et al. [3]	$2T_{exp} + 4T_h + 2T_s + T_e$	$2T_{exp} + T_d + T_{bio} + 4T_h + 3T_s$	$4T_{exp} + T_d + 8T_h + T_e + T_{bio} + 5T_s$
Proposed scheme	$2T_{ec} + 4T_h + 2T_s + T_e$	$2T_{ec} + T_d + T_{bio} + 4T_h + 3T_s$	$4T_{ec} + T_d + 8T_h + T_e + T_{bio} + 5T_s$

Now, we consider the following notations:*EC*: Total number of elliptic curve operations to calculate multiplication of two points, *EXP*: Total number of modular exponent operations, *D*: Total number of modular decryption exponent (d) operations, *E*: Total number of the modular encryption exponent (e) operations, *S*: Total number of encrypt/decrypt operations using the symmetric key, *H*: Total number of hash function operations, *BIO*: Total number of biometric comparison $\sigma()$ functions, *MUL*: Total number of modular multiplication operations, *XOR*: Total number of XOR operations. The total computational time per operation type is captured in Fig. 2.

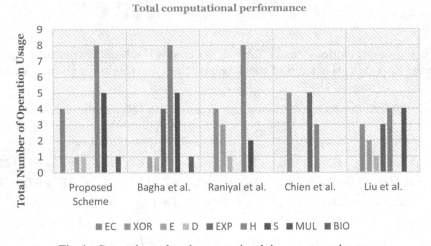

Fig. 1. Comparison of total computational time per operation type.

As shown in Fig. 1, the total computational time of the proposed scheme is higher than that of other schemes. This is due to the use of the EC key exchange algorithm. However, to prevent Rainbow attacks, our proposed scheme uses combined hash functions to protect the data in case of database exposure, making the raw data extraction very difficult.

In terms of storage requirements, in our proposed scheme, each user node is required to store $(ID_i, OTT_i, g, e, N, h, \Delta T, E_P, F_P)$. We have used SHA3-512 as hash function and the output of SHA3 512 is 512 bits. By applying these settings, we have obtained $|ID_i| = |OTT_i| = 512$ bits while $|F_p|$ was assumed to be 256 bits for security purpose. The E_P indicates with standard elliptic curve we are using and can be stored as an Enum (i.e., 8 bits). The g is the starting point of the elliptic curve so an integer variable (i.e., 32 bits) can be used for storing it. Also, ΔT is saved as a 32 bits integer value. On the other hand, we need to store $(p, q, r1, r2)$ as server RSA private key, (E_P, F_P) as EC parameters along with (ID_i, OTT_i, B_i) for each user. The size of B_i is dependent on the type of biometric factor impression, which in our implementation was assumed to be a compressed image of the user's face for face recognition purpose. Hence, B_i can be stored in $|B_i|$ bits. Hence, the total storage required by each user node U_i is $(1384 + |e| + |N|)$ bits, and the total storage required by the server is $(n \times (1024 + |B_i|)) + |(p, q, r1, r2)| + 72$, where n is the number of registered users.

In terms of communication overhead, in the authentication transmissions, the user sends $U_i \rightarrow server : \langle OTT_i, C_1 \rangle$ in the first step, where OTT_i is 512 bits and C_1 includes the EC public parameter of the user, the timestamp T and tsk_i, so C_1 is $256 + 32 + 256$ bits length. The user also sends $U_i \rightarrow server : \langle C_3 \rangle$ in the Step 3, where C_3 includes $\{P_3, B_i^*, T\}$ and P_3 is the output of the hash function (SHA3-512) i.e. 512 bits long; and B_i^* is the biometric impression of the attempting user. On the other hand, the server needs to send $server \rightarrow U_i : \langle C_2 \rangle$ where C_2 is the symmetrically encrypted message containing the 512-bit new one-time token, the 32-bit timestamp, the 256-bit EC public parameter of the server, and P_2 the output of the hash function (SHA3-512) which is 512 bits long. The overall server-to-user communication overload is therefore equal to $(256 + 512 + 512 + 32)$.

5 Informal Security Analysis

5.1 Confidentiality

In the proposed EC-B-ASH-S scheme, all the messages are encrypted either by RSA or a symmetric key except for OTT_i, which is a one-time token updated upon each authentication completion. This value is only used for initiating the user-server communication so that the server could identify the user. Sending OTT_i without encryption enables the server to distinguish DOS vs. DDOS attacks before decrypting any messages, which make the procedure faster and ensures the availability of the server. Even if the attacker somehow gains access to tsk_i which is not stored in the database in anyway, it is not possible to extract the session key since in order to access the session key, either a_i or b_i is needed. Hence p_{ec} is a prime number and based on the on elliptic curve discrete logarithm [18], retrieving b_i from $b_i g \ mod(p_{ec})$ is a NP-hard (non-deterministic polynomial-time) problem.

5.2 Masquerade Attack

In the proposed EC-B-ASH-S scheme, the user is safe from any attempts of a masquerade attack since there are no parameters sent in a plaintext format other than the OTT_i, which gets regenerated with each session. Even when the attacker gains access to the token, there is no way for he/she to masquerade the user's biometric impression and the password. Hence, in order for the attacker to gain access to the session key with which the user-server communication is encrypted with, he/she requires access to the server's private key as well as one of the session independent random exponents chosen by the server or the user.

5.3 Replay Attack

In the proposed scheme, not only each session has a new key, but also all the messages include a timestamp T which are valid for a short amount of time and are never sent in a plaintext format.

5.4 Denial of Service (DoS) and Distributed Denial of Service (DDoS) Attacks

Upon receipt of an authentication request, the server only needs to validate OTT_i to distinguish a valid request from an attack. Even if the attacker has access to a valid OTT_i, the server can easily identify the particular user, then set short-term firewall rules to ignore the requests from that user and temporary ban the user's access.

5.5 Perfect Forward Secrecy

As described earlier, the proposed EC-B-ASH-S scheme uses a fresh key for each session. (b_i, a_i) which are the secret parameters of the key exchange algorithm, will never be saved, therefore even if the private key of the server is compromised, the session keys will not be exposed since the attacker cannot obtain a session key unless he/she has access to either b_i or a_i of that session.

5.6 Man-in-the-Middle (MITM) Attack

In the proposed EC-B-ASH-S scheme, the initial authentication message contains a challenge that would be validated by the user-side application to authenticate the server. This initial message is encrypted with the server's RSA public key, it can only be decrypted by the server. This feature of the scheme makes impossible the access to the challenge unless the attacker has access to the server's RSA private key.

5.7 Password Guessing Attack

In the proposed scheme, to perform password guessing attack, the attacker needs to decrypt the last authentication message, which is infeasible considering the encryption of the message. Even if the attacker gets access to the private key as well as the database and successfully decrypts it, because of the fact that $h(h(PW_i), ID_i)$ was saved in the database, he/she cannot get access to the $h(PW_i)$ in a reasonable amount of time. Indeed, using ID_i as a Salt in password hashing enables us to prevent the rainbow attack. Even if the attacker in some way gets access to the password, he/she requires the user's biometric impression and his/her smartphone to get authenticated from the server.

5.8 Device Loss Attack

In case of user's device loss, the attacker must break through the smartphone's operating system to get the user's ID_i but by knowing only ID_i, he/she is not able to get authenticated, because the authentication procedure requires the user's password along with his/her biometric impression, which are never saved on the device.

6 Proof-of-Concept

To implement the proof of concept of the proposed scheme we used Apple iPhone 7 Plus smartphone on the client-side with iOS 12.4, running as operating system which has Quad-core ($2\times$ Hurricane $+ 2\times$ Zephyr) CPU with 1.64 GHz frequency. The smartphone is equipped with a front-facing camera which enabled us to implement face recognition as the biometric authentication factor of our proposed scheme. The user-side application was implemented using Swift 4 [19], a native language for iOS application development. On the server-side we used a shared host with CloudLinux 6.x [20] as running operating system, which has Dual Intel(R) Xeon(R) CPU E5-2660 v4 with 2.00 GHz frequency. Considering that the server is running over a shared host, all the resources such as CPU and RAM are not completely available. The server-side implementation is over PHP [21] version 7.2, MySQL 10.1.41-MariaDB-cll-lve [22] and for the face recognition functionality, we used FaceX API [23].

In both client and server-sides, the RSA encryption was implemented for a key length of 2048 bits using OpenSSL Lib v.1.1.1 [24] and to implement the symmetric encryption, we used AES-256-GCM [25]. For security purposes, each session independently relies on security of AES-256-GCM. It should be emphasized that even with Frontier [26], the most powerful and fastest supercomputer in the world, which is going to be operational in 2021, it will take millions of years to crack the 256-bit AES encryption. Also, for the Elliptic Curve Diffie Hellman key exchange algorithm, 256 bits long prime number p_{ec} has been considered.

The proof-of-concept implementation consists of two phases: Registration phase and Login and authentication phase as described in the sequel.

6.1 Registration Phase

The proof of concept is implemented on Apple iOS platform. The biometric factor in the implemented proof of concept is face recognition using a two-dimensional picture due to the fact that the current smartphone operating systems do not provide raw access to the device biometric authentication technologies such as fingerprints or depth-powered face capturing. The iOS supported devices have high-resolution front cameras which result in higher face recognition accuracy. The face recognition process is used both in registration and authentication phases. The user captures a picture using the front camera of his/her devices, the client-side application then detects and crops the face in the picture using the iOS Core APIs [19], for efficiency purposes. The user then chooses a secure password as the "what you know" factor. The cropped picture is then encoded into a Base64 format [27], for simplicity, and then sent and saved to the server along with the SHA3-512 [28] hash of the chosen password. Upon receipt, the server generates two 512-bits long unique random values, one of which is ID_i, and the other one is OTT_i. The server then generates the SHA3-512 hash of ID_i combined with the received hashed-value of the user password. The generated value, OTT_i and the Base64 formatted user face image are then stored into the server's database. The server returns the user ID_i, as well as the one-time token to the client application. All the incoming and outgoing data in the registration process is assumed to be sent over a secure channel. It should be noted that the raw value of the password is never saved in the client nor the server side. The user ID_i, i.e. "what you have" factor is also only stored in the device's operating system secure storage unit. The steps of this phase are shown as below in Fig. 2.

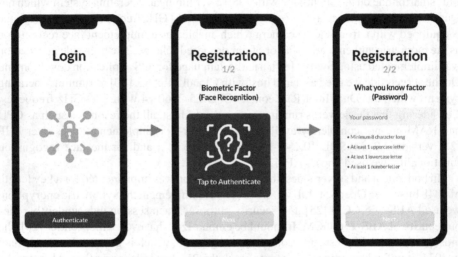

Fig. 2. Proof of concept registration process.

6.2 Login and Authentication Phase

If the user has registered and the ID_i is stored on the device, the user must be authenticated using his/her biometric impression as well as the selected password. The steps are as illustrated in Fig. 3.

After the key exchange is completed, the client side and server-side have both agree on the same fresh session key, the authentication can proceed. The user application takes the face image, the inputted password and ID_i to create an encrypted authentication request using the session key and then sends the resulting request to the side. If either the biometric impression or the password does not match with the stored record from the server's database, the server declines the authentication request and the client-side application will transfer the user to the previous screen.

Once the user authenticates him/her identity using the authentication process, himself/herself can have access to the Home page and the Settings page in which he/she is able to change his/her password and/or biometric impression. The user also able to destroy the current session, turn the debug mode on or off. It should be noted that the

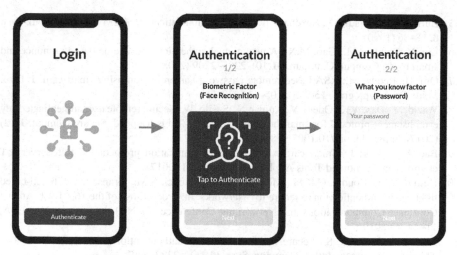

Fig. 2. Proof of concept login and authentication process.

debug mode enables the user to view all the outgoing and incoming packages, the agreed session key, and the secret random parameters, for demonstration purpose.

7 Conclusion

We have proposed a new EC-biometric based authentication scheme for smart-homes using smartphone (called EC-B-ASH-S). Its formal analysis using the BAN Logic is provided, showing that the proposed scheme achieves the perfect forward secrecy by utilizing a fresh encryption key for each session. As future work, one can redesign the initialization step of the proposed scheme in such a way as to strengthen its computational efficiency. One can also include in this design a new authentication layer meant to detect anomalies based on the behavioral patterns of the users. Considering the direction of the technologies in this sector and the progress in machine learning areas, the future of behavioral pattern recognition is promising, especially in the IoT world.

References

1. Miraz, M.H., Ali, M., Excell, P.S., Picking, R.: A review on Internet of Things (IoT), Internet of Everything (IoE) and Internet of Nano Things (IoNT). In: Proceedings of IEEE Internet Technologies and Applications (ITA). Glyndwr University, Wrexham, North East Wales, UK (2015)
2. Stobert, E., Biddle, R.: Workshop on Home Usable Privacy and Security (HUPS). Workshop on Home Usable Privacy and Security (HUPS), 24 July 2013. http://cups.cs.cmu.edu/soups/2013/HUPS/HUPS13-ElizabethStobert.pdf. Accessed on 8 July 2019
3. Raniyal, M.S., Woungang, I., Dhurandher, S.K.: An RSA-Biometric Based User Authentication Scheme for Smart Homes using Smartphone. Toronto (2019)
4. Raniyal, M.S., Woungang, I., Dhurandher, K.: An RSA-Based User Authentication Scheme for Smart-Homes Using Smart Card. Ryerson University, Toronto, Ontario (2018)

5. Burrows, M., Abadi, M., Needham, R.: A logic of authentication. ACM Trans. Comput. Syst. **8**, 18–36 (1990)
6. Liu, Y., Zhou, A.M., Gao, M.X.: A new mutual authentication scheme based on nonce and smart cards. Comput. Commun. **31**(10), 2205–2209 (2008)
7. Om, H., Reddy, M.: RSA based remote password authentication using smart card. J. Disc. Math. Sci. Cryptograp. **15**(2–3), 105–111 (2012)
8. Wazid, M., Das, A.K., Odelu, V., Kumar, N., Susilo, W.: Secure remote user authenticated key establishment protocol for smart home environment. Trans. Depend. Secure Comput. **17**(2) (2017). https://doi.org/10.1007/978-3-030-03712-3_2
9. Bae, W., Kwak, J.: Smart card-based secure authentication protocol in multi-server IoT environment. Multimed Tools Appl. **79**, 15793–15811 (2017)
10. Dammak, M., Boudia, O.R.M., Messous, M.A., Senouci, S.M., Gransart, C.: Token-based lightweight authentication to secure IoT Networks. In: Proceedings of the 16th IEEE Annual Consumer Communications and Networking Conference (CCNC), Las Vegas, NV, USA, 11–14 Jan 2019
11. Dhillon, P.K., Kalra, S.: Secure multi- remote user authentication scheme for Internet of Things environments. Intl. J. Commun. Syst. **30**(16), e3323 2017
12. Yang, W.H., Shieh, S.P.: Password authentication schemes with smart cards. Comput. Secur. **18**, 727–733 (1999)
13. Fan, L., Li, J.H., Zhu, H.W.: An enhancement of timestamp based password authentication scheme. Comput. Secur. **21**, 665–667 (2002)
14. Yang, C.C., Wang, R.C., Chang, T.Y.: An improvement of the Yang-Shieh password authentication schemes. Appl. Math. Comput. **162**, 1391–1396 (2005)
15. Om, H., Kumari, S.: Comment and modification of RSA based remote password authentication using smart card. J. Disc. Math. Sci. Cryptograp. **20**(3), 625–635 (2017)
16. Shen, J.J., Lin, C.W., Hwang, M.S.: Security enhancement for the timestamp-based password authentication scheme using smart cards. Comput. Secur. **7**(22), 591–595 (2003)
17. Chien, H.Y., Jan, J.K., Tseng, Y.M.: An efficient and practical solution to remote authentication: smart card. Comput. Secur. **21**(4), 372–375 (2002)
18. Silverman, J.H., Suzuki, J.: Elliptic curve discrete logarithms and the index calculus In: Dingyi Pei, K.O. (ed.) Advances in Cryptology—ASIACRYPT'98. Lecture Notes in Computer Science, pp. 110–125. Springer, Berlin (1998). https://doi.org/10.1007/3-540-49649-1_10
19. Swift: Apple Inc. https://swift.org. Accessed on Sept 2019
20. CloudLinux, Inc.: CloudLinux OS CloudLinux, Inc. (2010). https://www.cloudlinux.com. Accessed on 8 2019
21. The PHP Group: PHP, The PHP Group. https://www.php.net
22. MariaDB Foundation: MariaDB Foundation. https://mariadb.org. Accessed on Sept 2019
23. FaceX : Face Recognition APIs, FaceX (2018). https://facex.io. Accessed on 8 Sept 2019
24. OpenSSL Software Foundation: OpenSSL Software Foundation. https://www.openssl.org. Accessed on 8 Sept 2019
25. Dworkin, M.J., et al.: Advanced Encryption Standard (AES), Federal Information Processing Standards Publication, 26 Nov 2001
26. Oak Ridge National Laboratory (2018). https://www.olcf.ornl.gov/2018/02/13/frontier-olcfs-exascale-future/. Accessed on Sept 2019
27. Muła, W., Lemire, D.: Faster Base64 encoding and decoding using AVX2 instructions. ACM Trans. Web (TWEB) **12**(3), 1–26 (2018)
28. Dworkin, M.J.: SHA-3 Standard: Permutation-Based Hash and Extendable-Output Functions, p. 202. Federal Information Processing Standards Publication (2015)

Efficient Subchannel and Power Allocation in Multi-cell Indoor VLC Systems

Sylvester Aboagye$^{(\boxtimes)}$ ⓘ, Telex Magloire N. Ngatchedⓘ, and Octavia A. Dobreⓘ

Memorial University of Newfoundland, St. John's, NL A1C 5S7, Canada
{sbaboagye,odobre}@mun.ca, tngatched@grenfell.mun.ca

Abstract. Visible light communication (VLC) is seen as a promising technology to improve the performance of indoor communication systems. However, the issues of inter-cell interference (ICI) and blockage effects are seen as crucial problems that could result in performance deterioration for VLC systems. This paper investigates the joint subchannel allocation (SA) and power allocation (PA) optimization problem to overcome ICI and blockage effects in the downlink of an orthogonal frequency-division multiple access based multi-cell VLC system. This is a non-convex problem, and no efficient algorithm exists to obtain the globally optimal solution. To obtain an efficient solution, the original problem is first separated into the SA and PA problems. A simple yet efficient SA procedure based on the quality of the channel conditions is proposed. Then, the quadratic transform approach is exploited to develop a PA algorithm. Finally, simulation results are used to demonstrate the effectiveness of the proposed solution in terms of its fast convergence and overall performance.

Keywords: Subchannel allocation · Power allocation · Inter-cell interference · Visible light communication · Quadratic transform

1 Introduction

The last decade has witnessed a continuous emergence of high data rate services and bandwidth-hungry applications. This has contributed to the massive growth in the demand for higher capacity cellular networks. At the same time, the radio frequency (RF) spectrum for cellular communications has become oversaturated, requiring network operators to find alternatives to meet this data demand. Visible light communication (VLC) has attracted extensive research interest as a key enabling technology for the next generation of wireless communication networks due to the vast and unregulated bandwidth in the visible light spectrum

This work was supported by the Natural Science and Engineering Research Council of Canada (NSERC) through its Discovery Program, and the Memorial University VPR Program.

T. M. N. Ngatched and I. Woungang (Eds.): PAAISS 2021, LNICST 405, pp. 237–247, 2022.
https://doi.org/10.1007/978-3-030-93314-2_15

[1]. Recent studies have investigated the resource allocation problem with various objectives for VLC systems. In [2], a spectral efficiency (SE) optimization problem was considered for a time division multiple access (TDMA)-based VLC system. In [3], the energy efficiency (EE) and SE performances of a three-tier heterogeneous network (HetNet), consisting of a macro base station (BS), multiple pico BSs, and many indoor VLC access points (APs), were investigated. The joint problem of AP assignment and power allocation (PA) for a hybrid RF/VLC HetNet was studied in [4]. The issue of subchannel allocation (SA) and PA for an orthogonal frequency division multiple access (OFDMA) based RF/VLC HetNet was explored in [5,6]. The PA problem to maximize the EE was studied for an aggregated RF/VLC system in [7].

The above-mentioned works (i.e.,[2–4,6,7]) focused on multi-user VLC systems with one light-emitting diode (LED) array (i.e., single-cell VLC system). However, a single light source is typically not able to provide sufficient illumination in large indoor environments (e.g., conference rooms), and as a consequence, has limited coverage capability. Moreover, VLC relies heavily on line-of-sight (LoS) communication links as the non-LoS (i.e., reflected) signals are usually much weaker than the LoS signals and thus can be neglected. In single-cell indoor VLC systems, blocking effects resulting from the LoS light paths encountering obstructions will compromise the performance of the VLC system. Note that multiple LED arrays, with overlapping illumination regions, are typically deployed in indoor environments to guarantee uniform illumination and overcome blockage effects. As a result, a multi-cell structure is naturally obtained in VLC systems. Although [5] considered a multi-cell VLC system, the authors assumed that the multiple LED arrays (i.e., APs) transmit the same signal simultaneously. Consequently, the proposed approaches in [2–7] are not appropriate for indoor environments with the multi-cell structure, where any resulting interference needs to be considered and mitigated.

Few research works have considered resource allocation problems for multi-cell VLC systems [8–11]. A fuzzy-logic based AP assignment scheme was proposed in [8] for a hybrid light-fidelity (LiFi) and wireless-fidelity network. In [9,10], the optimization problem of AP assignment and time slot resource allocation was proposed for a TDMA-based hybrid RF/Li-Fi indoor network. In [11], a multi-user VLC system based on OFDMA, where a multi-cell structure is used to support a high density of users, was investigated. In multi-cell VLC systems, users residing in different cells may experience inter-cell interference (ICI) since the same subchannel sets are typically reused across the cells. This can have a significant impact on the achievable data rate of users in the VLC system. To the best of the authors' knowledge, the joint optimization of PA and SA for an OFDMA-based indoor VLC system has not appeared in many studies. This paper investigates this resource allocation problem for multi-cell indoor VLC systems bringing the following major contributions:

- We consider the downlink of a multi user multi-cell OFDMA-based indoor VLC system and investigate the SA and PA optimization problem to maximize the sum-rate.
- The initial joint problem is a combinatorial optimization problem. Hence, we optimize the SA and PA problems separately to reduce the overall computational complexity. The separate SA and PA optimization problems are both non-convex.
- A simple yet efficient algorithm that assigns subchannels to users according to the quality of the channel condition is first proposed. Given the SA solution, the quadratic transform approach is exploited to recast the original non-convex PA problem into a series of convex problems that can be efficiently solved in an iterative manner to obtain at least a stationary point.
- We demonstrate that the proposed SA and PA solution outperforms the considered benchmark scheme and evaluate the impact of varying key system parameters such as the transmit power on the performance of the proposed scheme.

The rest of the paper is organized as follows. Section 2 discusses the system and channel models. Section 3 formulates the optimization problem and Sect. 4 details the proposed solution approach. Simulation results are presented in Sect. 5, followed by conclusion in Sect. 6.

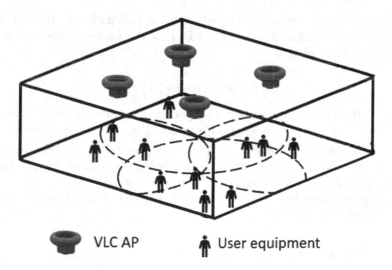

Fig. 1. Multi-user indoor VLC system consisting of multiple APs with overlapping coverage areas.

2 System Model

2.1 VLC Network

An indoor VLC system that consists of multiple APs and serves many user devices equipped with photodetectors (PD) is considered. As shown in Fig. 1, each AP is composed of five LED arrays and its coverage area (i.e., cell) is defined by the illumination region of the LED arrays of that AP. To better serve the users, the illumination regions of the APs are overlapping. The number of APs and users in the indoor environment are represented by the sets $\mathcal{A} = \{1, 2, \ldots, a, \ldots, |\mathcal{A}|\}$ and $\mathcal{U} = \{1, 2, \ldots, u, \ldots, |\mathcal{U}|\}$, respectively. Any AP a in the VLC system is assigned a predefined number of OFDMA subchannels which is represented by the set $\mathcal{S}_a = \{1, 2, \ldots, s, \ldots, |\mathcal{S}_a|\}$. Any user u can be served by a single AP according to the strongest channel gain rule. All the APs in the indoor environment are connected to a central control unit via backhual links.

2.2 VLC Channel Model

By focusing on the LoS paths, the channel gain between AP a and user u on the subchannel s is given by [5]

$$G_{s,u}^a = \rho_{u,s} \frac{A_{\text{PD}}(m+1)}{2\pi d_{a,u}^2} \cos^m(\Phi_{a,u}) T(\Psi_{a,u}) G(\Psi_{a,u}) \cos(\Psi_{a,u}), \tag{1}$$

where $\rho_{u,s}$ indicates the probability of having a LoS path on subchannel s for user u, A_{PD} is the physical area of the PD, m is the Lambertian emission order which can be calculated as

$$m = -\log_2\left(\cos\left(\phi_{\frac{1}{2}}\right)\right)^{-1}, \tag{2}$$

with $\phi_{\frac{1}{2}}$ as the LED's semi-angle at half power, $d_{a,u}$ is the distance between the AP a and user u, $\Phi_{a,u}$ is the angle of irradiance, $\Psi_{a,u}$ is the angle of incidence, $T(\Psi_{a,u})$ is the optical filter gain, $G(\Psi_{a,u}) = \frac{f^2}{\sin^2 \Psi_{\text{FoV}}}, 0 \leq \Psi_{a,u} \leq \Psi_{\text{FoV}}$, is the gain of the non-imaging concentrator, with f being the ratio of the speed of light in vacuum to the velocity of light in the optical material.

The signal-to-interference-plus-noise ratio (SINR) of user u on subchannel s of AP a is given as

$$\text{SINR}_{s,u}^a = \frac{p_{s,u}^a \left(R_{\text{PD}} G_{s,u}^a\right)^2}{\sum\limits_{u' \neq u} \left(\sum\limits_{a' \neq a} p_{s,u'}^{a'} \left(R_{\text{PD}} G_{s,u'}^{a'}\right)^2\right) + \sigma^2}, \tag{3}$$

where $p_{s,u}^a \left(R_{\text{PD}} G_{s,u}^a\right)^2$ is the total electrical power received by the PD of user u on subchannel s from the AP a with $p_{s,u}^a$ being the electrical transmit power on subchannel s of AP a for user u, a is the serving AP and a' denotes other APs that reuse the subchannel s, R_{PD} is the responsivity of the PD, u' represents users other than user u that employ subchannel s, a' denotes other APs reusing subchannel s, and σ^2 is the electrical additive white Gaussian noise power. The corresponding achievable data rate for user u on subchannel s of AP a can be computed by [12].

$$R_{u,s}^a = \rho_{u,s} B \log_2 \left(1 + \frac{\exp(1)}{2\pi} \mathrm{SINR}_{s,u}^a \right), \tag{4}$$

where B is the bandwidth of a subchannel.

3 Sum-Rate Optimization

The joint optimization of PA and SA to maximize the sum-rate for the considered indoor multi-cell VLC system is formulated as follows:

$$\max_{\mathbf{x},\mathbf{p}} \sum_{a \in \mathcal{A}} \sum_{u \in \mathcal{U}} \sum_{s \in \mathcal{S}_a} R_{u,s}^a$$

s.t.

$$
\begin{aligned}
&C1: \sum_{s \in \mathcal{S}_a} R_{u,s}^a \geq R_{\min}, \forall u \in \mathcal{U} \\
&C2: p_{s,u}^a \leq x_{s,u}^a P_a^{\max}, \forall u \in \mathcal{U}, \forall s \in \mathcal{S}_a, \forall a \in \mathcal{A}, \\
&C3: \sum_{u \in \mathcal{U}} \sum_{s \in \mathcal{S}_a} p_{s,u}^a \leq P_a^{\max}, \forall a \in \mathcal{A} \\
&C4: \sum_{u \in \mathcal{U}} x_{s,u}^a \leq 1, \forall s \in \mathcal{S}_a, \forall a \in \mathcal{A} \\
&C5: x_{s,u}^a \in \{0,1\}, \forall u \in \mathcal{U}, \forall s \in \mathcal{S}_a \\
&C6: p_{s,u}^a \geq 0, \forall u \in \mathcal{U}, \forall s \in \mathcal{S}_a, \forall a \in \mathcal{A}
\end{aligned}
\tag{5}
$$

where $\mathbf{x}$ and $\mathbf{p}$ are the vectors of optimization variables for SA and PA, respectively, and $R_{\min}$ is the required minimum rate. The physical interpretation of the sets of constraints for the optimization problem in (5) is as follows. $C1$ is the quality-of-service (QoS) requirement. $C2$ limits the transmit power on any subchannel to the available maximum power $P_v^{\max}$ of any AP v. $C3$ represents the power budgets for the APs. $C4$ ensures each subchannel of any AP is allocated to at most one user. $C5$ denotes the fact that the SA variables are binary and $C6$ indicates that the PA variables are non-negative.

4 Proposed Sum-Rate Optimization Solution

The optimization problem in (5) is NP-hard due to the presence of both binary variables $\mathbf{x}$ and continuous variables $\mathbf{p}$. It is challenging to obtain the globally optimal solution within polynomial time. To find a tractable solution, problem (5) is decomposed into two separate problems (i.e., SA problem under fixed PA and PA problem under fixed SA). The SA problem is solved by allocating subchannels to users according to the quality of the channel condition. For a given SA, the quadratic transform approach is exploited to solve the PA problem to obtain at least a stationary point solution. Note that this solution method is a centralized scheme, where all computations and decisions are made by a central control unit. The control unit then broadcasts the solution to the joint problem to all the APs via backhaul links dedicated for control signals. The VLC APs and the control unit require a complete knowledge of the downlink channel state information and it is assumed that this information can be reliably obtained.

4.1   Subchannel Allocation (SA) Procedure

The SA subproblem is solved for a given PA. Note that the equal PA (EPA) policy, for which each AP equally shares the total available power to all of its subchannels, can be employed at this stage. The main idea of the SA procedure is that each subchannel of an AP should be allocated to the user with the highest power gain. This idea can be mathematically expressed as

$$x_{s^*,u^*}^a = \begin{cases} 1, & (s^*, u^*) = \arg\max_{s,u} G_{s,u}^a \\ 0, & \text{otherwise.} \end{cases} \tag{6}$$

Although this SA procedure can lead to instances whereby not every user is assigned subchannel(s) because of the channel condition experienced on all the available subchannels, this is beneficial to the network performance as resources are only allocated to users such that the network performance is maximized. Allocating resources to users with bad channels will lead to their inefficient usage. The admission control scheme will deny such users access to the network, and they can try again later.

4.2   Power Allocation (PA) by the Quadratic Transform Approach

Given the solution to the SA optimization problem, the PA optimization problem can be formulated as

$$\max_{\mathbf{P}} \sum_{a \in \mathcal{A}} \sum_{u \in \mathcal{U}} \sum_{s \in \mathcal{S}_a} R_{u,s}^a$$

s.t.

$$C1 : \sum_{s \in \mathcal{S}_a} R_{u,s}^a \geq R_{\min}, \forall u \in \mathcal{U}$$

$$C2 : p_{s,u}^a \leq x_{s,u}^a P_a^{\max}, \forall u \in \mathcal{U}, \forall s \in \mathcal{S}_a, \forall a \in \mathcal{A}, \tag{7}$$

$$C3 : \sum_{u \in \mathcal{U}} \sum_{s \in \mathcal{S}_a} p_{s,u}^a \leq P_a^{\max}, \forall a \in \mathcal{A}$$

$$C6 : p_{s,u}^a \geq 0, \forall u \in \mathcal{U}, \forall s \in \mathcal{S}_a, \forall a \in \mathcal{A}.$$

The problem in (7) is still a non-convex optimization problem due to the SINR term in the objective function and the constraint set $C1$. The quadratic transform approach, introduced in [13] for solving fractional programming problems, is exploited to transform the non-convex problem in (7) into series of convex optimization problems.

In order to solve (7) using the quadratic transform approach, the auxiliary variable $\boldsymbol{\lambda}$ is first introduced. Then, according to this approach, each SINR in (7) can be replaced by the quadratic term

$$\mathrm{SINR}_{s,u}^{a^*} = 2\lambda_{s,u}\sqrt{p_{s,u}^a \left(R_{\mathrm{PD}}G_{s,u}^a\right)^2} - \lambda_{s,u}^2 \left(\sum_{u'\neq u}\left(\sum_{a'\neq a} p_{s,u'}^{a'}\left(R_{\mathrm{PD}}G_{s,u'}^{a'}\right)^2 \right) + \sigma^2 \right),$$

$$(8)$$

and the corresponding achievable data rate for user u on subchannel s of AP a can be computed by

$$R_{u,s}^{a^*} = \rho_{u,s}B\log_2\left(1 + \frac{\exp(1)}{2\pi}\mathrm{SINR}_{s,u}^{a^*}\right). \qquad (9)$$

An equivalent optimization problem for (7) can be expressed as

$$\max_{\mathbf{p},\boldsymbol{\lambda}} \sum_{a\in\mathcal{A}}\sum_{u\in\mathcal{U}}\sum_{s\in\mathcal{S}_a} R_{u,s}^{a^*}$$

s.t.

$$C1: \sum_{s\in\mathcal{S}_a} R_{u,s}^{a^*} \geq R_{\min}, \forall u\in\mathcal{U} \qquad (10)$$

$$C2,\ C3,\ \text{and}\ C6,$$

where $\lambda_{s,u}$ is an auxiliary variable introduced by the application of the quadratic transform to the SINR of each user and subchannel. The proof of the equivalence of (7) and (10) can be obtained by following the approach in [13]. Problem (10) is non-convex when $\boldsymbol{\lambda}$ and $\mathbf{p}$ are jointly considered. However, for a fixed $\boldsymbol{\lambda}$, the optimization problem in (10) becomes convex and can be solved to obtain the optimal solution. For a fixed $p_{s,u}^a$, the optimal $\lambda_{s,u}$ can be obtained by setting $\partial\mathrm{SINR}_{s,u}^*/\partial\lambda_{s,u}$ to zero, and is given by

$$\lambda_{s,u}^* = \frac{\sqrt{p_{s,u}^a\left(R_{\mathrm{PD}}G_{s,u}^a\right)^2}}{\sum_{u'\neq u}\left(\sum_{a'\neq a} p_{s,u'}^{a'}\left(R_{\mathrm{PD}}G_{s,u'}^{a'}\right)^2 \right) + \sigma^2}. \qquad (11)$$

Then, the optimal $\mathbf{p}$ for fixed $\boldsymbol{\lambda}$ can be found by solving the resulting convex problem in (10). The variables $\boldsymbol{\lambda}$ and $\mathbf{p}$ are optimized iteratively. This PA method is summarized in Algorithm 1.

Algorithm 1. The PA algorithm.

---

1. $\mathbf{p}$ is initialized to any feasible value;
while *no convergence* **do**
   2. Update the auxiliary variable $\boldsymbol{\lambda}$ according (11);
   3. Update $\mathbf{p}$ by solving (10) for the given $\boldsymbol{\lambda}$.
end while

Table 1. Simulation parameters.

Parameter	Value
Maximum transmit power per AP, $P_a^{\max}$	4 W
Height of VLC APs	2.5 m
Noise power spectral density, σ^2	10^{-21} A^2/Hz
Photodetector responsivity, R_{PD}	0.53 A/W
LED semi-angle at half-power, $\phi_{\frac{1}{2}}$	60°
Gain of the optical filter, T	1
Refractive index, f	1.5
FOV of a photodetector, Ψ_{fov}	70°
Physical area of the photodetector, A_{PD}	$1\,cm^2$

5   Simulation Results and Discussions

In this section, the performance of the proposed SA and PA solution method is investigated for the system model in Fig. 1. A practical room dimension of $15 \times 15 \times 3$ m^3 with 4×4 uniformly distributed APs is considered. The users are randomly distributed in the indoor environment according to a uniform distribution. Each user device is fitted with a PD and an assumption is made that it is vertically facing upwards. Each AP has been allocated 25 subchannels and this same set of subchannels is reused by all the APs. A system bandwidth of 1 GHz is used. The QoS requirement is set as 50 Mbps. Unless otherwise noted, the related parameters used to obtain the results are summarized in Table 1. For comparison purposes, EPA is considered as a benchmark scheme.

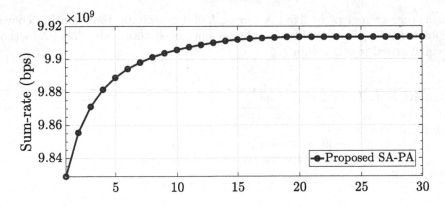

Fig. 2. Sum-rate versus number of iterations.

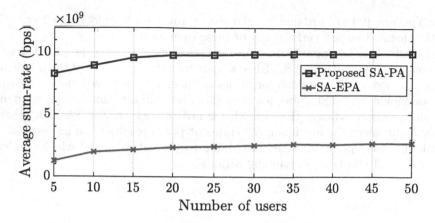

Fig. 3. Average sum-rate versus different number of users.

Figure 2 depicts the convergence rate of the proposed SA-PA solution for a total of 40 users. It can be observed from this figure that the proposed solution has reached convergence after iteration number 19. Hence, it has a fast convergence rate and is suitable for practical implementation.

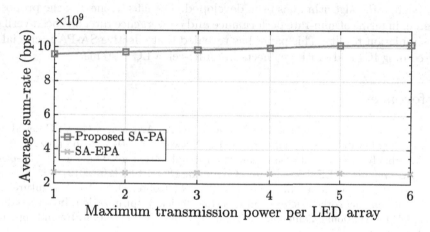

Fig. 4. Average sum-rate versus maximum transmitting power.

Figure 3 illustrates the sum-rate performance of the proposed SA-PA solution and the SA-EPA benchmark scheme for different number of users. It can be observed that the sum-rate performances for both schemes increase with increasing number of users. The reason is that with more users, each subchannel has more candidates to choose from. Hence, the subchannel resources are efficiently utilized. The proposed scheme achieves superior sum-rate performance (i.e., a gain of around 325%) than the SA-EPA, highlighting the importance of performing PA in VLC systems. This is because the proposed PA algorithm effectively manages any ICI at overlapping regions and any resulting blocking effects. The EPA scheme does not perform any of these operations.

Finally, Fig. 4 compares the sum-rate performance of the proposed SA-PA scheme and the benchmark SA-EPA scheme for different values of the maximum transmit power. This is done for 40 users. It can be observed that increasing the maximum transmit power leads to an increase in the sum-rate performance for the proposed scheme. However, this is not the case for the SA-EPA scheme since augmenting the maximum AP transmit power results in an increase in the available power per subchannel (according to the EPA scheme) which can lead to higher ICI effects in overlapping regions.

6 Conclusion

In this paper, the downlink of a multi-user multi-cell OFDMA-based indoor VLC network was studied. The joint optimization problem of SA and PA to maximize the sum-rate while considering ICI and blockage effects has been formulated and an efficient solution has been proposed. In particular, the initial joint problem was separated into two subproblems to reduce the complexity of solving this mixed integer nonconvex problem. A SA solution based on the quality of the channel condition has been proposed. By exploiting the quadratic transform approach, a PA algorithm has been developed. The effectiveness of the proposed scheme, in terms of sum-rate performance and convergence rate, has been verified via simulation results. This paper has revealed that effective SA-PA is crucial in overcoming ICI and blockage effects in multi-cell VLC systems.

References

1. Ndjiongue, A.R., Ngatched, T.M.N., Dobre, O.A., Armada, A.G.: VLC-based networking: feasibility and challenges. IEEE Networks **34**(4), 158–165 (2020)
2. Abdelhady, A.M., et al.: Downlink resource allocation for dynamic TDMA-based VLC systems. IEEE Trans. Wirel. Commun. **18**(1), 108–120 (2019)
3. Aboagye, S., Ibrahim, A., Ngatched, T.M.N., Dobre, O.A.: VLC in future heterogeneous networks: energy- and spectral-efficiency optimization. In: Proceedings IEEE International Conference Communications (ICC), Dublin, Ireland, pp. 1–7, June 2020
4. Aboagye, S., Ngatched, T.M.N., Dobre, O.A., Ibrahim, A.: Joint access point assignment and power allocation in multi-tier hybrid RF/VLC HetNets. IEEE Trans. Wirel. Commun. **20**(10), 6329–6346 (2021, early access)
5. Zhang, H., Liu, N., Long, K., Cheng, J., Leung, V.C.M., Hanzo, L.: Energy efficient subchannel and power allocation for software-defined heterogeneous VLC and RF networks. IEEE J. Sel. Areas Commun. **36**(3), 658–670 (2018)
6. Kashef, M., et al.: Energy efficient resource allocation for mixed RF/VLC heterogeneous wireless networks. IEEE J. Sel. Areas Commun. **34**(4), 883–893 (2016)
7. Ma, S., Zhang, F., Li, H., Zhou, F., Alouini, M.-S., Li, S.: Aggregated VLC-RF systems: achievable rates, optimal power allocation, and energy efficiency. IEEE Trans. Wirel. Commun. **19**(11), 7265–7278 (2020)

8. Wu, X., Safari, M., Haas, H.: Access point selection for hybrid Li Fi and Wi-Fi networks. IEEE Trans. Commun. **65**(12), 5375–5385 (2017)
9. Wang, Y., Basnayaka, D.A., Wu, X., Haas, H.: Optimization of load balancing in hybrid LiFi/RF networks. IEEE Trans. Commun. **65**(4), 1708–1720 (2017)
10. Wang, Y., Wu, X., Haas, H.: Load balancing game with shadowing effect for indoor hybrid LiFi/RF networks. IEEE Trans. Wirel. Commun. **16**(4), 2366–2378 (2017)
11. Lian, J., Pearce, M.B.: Multiuser visible light communication systems using OFDMA. J. Lightw. Technol. **38**(21), 6015–6023 (2020)
12. Aboagye, S., Ngatched, T.M.N., Dobre, O.A., Armada, A.G.: Energy efficient sub-channel and power allocation in cooperative VLC systems. IEEE Commun. Lett. **25**(6), 1935–1939 (2021)
13. Shen, K., Yu, W.: Fractional programming for communication systems-Part I: power control and beamforming. IEEE Trans. Sig. Process. **66**(10), 2616–2630 (2018)

Autonomic IoT: Towards Smart System Components with Cognitive IoT

Justice Owusu Agyemang[1]([⊠]), Dantong Yu[2], and Jerry John Kponyo[1]

[1] Kwame Nkrumah University of Science and Technology, Kumasi, Ghana
jay@sperixlabs.org, jjkponyo@ieee.org
[2] New Jersey Institute of Technology, Newark, USA
dtyu@njit.edu

Abstract. The Internet of Things (IoT) describes physical objects or subsystems enhanced by sensors, actuators, transducers, softwares, communication interfaces, and data exchange mechanisms among peers over the Internet. It has emerged as a critical component of modern distributed systems. The concept of "things" has a broad definition that includes any physical object in the real world such as a lightbulb, a cellphone, a refrigerator, a desktop computer, a Nano device, and something as large as a supercomputer, or even a smart city. Self-awareness and machine intelligence are essential to cope with the increasing complexity of IoT and extend IoT to handle complex systems. Our paper introduces a novel concept of autonomous IoTs, referred to as the "Internet of Smart Things (IoST)" that incorporates autonomic computing functions and embedded Knowledge Engine (KE) for self-awareness and autonomy in responding to dynamic changes. The KE is an embedded computing element optimized for lightweight machine learning, fuzzy rule-based systems, and control functions to enable the IoST to perform intelligent functions, such as initiating or responding to machine-to-machine communications and performing autonomic functions (self-healing, self-optimization, and self-protection). This paper discusses the possibility of using a Software-Defined Framework (SDF) to separate the knowledge engine from the underlying physical IoT device which enables the knowledge subsystem and the physical device to evolve and scale independently.

Keywords: IoT · Smart-IoT · Autonomous · Self-aware · Machine learning

1 Introduction

Recently, an increasing number of sensors and measurement devices have been connected to existing and new infrastructures of today's data-intensive applications and sectors, such as agriculture, manufacturing, healthcare, etc. This technological advance acknowledges the transition towards 'smart' and 'smarter'

T. M. N. Ngatched and I. Woungang (Eds.): PAAISS 2021, LNICST 405, pp. 248–265, 2022.
https://doi.org/10.1007/978-3-030-93314-2_16

systems. The rapid growth of smart devices and high-speed communication networks has led to the emergence of the Network of Things (NoT) that generalizes the IoT and uses private or public networks to interconnect "things" and embedded devices with sensors. IoT is an instantiation of NoT; more specifically, IoT has its 'things' tethered to the Internet. The information sharing among the devices then takes place through the network with the standard protocols of communication. A different type of NoTs resides in a Local Area Network (LAN), with none of its 'things' connected to the Internet. The smart connected devices or 'things' range from simple wearable accessories to large machines, each containing sensor chips or micro-controllers [10]. The data collected through these devices may be processed in real-time to improve the entire system's efficiency.

The primitives of an IoT are 1) **Sensor**, 2) **Aggregator**, 3) **Communication channel**, 4) external utility (**eUtility**), and 5) **Decision Trigger**. Some commonly used IoTs might not contain all these components. Figure 1 shows that these IoTs only involve *sensing*, *computing*, *communication*, and *actuation*. This type of IoT follows a layered architecture comprising of three main layers: Perception layer that includes physical objects and sensing devices, Network layer for transmitting data between physical objects and the gateway/edge of the network, and Application layer that supports applications/services per user demand [5,14,17,24].

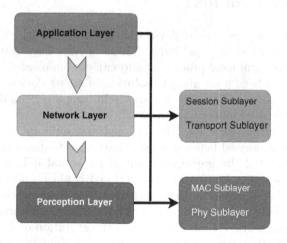

Fig. 1. Traditional IoT architecture model.

The myriad implementation of IoT extends the Internet connectivity among billions of devices. The connected devices produce a considerable amount of data, hence the need for intelligent control and management solutions. Many solutions have been confronted with solving existing issues in the current IoT paradigm. However, traditional networks cannot handle the enormous number of devices in the smart and connected world and associated data manipulation. Software-Defined Systems (SDS) is considered a revolutionary technology by separating the control system from its physical system and enable the flexible control plane to support heterogeneous systems with machine intelligence, rapid evolution, and dynamism.

The concept of SDS involves programmable planes (control and physical planes) [6,7,11,12,16,19,21,25]. The logical separation of the control and physical planes introduces flexibility and reconfigurability and enables the system to scale efficiently and adapt to various application needs. This paper adopts the SDS concept in designing the IoST, i.e., dividing the device-level architecture of IoT into two planes: the physical plane and the knowledge (control) plane. This division enables the knowledge plane of the device to evolve independently of the physical plane. This evolution will allow the devices to cater to various needs or implementations and acquire machine learning-assisted autonomy in their operations compared to current IoT devices that only operate on a fixed (modest) set of hardware resources and predefined instructions.

The research paper is organized as follows: Sect. 2 discusses the concept of IoST. Section 3 presents a detailed device-level architecture of an IoST device. It also describes the possible hardware implementations, communication network topologies, and technologies used in IoST. Section 4 presents possible case-studies where the proposed concept can be applied and Sect. 5 concludes the paper.

2   The Concept of IoST

The core of IoT comprises smart devices [2,18]; objects with moderate computation and communication capabilities. These devices have some data storage capability, can perform local processing and can communicate with other smart devices. There has been a significant evolution of smart devices over these past few years. This evolution is geared towards achieving a certain degree of *smartness* also termed as *social consciousness* [3].

Most IoT solutions were initially designed and built in isolation, resulting in limited and fragmented heterogeneous smart objects disconnected from each other. This prevented the implementation of an actual IoT ecosystem on top of which other systems (composite applications) could be developed. Through enabling technologies, smart objects were able to communicate with the external world by relying on web protocols and communication paradigms based on the current Internet of services. This marked the evolution of smart objects into smart devices. Furthermore, embedded software solutions and sensorial capabilities, made smart objects able to develop a spontaneous networking infrastructure based on the information to be disseminated other than information on the smart devices themselves. The future evolutionary step seeks to answer the question, are there new potentials that smart devices are still expected to manifest? Current research works seek to improve the intelligence of smart devices by leveraging enabling technologies such as artificial intelligence [23] to realize context-awareness and autonomy [20].

The architecture of the current IoT devices interleaves the control and physical planes, making its evolution in terms of intelligence and autonomy difficult.

Recently, machine learning and deep learning have gained successes in industrial automation and manufacturing analytics. These solutions are subject to the centralized paradigm where data is uploaded into the cloud for model development, training, and inference; consequently, model training and parameter tunings become roadblocks for online and real-time device control. On the other hand, lightweight machine learning software libraries and low-cost and energy-efficient hardware are available for real-time in-situ machine learning and inference. Figure 2 shows the idea of the IoST framework in comparison to the International Telecommunication Union (ITU) IoT reference framework and current SDN-Enabled IoT framework. The knowledge plane in the reference design of IoST is dynamic and evolves independently from underlying physical systems. The dynamism associated with the knowledge plane enables devices to perform tasks such as learning to control, communication, intelligence, security, maintenance, and optimization. We consider that each IoST device has computational and storage capability to support self-management without relying on external intelligent controllers. This paradigm enables IoT devices to realize machine intelligence (such as classic machine learning algorithms, deep learning, deep reinforcement learning) to perform autonomic or self-managed and event-driven operations.

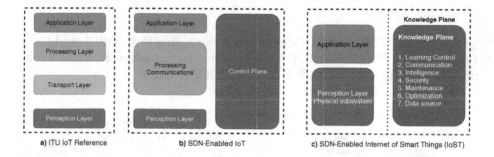

Fig. 2. The concept of IoST.

Our concept of IoST is focused on realizing self-management and autonomic capabilities. We discuss the device-level architectural components of IoST in Sect. 3.

3   Device-Level Architecture for IoST

Figure 3 shows the device-level architecture of an IoST device. It consists of two sections (modelled after the concept of SDS): 1) Physical/Mechanical Plane, and the 2) Knowledge Plane; shown in Fig. 3. The mechanical plane consists of sensors, actuators and transducers. The control plane consists of a micro-controller and the knowledge plane consists of a heterogeneous computing hardware/engine

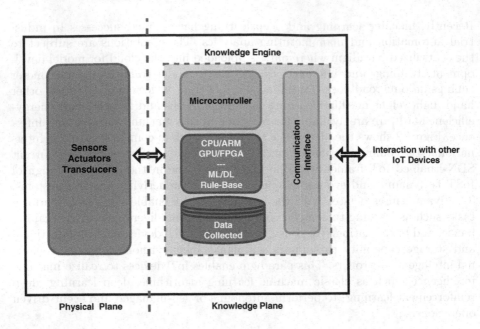

Fig. 3. Device-level architecture of IoST.

(Advanced RISC Machine (ARM), Graphics Processing Unit (GPU), and Field-Programmable Gate Array (FPGA)), an archive for dataset storage and a communication interface to other IoT devices; shown in Fig. 4.

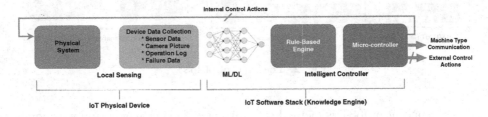

Fig. 4. Device-level architecture pipeline of IoST.

3.1 Physical/Mechanical Plane

The mechanical subsystem (consisting of sensors, actuators, and transducers) enables the IoST device to interface with other devices to perform event-driven tasks and other control functions. The generalized sensors are assumed to have the following characteristics: 1) They are connected to physical devices via wire, probe, data reader, writer, and signal detectors; some may have Internet access capability, 2) each sensor might have an identity or have the identity of the 'thing' to which they are attached, 3) some low-level passive sensor has little or no computing, software, and data analysis functionalities; more advanced sensors may have device drivers, software functionality and computer power, 4) They may be heterogeneous, come from different manufacturers, and collect data with varying levels of data integrity, 5) They may be associated with fixed geographic locations or mobile, 6) They acquire data via multiple modes, i.e., asynchronous, event-driven interruption, synchronous, manual input, command-driven or periodical sampling, and 7) The data are sent and received to/from multiple IoT devices via peer-to-peer communications.

3.2 Knowledge Plane

The knowledge plane consists of: 1) The Control System, 2) System Software, and 3) the Knowledge Engine. It enables the IoT to make decision to handle unfamiliar situations.

Control System. The control system consists of intelligent micro-controller hardware that includes: 1) the central Central Processing Unit (CPU) core with the arithmetic logic unit, the control unit, and the registers (stack pointer, program counter, accumulator register, and register files: 2) A Direct Memory Access (DMA) controller that handles data transfers between peripheral components and the main memory; and 3) Digital and Analog Input/Output (I/O) interfaces which are linked to the mechanical plane for data acquisition and actuating event-driven responses. The intelligent controller is responsible for the on-device processing of information and handling event-driven tasks/processes. It also implements a mechanical plane control function, acts as a coordinator, allocates computing/storage resources, and includes arbitrary southbound functions for servicing the physical plane. The control subsystem can also perform knowledge inference to achieve autonomy [8] through the use of knowledge-based logic systems realized with the combination of Machine/Deep Learning and fuzzy expert systems.

System Software for Knowledge Engine. The system software consists of application programs, device drivers, run-time libraries and kernels, compilers, and real-time operating systems. Each type of software performs an entirely different job, but all three work closely to perform defined controls and data collection tasks and implement high-level knowledge engine.

The software stack runs on heterogeneous embedded architectures with different accelerators, for example, GPU, multi-core CPU, FPGA. The software stack shown in Fig. 5 reflects the diversity of supportive hardware. The software stack consists two main components: a core layer and an over-the-top layer. The core layer consists of three sub-layers: Lightweight Machine Learning (ML) sub-layer, IoT engine, and the IoT hardware (HW) accelerators. An IoST device uses the HW accelerators and the ML libraries to infer and predict based on current states and export prediction results to generate rule-based decisions required to initiate control actions and perform relevant autonomic/event-driven tasks. The decision rules will be dynamically loaded into the microcontroller for device actuation and sensing.

The ML sub-layer of the software stack in Fig. 5 directly interacts with IoT applications and consists of a series of machine learning tasks and model repositories for a composable design of high-level IoST applications. Many ML tasks in IoT are inference-only, while the model training occurs in cloud or remote servers. The recent development in Deep Learning (DL) and Deep Reinforcement Learning (DRL) requires model training and policy updates to take place locally. The machine learning tasks depend on ML/DL library to ease the model development and tuning. Machine learning libraries and deep learning packages must be lightweight due to the limited resources in the embedded computer, the low latency requirement for fast inference, and the energy efficiency. For example, various deep learning platforms, such as Google Tensorflow, Keras, Pytorch, and MXNet, provide model converters to perform weight pruning and quantization on large models and even reduce their parameters and number of network layers for the latency and efficiencies.

The IoT systems are all equipped with ARM CPU cores and have the same Operating systems (for example, Linux) as many other Intel-based computers and servers. In addition to the standard OS components, IoT uses a microSD storage card with one Terabyte space that is sufficient to host large local databases of sensor data, real-time operating systems (RTOS) to speed up control and provide QoS supports for events, fuzzy logic fuzzification for rule generations, and rule-based engine. The Realtime operating system (RTOS) leverages the codes and software paradigms in Robotic Operating System (ROS) [13] to execute tasks on the resource-constrained microcontrollers that interact with external devices.

The IoT Hardware Accelerators in the core layer of Fig. 5 have heterogeneous architecture: GPU, FPGA, Tensor Processing Unit (TPU), and Application-Specific Instruction Set (ASIC). The Open Computing Language (OpenCL) standard [15] is proposed to mitigate the complexity of programming hardware. OpenCL supports heterogeneous hardware architectures with the same programming standard and allows programmers to choose a set of programming languages (C and Python), APIs, and Integrated Development Environment (IDE) to program these devices, control the platforms and execute programs between the central processor and accelerating devices. The kernel libraries are cross-compiled in the IDE and deployed into the targeted hardware accelerators: Unified Device Architecture (CUDA) GPU, FPGA, TPU, and ASIC.

The core layer enables numerous over-the-top applications to be realized. In the instance of context-awareness and event-driven tasks, several simulations can be done on-device to generate optimal solutions to a given problem through the application of techniques such as reinforcement learning and other estimation techniques. The generated models can then be shared with other IoST devices communicating in a well-defined topology. Furthermore, composite applications

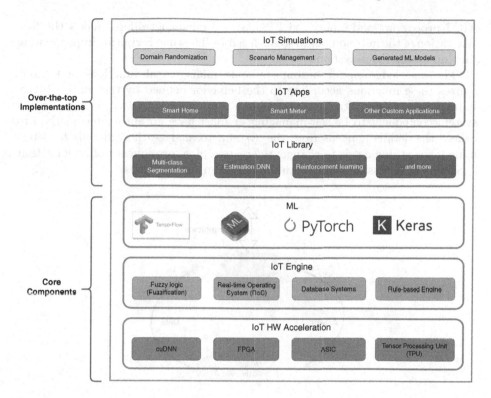

Fig. 5. Software stack.

can be built on the core layer and reconfigured to suit various application needs using the same IoST device.

Knowledge Engine. The knowledge engine (KE) shown in Fig. 4 forms the critical component of autonomic computing—a framework that supports the paradigm of intelligent computing systems that are self-aware and self-managing once given high-level objectives of the system's operators and administrators. The IoST proposed in this paper rests upon an autonomy-enabled knowledge engine and its unique self-aware properties and capabilities that mimic the nervous systems, i.e., self-configuration, self-healing, self-optimization, and self-protection. Table 2 summarizes the difference between classical IoT and IoST and the key value added by the knowledge plane.

Scientifically, defining appropriate abstractions and models for understanding, controlling, and planning emergent behavior in conventional autonomic systems is a difficult task to achieve. The autonomic computing concept was first introduced two decades ago in [4] but could not be fully realized because of a lack of essential computing software and hardware primitives. Recently, rapid advancements in Artificial Intelligence (AI), Machine Learning, distributed Learning, neuroscience, and heterogeneous low-power hardware, such as GPUs,

ARM processors, and embedded FPGAs and microcontrollers, makes the first generation of the autonomous systems feasible. The time is ripe for implementing such an autonomous systems.

The knowledge engine automates some management functions and externalizes these functions according to the behavior defined by the control plane. It implements the control loop to achieve autonomy, as shown in Fig. 6. For a system component to be self-managing, it must have an automated method to collect the details it needs from the system; to analyze those details to determine if something needs to change; to create a plan, or sequence of actions, that specifies the necessary changes; and to perform those actions.

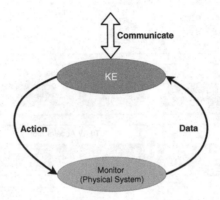

Fig. 6. Implementation of control loop to achieve autonomy.

A knowledge source entails a registry, dictionary, database, data repository and provides access to knowledge according to the interfaces prescribed by the architecture. It is required to realize autonomy. In an autonomic system, knowledge consists of a particular type of data with predefined syntax and semantics, such as symptoms, policies, change requests, and change plans; this knowledge can be stored in a knowledge database and shared among IoST nodes in communication topologies. The topology can be centralized with a hub for distributing messages, decentralized, hierarchical, and ad-hoc or self-organizing (as shown in Fig. 7).

The source of knowledge, in this case, is acquired from training acquired data using lightweight Machine Learning (ML) and Deep Learning (DL) algorithms. Examples of these lightweight ML/DL libraries include TensorFlow Lite and Fast and Lightweight AutoML (FLAML). IoST applications use the outputs of the prediction algorithms to generate rule-based decisions and interpret information and knowledge effectively during interaction with the external environment. Besides the local data being used as a source of knowledge, the IoST device also obtains its knowledge from other IoST devices through peer-to-peer information exchange. Peer-to-peer communication further enables complex ML problem solving by applying federated machine learning to decompose complex

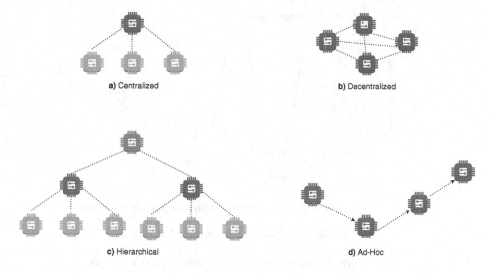

a) Centralized

b) Decentralized

c) Hierarchical

d) Ad-Hoc

Fig. 7. Possible topology configurations.

problems into small ones [9] and train a meta-model on the entire data source and individual model on each partition. The KE takes the output of ML, compiles the rules, and sends the actions to the physical plane to perform event-driven tasks. The ML output can be 'fuzzified'. For instance, a supervised machine learning algorithm consists of two classes: regressions for generating numeric outputs and classification methods that output discrete values with probability. However, real-world controllers often use the analog signal that aligns with human intelligence. The standard controller uses Analog-to-Digital/Digital-to-Analog (AD/DA) logic to convert between two regimes. However, a brute force conversion from a digital signal to an analog might generate abrupt actions and even damage physical devices. Fuzzy logic will bridge the gap and use Fuzzy control tables (as shown in Table 1) and member functions (Fig. 8) to translate signals smoothly from machine learning outputs to actions.

Table 1. An example of fuzzy controller table.

	NB	NS	ZZ	PS	PB
NB	ZZ	PS	PB	PB	PB
NS	NS	ZZ	PS	PB	PB
ZZ	NB	NS	ZZ	PS	PB
PS	NB	NB	NS	ZZ	PS
PB	NB	NB	NB	NS	ZZ

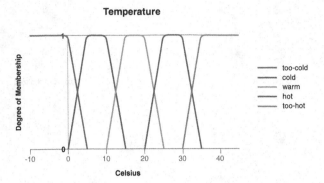

Fig. 8. An example of a fuzzy logic temperature member function.

Table 2. Self-awareness in smart IoT

Concept	Current Internet of Things	Internet of Smart Things
Self-configuration	Manual configuration with static workflows	Automatically turn the high-level services requirements into the integrated multiple services in one or more KEs
Self-optimization	Manual adjust system settings of one or more components	Dynamic improvement of performance and efficiency using Machine learning and expert systems rules
Self-healing	Systems report errors, faults, and malfunctions and the system is shut for repairs or updates	Automatically diagnose, detect, and repair software and hardware. Predictive maintenance
Self-protection	Scheduled or manually configured security workflows	aromatically detect intrusions, raise alarms, and change firewall configurations

3.3　Hardware Implementations

Currently, there are many types of IoT devices with different computational capabilities. We considered a number of these devices are capable of realizing the IoST concept.

There are five possible types of the embedded hardware implementation: NVIDIA Jetson, Raspberry Pi, Google Coral, SmartPhone, and Intel Movidius Neural Computing Stick (NCS). These five implementations use different ML/DL inference accelerator technology, including ASIC, FPGA, Neural Engine, and NVIDIA CUDA. NVIDIA Jetson consists of multi-core ARM Cortex CPU processors, NVIDIA GPU for vision processing and machine learning, and external bus to peripheral devices. Similarly, Google Coral is an edge System-on-

Fig. 9. Raspberry Pi does not have in-chip ML/DL accelerator and requires an external hardware for Neuron Engine. Intel Movidius provides a good ML accelerator hardware for Raspberry Pi.

Modules (SoM) that consists of Quad-core Cortex ARM processors, GPU, Vision Processing Unit (VPU), Google TPU ML (ASIC based accelerator co-processor), and Peripheral Component Interconnect express (PCIe) Bus. The smart mobile platforms (such as iPhone, Android, Samsung, and Huawei) and recent Apple M1 iPad adopt a similar processor architecture. multi-core ARM CPU processors for high-performance computing jobs and high efficient tasks, multi-GPU cores with Single instruction, multiple data (SIMD) for PC quality graphical processing, Neural Engine performing deep learning on the processing Chip.

Intel Movidius Neural Compute Stick (An ASIC ML Accelerator): Intel Movidius ASIC is also an ASIC-based Vision Processing Unit (VPU) designed to accelerate machine learning and artificial intelligence tasks, including image processing and recognition. Intel Movidius has a comparable throughput to the state-of-the-art NVIDIA Jetson Nano embedded system, at one-third of power. The ASIC design makes Intel VPU energy efficient and can be plugged into any ARM-based embedded system to add and enhance the machine learning capability at the edge.

Raspberry Pi: Raspberry Pi is the most cost-effective IoT module and has four generations and more than ten models ((RPi 1, 2, 3 &4) over the past decade. Raspberry Pi uses the ARM-based CPU processor used by many mobile phones (Samsung, Apple, and Qualcomm) and supports many operating systems, including Linux and Windows). The current Raspberry Pi 4B provides a suitable desktop replacement that handles most desktop applications, including browser, email, and visualizations. In Fig. 9, Raspberry Pi uses Intel Movidius NCS to run machine learning and deep learning models and provides an energy-efficient and cost-effective IoT solution for self-awareness and automation.

NVIDIA Jetson: NVIDIA Jetson consists of multi-core ARM Cortex CPU processors for general purpose tasks, NVIDIA GPU for vision processing and machine learning, and the external bus to control interfaces and peripheral devices. The System-on-Chip (SoC) in Fig. 10 consists of an 8-core ARM processor and 512-core GPU for both training and inference. The embedded system

Fig. 10. NVIDIA Jetson.

has 32 GB memory and 32 GB NAND flash memory. It also supports expandable PCIe Solid State Drive (SSD) for high-speed data I/O. The default OS is Ubuntu. The Jetson Xavier offers unprecedented computing power and functions as a workstation replacement for training jobs, data analysis and, and model inferences while being portable ($4 \times 4 \times 2.5$ in.) and serving as an add-on to network equipment. We propose to deploy Tensorflow and Deep Reinforcement Learning on NVIDIA embedded system for the proposed intelligence control layer.

Xilinx Kria: Many IoT applications require real-time signal transmission and control; the GPU co-processor does not meet the timing requirement. On the other hand, the ASIC is too rigid and does not allow customization. The ASIC-based control system is not appropriate because the Quantum network device is still in the prototype development stage and requires its control interface and protocols to adapt to constant changes. The FPGA SoC and embedded systems are mainly used in the south-bound interface in the SDN paradigm.

The Xilinx FPGA SoC consists of four ARM Cortex CPU cores and 600K Logic cells, half-million Flip-flops, and 300K LUTs. Xilinx Kria essentially functions as a full-featured computer, in addition to its FPGA that is pre-installed with Intellectual Properties (IPs) or dynamically loaded run-time kernels. The board contains the pre-built PCIe and 100 Gbps Ethernet IPs in its programmable logic. We choose Ubuntu as the operating system of the proposed FPGA embedded system, i.e., the Xilinx Kria embedded system. Only a few attempts were made to deploy any SDN software stack on the FPGA-based embedded system. We will customize SDN and provide real-time support and control to the attached device.

The key difference between GPU-based IoT and FPGA is that GPU communicates with other onboard modules via DDR while Xilinx uses a pipeline that accesses DDR at its beginning and ending stages and eliminates the memory I/O.

3.4 Communication Technologies

The implementation of autonomous IoT requires communication technologies. The choice of communication technologies depends on the considered use case; hence we can support either Intra-/Inter-IoST communication. Commonly, the communication technologies for realizing IoST can be categorized into 1) Low Power Wide Area Network (LPWAN), and 2) Short-range network [1]. The LPWAN consists of technologies such as SigFox and Cellular. The short-range network consists of technologies such as 6LoWPAN, ZigBee, WiFi, BLE, and Z-Wave. The interconnection between smart IoTs in particular environments, such as Industrial automation, may require networks and protocols that are yet to be developed to operate at an acceptable performance.

4 Case-Studies

With IoT revolutionizing sectors such as energy, health, transportation, agriculture, and cyber-physical systems (CPS), the concept of IoST can also be applied in these sectors. In this section, we explore the application of IoST in energy and Cyber-Physical Systems.

4.1 IoST in Energy

With the current push for renewable energy and ubiquitous IoT integration with Active Distribution Networks (ADN), cloud services are commonly regarded as promising solutions for data acquisition, processing, and storage, providing data-driven opportunities for centralized management in ADN. However, existing cloud-based centralized energy management schemes are often criticized for large communication overheads (i.e., the breakdown of cloud servers leads to the collapse of the entire decision-making process) and poor physical scalability. The concept of IoST can be applied to address this point-of-failure problem by adopting a decentralized IoT infrastructure for distributed management of energy resources.

The current demand for reliable energy supply and the push for green energy has resulted in an uptaking trend of adopting renewable energy systems. In many developing countries, the most common form of renewable energy being deployed is solar Photovoltaic (PV). Most energy companies resort to Small-Scale Modular Solar PV Containers (SSMoC) for residential and commercial environments. In such systems, the customers need to know their consumption patterns and characterize the power usage of customers in conjunction with the main power supply from the grid. The current systems deployed and available in the market enables users to have constant internet access where the SSMoC units relay their data to an online server for data processing and optimizing their operations. One challenge facing most developing countries is the constant availability of the Internet. The concept of IoST can be applied to provide on-device intelligence through processing and training of the acquired data and can be used for forecasting consumption patterns. Its intelligence can be updated once in a while, which alleviates the burden of having constant internet access for most of the SSMoC units to operate.

Furthermore, this base concept of IoST can be integrated into the current smart metering infrastructure. The smart meters deployed at customers' premises cannot learn and evolve their intelligence on their own. Most power operators tend to replace the entire unit in instances where some deficits are found due to their inability to execute some specific tasks. The IoST concept enables the knowledge or base algorithm used by these smart meters to evolve depending on the required use case or scenario.

4.2   IoST in Cyber-Physical Systems

Cyber-Physical Systems (CPSs) focus on the interaction between physical, networking, and computation processes. However, interconnecting the cyber and physical worlds gives rise to new dangerous security challenges (i.e., cyber or physical security threats). The heterogeneous nature, reliance on private and sensitive data, and large-scale deployment are significant factors contributing to the identified challenges in CPS. Intentional or accidental exposure of these systems results in catastrophic effects, which makes it critical to put in place robust security measures [22]. In ensuring the rapid recovery from cyber attacks, automatic reconfiguration of CPS has become crucial in fighting against cyber threats. Once again, the concept of IoST becomes a suitable and convenient solution.

5   Conclusion

This paper introduced a new concept that enables IoT devices to evolve and self-learn by leveraging on lightweight ML algorithms, fuzzy rule-based systems, and control functions to perform intelligent and autonomic functions through the adoption of SDF. We discussed the device-level components of IoST and provided possible implementations for current IoT devices. We also offered potential scenarios where this concept can be applied. Even though this new concept seeks to revolutionize current smart devices, its base requirements prevent its realization in resource-constrained IoT devices; hence a limitation.

The future works will focus on the implementation of the composite software stack to realize this new IoST concept. We will further apply this concept in energy systems and CPSs to provide self-optimization and self-protection for IoT devices and the entire system. We will further evaluate the performance of the proposed concept using different communication technologies and topologies.

List of Abbreviations

IoT Internet of Things
IoST Internet of Smart Things
KE Knowledge Engine
SDF Software-Defined Framework
SDS Software-Defined Systems
SDN Software-Defined Networking
NoT Network of Things
LAN Local Area Network
ITU International Telecommunication Union
ARM Advanced RISC Machine
RISC Reduced Instruction Set Computing
ASIC Application-Specific Instruction Set
CPU Central Processing Unit
GPU Graphics Processing Unit
FPGA Field-Programmable Gate Array
ML Machine Learning
DL Deep Learning
FLAML Fast and Lightweight AutoML
DMA Direct Memory Access
I/O Input/Output
DRL Deep Reinforcement Learning
RTOS Realtime operating system
ROS Robotic Operating System
TPU Tensor Processing Unit
OpenCL Open Computing Language
IDE Integrated Development Environment
CUDA Compute Unified Device Architecture
ML Machine Learning
AI Artificial Intelligence
DNN Deep Neural Network
cuDNN CUDA Deep Neural Network
AD/DA Analog-to-Digital/Digital-to-Analog
NCS Neural Computing Stick
VPU Vision Processing Unit
PCIe Peripheral Component Interconnect express
SSD Solid State Drive
LUTs Lookup Tables
DDR Double Data Rate
LPWAN Low Power Wide Area Network
6LoWPAN IPv6 over Low Power Wireless Personal Area Network
WiFi Wireless Fidelity
BLE Bluetooth Low Energy
ADN Active Distribution Networks
PV Photovoltaic
SSMoC Small-Scale Modular Solar PV Containers
CPSs Cyber-Physical Systems
SoC System-on-Chip
IPs Intellectual Properties

References

1. Al-Sarawi, S., Anbar, M., Alieyan, K., Alzubaidi, M.: Internet of Things (IoT) communication protocols: review. In: 2017 8th International Conference on Information Technology (ICIT), pp. 685–690 (2017). https://doi.org/10.1109/ICITECH.2017.8079928
2. Alam, T.: A reliable framework for communication in internet of smart devices using IEEE 802.15.4. ARPN J. Eng. Appl. Sci. (2018). https://ssrn.com/abstract=3684655
3. Atzori, L., Iera, A., Morabito, G.: From "smart objects" to "social objects": the next evolutionary step of the Internet of Things. IEEE Commun. Mag. 52(1), 97–105 (2014). https://doi.org/10.1109/MCOM.2014.6710070
4. An Architectural Blueprint: An Architectural Blueprint for Autonomic Computing, 4th edn (2006)
5. Di Martino, B., Rak, M., Ficco, M., Esposito, A., Maisto, S., Nacchia, S.: Internet of Things reference architectures, security and interoperability: a survey. Internet Things 1–2, 99–112 (2018). https://doi.org/10.1016/j.iot.2018.08.008. https://www.sciencedirect.com/science/article/pii/S2542660518300428
6. Kakiz, M.T., Öztürk, E., Çavdar, T.: A novel SDN-based IoT architecture for big data. In: 2017 International Artificial Intelligence and Data Processing Symposium (IDAP), pp. 1–5 (2017). https://doi.org/10.1109/IDAP.2017.8090186
7. Karmakar, K.K., Varadharajan, V., Nepal, S., Tupakula, U.: SDN-enabled secure IoT architecture. IEEE Internet Things J. 8(8), 6549–6564 (2021). https://doi.org/10.1109/JIOT.2020.3043740
8. Kephart, J.O., Chess, D.M.: The vision of autonomic computing. Computer 36(1), 41–50 (2003). https://doi.org/10.1109/MC.2003.1160055
9. Khan, L.U., Saad, W., Han, Z., Hossain, E., Hong, C.S.: Federated learning for Internet of Things: recent advances, taxonomy, and open challenges (2020)
10. Khan, M.A., Salah, K.: IoT security: review, blockchain solutions, and open challenges. Future Gener. Comput. Syst. 82, 395–411 (2018). https://doi.org/10.1016/j.future.2017.11.022. https://www.sciencedirect.com/science/article/pii/S0167739X17315765
11. Li, J., Altman, E., Touati, C.: A general SDN-based IoT framework with NVF implementation. ZTE Commun. 13(3), 42–45 (2015). https://hal.inria.fr/hal-01197042
12. Li, Y., Su, X., Riekki, J., Kanter, T., Rahmani, R.: A SDN-based architecture for horizontal Internet of Things services. In: 2016 IEEE International Conference on Communications (ICC), pp. 1–7 (2016). https://doi.org/10.1109/ICC.2016.7511053
13. Maruyama, Y., Kato, S., Azumi, T.: Exploring the performance of ROS2. In: 2016 International Conference on Embedded Software (EMSOFT), pp. 1–10 (2016). https://doi.org/10.1145/2968478.2968502
14. binti Mohamad Noor, M., Hassan, W.H.: Current research on Internet of Things (IoT) security: a survey. Comput. Netw. 148, 283–294 (2019). https://doi.org/10.1016/j.comnet.2018.11.025. https://www.sciencedirect.com/science/article/pii/S1389128618307035
15. Munshi, A., Gaster, B., Mattson, T.G., Fung, J., Ginsburg, D.: OpenCL Programming Guide, 1st edn. Addison-Wesley Professional (2011)
16. Ojo, M., Adami, D., Giordano, S.: A SDN-IoT architecture with NFV implementation. In: 2016 IEEE Globecom Workshops (GC Wkshps), pp. 1–6 (2016). https://doi.org/10.1109/GLOCOMW.2016.7848825

17. Radoglou Grammatikis, P.I., Sarigiannidis, P.G., Moscholios, I.D.: Securing the Internet of Things: challenges, threats and solutions. Internet Things **5**, 41–70 (2019). https://doi.org/10.1016/j.iot.2018.11.003. https://www.sciencedirect. com/science/article/pii/S2542660518301161
18. Risteska Stojkoska, B.L., Trivodaliev, K.V.: A review of Internet of Things for smart home: challenges and solutions. J. Clean. Prod. **140**, 1454–1464 (2017). https://doi.org/10.1016/j.jclepro.2016.10.006. https://www.sciencedirect. com/science/article/pii/S095965261631589X
19. Shamsan, A.H., Faridi, A.R.: SDN-assisted IoT architecture: a review. In: 2018 4th International Conference on Computing Communication and Automation (ICCCA), pp. 1–7 (2018). https://doi.org/10.1109/CCAA.2018.8777339
20. Silverio-Fernández, M., Renukappa, S., Suresh, S.: What is a smart device? - a conceptualisation within the paradigm of the Internet of Things. Vis. Eng. **6**(1) (2018). Article number: 3. https://doi.org/10.1186/s40327-018-0063-8
21. Tayyaba, S.K., Shah, M.A., Khan, O.A., Ahmed, A.W.: Software defined network (SDN) based Internet of Things (IoT): a road ahead. In: Proceedings of the International Conference on Future Networks and Distributed Systems, ICFNDS 2017. Association for Computing Machinery, New York (2017). https://doi.org/10.1145/3102304.3102319
22. Yaacoub, J.P.A., Salman, O., Noura, H.N., Kaaniche, N., Chehab, A., Malli, M.: Cyber-physical systems security: limitations, issues and future trends. Microprocess. Microsyst. **77**, 103201 (2020). https://doi.org/10.1016/j.micpro.2020.103201. https://www.sciencedirect.com/science/article/pii/S0141933120303689
23. Yazici, M.T., Basurra, S., Gaber, M.M.: Edge machine learning: enabling smart Internet of Things applications. Big Data Cogn. Comput. **2**(3) (2018). https://doi. org/10.3390/bdcc2030026. https://www.mdpi.com/2504-2289/2/3/26
24. Yousuf, O., Mir, R.N.: A survey on the Internet of Things security. Inf. Comput. Secur. **27**(2), 292–323 (2019). https://doi.org/10.1108/ICS-07-2018-0084
25. Zheng, S.: Research on SDN-based IoT security architecture model. In: 2019 IEEE 8th Joint International Information Technology and Artificial Intelligence Conference (ITAIC), pp. 575–579 (2019). https://doi.org/10.1109/ITAIC.2019.8785456

Study of Customer Sentiment Towards Smart Lockers

Colette Malyack$^{(\boxtimes)}$, Cheichna Sylla, and Pius Egbelu

New Jersey Institute of Technology, Newark, NJ, USA
{ctm22,cheickna.sylla,pius.j.egbelu}@njit.edu

Abstract. Understanding customer sentiment associated with delivery solutions, such as smart lockers, is an area of increasing interest for package delivery companies. Applications of this data could result in cost savings through vehicle route planning, cross docking, fleet size optimization, and increased placement of smart locker technology for stop reduction. However, there has been little effort applied to gathering information related to public sentiment applications to last mile package delivery. Therefore, through a survey instrument we gather sentiment data related to smart lockers for review and analysis. Sentiment analysis by region (suburban, urban, and rural) is accomplished through a survey instrument with the goal of understanding the difference in sentiment by region and the effects of COVID-19 on customer sentiment towards the use of smart lockers. Some significant findings were that suburban residents were willing to travel further to pick-up a package from a smart locker ($\alpha = 0.01$) and previous experience was correlated with increased sentiment ($\alpha = 0.05$).

Keywords: Smart locker · Statistical analysis · Survey instrument · Omnichannel delivery network

1 Introduction

Movement of goods through package delivery services has become a requirement of modern life. Especially during the COVID-19 pandemic, where movement of goods by logistics companies increased 13% at the beginning of the pandemic alone [1]. While customers do not usually think about the process behind package delivery, logistics companies like UPS and USPS (United States Postal Service) rely on obtaining new package deliveries through maintaining high quality of service and customer sentiment.

Smart lockers provide a new opportunity to increase customer sentiment, reduce the number of stops necessary for delivery, and provide a contactless method of delivery during a pandemic. The main problem resolved by smart lockers is known as the "last mile delivery problem", this final step accounts for up to 53% of the total shipping cost [2]. Reducing this cost would benefit companies and their customers, who could see a reduction in shipping costs, incentives to use smart lockers, or increased security through their use and application. These lockers also provide other benefits for customers such as avoiding the need for repeat delivery calls and contactless delivery during a pandemic.

© ICST Institute for Computer Sciences, Social Informatics and Telecommunications Engineering 2022
Published by Springer Nature Switzerland AG 2022. All Rights Reserved
T. M. N. Ngatched and I. Woungang (Eds.): PAAISS 2021, LNICST 405, pp. 266–277, 2022.
https://doi.org/10.1007/978-3-030-93314-2_17

However, understanding customers and their willingness to use this resource is vital to optimize their application within the network. The launching of Amazon's smart lockers in the early 2010s allowed a growing population access to shared and secure package storage, with lockers currently in over 900 cities and towns across the United States [3, 4]. However, there is no understanding of customer sentiment towards this service being collected or analyze for last mile delivery purposes.

Lack of customer sentiment collection is likely due to lack of access to information relating to the topic and limited sources of reliable data. An approach to remedying this problem is the use of survey instruments to gather and analyze data on customers' sentiments. Survey instruments based on Likert scale is a proven method used in marketing research and related business studies in strategic management. Typically, this process requires asking customers to answer questions designed using Likert scale, as well as open ended questions regarding their preferences and sentiments, which can be analyzed to confirm the results. These responses could allow companies to gain real-world insights into how their products are being viewed and where to focus marketing strategies. In this case, the results of such a survey could be used to optimize smart locker locations and increase customer satisfaction.

The rest of this paper is organized as follows: Sect. 2 contains a "Literature Review", Sect. 3 provides the "Research Objectives", Sects. 4 and 5 review the "Survey Description and Distribution" and "Methodology" respectively, Sect. 6 provides an overview of "Results", and Sects. 7, 8, and 9 contain the "Discussion", "Limitations", and "Conclusions".

2 Literature Review

To our knowledge, there has been no previous work done on the analysis of customer sentiment through a survey instrument relating to the use of smart lockers. However, there have been many previous accomplishments relating to the incorporation of customer sentiment in other industries through customer written corpus sentiment analysis.

Sentiment analysis can be defined as the association of an emotion to text using various analysis techniques to interpret the true meaning of the text and then classify the content within the given text passage [5]. These passages, referred to as a "corpus", can vary in size from a couple of words to full documents, and can include words of any language, slang, punctuation, emojis, or combination of these attributes depending on the source of the corpus. Further complicating sentiment analysis, results can be formatted in multiple methods ranging from classification into an emotional category or polarity (positive vs. negative) to a numerical scale determining the polarity and level of sentiment within the corpus [6]. However, the end goal of all sentiment analysis remains to associate a classification or numerical value representing the feelings of the individual who has written the given corpus.

While sentiment analysis remains a largely subjective field relying on natural language processing (NLP), machine learning, and artificial intelligence to identify meaning from words and phrases, the results of this analysis can be vital to various industries. Real-world applications of sentiment analysis are varied and range from customer understanding to stock market trend forecasting. One study carried out in 2014 applied the use of emotional sentiments (e.g., feelings, opinions, preference, etc.) from blog posts to the reactions of the stock market, determining there were applicable trends between negative sentiment and prediction of stock changes [7]. Other studies, including two articles related to product sales, have gathered text through online product reviews with the goal of determining their effect on the sales of those products [8, 9]. There are many other real-world applications for businesses including public relations, churn, marketing, political campaigning, etc., but one of the main real-world applications is through publicly sourced corpuses is for disaster and emergency response [10].

State-of-the-art sentiment analysis has been done in the past on microblogging site contents using a Support Vector Machine (SVM). The goal of this project was to detect the sentiment of the overall corpus and terms within the corpus [11]. However, unlike the state-of-the-art method described, microblogging contents in this paper are analyzed using n-grams and word tagging. While this method does learn associations with words and sentiments, no SVM or other advanced model is applied to obtain results.

Regardless of sentiment analysis purpose, all results start with unstructured data, which is believed to makeup approximately 80% of all existing data at this time [12]. There are two main methods for the gathering of text-based corpuses for the purpose of sentiment analysis. Either this information can be directly solicited through a survey instrument in an open-ended question format or data can be gathered through secondary sources based on available resources without solicitation.

3   Research Questions

With the goal of attaining an understanding of public sentiment for smart lockers, we collected customer sentiment data through the distribution of a survey instrument and analysis of results. Unfortunately, there is no known research related to obtaining customer sentiment towards smart lockers. As a result, we apply the Technology Acceptance Model (TAM) and aim to measure perceived usefulness and ease of use [13]. To accomplish this goal, we look at the results of the survey with the following hypotheses, which are also illustrated in Fig. 1 below.

- H1: Higher density leads to higher acceptance levels.

  - o A: Customers living in higher density regions (urban vs. rural) will have increased perceived ease of use related to smart lockers.
  - o B: Customers living in higher density regions (urban vs. rural) will have increased perceived usefulness related to smart lockers.

- H2: Consideration for the COVID-19 pandemic leads to higher acceptance levels.

  - o A: Consideration for the COVID-19 pandemic will result in increased perceived ease of use related to smart lockers.
  - o B: Consideration for the COVID-19 pandemic will result in increased perceived usefulness related to smart lockers.

- H3: Previous experience leads to higher acceptance levels.

o A: Previous experience with smart lockers will result in increased perceived ease of use related to smart lockers.

o B: Previous experience with smart lockers will result in increased perceived usefulness related to smart lockers.

4   Survey Description and Distribution

The region selected for sentiment data collection was Northern New Jersey. Sentiment data about smart lockers for the public was gathered using a survey that contained questions directly related to sentiment (Likert Scale), factors effecting sentiment (multiple choice questions), and open-ended responses mimicking a Twitter/MS post. The survey was distributed from December 31st, 2020 to February 20th, 2021 through community leaders, email was used to send the survey to those in the population and response participation was voluntary for members of the community. A Google Forms survey was created for distribution and response gathering purposes [14]. Results were gathered for 102 individuals prior to closing the survey and performing analysis.

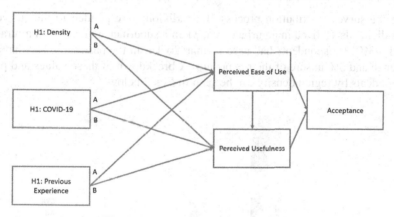

Fig. 1. Hypothesis connection to TAM

5   Methodology

Open-ended question responses were gathered from 90 of the 102 participants, the other 12 participants did not provide a response to this section. Sentiment analysis was then accomplished using the TextBlob python package [15]. This python library contains a pre-trained sentiment analysis model that analyzes corpuses using n-grams and word tagging. Using machine learning and artificial intelligence the unlabeled corpuses are then given a sentiment polarity (with 0 representing neutral sentiment) based on the pre-trained natural language processing model. Once this was accomplished the data was aggregated for analysis and understanding of customer sentiment towards smart lockers.

The six Likert scale questions (scale of 1–6), maximum distance willing to travel, and sentiment analysis results of the open-ended question were all analyzed using a two-tailed T-test and Wilcox test. Results of the factors most likely to affect smart locker use (multiple choice question) are also provided for review and application to understanding these results.

A major portion of this study involves the understanding of customer sentiment towards smart lockers and, therefore, smart system features provided. To accommodate this, several attributes were described for respondents including touchless package pickup, security through passcodes, access to lockers, etc. Once these system features were understood respondents were asked to fill out the described survey instrument.

6   Results

Here we present a breakdown of results for each survey question. The importance of these results is discussed later in the Discussion section.

6.1   Respondent Breakdown

During the survey distribution process 102 individuals responded to the sur-vey. Of these individuals 18 lived in an urban area, 81 in a suburban area, and 3 in a rural area. Overall, 63% of respondents had used a smart locker in the past, with 34% having no experience and 3% unsure of their exposure. A breakdown of these values and percent of respondents by region density can be seen in Fig. 2 below.

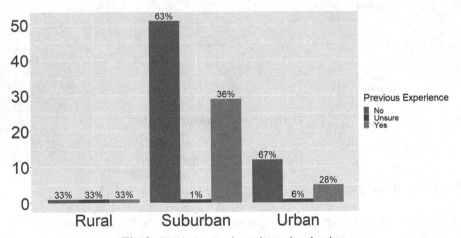

Fig. 2. Previous experience by region density

6.2   Likert Scale Question Analysis

The box plot (Fig. 3) below contains a distribution of responses by density for one of the Likert scale questions. This figure is representative of the responses to all 6 questions across all regions. Contrary to our expectations, the T-test and Wilcox test results did not reveal any statistically significant difference in responses to these six questions when comparing respondents in different density regions.

An interesting second question resulting from these six questions is whether opinions changed when considering COVID-19 and after customers were provided with the added understanding that pickup without physical contact was possible. To test whether sentiment changes occurred a paired T-test was applied. Both the difference between general sentiment and sentiment when considering COVID-19 (average of 0.39-point decrease in sentiment) and the difference between COVID-19 in general and considering pickup without physical contact (average 0.39-point increase in sentiment) were found to be significant, $\alpha = 0.01$ with p-values of 0.003 and 3.845e−06 respectively.

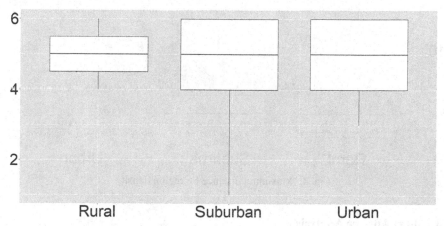

Fig. 3. General sentiment towards smart locker by region density

6.3 Maximum Distance Analysis

The next data point requested from respondents was maximum distance they would be willing to travel to obtain a package from a smart locker. A breakdown of these responses by density can be seen in Table 1. As shown in Fig. 4 below, suburban respondents are willing to travel further to pick up a package from a smart locker than urban respondents. This was supported by the results of both the T-test and Wilcox test, $\alpha = 0.01$ with p-values of 0.0007 and 0.01 respectively. Contrary to our expectations, the difference between rural regions and either of the other density definitions was not considered significant. This is likely due to the lack of respondents from rural regions.

Table 1. Maximum distance responses

Region density	Mean	Median	Mode
Rural	2	1	5
Suburban	4.23	3	5
Urban	2.11	1.25	1

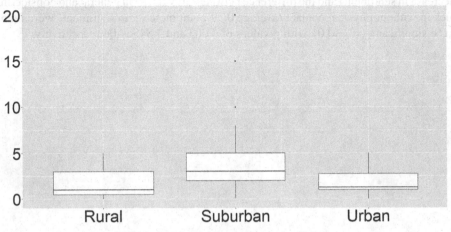

Fig. 4. Maximum distance by region density

6.4   Short Answer Analysis

As described above, respondents were asked to create a short message to share with others related to smart lockers and sentiment analysis was performed on these corpuses. To analyze these short answers the TextBlob python package was applied. This package (described in Sect. 5) employs the use of NLP and machine learning to analyze short corpuses and apply a value between -1 and 1, with 0 representing neutral sentiment. Once these numeric values were applied they were analyzed by geographic region and previous experience to further understand the attributes that effect sentiment.

For the region density breakdown, no difference was found between the sentiments in the short messages. This can be further seen in Fig. 5 below, where all mean values are around the same point for sentiment. Additionally, this result validates the results of the Likert scale questions, which also resulted in no difference in sentiment between density regions.

Finally, the sentiments in the short messages were analyzed to see if there was a difference based on previous experience with smart lockers. This analysis showed there was a statistically significant difference in sentiment between those who answered "Yes" and those who answered "No". This was supported by the results of both the T-test and Wilcox test with $\propto\ = 0.05$ and can be seen in Table 2 and Fig. 6 below.

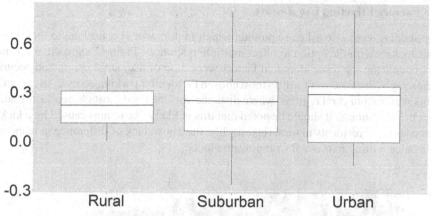

Fig. 5. Short text sentiment distribution by region density

Table 2. Previous experience short message T-test and Wilcox test results

Previous experience comparison	T-test result	T-test P-value	Wilcox result	Wilcox P-value
Yes vs. No	Difference	0.04	Difference	0.03
Yes vs. Unsure	No difference	0.35	No difference	0.15
No vs. Unsure	No difference	0.57	No difference	0.62

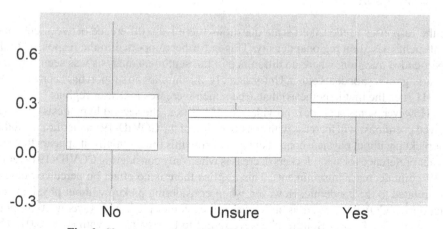

Fig. 6. Short text sentiment distribution by previous experience

6.5   Factors Effecting Use Results

Respondents were also asked to provide which factors would contribute to their use of smart lockers with the option to select multiple responses. Figure 7 shows that for most respondents the top three identified factors were ease of use, notification, and security. Interestingly, distance was the fifth most chosen factor after parking access. An exception to this was seen in rural regions, where distance was the third most chosen factor ahead of security. Although it should be noted that this is likely due to bias caused by a lack of responses from residents in rural regions, like the above lack of difference in responses to distance willing to travel for rural respondents.

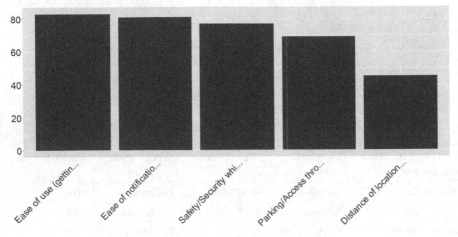

Fig. 7. Top factors for all regions

7   Discussion

In the responses to the Likert scale questions there is no difference between customer sentiments based on regional density. This is further supported in the responses to the open-ended question, where no difference in the sentiment analysis was seen for these groupings of respondents either. Unfortunately, this implies no support has been provided for H1 (i.e., the first hypothesis) that acceptance increases in denser regions.

However, some support is provided for H2 B (i.e., the second hypothesis) that perceived usefulness will increase with consideration of the COVID-19 pandemic and ability for pickup without physical contact options during this time. Initially, it appears that customer preference for smart lockers decreases when only considering COVID-19 (average 0.39-point decrease in sentiment). This implies there is no effect on perceived ease of use related to the pandemic. However, when considering pickup without physical contact during COVID-19 there is an increase in customer preference (average 0.39-point increase in sentiment). Both results were found to be significant with $\alpha = 0.01$. This shows that respondents were likely concerned about using a shared resource during a pandemic and felt more secure after being informed of pickup without physical contact options. In other words, the perceived usefulness of the smart lockers increased with the knowledge that packages could be picked up without physical contact. Analyzing how customers view shared resources in a pandemic could assists in understanding the respondent's overall preference towards the use of lockers and willingness to recommend the resource to others. These results indicate that with touchless pickup customers maintain at least the same sentiment towards smart lockers as they had prior to the pandemic. Factors indicated to contribute to smart locker use in Sect. 6.5 also support H2 B. Since package security was in the top three considerations, it is reasonable to conclude that customers might also be concerned about their security when using delivery technology, a sentiment that would also affect perceived usefulness for smart locker technology.

Additionally, support is provided for H3 (the third hypothesis) that acceptance will increase for those who have previous experience with smart locker technology. There was a statistically significant difference in sentiment supported by both the T-test and Wilcox test with $\alpha = 0.05$. Respondents having increased sentiment towards smart lockers when they had previous experience indicates there is perceived ease of use and perceived usefulness for those with a better understanding of the technology. A conclusion also supported by the presence of ease of use, notification, and available parking being indicated as three of the top five factors contributing to smart locker use. These factors all highlight that respondents are uncertain about the ease of use related to accessing a smart locker to obtain their packages.

8 Limitations

There is insufficient research in the available literature related to the topic of applying customer sentiment to the omnichannel delivery network and delivery technologies. This limits the available information and best practices to be applied to the amount and quality data and survey questions as well as the implications of the results. Previous research would allow for comparison of results and additional insights into the potential to understand why customers have certain sentiments. However, this also allows us to fill in a gap in the literature and provide information for future studies.

This paper is aimed at shedding more lights into the unexplored but important area of research on customer sentiment to help the design and choices of smart locker technology. The main limitation of the present study is the sample size and survey distribution methodology. The survey was distributed at random through community leaders with no incentive to provide responses. This makes it likely large demographics of the population are not represented, or are underrepresented, in the results of this analysis. Even in the current analysis rural respondents are underrepresented, leading to an inability to determine if there is a difference in customer sentiment for this population segment.

9 Conclusion

Through this research we have provided a review of survey data collected to analyze customer sentiment related to smart lockers using the TAM. We collected results related to smart locker sentiment, likelihood of use, likelihood of recommendations, and consideration for the COVID-19 pandemic from December 31st, 2020 to February 20th,

2021. The results of this survey did show an increase in sentiment towards smart locker technology with previous experience, supporting to our third hypothesis. It was also shown that the COVID-19 pandemic effected customer sentiment as well. Initially this consideration decreased sentiment until touchless pick-up information was provided, which returned sentiment to the levels prior to COVID-19 consideration. This lends limited support to our second hypothesis. Unfortunately, the results did not support our first hypothesis that customers living in areas with different density (urban, suburban, and rural) will have different sentiment levels towards the use of smart lockers. Figure 8 below shows the connections that were supported and how they relate to the TAM.

Future studies in this area should continue to focus on the concept of popularity by region for application to the last mile delivery problem. Results of this survey indicated that exposure to smart lockers could be applied to adjust customer preference in regions where smart locker technology would be of the greatest assistance to logistics companies. This would then result in increased perceived ease of use, connection shown in Fig. 8 below. This conclusion is based on the support of H2 B and H3, which revealed customer perceived usefulness increased after obtaining more information related to smart lockers and perceived ease of use increased with previous experience (or a better understanding of how the technology functions). Additionally, factors indicated by the respondents in Sect. 6.5 as effecting their preference were also related to uncertainty around smart lockers and interaction with the technology. Once the reasons behind perceived ease of use and usefulness are understood, it may be possible to work with customers to increase their preference and/or comfort towards smart lockers with the goal of saving delivery resources through the increased acceptance. In the future, it would be interesting to apply these results with the goal of optimizing omnichannel delivery network based on customer sentiment.

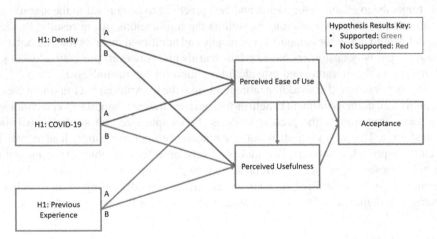

Fig. 8. Hypothesis connection to TAM with hypothesis support indication

References

1. Shipment Stats Continue to Grow During Pandemic, 20 April 2020. https://www.sdcexec.com/transportation/press-release/21129418/consignor-shipment-stats-continue-to-grow-during-pandemic
2. Dolan, S.: The challenges of last mile delivery logistics and the tech solutions cutting costs in the final mile, 10 May 2018. https://www.businessinsider.com/last-mile-delivery-shipping-explained
3. CBS San Francisco: Amazon Offering Lockers for Secure Product Delivery, 07 August 2012. https://sanfrancisco.cbslocal.com/2012/08/07/amazon-offering-lockers-for-secure-product-delivery/
4. Holsenbeck, K.: Everything you need to know about Amazon Hub Locker, 21 June 2018. https://www.amazon.com/primeinsider/tips/amazon-locker-qa.html
5. Li, N., Wu, D.D.: Using text mining and sentiment analysis for online forums hotspot detection and forecast. Decis. Support Syst. **48**(2), 354–368 (2010)
6. Hu, X., Tang, J., Gao, H., Liu, H.: Unsupervised sentiment analysis with emotional signals. In: Proceedings of the 22nd International Conference on World Wide Web, pp. 607–618, May 2013
7. Li, Q., Wang, T., Li, P., Liu, L., Gong, Q., Chen, Y.: The effect of news and public mood on stock movements. Inf. Sci. **278**, 826–840 (2014)
8. Fan, Z.P., Che, Y.J., Chen, Z.Y.: Product sales forecasting using online reviews and historical sales data: a method combining the Bass model and sentiment analysis. J. Bus. Res. **74**, 90–100 (2017)
9. Li, X., Wu, C., Mai, F.: The effect of online reviews on product sales: a joint sentiment-topic analysis. Inf. Manag. **56**(2), 172–184 (2019)
10. Beigi, G., Hu, X., Maciejewski, R., Liu, H.: An overview of sentiment analysis in social media and its applications in disaster relief. In: Pedrycz, W., Chen, S.-M. (eds.) Sentiment analysis and ontology engineering. SCI, vol. 639, pp. 313–340. Springer, Cham (2016). https://doi.org/10.1007/978-3-319-30319-2_13
11. Mohammad, S.M., Kiritchenko, S., Zhu, X.: NRC-Canada: building the state-of-the-art in sentiment analysis of tweets. arXiv preprint arXiv:1308.6242 (2013)
12. Gupta, S., Gupta, S.K.: Natural language processing in mining unstructured data from software repositories: a review. Sādhanā **44**(12), 1–17 (2019). https://doi.org/10.1007/s12046-019-1223-9
13. Davis, F.D.: Technology acceptance model: TAM. In: Al-Suqri, M.N., Al-Aufi, A.S. (eds.) Information Seeking Behavior and Technology Adoption, pp. 205–219 (1989)
14. Malyack, C.: Smart Locker Opinion Survey [Google form] (2021). https://docs.google.com/forms/d/18eyPCKKAY8sG_opy46OImbiW_v47eRaJJGnuvOg2s58/edit
15. Loria, S.: TextBlob: Simplified Text Processing — TextBlob 0.15.2 documentation. Textblob.readthedocs.io (2018). https://textblob.readthedocs.io/en/dev/

Author Index

Aboagye, Sylvester   237
Agyemang, Justice Owusu   248
Auguste, Mboule Ebele Brice   55, 120

Bagha, Amir Mohammadi   219
Bosman, Anna S.   169

Dhurandher, Sanjay Kumar   219
Dickson, Matthew C.   169
Dobre, Octavia A.   237

Ebele, Brice Auguste Mboule   137
Egbelu, Pius   266
Essoh, Serge Leonel Essuthi   137
Etoua, Oscar Vianney Eone   137
Etoua, V. Eone Oscar   55

Fashoto, Stephen   182

Genders, Emma   150
Gwetu, Mandlenkosi   18, 33, 74, 108

Jackpersad, Kishan   74

Kaulasar, Liresh   108
Kenfack, Hippolyte Michel Tapamo   55, 137
Kponyo, Jerry John   248

Leonel, Essuthi Essoh Serge   55, 120

Mafumbate, Racheal   182
Makurumure, Leenane Tinashe   33
Malan, Katherine M.   169
Malyack, Colette   266
Mbietieu, Amos Mbietieu   137
Mbietieu, Mb. Amos   55
Mbietieu, Mbietieu Amos   120
Mbunge, Elliot   182
Michel, Tapamo Kenfack Hippolyte   120
Mienye, Ibomoiye Domor   94
Molefe, Mohale Emmanuel   203

Ngatched, Telex Magloire N   237
Nxumalo, Sanelisiwe   182

Seedat, Yusuf   3
Sun, Yanxia   94
Sylla, Cheichna   266

Tapamo, Jules-Raymond   203
Traore, Issa   219

Vambe, Trevor Constantine   18
van der Haar, Dustin   3
Vianney, Eone Etoua Oscar   120
Viriri, Serestina   18, 150

Woungang, Isaac   219

Yu, Dantong   248

Printed in the United States
by Baker & Taylor Publisher Services